AMERICAN ORIENT

American Orient

Imagining the East from
the Colonial Era through the
Twentieth Century

David Weir

University of Massachusetts Press

AMHERST AND BOSTON

LC 2011014407
ISBN 978-1-55849-879-2 (paper); 878-5 (library cloth)

Designed by Dennis Anderson
Set in Sabon by House of Equations, Inc.
Printed and bound by Thomson-Shore, Inc.

Library of Congress Cataloging-in-Publication Data

Weir, David, 1947 Apr. 20–
American Orient : imagining the East from the colonial era through the
twentieth century / David Weir.
          p. cm.
Includes bibliographical references and index.
ISBN 978-1-55849-879-2 (paper : alk. paper)—
ISBN 978-1-55849-878-5 (library cloth : alk. paper)
1. East Asia—Foreign public opinion, American.   2. East Asia—Relations—United States.
3. United States—Relations—East Asia.   4. Orientalism—United States—History.
5. United States—Intellectual life.   6. East Asia—In literature.
7. American literature—History and criticism.   8. United States—Civilization—
East Asian influences.   9. East and West—History.   10. Public opinion—United States—
History.   I. Title.
DS518.8.W356 2011
303.48'27305—dc22
                                  2011014407

British Library Cataloguing in Publication data are available.

"The stalk of the lotus may be broken,
and the fibres remain connected."
—*Hitopadesa*

In memory of David Geoffrey Weir
(1973–1991)

CONTENTS

ACKNOWLEDGMENTS

THE ONLY transcendental experience available at the Cooper Union is in the classroom, so thanks are due to the transcendent students in my seminar on the American Orient, especially Janice Chu, Ugla Hauksdóttir, and Galen Wolfe-Pauly. I am also grateful to my longtime student Ana Becker, who was as conscientious and perfectionist as my research assistant as she is in her day job as a graphic designer. And since I completed the bulk of this book while on sabbatical, I must thank the Cooper Union Federation of College Teachers for negotiating the contract with a recalcitrant administration which made the sabbatical possible.

I am also grateful to Sig. Matthew Woods, Sig. Nathaniel Osborn, and Sig.ra. Aimee Bayles of the Pisticci Foundation; and to Mssrs. Olivier Filograsso and David Maher of the Balthazar Institute: oenological scholars, all.

Outside the confines of Cooper Union and New York City, I owe the greatest debt of gratitude to the two professors who read *American Orient* in manuscript: Richard Millington of Smith College and Christopher Benfey of Mount Holyoke College. Their suggestions and corrections have certainly made this book better than it would have been otherwise, even though I fear it falls short of the level of excellence exemplified by their own work.

It seems like more than a *manvantara* ago that my editorial guru Clark Dougan of the University of Massachusetts Press guided my first book into print. I am deeply grateful to him and to the editorial yogini Carol Betsch for their help in seeing this one through the press.

Finally, I remain thankful both to and for my wife Camille, a bit of a yogini herself, and in more than one way.

 AMERICAN ORIENT

Introduction

DURING THE days of Lewis and Clark, Americans held out the hope of an easy way west, a path across the continent to the Pacific that would unify the nascent nation and connect its western verge to the wealthy, civilized cities of the Atlantic coast. The quest for the Northwest Passage was also driven by the dream of reaching the Far East, of extending the western reach of America so far that it became east again, a destiny more mingled than manifest, perhaps, but one that would at last achieve what Columbus had set out to accomplish. For centuries America was what you got instead of China or Japan: the long voyage west from Europe ended in still more West, so much West, in fact, that the East receded as a real place and became instead a country of the mind and the imagination. In America, that phase ended with the completion of the transcontinental railroad in 1869, not because it brought America to Asia but because it brought Asia to America, in the form of actual Asians. The Chinese immigrants who laid the rails were, for most nineteenth-century Americans, the first "Orientals" they had seen with their own eyes. Prior to this experience, reality rarely entered the picture when Americans imagined the Orient. In this respect they were not unlike their European counterparts of an earlier era.

In Europe, the East became not so much *terra incognita,* as the old maps had it, but *terra fantastica,* at least in the days before the missionaries and the trading companies traveled to China and India in the seventeenth century. Once they did, the distant East assumed new meaning in the mind of Europe, as the Christian and commercial missions proved to be remarkably compatible. The missionaries had no difficulty determining that the people of the East were ignorant and superstitious, in desperate need of Christian conversion; the traders, likewise, were quick to notice that those ignorant and superstitious people had somehow managed to produce enormous wealth, in desperate need of removal from those who had produced it. The exchange of Eastern riches for European religion between parties unequal in power forms the context of the term *orientalism,* a word of surprisingly recent vintage. Per the Oxford English Dictionary, as a description of Oriental style it dates from 1769; as a scholarly designation, from 1811; and as a Western representation of the Orient, only from 1978—the publication date of the book *Orientalism* by Edward Said. The stylistic, scholarly, and ideological meanings of *orientalism* would not have been possible, of course, without the earlier word *oriental,* based on the Latin *orientālis,* which simply means "eastern" or "easterly" and was used as early as 1400 by Chaucer, who spelled the word as we do today (OED).

The word *orientalism,* then, can hardly be said to "derive" from *oriental,* since the older word was simply a directional or geographical designation. Rather, it might be said that the elder term now owes a debt of derivation to the younger: today, no Western prospect exists from which to view the East that does not cast the line of vision through clouds of culture and mists of ideology. This is the sense in which I wish my oxymoronic phrase "American Orient" to be understood: as a version and a vision of the East that can be apprehended only through the distorting lens of the Western eye. For Said, the distortion takes specific form as an ideology of otherness, a false consciousness that construes the East as something that the West cannot possibly be—its opposite, in fact: "The Orient has helped to define Europe (or the West) as its contrasting image, idea, personality, experience."[1] Hence, the Orient is a "European invention," a place of exotic peoples and experiences so much at variance with Western "norms" that it beggars description and begs for exploitation. Orientalism therefore derives its conceptual complexity from its status as a representation, an artifact of European consciousness, and the Oriental becomes an emblem of something radically different from Western man, an Other who "invites" colonial conquest, whether commercial, cultural, or sexual (Said, 190).

For the American no less than the European, the Orient was a representation of exotic otherness, but the American Orient was quite unlike the European one that Said describes, mainly because the United States was not a colonial power. Indeed, colonial subjugation was itself a part of the American experience, so eighteenth- and nineteenth-century Americans experienced the Orient in a fundamentally different way than the Europeans did. Said acknowledges early on that "Americans will not feel quite the same about the Orient" as will the British and the French (1), not least because the imperial might of the United States was not unleashed until fairly late in its history. The country did not exercise its military power against an Asian nation until the gunboat diplomacy of 1853, when Commodore Matthew Perry sailed into Japan's Edo Bay. In the years succeeding, notably 1898, American might was confined either to its own hemisphere (Cuba and, later, Panama, Puerto Rico, and the Virgin Islands) or to areas formerly occupied by older colonial powers (such as the Philippines). Americans were colonial subjects themselves for the better part of two centuries, and America itself emerged out of the same commercial spirit that led Great Britain, France, Belgium, Holland, and other European nations to form trading companies in the Far East (less than a decade separates the chartering of the British East India and the Virginia Companies). Indeed, the East India trade makes Said's choice of "the late eighteenth century as a very roughly defined starting point" for orientalism (3) seem a bit arbitrary. But regardless of the European starting point, American imperial force was not felt as fully in Asia as that of the traditional colonial powers until World War II.

For a variety of reasons, then, the American experience of the Orient is fundamentally different from that of Great Britain, France, and other European nations. In eighteenth-century America the East was, paradoxically, a means of reinforcing the enlightenment values of the West: Franklin, Jefferson, and other American philosophes found in Confucius a complement to their own political and philosophical values. In the nineteenth century, with the U.S. shift from an agrarian to an industrial economy, the Hindu Orient emerged as a mystical alternative to American reality. During this period, for Ralph Waldo Emerson, Henry David Thoreau, and other transcendentalists, the Oriental was not an exotic Other but an idealized one, an Other who was oddly the Same: the American not as he was but as he should be, stripped of all the components of commercialism and materialism that now set him apart from the ideal he had of himself. In this formulation the American is the Other of himself, alienated from what his Puritan origins say he should be. A structurally similar sense of Orient otherness informed the aesthetic discoveries of the early twentieth century, as Ezra Pound, T. S. Eliot, and other American poets found in Chinese and Japanese literature an artistic purity and intensity absent from Western tradition. The experience of the East on the part of such authors amounts to a kind of idealized reaction formation, in which the "Oriental" becomes the fantasy mechanism whereby they overcome something objectionable—either in themselves or in the American culture of which they are a part—in order to attain some freer, more genuine form of artistic expression. Perhaps the Orient Other of the American imagination, then, is a source not so much of exoticism as of authenticity.

The idea that Americans somehow recovered something authentic in themselves—or remade themselves as they wished they were—by taking inspiration from the Far East is the basic argument of this book. But the claim needs to be qualified in several ways. First, as the Eurocentric term "Far East" implies, an American Orient that confers spiritual and artistic benefits to its adherents and enthusiasts makes it fundamentally different from that other Orient which is, properly speaking, the subject of Edward Said's critique: the "Near East." The Near East, also known, oddly, as the "Middle East," could never offer the kind of spiritual and aesthetic satisfaction that came to be associated with the Far East, for the very good reason that the Near East was overrun by pagan infidels. The Ottoman Empire held sway over the "Holy Land," so naturally the Near Eastern Orient was subject to Christian disapproval in a way that the Far Eastern Orient was not. For one thing, Christian missionaries faced far less resistance from Hindus and Buddhists in faraway Asia than they did from Turks and Arabs on the doorstep of Europe. More important, Hinduism and Buddhism were *comparable* to Christianity and, at least among Unitarians and other liberal theologians, possibly even superior to it. The Near Eastern Orient was therefore more "pagan," more erotic, and more worthy of Christian censure than the Far Eastern Orient.

The focus of this book is on the Far East because the American notion of the Near East does not differ appreciably from the British and French conceptions, as a rare exploration of "Orientalism" from an 1853 issue of the *Knickerbocker Magazine* shows. After admitting that the subject is "so general and indefinite" as to resist definition, the author seeks to impose "some limitation of the term" *orientalism* by "represent[ing] it pictorially," though to do so risks breaking "all artistic unity":

> We frame to ourselves a deep azure sky, and a languid, alluring atmosphere; associate luxurious ease with the coffee-rooms and flower-gardens of the Seraglio at Constantinople; with the tapering minarets and gold-crescents of

Cairo; with the fountains within and the kiosks without Damascus—settings of silver in circlets of gold. We see grave and reverend turbans sitting cross-legged on Persian carpets in baths and harems, under palm-trees or acacias, either quaffing the cool sherbet of roses, or the aromatic Mocha coffee, sipped from the fingan poised in the zarf. . . . We perceive the spirit of silence brooding over the turbaned tomb-stones of the cemetery, enamored of its cypress-home and the cool shadow; Nubian slaves, with stealthy tread, following their veiled mistresses through the bazaars. . . . We feel the power of the Sultan and the creed of Mahomet, through Emir and Dervish sweeping over the Orient, giving at least some unity to the scene; we then bespread over all a sort of Arabian night-spell, with its deep sapphire star-light and its nightingale-music from the crown of the palm-tree or liquorice-bush; or in dreamy repose we seem transported to some Swerga of bliss . . . and we call this—Orientalism![2]

This "Orientalism," the author goes on to say, "as it swims before the sensuous imagination[,] is too unreal to be defined" (479). But there is another orientalism more real and tangible than the sensuous one because, paradoxically, it is spiritual. The Orient of minarets, bazaars, sherbets, and seraglios is unreal because it can be only pictured, not felt, unlike the "rich stream of poetry which flows through the Bible, and penetrates our best emotions," and which "springs from the Orient, inspired by God." This Orient, "because spiritual, [is] no longer local" (480). The Judeo-Christian tradition, in other words, "springs from the Orient" only to transcend it: by becoming universal, it ceases to be Oriental. The "local" Arabs and Ottomans are left behind in the fantasy land of the Near East, immune to Christian conversion and bereft of any meaningful spiritual traditions of their own. In the Far East, these formulations did not apply with anything like the force that they had in the Near East. While most Americans could muster no sympathy at all for the Muslims, they might make an effort to understand the Confucians, the Hindus, or the Buddhists on their own terms.

The greater openness to the Far Eastern Orient may owe something to the fact that the United States did not fully assert itself as a colonial power until the late nineteenth century. But as the *Knickerbocker Magazine* essay makes clear, the absence of colonialist ambition did not exempt Americans from many of the same political and cultural misconceptions that their European contemporaries took for granted as Oriental reality. Most Americans, after all, were Anglo-Europeans who took great pride in their Aryan heritage, especially in the latter part of the nineteenth century, and they were deeply suspicious of all Asian peoples as inherently un-Christian and therefore uncivilized. The European stereotype of the devious, uncivilized Oriental was kept alive in the United States through the popular press, even as members of the cultural elite found inspiration in Indian antiquity and ancient China. But the American reaction to Asian cultures is more complex than this formulation allows: the matter cannot be fully explained as yet another conflict of low culture and high. In fact, that conflict was overlaid by another: namely, the seeming contradiction between ancient wisdom and contemporary reality. Indeed, at the same time that the "Buddhist vogue" was sweeping the country in the 1880s, inspired by Sir Edwin Arnold's *The Light of Asia,* the first exclusion laws were being enacted to restrict the immigration of Asian workers. This fact leads to another point of qualification: the idealization of "Orientals" was no guarantee against the hatred and debasement of Asian peoples. Not surprisingly, the admiration of Asian culture and the parallel antagonism toward Asian people intensified as immigration became an increasingly uncomfortable fact of American life.

Although eighteenth-century philosophes such as Jefferson and Adams had admired Confucian China, and nineteenth-century Brahmins such as Emerson and Thoreau had admired Hindu India, none of these men had ever encountered a Chinese or Indian person in the flesh. Not until the latter half of the nineteenth century did Americans come face to face with any of the Orientals they had hitherto known only from books. The contact came on two fronts: the Chinese construction workers who were recruited by railway agents to work on the transcontinental line, and the Japanese students whom American professors taught in Japan during the period of the Meiji modernization. Once the railroad work ended and the Chinese workers tried to enter other sectors of the labor market, they drew fire from the unions, which succeeded, with the aid of pressmen and politicians, in demonizing the Chinese as a threat to the American way of life. The Japanese, by contrast, were represented by those who had taught them at Tokyo University as model students eager to emulate Western ways. Even as mobs were stoning Chinese men and women in California, genteel audiences in New England were listening to lectures about the exotic, aesthetic Japanese. And at the same time, American scholars were fairly obsessed with the Sanskrit language and the Vedic culture of their Aryan ancestors from ancient India. Evidently, the "bad" Oriental could be distinguished from the "good" one on the basis of the latter's geographical and temporal removal from the continental limits of the United States. Problems arose when people of Asian origin tried to participate in American life, as the Chinese did in San Francisco, Denver, and other towns throughout the West in the 1850s and 1860s. The problems intensified in the 1870s, not only because the transcontinental railway was complete but also because the mining industry had collapsed, especially in Nevada.[3] Chinese laborers looked for other types of work and found them, accepting wages well below union scale, and thus began the long, sorry saga of exclusion legislation.

The first such legislation was the Chinese Exclusion Act, passed in 1882, which, as the name indicates, specifically targeted Chinese immigrants. The law "suspended . . . the coming of Chinese laborers to the United States" and prohibited any "State court or court of the United States" from admitting "Chinese to citizenship." A further refinement on the policy came with the Scott Act of 1888, which prohibited Chinese nationals, even longtime legal residents, from reentering the United States after a visit to China. Despite the restrictions on immigration and travel, Chinese people continued to enter the United States illegally, mainly through Vancouver, Canada. In 1892, Congressman Thomas J. Geary of California introduced legislation extending exclusion for another ten years and mandating that all Chinese people legally resident in the country obtain "a certificate of residence" from "the collector of internal revenue" within a year of passage, upon penalty of immediate deportation. When the Geary Act expired in 1902, President Theodore Roosevelt encouraged Congress to make exclusion permanent and extend the policy to cover Hawaii and the Philippines. Later, the 1917 Immigration Act, also known as the Asiatic Barred Zone Act, imposed limits and restrictions (including a literacy test) on all groups of immigrants but targeted Asians in particular: "persons who are natives of islands not possessed by the United States adjacent to the Continent of Asia . . . or who are natives of any country, province, or dependency situate on the Continent of Asia" were prohibited from entering the country. The act specified zones based on lines of latitude and longitude that barred immigration from Indonesia and India (exclusion of Chinese immigrants remained in force because of the 1902 act).[4] The Immigration Law of 1924 allowed immigration but established annual quotas equivalent to 2 percent of the population of groups resident in the United States according to the 1890 census, or a minimum of 100 persons per nation. In his proclamation based on the 1924 law, President Calvin Coolidge used the percentile figure for European countries (in the case of Great Britain and Northern Ireland, for example, the quota worked out to 34,007), but for all Asian nations the minimum figure was used instead.[5] Exclusion ended in 1943 with the Magnuson Act, but the quota system established in 1924 was maintained until 1965, when the Hart-Cellar Act abolished all quotas based on national origin.

The cultural activities that run parallel to these critical moments of immigration legislation are both expected and surprising. Readers who know only the alternative title of Bret Harte's famous poem "Plain Language from Truthful James"—"The Heathen Chinee"—might be surprised to learn that the poem itself and, more important, several of Harte's short stories represent Chinese-American relations in California in an unusually vivid, documentary fashion. The stories, especially (such as "Wan Lee, the Pagan"), accurately capture the realities that led to exclusion despite, or possibly because of, Harte's gifts for caricature.[6] After the exclusion act of 1882, P. T. Barnum exhibited the Chinese giant Chang Yu Sing as both a freak of nature and a cultural anomaly: a Chinese man who, despite his great size, posed no threat at all because he had adapted to Western ways. The year after passage of the Geary Act, American audiences responded enthusiastically to Asian speakers who presented their various beliefs at the World's Parliament of Religions, held in conjunction with the Columbia Exposition in Chicago. A decade later, after the exclusion policy had been made permanent, Shaku Soen, one of the speakers at the Parliament, returned to the United States to lecture on Zen Buddhism, accompanied by his student and translator, D. T. Suzuki.

The American appetite for Asian wisdom also coincided with the 1917 legislation: Rabindranath Tagore's celebrated lecture tour of 1916–17 harmonized with the reelection campaign of Woodrow Wilson, who had campaigned as a pacifist internationalist, precisely the message and image presented by the saintly Tagore. Things turned ugly when the immigration law passed in February 1917 and America declared war on Germany in April. And things turned even uglier after the war, at least for Asian immigrants, with the passage of the 1924 law. Nonetheless, American curiosity about Asian culture continued unabated, notable successes being the popularizations of Buddhism published by Jiddu Krishnamurti in the 1920s.

During the 1930s, the novels of Pearl S. Buck and the Hollywood version of the most famous of those novels, *The Good Earth*, almost certainly helped to change American attitudes toward China and Chinese Americans, culminating in the Magnuson Act of 1943. When the remaining strictures against Asian immigrants and Asian residents were lifted with the 1965 Hart-Cellar Act, Eastern culture—of both the "high" and the "low" variety—fairly flooded into the United States. Much of the counterculture of the late 1960s was fueled by this new Asiatic awakening, and much of that counterculture became part of the commercial mainstream: yoga workshops, martial arts centers, feng-shui advisers, New Age gurus, and the rest are now the stuff of late-night infomercials and regular features of middle-class American life. The self-help industry's reliance on Asian traditions, however debased, is only the most recent instance of a long-standing tendency in the United States to find Oriental remedies for American ills. The trend began even before the country did, in the colonial period, and underwent many changes as American interest and involvement with Asian culture developed and ramified over the centuries.

Basically, the history of the American Orient falls into three major phases: (1) the period before contact with Asian peoples, which runs up to 1853, when Commodore Perry sailed into Edo Bay; (2) the period after contact but before the Magnuson Act of 1943, when exclusion finally ended; and (3) from 1943 to the present. The rationale for these divisions is based on the "ontological" status of the Oriental from the American perspective. In the first period, the Oriental may hardly be said to exist at all, except as a philosophical idea or a theological construction. This version of the Oriental hardly disappeared during the second period, especially among the scholars, but was joined by other versions, Orientals who were Other in different ways: San Franciscans had never seen anything like the Chinese "celestials" who worked the mines and rails, and the Bostonians found the Japanese they encountered strange beyond description. Asians remained aliens in America after 1943 of course, but the end of exclusion began a process of assimilation that became all but complete by the early twenty-first century.

Paradoxically, the process began not only with the Magnuson Act but also with Japanese internment during World War II. That injustice continues to resonate as one of the most shameful episodes in American history precisely because the people of Japanese ancestry (half of them children) in the internment camps were U.S. citizens or permanent legal residents.[7] The racist rationale for the camps, while obvious (no German Americans or Italian Americans were rounded up, despite their status as "Axis" groups), was actually quite complex. Lobbyists for West Coast growers' associations urged the government to "kick the Japanese out," as one of them testified before Congress, not from "fear of sabotage" but for "economic reasons."[8] The government's response to this kind of reactionary, nativist thinking was, at the time, promoted as a progressive, liberal solution to the Japanese problem. The War Relocation Authority (WRA) was, after all, a civil agency of the Roosevelt era modeled on the Civilian Conservation Corps and the Works Progress Administration. Its purpose was partly to protect Japanese Americans from their xenophobic Caucasian neighbors in Washington, Oregon, and California, and partly to exploit their agricultural skills to reclaim exhausted farmlands in the remote regions of the West where they were relocated. The "progressive" nature of Japanese internment is captured by the title of the report on its wartime activities that the WRA published in 1946, *A Story of Human Conservation*.[9] But regardless of the rationale, one fact is clear: the people in the camps were as American as the guards who kept them confined or the politicians who ordered their confinement in the first place.

This basic truth makes the distinction between "Americans" and "Orientals" harder and harder to sustain in the postwar period. Partly for this reason, and partly because the enormity of the topic requires restriction, this book deals mainly with the first two phases sketched out above and describes the American Orient from the Enlightenment era to the end of exclusion in 1943. The shifting intellectual and cultural attitudes over these two centuries are manifold and complex, but I have tried to organize them into an interconnected chain of changes: from politics to theology; from theology to scholarship; from scholarship to aesthetics; from aesthetics to modernism; and from modernism to mass culture.

The first chapter examines the attitudes of the American philosophes Franklin, Jefferson, and Adams toward ancient Confucian China and, to a lesser extent, Hindu India. What the founding fathers find in Confucius is not altogether compatible with revolutionary politics, so it is not surprising that the least revolutionary of them—Benjamin Franklin—should have taken the greatest interest in the Chinese sage. After the Revolutionary War period, the Chinese Orient gives way to the Indian, as American interest in the Far East shifts from politics to theology, a transition charted in this first chapter.

The second chapter, "The Nineteenth Century: From Theology to Scholarship," tracks the changes not only in the meaning of the American Orient but also in its cultural focus: Confucianism gives way to Hinduism as the Orient of choice; the philosophe is succeeded by the Brahmin. During this period, when Unitarian theologians enlist the Hindus to support their arguments against their Congregationalist neighbors, a great deal of confusion initially exists about the basic facts of Eastern religion (Emerson, for example, thinks the *Bhagavad-Gita* is a book of Buddhism). Ignorance, however, is no impediment to the emerging American impulse to find in Eastern religion a means of supplementing an American experience starved for spirit. Yet, as the century proceeds, more reliable facts begin to accrue when the American Orient enters the academy. With the founding of the American Oriental Society in 1842, the American age of Oriental scholarship finally begins. The professionalization of Oriental studies, confined at first to the study of languages, broadens into archaeology and even geology, as the cultural focus shifts again, this time from India to Japan.

Chapter 3, "The Fin de Siècle: From Scholarship to Aesthetics," follows this shift into the Japan of the Meiji period, when Americans such as Edward Morse and Ernest Fenollosa were invited to Tokyo and other universities to teach modernity to the Japanese (Morse taught Darwin;

Fenollosa, Hegel and Spencer). The Americans of this period were the first to experience any Asian culture firsthand, with the partial exception of Baptist missionaries who went to India in the early nineteenth century (but who were more interested in getting the Hindus to experience Christian culture than in experiencing Hindu culture themselves). For American professors at Tokyo Imperial University during the Meiji era, it is hard to say what was more important: teaching Western science and philosophy to the Japanese or learning Eastern art and aesthetics from them.

The transmission of Eastern aesthetics to modernist writers is the subject of chapter 4, "The Twentieth Century: From Aesthetics to Modernism," a title that may seem a bit baffling at first, but what I mean by it is that the modernists got more from the Orient than aesthetics alone. Indeed, the artistic careers of T. S. Eliot, Ezra Pound, and others argue that the modernists not only pursued aesthetic doctrines partly inspired by the Far East; they also revived the political and theological values of the American Orient that had fascinated earlier ages. The final chapter moves from "Modernism to Mass Culture," a movement that can be explained only by stepping back to the nineteenth century and looking at the place of popular culture in the American Orient, elements of which also contribute to the development of modernism.

The book ends with a brief afterword that traces the permutations of the American Orient over the fifty years or so from the Beat Generation to the New Age conflation of mysticism and consumerism.

Perhaps because of the dominance of Edward Said's European focus on the topic, very few books have explored orientalism from an American perspective. That perspective, however, formed the basis of two art exhibitions in recent years: *Noble Dreams, Wicked Pleasures: Orientalism in America, 1870–1930,* an exhibition at the Sterling and Francine Clark Art Institute, Williamstown, Massachusetts, from 6 June to 4 September 2000; and *The Third Mind: American Artists Contemplate Asia, 1860–1989* at the Solomon R. Guggenheim Museum in New York City, from 30 January to 19 April 2009.[10] The exhibition at the Clark Institute focused on American responses to the Islamic tradition by artists and collectors, with some attention paid to the exploitation of that tradition in popular culture (Camel cigarette advertisements, Rudolph Valentino films, and the like). The Guggenheim exhibition presented American artistic responses to the Far East from the fin de siècle period (e.g., Whistler, Mary Cassatt, Arthur Wesley Dow) to the modernist era (e.g., Georgia O'Keeffe, Arthur Dove, Morris Graves) and beyond (including the action painters of the 1950s, pop artists of the 1960s, and performance artists of more recent years). Curiously, both exhibitions pegged the origins of the American Orient to the same decade, roughly, in the nineteenth century, even though American interest in the East, both "Near" and "Far," began much earlier.

The nineteenth century is also emphasized in what appear to be the only two book-length studies of American orientalism: Carl T. Jackson's *The Oriental Religions and American Thought: Nineteenth Century Explorations* (1981), and Beongcheon Yu's *The Great Circle: American Writers and the Orient* (1983).[11] As his title indicates, Jackson focuses on the role of Eastern religions in American intellectual history over the nineteenth century alone, whereas Yu traces the American literary interest in Asia over another 100-year span, from the mid-nineteenth century to the mid-twentieth, or from Emerson to the Beats. Neither book, then, takes as comprehensive an approach as the one attempted here, which includes the early American period at the beginning as well as a sketch of recent developments at the end. My approach is inclusive in another way as well, since I do not limit my discussion to religion alone, as Jackson does, or to literature alone, as Yu does. In addition to the theological and aesthetic topics they address, I try to give adequate coverage to the political and scholarly dimensions of the American Orient.[12]

Although overall treatments of American orientalism are scarce, aspects of the topic have been the object of specialized analysis for many years. For example, Owen Aldridge's *The Dragon and the Eagle: The Presence of China in the American Enlightenment* (1993) surveys early American interest in China from the birth of Franklin in 1706 to the death of Jefferson in 1826 (evidently the only book to do so). Thomas A. Tweed's *The American Encounter with Buddhism* (1992) covers the years 1844–1912 and overlaps, chronologically but not conceptually, with Lawrence Chisolm's *Fenollosa: The Far East and American Culture* (1963), which remains a valuable source on American participation in the Meiji modernization and other topics. More recently, Judith Snodgrass's *Presenting Japanese Buddhism to the West* (2003) sheds new light on the 1893 Parliament of Religions, while Christopher Benfey's *The Great Wave* (2003) freshens the story of Americans in Meiji Japan. Colleen Lye's *America's Asia: Racial Form and American Literature, 1893–1945* (2005) focuses on representations of Asians and Asian Americans by white authors such as Pearl S. Buck and John Steinbeck in the context of U.S. economic and immigration policies.[13]

But aside from Jackson and Wu, no critic or historian has given comprehensive treatment to American orientalism, despite sometimes exhaustive examination of particular aspects of it. Certainly the relationship of the American transcendentalist writers to Far Eastern thought is ground that has been gone over many times. The same might be said of the widely studied Oriental enthusiasms of modernist authors. But such topics have largely remained discrete, with little or no discussion of commonalities that might connect them. What I hope to bring to the conversation about the American Orient is a sense of context and connection and, at the same time, to introduce areas of study that appear to have been genuinely neglected. The relationship of early American thinking to Far Eastern thought is one area of scholarly neglect, as is the role of orientalism in mass culture. The subject is indeed manifold and multifaceted.

My approach to the manifold nature of American orientalism recalls, in some ways, the one that Ezra Pound called "ideogramic," after his rather limited notion of the way the Chinese writing system works. Pound mistakenly assumed that Chinese characters were more pictographic than they are in fact, but he took away from the Chinese "ideogram" the interesting notion that knowledge of something is made more complete by multiple perspectives on it, provided those perspectives are concrete, grounded in reality. For example, Pound saw in the character for "red" several concrete elements whose meanings contribute to a better understanding of "red" than could ever be gained by abstract definition: "rose," "rust," "cherry." Similarly, the "ideogram" of the American Orient can best be understood as a combination of the various "radicals" I have identified: politics, theology, scholarship, aesthetics, modernism, and mass culture. But the main way that this book differs from earlier efforts to describe orientalism in America is the argument: what the American hoped to find in the Far East was another way of being American. If Europeans were mainly intent on overcoming the Oriental in some actual East, the Americans wished instead not to overcome but to become, to experience the Oriental in themselves. The experience, in turn, need not occur in any actual Orient, but in some political, spiritual, or aesthetic East that can only be found in the West, and can only be called American Orient.

The Eighteenth Century

From Politics to Theology

IN EARLY AMERICA, Benjamin Franklin, Thomas Jefferson, and John Adams, no less than their European counterparts, all took an interest in the various Orients of the eighteenth century. All three were aware of the political import of Confucius, who entered into American political thought mainly by way of the great European philosophes that the nation's founders admired and respected: Leibniz, Condorcet, Voltaire, and others. Jefferson, for example, appears to have derived some of his ideas about education from accounts of the Confucian system that found their way into the enlightened discourse of the Europeans. But Confucian thought ultimately proved irrelevant to the revolutionary shift from colony to nation that the founding fathers accomplished. After the revolution, Americans ceased to be interested in the old Chinese Orient that the French had discovered; instead, they turned their attention to the "new" Sanskrit East that was beginning to excite their British contemporaries. Adams, for one, expressed a keen interest in the way the antiquity of the Hindu faith energized the mythographic debates of the age. Franklin was philosophically less inclined to enter such debates, but he did know and admire the great orientalist William Jones, who had visited him at Passy. Jefferson also took an interest in Jones's translations from the Sanskrit and other Asiatic languages, though he appears to have shown little curiosity about the aesthetic shift such translations occasioned. In fact, the full impress of the Asiatic awakening on American literature had to wait for the transcendentalists of the mid-nineteenth century. By that time, Confucius and the political meanings invoked in his name had receded from the American scene, even as theological and scholarly values became increasingly intertwined.

The well-known orientalism professed by Emerson and his circle in the 1840s (which grew out of Unitarian interest in Hinduism in the 1820s) was the second wave of Asian influence in America, although to divide that influence into waves or phases risks understating just how steady and widespread it was. While Eastern interests among the intellectual elite may have shifted from political to theological, and from Chinese to Indian, during the first century or so of the American Orient, that characterization ignores the growing acquaintance with Oriental culture that followed from the regular arrival of goods from the East in the maritime cities of Salem and Boston. With material riches arriving from China, Turkey, Persia, India, and even Japan (via Dutch traders), the question that presents itself is why India should have eventually emerged in the mid-nineteenth century as the Orient of choice among poets and intellectuals. Classics of Chinese and Persian literature were known in Europe long before the Vedantic literature of India was even translated, so it becomes something of a surprise that Emerson and the transcendentalists in the nineteenth century were already following an earlier American tendency when they began to merge their native New England culture with Vedic tradition. Years before the meeting of Calcutta and Concord, Jefferson acquired a copy of Sir William Jones's 1789 translation of Kalidasa's poetic drama *Sakuntala*. This work, along with Jones's *Poems, Consisting Chiefly of Translations from the Asiatic Languages* (1772) and his *Poeseos Asiaticae Commentariorum* (1774; also owned by Jefferson), were finding their way into American libraries prior to 1800.[1] But eighteenth-century American forays into Hindu literature now appear anticipatory only, motivated largely by the kind of disenchantment with classical tastes that led American readers, including Jefferson, to James Macpherson's *Poems of Ossian* (1773), the spurious epic based on an ancient but nonexistent Gaelic manuscript. Only after 1800 did the Indian East eclipse the more established Orient of China. And it was that Orient that first attracted the attention of Colonial Americans.

I

The initial interest in the Chinese Orient was motivated by politics; at least as represented by the European philosophes, Confucian China was a model society based on virtue and the rule of law. The model, however, was obviously not republican, so the political appeal of China declined as America emerged from the revolutionary period. Paradoxically, the shift toward the theological Orient of India was also motivated, at least in part, by political considerations. Not only did Americans and Indians share the experience of colonial subjugation (the Virginia and East India Companies had been chartered around the same time); they also shared the experience of Sir William Jones, who was known in America for his revolutionary politics even before he was known in India for his Asiatic researches. No single individual did for the Chinese Orient what Jones did for the Indian, but the Chinese Orient probably dominated the early American scene precisely for that reason: any number of European authorities recommended China as the paradigm of an enlightened society.

Jesuit missionaries had begun to convey detailed information to Europe about Chinese culture as early as the seventeenth century. The first introduction to Confucius was provided by Matteo Ricci in his journal covering the years 1583–1610. Ricci's journal has been called one of the most influential works of the seventeenth century: "It probably had more effect on the literary and scientific, the philosophical and religious, phases of life in Europe than any other historical volume" of the period.[2] Accounts of Chinese society by Ricci and, later, by Jean-François Foucquet (1663–1739 or 1740), another Jesuit missionary, exercised an important influence on such Enlightenment philosophes as Voltaire. In his *Philosophical Dictionary* (1764), Voltaire used Foucquet's sympathetic understanding of China as the basis for his "Catéchisme chinois," a dialogue between Cu-su, a disciple of Confucius, and Prince Kou, a young potentate. Cu-su praises his master as a model of wisdom and restraint: "There isn't a virtue he doesn't inspire." When Cu-su quotes Confucius—"Acknowledge kindnesses with kindnesses, and never avenge injuries"—Voltaire makes a comparative comment: "What maxim, what law, could the people of the Occident match against a morality so pure? In how many places Confucius recommends humility! If people practiced this virtue, there would never be a quarrel in the world." Elsewhere in the *Philosophical Dictionary* the Chinese empire is said to be "the best in the world, the only one founded entirely on paternal power," a society well in advance of Europe: "Four thousand years ago, when we couldn't even read, the Chinese knew all the absolutely useful things we boast about today."[3]

Unlike the Protestant missionaries to China of the nineteenth century, the Jesuits respected the Confucian tradition as a kind of cognate to Judaism: that is, as a monotheistic religion that might usefully serve as a basis for conversion to Christianity. The Jesuit conversion strategy was further aided by the tactical claim that neo-Confucianism, because of the added element of Buddhist mysticism, was a corruption of the original Confucian philosophy. Were Confucius himself alive in the seventeenth century, the Jesuit argument ran, he would opt not for contemporary neo-Confucianism but for Catholicism, which bore a greater resemblance to his own ideas.[4] However successful the Jesuits' strategy may have been in China, in Europe their representation of ancient Confucian culture had a different result. The sympathetic attitude toward Confucian thought had the paradoxical effect of turning China into a paradigm of an enlightened society based not on the moral and religious precepts of Christianity but on natural religion and human reason. The Chinese as the Jesuits represented them in the eighteenth century, then, might be used for the non-Jesuitical purpose of "converting" Europe from Christian superstition to enlightened rationality. The philosophe Pierre Poivre (1719–1786) said as much when he claimed that "China offers an enchanting picture of what the whole world might become, if the laws of that empire were to become the laws of all nations."[5] Likewise, Leibniz conveyed the elevated status of the Chinese as practitioners of natural religion when he wrote, "I almost think it necessary that Chinese missionaries should be sent to us to teach us the aim and practice of natural theology, as we send missionaries to them to instruct them in revealed theology."[6]

Given the political idealization of China that prevailed during the eighteenth century, it may seem surprising at first that Enlightenment thinkers in America did not take up the French view of the Chinese as the precursors of the kind of ordered, tolerant society that such philosophes as Voltaire encouraged. This type of "Chinese" society may have been philosophically consonant with the American Enlightenment, but the emphasis on what Voltaire called "paternal power" was not compatible with American politics. In France, the conception of Confucian society that obtained through Jesuit accounts took shape well before republican ideas developed, so that no inconsistency between politics and philosophy emerged when the enlightened despot was encouraged to model himself on Chinese virtue. Also, by the eighteenth century the trade in Chinese porcelain and textiles had made Chinese decorative design fashionable with the European aristocracy. Chinese influences in design led to the vogue of *chinoiserie* and the rise of rococo art, the official style of the ancien régime.[7] To some extent the enlightened intellectual culture that came out of China in the eighteenth century was offset by the elaborate material culture that contributed to the rococo style. This tension was no doubt more evident in France than in America, where chinoiserie and rococo art were hardly as fashionable as they were in Europe. Still, the contrast between an ancient philosophical tradition that emphasized virtue and restraint and a recent decorative tradition that encouraged decadence and indulgence is striking. After the revolution, there would be little room in American society for either type of "Chinese" culture, whether intellectual or material. Indeed, aside from a few nineteenth-century forays into Confucian ethics, American interest in China would not be aroused again until early in the twentieth century.

II

A major exception to the gradual erosion of early American interest in the Chinese Orient is Benjamin Franklin, who remained a royalist through much of his long life and held out hope for the continued union of the colonies and Great Britain as late as 1775.[8] Franklin turned to Confucius for support of the principle of enlightened despotism fairly early on, when he printed extracts from the "*Ta hio,* or *The Great Science*" in a March 1738 issue of the *Pennsylvania Gazette*. In an article titled "From the Morals of Confucius," Franklin cites a passage in which the ancient Chinese sage claims that if "the Understanding of a Prince is well enlighten'd, his Will will incline only to Good." The passage continues in a way that confirms the politics of enlightened despotism, with the goodwill and reason of the prince radiating outward to the entire kingdom:

> His will inclining only to Good, his soul will be entirely rectified, there will not be any Passion that can destroy his Rectitude: The Soul being thus rectified, he will be composed in his exterior, nothing will be observ'd in his Person that can offend Complaisance. His Person being thus perfected, his Family, forming it self according to this model, will be reform'd and amended. His Family being arriv'd at this Perfection, 'twill serve as an Example to all Subjects of the particular Kingdoms, and the Members of the particular Kingdoms to all those that compose the body of the Empire. Thus the whole Empire will be well govern'd.[9]

Since in 1738 the colonies were indeed one of the "kingdoms" of the Crown, the selection makes sense in the early American context.

That same context, though with a different emphasis, came into play when Franklin invoked Confucius again to counsel his friend George Whitefield on the best means of gaining converts. In 1749 Franklin wrote to the celebrated evangelist and commended the practice of "preaching among the greats": "On this principle, Confucius, the famous Eastern reformer, proceeded. When he saw his country sunk in vice, and wickedness of all kinds triumphant, he applied himself first to the grandees; and having, by this doctrine, won *them* to the cause of virtue, the commons followed in multitudes."[10] Franklin is also likely to have been the author of the preface to the premier volume of the American Philosophical Society's *Transactions* (1771), in which Americans were encouraged to imitate the industriousness of the Chinese and to emulate "their arts of living" in general.[11] After the Revolutionary War, and near the end of his stay in Passy as the American ambassador to France, Franklin wrote to his daughter to express dismay over plans in the new republic to establish "Ranks of Nobility . . . and form an order of *hereditary Knights*." He counters the thinking behind the proposed "Order of Cinncinatus" by citing the example of China:

> Among the Chinese, the most ancient, and from long Experience the Wisest of Nations, honour does not *descend*, but *ascends*. If a Man from his Learning, his Wisdom, or his Valour, is promoted by his Emperor to the Rank of Mandarin, his Parents are immediately entitled to all the same Ceremonies of Respect from the People, that are establish'd as due to the Mandarin himself; on the supposition that it must have been owing to the Education, Instruction, and good Example afforded him by his Parents, that he was rendered capable of serving the Publick.[12]

Franklin had long encouraged the "Chinese" virtues of humility, respect for ancestors, and public service. Indeed, many of the axioms in the Confucian texts suggest that the ancient Chinese philosopher and the early American philosophe had certain moral and political values in common. More important, Franklin's use of Confucius is an early instance of a general pattern in the growth of the American Orient: time and again, Eastern values, beliefs, and ideas are used to supplement American political, theological, or aesthetic interests. In Franklin's case, the appeal to Chinese antiquity for moral and political reasons serves to convey an authority that any spokesman for so young a nation would naturally lack.

Franklin's lifetime interest in China reached a kind of culmination in 1771, when he suggested a number of practical proposals for the improvement of America based on comparisons with China. The preface to the first volume of the *Transactions of the American Philosophical Society*[13] explains that "*Philadelphia* lies in the 40th degree of north latitude, the very same as *Pekin* in *China*."[14] The two cities are also on the eastern side of their respective continents and as a result have a similar climate. The author further observes that the plant life of the two countries has much in common; ginseng, for example, is found only "to the westward of *Pekin*" and "within the same degrees of latitude in *America.*" Franklin had his fellow Pennsylvanian John Bartram to thank for the discovery of ginseng in colonial America, having announced the botanist's find more than thirty years earlier in the *Pennsylvania Gazette* of 27 July 1738, the same year he had published his article on the morals of Confucius (Bartram was also enthusiastic about Confucius and even wrote a brief biography of the Chinese sage).[15] The presence of ginseng on both continents and other agricultural resemblances between ancient China and the New World give rise to the hope that "Tea, so much in use among us, and now become so necessary a part of our diet, might be found in *America*" (Pref., v). The comparison is not limited to agricultural prospects; China might also serve as a model for America to follow in other ways: "And could we be so fortunate as to introduce the industry of the *Chinese,* their arts of living and improvements in husbandry, as well as their native plants, *America* might become as populous as *China,* which is allowed to contain more inhabitants than any other country, of the same extent, in the world" (Pref., vii). All these comparisons are made in the context of pre-Revolutionary America and in the spirit of scientific inquiry. The China-America connection is made with an eye not to strengthening an independent nation but to expanding the British Empire, a purpose consistent with Franklin's earlier publication of Confucian texts in the *Pennsylvania Gazette.*

Precisely what early American thinkers such as Franklin meant when they said "Confucius" is not easy to ascertain. Although Latin translations of Confucian works began appearing as early as 1662, it would be some time before they would be understood as distinctively Chinese.[16] Franklin pretty clearly regarded Confucius in the same way as his Continental counterparts did: as a model of reasoned virtue and enlightened governance. But Franklin appears to have discovered Confucius fairly early on: the commentaries and translations he published in the *Pennsylvania Gazette* anticipate Voltaire's "Catechisme chinois" in the *Dictionaire philosophique* (1764) by almost thirty years. And there is no doubt that the passages from the *Da xue* that Franklin published are, in fact, translations, though not, of course, from the Chinese; the fragments from the classic text that Franklin quotes in the *Gazette* are probably translated from *Confucius Sinarum Philosophus* (1687), a Latin work by the Jesuit Philippe Couplet. The fact is remarkable in itself, since the first English translations of Confucius are usually dated from the early nineteenth century.[17] How Franklin came to be the first American to publish an English translation of Confucius, however, is not completely clear. He was friends with the Philadelphia bibliophile James Logan, who is known to have acquired a copy of Couplet's *Confucius Sinarum Philosophus* in 1733.[18] Hence, Franklin could have been not only the first American publisher of Confucius but also the first American translator (from Latin, not Chinese). That possibility is mitigated, however, because the article that appeared in the *Pennsylvania Gazette* is partly copied from *The Morals of Confucius, a Chinese philosopher*, a pamphlet published in London in 1691, which, in turn, was translated from a French work, *Lettre sur la morale de Confucius, philosophe de la Chine* (Paris, 1688).[19] (An 1807 catalogue of the holdings of the Library Company of Philadelphia lists a 1724 edition of the London pamphlet but does not indicate the date of acquisition).[20]

Despite these questions about the provenance of Franklin's 1738 presentation of Confucius, the fact remains that no American after him attempted a translation of the *Da xue* until Ezra Pound did so in the twentieth century, even though other English translations did appear in revolutionary America. Late in the eighteenth century the sense of Confucius shifted, at least in part, from the reasonable, enlightened meanings that Franklin cultivated to something closer to the ideas that the Jesuits had promoted for so long: namely, that there was some kind of analogy between Confucius and Christ. Even the great orientalist William Jones, a tireless advocate for Asian cultures, was content with a Confucius who is a precursor of Jesus. In the last anniversary address he gave before the Asiatic Society in Bengal, only two months before his death in 1794, Jones made a wide-ranging comparison of "the philosophy of the Asiaticks" with classical and Christian thought. In this address, he claims that the Golden Rule—"that *we must act in respect of others, as we should wish them to act in respect of ourselves*"—is expressed "word for word in the original of CONFUCIUS, which I carefully compared with the Latin translation."[21] The comment makes clear that some kind of Latinized, Christianized Confucius was circulating in the scholarly world at the end of the eighteenth century.

That same Confucius had found his way into American newspapers by the early nineteenth century, as shown by a clipping that appears in the scrapbook Thomas Jefferson kept. The scrapbook covers the years 1800–1808 and includes "A Very Ancient Chinese Ode" done into English from the Latin of Jones, the original of which is said to be "quoted in the Ta Hio of Confucius,"[22] the same work Franklin quoted in 1738. The poem first appeared in Jones's *Poeseos Asiaticae Commentariorum* (1774), a book Jefferson owned, accompanied by the original Chinese with a character-by-character Latin gloss, along with a full translation, also in Latin.[23] The same poem is featured in Jones's 1790 essay, "On the Second Classical Book of the Chinese," this time with a literal translation and a versified paraphrase, both in English.[24] As the headnote to the poem in the scrapbook indicates, the translator, one John Collegins, would have had the benefit of Jones's

English version. In any event, Jefferson, who was president at the time, may have clipped the poem because it extols the political benefits of virtuous humility. According to the Confucian "ode," the prince molds the people by the example of his virtue and so refines the nation:

> In him the meek ey'd virtues join!
> Just as a patient carver will
> Hard ivory model by his skill,
> So his example has impress'd
> Benevolence in every breast. . . .
> Thus he in manners goodly great,
> Refines the people of his state.
>   (Gross, 163)

The clipping shows that Jefferson had some interest in Eastern thought but hardly justifies one commentator's claim that the third president "drew on the wisdom of Confucius for his own ideas about political leadership." Indeed, no volumes from Confucius made their way into Jefferson's library (Gross, 163n). The bibliographical absence is attributable to several factors: the gradual displacement of the Chinese Orient by the Indian one over the course of the eighteenth century; the limited relevance of Confucian ideas to revolutionary politics; and the relative scarcity of the texts themselves.

Nonetheless, the strong impression remains that Jefferson assimilated Confucian ideas into his own political thought. Two ideas in particular, one general, the other quite specific, point to some kind of indirect, mediated Confucian influence on him. The first is the general notion that social value rests on individual merit rather than on hereditary privilege. In a famous letter to John Adams from 1813, Jefferson distinguished between "a natural aristocracy among men," based on "virtue and talents," and "an artificial aristocracy, founded on wealth and birth, without either virtue or talents."[25] Franklin's letter to his daughter on the Chinese preference for ascending rather than descending honor expresses a similar political sentiment. Jefferson goes further, however, and makes the notion of natural aristocracy the rationale for a system of education designed to ensure the political welfare of the nation: "The natural aristocracy I consider as the most precious gift of nature for the instruction, the trusts, and government of society. . . . May we not even say that that form of government is the best, which provides the most effectually for the pure selection of these natural aristoi into the offices of government?" (A-J, 388). As one commentator puts it, "It would be difficult to epitomize the theory of the Chinese examination system more neatly."[26]

This second, highly specific correspondence between Jeffersonian and Confucian thought has been detailed at some length by H. G. Creel:

> Jefferson's plan [to establish a system of education] had three principles in common with the Chinese educational system: (1) Education was to be considered a principal concern of the state. (2) Students of outstanding ability were to be selected, by means of competitive examination, at three levels; students at the lowest level were to be selected from the small districts, and at the highest from the whole state (corresponding to the Chinese district, provincial, and national examinations). (3) A major purpose was to "avail the state" of the services, as officials, of the most talented of its citizens, whether they might be rich or poor and regardless of pedigree. It differed from the Chinese system in that it provided some free education for all, it called for the education of the talented wholly at public expense, and Jefferson would have required that his "natural aristocrats" must not only pass examinations but be elected to office, not appointed as in China. (*Confucius*, 276–77)

Jefferson's theory of education had its origins in the legislation he introduced into the Virginia House of Representatives in 1779. "A Bill for the More General Diffusion of Knowledge" proposed a system whereby certain citizens "whom nature has endowed with genius and virtue should be rendered by liberal education worthy to receive, and able to guard the sacred deposit of the rights and liberties of their fellow citizens."[27] The Virginia bill was so amended as to blunt its purpose, but Jefferson held out hope that his proposed system of education might one day be taken up by "some patriotic spirit" to "make it the key-stone of the arch of our government" (A-J, 390). Jefferson's language appears to echo, conceptually, that of François Quesnay (1694–1774), who called public education "the foundation of governments" and repeatedly singled out China as the only nation in history to have sufficiently recognized the importance of that foundation. In *Le Droit naturel* (1765), Quesnay insisted on "the establishment of public and domestic instruction" as the primary law "to which all others must conform": "Without this fundamental institution, government and personal action remain in confusion and disorder."[28] Elsewhere, Quesnay held up China as a model state because the Mandarins had made systematic education the basis of good governance: "China is a state founded on science and natural law, whose concrete development it represents."[29] Similar assessments of Chinese governance were a staple of Enlightenment discourse, and Jefferson could easily have been inspired by any of several accounts of the ancient nation which he is known to have read, such as the one in Voltaire's *Essai sur les moeurs et l'esprit des nations* (1756). He also owned a copy of the French edition of Louis Daniel le Compte's *Memoirs* (1697), an account of a journey through the Chinese empire, in which the Confucian system of education is described.[30]

If Jefferson shared the political opinion of Confucius so much in evidence among his French contemporaries and precursors, he also shared their skepticism of the value of revealed religion. Nowhere is this skepticism displayed more floridly than in *The Ruins* (1791), a popular book by the second-generation philosophe Constantin-François Chasseboeuf comte de Volney (1757–1820). *The Ruins; or, Meditation on the Revolutions of Empires* was widely read in the United States, where Volney lived for two years: starting in 1795 he traveled throughout North America in order to gather information for a geographical study of the continent.[31] During that tour he spent three weeks with Jefferson at Monticello, having met him earlier in Paris.[32] In 1787 Volney's *Voyage en Syrie et en Egypte* (1787) established his reputation as an orientalist. *The Ruins* contributed further to that reputation, since the work employed numerous Eastern faiths to make a strong political argument through mythographic means, namely, that religion works hand in glove with authoritarian government to limit liberty and subjugate citizens: "The heads of a nation, sometimes insolent and audacious, have forged its chains within its own bowels; and mercenary avarice has founded political despotism. Sometimes, hypocritical and cunning, they have called from heaven a lying power, and a sacrilegious yoke; and credulous cupidity has founded religious despotism."[33] No religion is exempt from the charge of complicity with political authoritarianism, and every religion is scorned for "ascribing merit to practices indifferent or ridiculous": "The Jew would rather die than *labour on the sabbath;* the Persian would endure suffocation, before he would *blow* the *fire* with his breath; the Indian places supreme perfection in besmearing himself with *cow-dung,* and *pronouncing* mysteriously the word *Aum;* the Mussulman believes he has expiated every thing in washing his head and arms; and disputes, sword in hand, whether the ablution should *commence* at the *elbow,* or finger's ends" (Volney, 1:102–3).

As this passage shows, Volney managed to convey some basic information about Asian religions despite the vitriolic tone, so Jefferson and other eighteenth-century Americans would have learned something about Hinduism and the rest in addition to following the author's main argument about the dangers of authoritarian politics and organized religion. This point is perhaps best made by the footnote that explains "the word *Aum*": "It is formed of three letters, of which the first, *a,* signifies the principle of all, the Creator, Brama; the second, *u,* the conservator, Vichenou [Vishnu]; and the last, *m,* the destroyer who puts an end to all, Chiven [Siva]. It is pronounced like the monosyllable om, and expresses the unity of those three Gods" (Volney, 1:103n). This is information, pure and simple, not polemic.

Jefferson and Volney have been described as "close acquaintances and regular correspondents," a fact borne out by Jefferson's decision to make his own translation of *The Ruins*. The project was carried out in secret, with Jefferson completing at least the first nineteen of the book's twenty-four chapters, probably in 1799. He sent the manuscript to Volney, who acknowledged receiving it in 1801 and then asked the American poet and diplomat Joel Barlow (1754–1812) to finish the job. *A New Translation of Volney's Ruins* was published in Paris in fall 1802 in a two-volume edition, the first volume being almost entirely Jefferson's work, the second all Barlow.[34] The two volumes have been usefully summarized as follows: "The first part of the book demonstrates the need to get rid of politically elite ruling classes in favor of representative democracies. The second part argues that conflicting religious beliefs—each one fanatically held to be the sole true faith by its followers—are the chief remaining source of human misery once political equality has been achieved."[35] Despite the greater focus on religion in the part of the book that Jefferson did not translate, we can be sure that he was thoroughly familiar with every page of this powerfully influential book. His involvement with the project shows that Jefferson would have been quite up to date in the Oriental knowledge of the day. But the secrecy associated with the translation, including his instructions to Volney that the manuscript of it be burnt, raises questions about Jefferson's attitude toward the material he translated.[36] Possibly, *The Ruins* was felt to be too sensational a work to be associated with the dignity of the office of president of the United States, which he had assumed in 1801. In any case, Jefferson's deep familiarity with *The Ruins* helps to explain his reluctance to entertain questions about Eastern religion with the kind of animation John Adams displayed late in life, when the two men renewed their friendship and began an exchange of remarkable letters.

Another point to be made about *The Ruins* is that Volney's comments on Confucianism are far less severe than his critiques of Hinduism, Islam, and Christianity. All he says is that "the follower of Confucius interrogates his destiny in the cast of dies and the movement of the stars" (Volney, 1:196), a fairly benign remark that hardly gainsays the earlier, more admiring comments about the political value of Confucius made by those first-generation philosophes, like Voltaire, whom Jefferson also read and admired.

III

Like Jefferson, John Adams made only incidental or indirect reference to Confucius as a political philosopher. In *Thoughts on Government,* a January 1776 argument for republican institutions, Adams names Confucius, along with "Zoroaster, Socrates, and Mahomet," as among the "sober inquirers after truth" who have "declared that the happiness of man, as well as his dignity, consists in virtue." And since "happiness, to the greatest number of persons, and in the greatest degree," is the overall aim of good government, that government is best which makes virtue its foundation.[37] After Independence, the name Confucius figures in another list from Adams's *Defense of the Constitutions of Government of the United States of America* (1787–1788): "The systems of legislators are experiments made on human life and manners, society and government. Zoroaster, Confucius, Mithras, Odin, Thor, Mahomet, Lycurcus, Solon, Romulus, and a thousand others, may be compared to philosophers making experiments in the elements."[38] This list differs from the earlier one in two respects: first, Adams has added legislators from classical antiquity, an addition most likely derived from Plutarch's *Lives*; second, and more significant, he includes figures that we would now describe as mythological rather than historical—namely, Odin and Thor.

The inclusion of Scandinavian deities in a list of legislators tells us that Adams must have been alert to the numerous mythographic studies that had begun to appear over the last third of the eighteenth century. Toward the end of his long life, Adams became deeply interested in the problems of religion that comparative mythographers such as Charles François Dupuis, Jacob Bryant, and Sir William Jones pursued.[39] But the comment from the *Defense of the Constitutions* suggests that Adams had already begun to develop an interest in mythography well before he retired to Quincy. Most likely, the inclusion of Odin and Thor owes something to Paul Henri Mallet's *Northern Antiquities,* published in French in 1755 and 1756 and translated into English in 1770. The work was the first to "introduce Norse mythology to a wide European audience" and was "read and admired by Gibbon, Walpole, and Voltaire."[40] Mallet describes Odin as an "extraordinary person" who "reigned in the north" and "made great changes in the government, manners, and religion" of ancient Scandinavia.[41] If not Mallet, then some similar source would have provided Adams with a wider view of the political past than classical antiquity alone could provide. Likewise, as the mythographic enterprise proceeded over the latter part of the eighteenth century, the perspective on religion was broadened to include the ancient faiths of many nations. The Indian Orient, in particular, became more richly detailed as a result of William Jones's Asiatic researches.

Adams began reading Jones in May 1817 and was particularly struck by the claims that Jones made in his eleventh anniversary discourse, "The Philosophy of the Asiaticks" (1794). There he argued for a number of parallels between Asiatic philosophy and Western values, especially with respect to "the metaphysicks and logick of the *Brāhmens*,"[42] a point of similitude that impressed Adams, as he noted in a letter to Jefferson of 26 May 1817: "In the 11th. discourse of Sir William Jones before The Asiatic Society Vol. 3. page 229. of his Works, We find that Materialists and Immaterialists existed in India and that they accused each other of Atheism before Berkly or Priestley, or Dupuis, or Plato, or Pythagoras, were born" (A-J, 517). Jones does rehearse the Platonic/Pythagorean argument for the idealist basis of matter in Hindu terms and also evokes Bishop Berkeley, though not by name, when he describes the idea "that existence and perceptibility are convertible terms" as "the fundamental tenet of the Vēdāntī school" (Pachori, 194). The accusation of atheism Adams mentions appears in Jones's discourse as the result of "the intolerant zeal of a missionary priesthood" that sought to discredit rival beliefs (Pachori, 194), language that would certainly have enforced Adams's estimate of the priesthood in his own day. But what Adams has more directly in mind when he mentions accusations of atheism is Joseph Priestley's response to Charles François Dupuis's *Origine de tous les cultes* (1795): "Dr. Priestley pronounced him an Atheist, and, his Work 'The Ne Plus ultra of Infidelity'" (A-J, 489).

Dupuis's mythographic study of world religions reduced them all to allegorized versions of fertility cults, priestly elaborations of the workings of contrary masculine and feminine principles. The theory, as Dupuis developed it, branched out into a kind of lower and higher form, as the contraries "male" and "female" were transformed into "sky" and "earth." Hence, religion—pagan and Christian alike—was explained allegorically as a combination of "sexual symbolism and astro-physical scientific truths."[43] Although Dupuis's analysis was not exclusively reliant on Asian religion, pride of place was given over to the East: "We shall therefore conclude that mythology is not the history of men and does not contain the most ancient annals of the human species disfigured by the hand of time"—which was more or less Volney's argument—"but the history of nature and of causes written in an allegorical style, in conformity with the genius and taste of the ancient philosophers and above all the Orientals."[44] Curiously, the pious Priestley himself seems to have relied on the atheistic Dupuis for a chapter titled "Licentious Rites of the Hindoo and other Ancient Religions" in his *Comparison of the Institutions of Moses with those of the Hindoos and other Ancient Nations* (1799), a work that Adams also read but which failed to fully satisfy his curiosity about the possibility that certain elements of the Hebrew and Christian faiths had their origins in India.[45]

Adams's frustration with Priestley's mythographic study is understandable: the book's aim is rather limited in that Hinduism serves mainly as a foil to advance the superior theology of the ancient Hebrews, whose monotheism presages the author's own Unitarian Christianity. Still, *A Comparison of the Institutions of Moses with Those of the Hindoos* is noteworthy for being the first book published in America to consider Hinduism in extended fashion. The tome comprises twenty-four chapters, or "sections," covering some 300 pages, with such titles as "Of the Veda's, and other sacred Books of the Hindoos," "Of the Bramins," "Of the Hindoo Doctrine of a future State," and so on. Another 100 pages (four sections) are taken up by "Remarks on Mr. Dupuis's Origin of All Religions"; an appendix attacking Nicholas Boulanger's etymological allegorizing of the Mosaic books; another appendix explaining the unique character of the Jewish faith; and, finally, an "Address to the Jews," in which Priestley praises the dispersed peoples of the Hebrew "nation" and predicts that the end of their sufferings is at hand. He reads biblical prophecy as confirmation of the revolutionary history of his own age and concludes that three events, allegedly in the process of unfolding, will herald the deliverance (and conversion) of the Jews: "the breaking up of the present European monarchies, the extinction of the papal power, and the overthrow of the Turkish empire."[46] No doubt Adams was drawn to Priestley because of the Englishman's revolutionary sympathies, not to mention the political persecution he had earlier suffered in Great Britain. After all, Priestley had immigrated to America after a "Church and King" mob burned down his house in Birmingham in 1791.[47] He relocated his laboratory and family to Northumberland, Pennsylvania, where he published *A Comparison* and lived out the remainder of his days as a political exile (he never became an American citizen).

The purpose of Priestley's mythographic comparison, as his title implies, was to affirm the integrity of "the institutions of Moses" over and against "those of the Hindoos." He did so because recent comparative analyses of Hinduism by Alexander Dow, John Holwell, William Jones, and many other authorities (all of whom Priestley quotes at length) had pointed out resemblances between the Hindu and Hebrew faiths and, given the antiquity of the former, also raised chronological questions about historical precedence and theological priority. Could it be that the laws of Moses were actually derived from those of Menu? Or perhaps Moses and Menu were really the same person, as the "etymological" similarity of their names suggested. Priestley does not shy away from making comparisons himself, relating the Hindu system not only to the Hebrew one but to many others as well, such as the Egyptian, the Chaldean, and the Druid—all of which are customarily understood as pagan, or "heathen," to use Priestley's favored term. The logic is simple: Hindu beliefs have much more in common with heathen superstition than with Jewish religion; therefore, Hinduism is a pagan cult. After almost 300 pages of exhaustive exposition and comparison, Priestley concludes that "the Hebrews had a religion perfectly rational," whereas "that of the Hindoos was absurd in the extreme" (*Comparison*, 279). Reason reduces any number of Hindu beliefs, such as reincarnation, to the grossest superstition: "That the souls of men have preexisted, and were sent down into mortal bodies for offences committed in a prior state, is what a man may easily *imagine,* but it is not what any man can *know.*" The Hebrew system is so much more rational than the Hindu one that it even provides proof of divine origin: "It is evident therefore, that true religion, consisting in the knowledge and sole worship of the one true God, and of the destination of man to survive the grave, must necessarily have been derived from revelation" (*Comparison*, 277, 284).

But this is not what Adams wanted to hear; he was disappointed with Priestley's study because the book failed to fully confirm his conviction that organized religion posed a threat to republican government. What he wanted was a broader analysis that would have included, for example, some discussion of the Hindu cognate of "the Trinity of Pythagoras and Plato" (A-J, 428) and other obscurities which have found their way into Christianity and have subsequently been exploited as a means to priestly power. The impulse behind Adams's reading of both Priestley and Dupuis was to find scholarly or "scientific" support for his deep-seated skepticism about institutionalized Christianity. The value of Dupuis's *Origine de tous les cultes* was the thoroughness with which the work was able "to discredit Corruptions and Impostures in Religion" (A-J, 499). Dupuis, Jones, and other mythographers provided Adams with "a compleat draught of the Superstition, Credulity and Despotism of our terrestrial Universe. They show how Science, Litteratur, Mechanic Arts, and those fine Arts of Architecture, Painting, Statuary, Poetry, Musick and Eloquence: which you [Jefferson] love so well and taste so exquisitely, have been subservient to Priests and Kings Nobles and common Monarchies and Republics. For they have all Used them when they could, but as the rich had them oftener than the Poor, in their power, the latter have always gone to the Wall" (A-J, 507). Adams's mythographic reading, not confined, to be sure, to the Orient alone, affirmed his deep-seated wariness of the political threat religious fanaticism posed for liberty and tolerance. As he wrote to Jefferson about a future that neither of them would live to see, "Questions without number will arise in this Country. Religious controversies, and Ecclesiastical Contests are as common and will be as Sharp as any in civil Politicks, foreign, or domestick. In what sense, and to what extent the Bible is Law, may give rise to as many doubts and quarrels as any of our civil political military or maritime Laws and will intermix with them all to irritate Factions of every sort" (A-J, 427).

Adams undertook his reading of Dupuis and Jones for the same reason that Jefferson undertook his translation of Volney: to find arguments to neutralize the political influence of traditional Christianity. And both of them found in mythography ample illustration of the ways in which the Asian faiths, no less than Christianity, had been used to legitimate and perpetuate political despotism. Thus, Jefferson and Adams explored the Orient for the same political reasons Franklin did, the critical difference being the historical circumstances under which their respective explorations were undertaken. In the pre-Revolutionary period, Confucius was admired as a model for reasoned, albeit autocratic, government. After the Revolution, the Oriental potentate emerged as a cautionary figure, a paradigm of the problems caused by a too close relationship of church and state and a warning to the young republic of the dangers of religious sectarianism. These are two rather different Orients, both of which add political meanings of special consequence to the image of the East in the American consciousness.

IV

As the references to Confucius on the part of Franklin, Jefferson, and Adams show, the gradual American removal from the French version of the Chinese Orient is understandable for ideological reasons. Those same reasons help to account for the initial interest in the English version of the Indian Orient that developed late in the eighteenth century and reached its zenith during the first half of the nineteenth. As it was for everyone else, the ancient culture of India was opened up for Americans by William Jones (1746–1794), the father of modern, comparative linguistics and the translator of numerous works from the Arabic, Persian, and Sanskrit languages. Jones is best known today as the founder of the Asiatic Society in Bengal (1784), the organization most responsible for first gathering, translating, printing, and disseminating to the West some of the most important works in the Indian tradition. Among the works that Jones and his associates translated and published were the *Bhagavad-Gita,* the *Hitopadesa,* and the *Sakuntala.* Jones's translation of Kalidasa's *Sakuntala* in 1789 was most significant to the formation of Western conceptions of an Indian literary canon that was seen as the equal of the works of Greek antiquity. Indeed, the period from 1785 (the date of Charles Wilkins's translation of the *Bhagavad-Gita*) to 1808 (the date of Friedrich von Schlegel's influential essay "On the Wisdom and the Language of the Indians") has been described as an "Oriental Renaissance," and no one is more responsible for this rebirth of a previously unknown culture than William Jones.[48] American fascination with the Indian researches of William Jones and the other members of the Asiatic Society might seem, at first, to be subject to the same ideological differences that sent the Chinese Orient underground for a century, since British imperial interests in India were irreconcilable with the ideals of the new republic. But William Jones is a special case: he had already made his reputation in America as a champion of liberty well before he went to India in 1783, and that reputation helped to assure an audience for his Asiatic investigations. Those investigations had aesthetic and theological ramifications that are harder to quantify than the more direct and immediate political impact that Jones had on his American contemporaries, but they are real and lasting nonetheless.

The political involvement of William Jones during the Revolutionary period dates from 1779, when he made the first of three trips to Paris as an agent of the British state to try to negotiate a compromise with the colonies and put an end to the hostilities. He arrived at Passy on 20 May for a meeting with Benjamin Franklin, but because Franklin was not at home, the meeting was delayed. In the interim Jones composed a classical allegory about the American Revolution titled "A Fragment of Polybius." The historical Polybius had authored a history of Rome from the First Punic War to the fall of Carthage, and Jones adopted the persona to construct an allegorical argument in which Athens (England) would accept the peaceful separation of the Islands (America) on condition that Athens maintain temporary control of the Islands but under a "commercial treaty" that would allow for eventual independence. Strangely, Jones concluded his imitation of Polybius by distancing himself from the compromise he had proposed: "While Athens is Athens, her proud but brave citizens will never *expressly* recognize the independence of the islands: their resources are no doubt exhaustible, but will not be exhausted in the lives of us and of our children: In this resolution all parties agree: I, who am of no party, dissent from them; but what is a single voice in so vast a multitude? Yet the independence of the united states was *tacitly* acknowledged by the very offer of terms."[49] When Franklin rejected the offer of terms, Jones began to be more open in his sympathy for the American cause and in 1780 published an opinion in which he said that the war "began with injustice, was pursued with malignity, and must end."[50]

The next year Jones expressed his opposition to the war and his support of American independence in his best-known political poem, "An Ode in Imitation of Alcaeus." The poem begins with the question "What constitutes a State?" and provides a most revolutionary answer:

> Men, who their *duties* know,
> But know their *rights*, and, knowing, dare maintain,

> Prevent the long-aim'd blow,
> And crush the tyrant while they rend the chain:
> *These* constitute a State,
> And sov'reign LAW, *that state's collected will,*
> O'er thrones and globes elate
> Sits Empress, crowning good, repressing ill;
> Smit by her sacred frown
> The fiend *Discretion* like a vapor sinks,
> And e'en th'all-dazzling *Crown*
> Hides his faint rays, and at her bidding shrinks.[51]

With its blatant attack on the tyranny of George III and its justification of chain-rending revolution, the poem became popular in America and was published there in broadside form as well as in anthologies. In 1783 Franklin had his grandson print it on his Paris press; the same year, broadside versions appeared in England as well, one notable edition published by the radical Society for Constitutional Information, which had elected Jones as an honorary member in 1782.[52] Jones's radical politics understandably antagonized the Tory government he had once represented and delayed his appointment to the Supreme Court in Bengal, a position he had sought for some time.[53] Jones was so certain his revolutionary sympathies had undercut his prospects in India that he made plans to immigrate to America, having received "an offer from some American leaders in several states to practice their old law among them and hold the pen in framing their new laws"—that is, to be a potential contributor to the Constitution of the United States. It was as an esteemed jurist that Jones made his preparations to immigrate, having already secured a letter of introduction to Thomas Jefferson written by his friend Benjamin Franklin. Had it not been for a series of accidents, Jones would have wound up in America rather than India in 1783, but his departure was delayed by illness and by the acceptance of his marriage proposal to Bishop Shipley's daughter Anna Maria. When the long-awaited judgeship in Bengal finally came through late in 1783, Jones's second career as an Indian researcher and translator was assured for posterity.[54]

William Jones's reputation in Revolutionary America as an advocate of republican government and individual liberty helped to secure a later audience for his Oriental writings. But the founders of America who either knew Jones personally or who knew of him through their associates nonetheless did not know him in the context of his Asiatic researches. Franklin's meetings with him in Paris took place at a time when Jones had put aside his investigations into Eastern languages. Though it is true that Jefferson owned that copy of Jones's translation of *Sakuntala,* he also owned *An*

Essay on the Law of Bailments (1781), Jones's study of British common law, which was much more in line with Jefferson's interests than was Kalidasa's Sanskrit drama. Jefferson and Franklin were men of the Enlightenment whose engagement with the practical affairs of nation-building left little room for the poetic myths of Hindu India. Not until the time of the transcendentalists would the Indian literature that Jones and other members of the Asiatic Society made available to Europe find a fully sympathetic audience in America or, at least, in New England. But to say that Jones's Asiatic researches had to wait for the arrival of transcendentalism before Indian literature could exercise its influence is to oversimplify the cultural interactions that occurred at the time. Western conceptions of Indian languages and literatures cannot be neatly set apart from the rise of the romantic movement, of which transcendentalism is part. Indeed, transcendentalism has been called "the offspring of a German father and a Hindu mother,"[55] a formulation that makes Jones the man most responsible for the "maternity" of the movement because of his linguistic and literary revelations of Indic culture.

Jones's contributions to the development of romanticism and its American variant, transcendentalism, were made directly in the form of his Indian translations and indirectly through his great insight that European and Asiatic languages shared a common origin. As for the impact of Jones's translations, there is much evidence to suggest that his work played a larger role in the development of romanticism than has been generally allowed. Extracts from James Macpherson's *Ossian* and Kalidasa's *Sakuntala,* identified as "an Oriental tale, text adapted from William Jones," were published together in the 1790s in the French journal *Décade philosophique,* an association that was repeated by Chateaubriand in his *Génie du Christianisme.*[56] The pairing of these two works, one a spurious and the other a genuine discovery of a form of literature previously unknown, shows that Jones's translation was read as an alternative to the ponderous classical tradition that had dominated eighteenth-century tastes. In England, the publication in 1787 of a series of hymns Jones had written to various Hindu deities was a literary event of some importance. Two years earlier Jones had become interested in Sanskrit and made rapid progress in the language by studying the mythical narrator Vishnu-Sarma's *Hitopadesa* with a native informant. A fine example of Hindu "wisdom literature," the *Hitopadesa* is a collection of fables said to illustrate "the art of practical living and upholding *dharma*"[57] ("dharma" refers to the customs of religious conduct that underlie a stable society). The study of Sanskrit through the *Hitopadesa,* in turn, was Jones's inspiration to compose the poems in praise of Hindu deities.

When Jones read the poems at a meeting of the recently formed Asiatic Society, Francis Gladwin, the East India Company's printer at Calcutta, suggested that they be published in a forthcoming collection of *"Original Productions, Translations, Fugitive Pieces, Imitations, and Extracts"* to be known as *The Asiatick Miscellany.* Jones accepted the invitation and published the hymns in the Calcutta edition of 1785. When *The Asiatick Miscellany* was reprinted in London in 1787, two years after the London publication of Charles Wilkins's translation of the *Bhagavad-Gita,* it helped to form the basis of the new romantic culture. Most literary histories treat the publication of Coleridge's and Wordsworth's *Lyrical Ballads* in 1798 as the seminal event in the English romantic movement, but the appearance of William Jones's Hindu poetry in 1787 must have had a role in the formation of the new literature, as these lines from "A Hymn to Nārāyena" suggest:

> Omniscient Spirit, whose all-ruling pow'r
> Bids from each sense bright emanations beam;
> Glows in the rainbow, sparkles in the stream,
> Smiles in the bud, and glistens in the flow'r
> That crowns each vernal bow'r;
> Sighs in the gale, and warbles in the throat
> Of ev'ry bird, that hails the bloomy spring,
> Or tells his love in many a liquid note,
> Whilst envious artists touch the rival string,
> Till rocks and forests ring . . .[58]

Despite the eighteenth-century diction, the poem anticipates the animist vision of nature found in Wordsworth and other English romantics, even as it looks forward to Emerson's cryptic poem "Brahma." The latter connection may be fairly ascertained by a comparison with Jones's remarks in the argument to the poem proper, where he says that Narayena is an epithet for "the spirit of GOD, . . . or *moving on the water*" and explains that "the whole Creation [is] rather an *energy* than a *work,* by which the Infinite Being . . . is present at all times and all places" (Jones, 51). Such ubiquity would seem to cover the case of Emerson's Brahma, for whom "Far or forgot to me is near; / Shadow and sunlight are the same."[59] The larger point here, of which Emerson is only one example, is that William Jones's Indian poetry and translations did not enter the Western tradition simply because of romanticism; rather, romanticism itself developed to some extent out of the Indian literature that Jones promoted and produced.

Jones's linguistic insights also helped to usher in the age of romanticism by casting doubt on the priority and prestige of the Western tradition. When he argued that Sanskrit, Latin, and Greek all developed from some common language (now known as Proto-Indo-European), Jones in one blow unseated the primacy of classical learning and introduced the possibility of a new conception of culture, one completely independent from European tradition and, in many ways, superior to it. Long before Jones delivered his celebrated "Third Anniversary Discourse" to the Asiatick Society on 2 February 1786, he had argued that various Oriental tongues were superior to European languages for certain artistic purposes. His "Une Traité sur la poësie orientale" (1769) argues that Persian and Arabic poetry are not bound by the conventions of English poetry and are therefore livelier. The two languages "are suited to poetry, permitting strong expressions, bold metaphors, animated pictures, and fiery sentiments."[60] The idea would be repeated in the twentieth century by Ezra Pound and other modernists, who saw some natural affinity between the Chinese language and poetic imagery, naively supposing that certain languages are better suited to literary expression than others. Thus, in retrospect, Pound's modernist bias in favor of the Chinese language as a medium for poetry merely repeats an earlier romantic inclination to regard Oriental languages as more expressive than Western languages.

Jones makes a similar kind of value judgment in the "Third Anniversary Discourse" when he presents the seminal idea that Indian and European languages are derived from a common language of great antiquity: "The *Sanscrit* language . . . is of a wonderful structure; more perfect than the *Greek*, more copious than the *Latin,* and more exquisitely refined than either, yet bearing to both of them a stronger affinity, both in the roots of the verbs and in the forms of grammar, than could possibly have been produced by accident; so strong indeed, that no philologer could examine them all three, without believing them to have sprung from some common source, which, perhaps, no longer exists" (Pachori, 175). Jones's high estimation of Sanskrit harmonizes with the general romantic impulse to find perfection in the past, an impulse that, in Europe, was prompted by political disillusion with the present, particularly after the failure of the French Revolution and the restoration of the Bourbon monarchy. Jones was, of course, speaking in Calcutta in 1786 well before these events occurred, but he was also speaking out of a sense of disillusionment with the politics of empire which prompted him to elevate the past over the present. Contemporary India may be in decline, but Jones finds no reason to doubt "how degenerate and debased so ever the *Hindus* may now appear, that in some early age they were splendid in arts and arms, happy in government, and wise in legislation, and eminent in various knowledge" (Pachori, 174).

Among many proofs adduced for the original splendor of Indian culture is the *Hitopadesa,* the collection of moral fables and axioms which, according to Jones, confirms the opinion of "the *Graecian* writers, that the *Indians* were the wisest of nations" (Pachori, 177). The *Hitopadesa* was translated by Jones's colleague Charles Wilkins in 1787 and entered American culture in 1842, when Emerson extracted axioms from it for publication in *The Dial* (see chapter 2). This work and Jones's translation of the *Manusmrti*—now known as the *Laws of Manu* but titled the *Institutes of Hindu Law; or, The Ordinances of Menu*—are probably more important to the development of American orientalism than Jones's poetic output. The original poems that Jones wrote based on his knowledge of Hindu literature break new ground in one sense, but they are couched in the archaic diction of eighteenth-century neoclassicism. So, too, are *The Ordinances of Menu,* but the formal diction in this instance only contributes to the sense that the wisdom literature of the Hindus is something to be respected for its great antiquity and authority.

The title of the work is somewhat misleading, for the "laws" that Manu, "a son or grandson of BRAHMĀ" (Pachori, 199), promulgates are spiritual, not juridical. The first chapter resembles the book of Genesis as, beginning with verse five, Manu explains the origins of the world:

5. This *universe* existed only *in the first divine idea yet unexpanded, as if involved* in darkness, imperceptible, undefinable, undiscovered *by reason, and* undiscovered *by revelation,* as if it were wholly immersed in sleep:
6. Then the *sole* self-existing power, himself undiscerned, but making this world discernible, with five elements and other principles of *nature,* appeared with undiminished glory, *expanding his idea, or* dispelling the gloom.
7. HE, whom the mind alone can perceive, whose essence eludes the external organs, who has no visible parts, who exists from eternity, even HE, the soul of all beings, whom no being can comprehend, shone forth in person. (Pachori, 203)

The conveyance of such elevated, spiritual matters in the balanced language of eighteenth-century rationalism made for a ready fit with New England Unitarianism, whose practitioners were among the first in the United States to give the sacred texts of India a sympathetic reading. But this is not the only reason to highlight the role of Jones in the emergence of American orientalism. Having come so close to being an American himself, Jones appealed to philosophes like Franklin because of his support of republican principles. His discovery of Hindu literature helped to usher in the new age of romanticism, and although that aspect of his influence may have been less important in America than in England, the break with tradition that the discovery entailed could only endear him to a nation in the process of forming its own traditions. Finally, the theological implications of the wisdom literature that Jones translated, and the language he used to convey that wisdom, were fully consonant with theological developments in the United States. No one before or since has managed to combine the political, theological, scholarly, and aesthetic variants of orientalism as fully as Sir William Jones, and no one is more important to the introduction of Hindu thought to America.

V

The American Orient around the end of the eighteenth century can be summed up by a glance at two seemingly unrelated texts: Hannah Adams's *Dictionary of All Religions and Religious Denominations* (1784, 1791, 1801, 1817) and Washington Irving's *A History of New York, from the Beginning of the World to the End of the Dutch Dynasty* (1809). What these two early nineteenth-century books have in common is that they are both indebted to the researches of eighteenth-century mythographers, though in very different ways. As one of the true founders of American literature, Washington Irving is widely known and thoroughly studied. Hannah Adams (1755–1831), a native of Medfield, Massachusetts, is, by contrast, hardly a household name, yet she shares with Irving the distinction of being one of the first Americans to earn her living by her pen (evidently the first American woman to do so).[61] Irving's *History* takes playful, satiric aim at the mythographic tradition, while Adams's *Dictionary* accepts the conclusions of the mythographers in an uncritical way, as did her distant relative John Adams, to whom she dedicated all but the first of the four editions of her wide-ranging account of Christian sects and pagan religions.

The first edition of this encyclopedic work was published in 1784 as *Alphabetic Compendium of the Various Sects Which Have Appeared from the Beginning of the Christian Era to the Present Day.* As that title implies, Hannah Adams's dictionary started its long life as a compendium of religion mainly limited to the variants of the Christian faith alone, although the book did include a short, separate section on non-Christian faiths, organized geographically.[62] In 1791 she changed the title to *A View of Religions, in two parts,* with the second part devoted to the religious practices of various "Pagan" groups, such as Greeks and Romans; Chaldeans and Phoenicians; and "Barbarians" (that is, Africans and Native Americans). Despite the severity of this scheme, Adams's treatment of different religions is generally tolerant and evenhanded. As she was careful to point out in the "Advertisement" that prefaced each edition of this popular book, one of the rules she set for herself was "to avoid giving the least preference of one denomination above another."[63] Something that sets Adams's approach off from that of other compilers was her refusal to categorize religions as simply "true" or "false," as Thomas Broughton (1704–1774) had done in *An Historical Dictionary of All Religions from the Creation of the World to this Present Time* (1742). Broughton, an Anglican clergyman, took such a hostile approach to dissenting and non-Christian beliefs that when Adams read him and others like him, she was inspired to do something different and more tolerant, as she noted in her *Memoir* (1832): "I soon became disgusted with the want of candor in the authors I consulted, in giving the most unfavorable descriptions of the denominations they disliked, and applying to them the names of heretics, fanatics, and enthusiasts."[64] Adams is generally true to her word, and her fairness extends to the presentation of Eastern religions no less than to Christian denominations: "In her description of Asian traditions," one commentator notes, "as throughout the volume, she always was more generous and judicious than the authors she consulted."[65] Her open-minded approach earned her recognition as one of the "true pioneers" in the comparative study of world religions.[66]

In 1801 Adams expanded her coverage of the Asian faiths by including a thirty-page survey in the second part of the third edition of her dictionary. For her account of Hinduism she relied mainly on articles by Sir William Jones from the *Asiatic Researches* and on one of Jones's most influential protégés, the Anglican churchman Thomas Maurice. Unlike Jones, Maurice had no knowledge of Sanskrit and no interest in understanding Hinduism on its own terms; rather, his concern was to defend Christianity as the one true faith against the claim that it was simply one more mythological system, no different from any number of such systems throughout the world. He was especially defensive over "Mr. Volney's impious attempt to mythologize the whole of the Christian system, by insisting that the history and miracles of Christ were borrowed from those of the Indian Chreeshna."[67] Consistent with her principles to avoid condemnation of any religion, Adams does not maintain Maurice's tone. But she does, unfortunately, relay Maurice's idea, common in the day, that Hinduism emerged as a distortion of the Hebrew faith, which was supposed to have been conveyed to India in pure form by Noah, his son Shem, or one of Shem's descendants—only to be corrupted later when the descendants of Noah's darker son Ham immigrated to India.[68] Despite this sort of backward thinking, the third edition of Adams's dictionary remains distinctive because it is the first attempt by an American author to offer a comprehensive account of Asian religions.

Also important is the contrast between the third and fourth editions, because the difference allows us to gauge how American knowledge of the Orient had changed in less than two decades. The third edition takes information—about India, for instance—from published sermons, from Montesquieu's *Spirit of Laws,* and from British religious periodicals such as the *Theological Repository.* Adams does cite two authorities on India of some repute: John Holwell and Nathaniel Halhed, the latter the author of *The Code of Gentoo Laws.* Nonetheless, the third edition is far less scholarly than the fourth, which shows that Adams was keen to keep up with the latest theological developments. The fourth edition includes more citations from Sir William Jones and other authorities whose understanding of Asiatic cultures was based on firsthand experience and knowledge of the languages in which those cultures were transmitted. Also, the kinds of sources that Adams uses in the fourth edition make clear that more information, and more reliable information, was making its way to the United States in 1817 than in 1801.

Most interesting, though, is the difference between the organization of the two editions. The third presents Oriental religions in the second of its two sections, the first devoted exclusively to Christian sects. Part two of the 1801 *View of Religions* separates "the Pagan[s], Mahometan[s], Jews, and Deists" from the Christians and claims that "the Pagan is the most extensive" of the non-Christian faiths.[69] The most extensive form of Paganism is "the worship of the *Grand Lama,*" which Adams seems to think dominates the entirety of the Far East. In her view, the "*Dailai Lama*" is an Oriental pontiff who commands respect from the Indians, the Chinese, and the Japanese, evidently because of the belief in "*Metempsychosis* as the most important article of their faith." The logic seems to be that because the soul of the Grand Lama "only quits a crazy habitation to look for another" (3rd ed., 277), passing from one body to the next, and because all the Asian faiths (according to Adams) subscribe to the doctrine of metempsychosis, all worship the Grand Lama as the perfect embodiment of the doctrine. Yet her exposition of the worship of the Grand Lama takes up only two pages of this section.

By the time the fourth and final edition of her dictionary appeared in 1817, Adams had abandoned the two-part structural division of religion into Christian and Pagan and included the entry on "Hindoos, or Hindus" among the many Western religions and sects she described. The entry is unusually long, covering some five pages (roughly twice as long as the entry for "Baptists" and about the same length as the entry for "Unitarians"). She begins with factual information about the textual origins of the faith the Hindus profess: "They pretend that their legislator, Brama, bequeathed to them a book, called the *vedas,* containing his doctrine and instructions. The shanscrit language, in which the vedas are written, was, for many centuries, concealed in the hands of the bramins; but has at length been brought to light, by the indefatigable industry of the late learned and ingenious Sir Wm. Jones and others" (4th ed., 106–7). Assuming that the word *pretend* conveys the now obsolete meaning "profess" (OED), the information is presented in an evenhanded manner. The next section of the entry borrows from Maurice's *Indian Antiquities* the narrative of an ancient Hebrew dispersion after the flood, culminating in the arrival of "the descendants of Ham [who] invaded and conquered India, and corrupted [the] ancient religion," by which is meant "the purest rites of the patriarchal religion" practiced by the descendants of Shem. Then follows an account of "the Hindoo theology" that is mostly cribbed from Jones, such as the description of "Brahme" as "the supreme, eternal, uncreated God" who takes on the three forms of Brahma, Vishnu, and Siva. Through Brahma, "the first created being," the uncreated God Brahme "made and governs the world, . . . assisted by Vishnu, the great preserver of men," and the "coadjutor" Siva, "the destroying power of God" (4th ed., 107). Adams also describes the Hindu belief in "the existence of good and evil" as a dynamic conflict of contrary powers necessitating "the doctrine of the metempsychosis, or transmigration of souls": "It is the invariable belief of the bramins that man is a fallen creature. Their doctrine of the transmigration of the soul is built upon this foundation" (4th ed., 108).

The entry includes information about Hindu religious traditions that are regressive and even shocking, such as *satī*—the practice of "wives burning themselves with the bodies of their deceased husbands"—or incomprehensibly superstitious, such as the "religious veneration . . . paid to the *cow* . . . as holding in the rotation of the metempsychosis the rank immediately preceding the human form" (4th ed., 110). A separate entry on "Yogeys" describes "Hindoo Devotees, who practise a variety of self-tortures"; these Yogeys are said to "cast themselves down on spikes[,] walk on fire, pierce themselves with pins" (4th ed., 322), and so on (the understanding of yoga as nothing more than a form of self-punishment was maintained well into the nineteenth century). This sort of information is set alongside the concept of a religion "originally pure," one that can stand beside any religion as worthy of veneration. In making her presentation, Adams puts the reader in the position of deciding between the narrow Christian perspective of Maurice and the enlightened view of Jones.

But toward the end of the entry she introduces a third authority, Nathaniel Halhed, whose translation of the *Code of Gentoo Laws* (1776) presents Hinduism as "the most tolerant of all religions." The argument proceeds by analogy: a God who creates a world of such astonishing natural diversity would surely welcome variety in the forms of worship directed at Him. As

Adams puts it, "Our author goes on to infer, from the varieties in created things, that the supreme Being has appointed and views different forms of religious worship with complacency." And she adds the authority of Jones to that of Halhed when she rehearses Jones's explanation for the reluctance of Hindus to convert to Christianity: "that they confound their own religion with it, and consider the advent of Christ, as nothing more than one of the incarnations of Vishnu" (4th ed., 111).

Adams concludes the entry by stating that communications from Baptist missionaries to India "fully confirm the above remarks" about Hindu tolerance and resistance to Christian conversion, although she does report that the Baptist mission at Serampore near Calcutta began to experience some success after the New Testament was translated into Bengali. In the end, the perspective is thoroughly Christian—Adams reports that "several of the natives" at Serampore "were baptized in the name of the Lord Jesus"—but other perspectives are on offer as well: Maurice's Judeo-centric mythography, Jones's universal theology, and Halhed's treatise on tolerance. Adams lays out the American sense of Hinduism in the early nineteenth century in all its facets, and what is most interesting about her account is the way she allows for competing opinions. Hardly compatible with the more informed and scholarly views of Jones and Halhed are the mythographic and missionary perspectives, but those were the ways in which Hinduism was understood during Hannah Adams's time.

Adams's presentation of other Asian faiths is not nearly as thorough as her explanation of Hinduism, a telling fact in itself. She treats Confucianism, for example, as one of three "sects" under the "Chinese," the other two being Chinese Buddhism (called "the sect . . . of *Foe*") and Taoism. In describing the religion of Confucius, Adams is well within the eighteenth-century convention of understanding the Oriental sage as an Eastern cognate of the enlightened philosophe: "This religion, which is professed by the literati, and persons of rank in China and Tonquin, consists in a deep inward veneration for the God, or King of Heaven, and in the practice of every moral virtue" (4th ed., 56). The terminology that Adams uses to describe Taoism is confused, but the description itself does not seem out of line with Taoist practice, even today: she claims that the morality of "*Tao-se,* or the followers of *Laokium* [Lao-tzu] . . . consists in calming the passions, and disengaging themselves from every thing which tends to disquiet the soul, to live free from care, to forget the past, and not be apprehensive for the future" (4th ed., 55). The entry, brief as it is, is nonetheless remarkable, because American interest in Taoism was extremely limited in the nineteenth century, with the partial exception of Bronson Alcott's and the total exception of the artist John La Farge's (see chapter 3).

The same might be said of Adams's explanations of Buddhism, which are necessarily confused, not least because none of her sources were written by authors with knowledge of Pali, the language of the canonical Buddhist texts. Her description of Chinese Buddhism as a form of "philosophical atheism" remained in place until the middle of the nineteenth century and beyond: "The internal doctrine of this sect . . . acknowledges no other god than the *void*, or *nothing*; and makes the supreme happiness of mankind to consist in a *total inaction*, an *entire insensibility*, and a *perfect quietude*" (4th ed., 56). The charge of atheism aside, the characterization of the spiritual state of Buddhist beatitude is hardly objectionable. In addition to describing Buddhism in China, Adams also provides entries for Burmese, Japanese, and Tibetan Buddhism, using the names, respectively, "Birmins," "Budso," and "Thibetians." The different varieties of Buddhism proved to be a source of confusion for Americans until well after the Civil War, when a kind of "Buddhist vogue swept the country," including the publication of Charles D. B. Mills's *The Indian Saint* (1876), the first book about the life of the Buddha by an American author.[70]

Despite its manifest and understandable shortcomings, Hannah Adams's *Dictionary* maintains its distinction as the first work by an American author to offer a comprehensive account of Asian religions. The knowledge about the Orient that Adams compiled is mostly reliant on that species of eighteenth-century mythography that sought to defend Christianity in the face of the challenge posed by the prior antiquity of Confucianism, Hinduism, and the rest. In her introduction she rehearses the familiar claim that "the deities of almost all nations were either ancient heroes, renowned for noble exploits and worthy deeds, or kings and generals who had founded empires, or women who had become illustrious by remarkable actions or useful inventions." Another familiar mythographic explanation is the one that sees the origins of all religion in astronomy: "As the sun, moon, and stars shine with a luster superior to that of all other material beings, they received religious homage from almost all the nations of the world" (4th ed., 7). Her sources in this instance are Jacob Bryant and William Jones, and one of the curious things about Adams's habits as a compiler is that she makes no distinction between the merits of these two authorities, the first a defender of the literal truth of the Bible, the second a learned scholar who based his knowledge of Asian culture on a reading of original texts in original languages. Adams's thinking is really much closer to that of the mythographers Bryant and Maurice than to that of the orientalists Jones and Halhed. For her, as for Bryant and Maurice, the origins of Christianity could not be explained by either the heroic or the astronomical theories. It was the one true faith, which "broke forth from the east like a rising sun, and dispelled the universal religious darkness which obscured every part of the globe" (4th ed., 11).

For the most part, Adams does try to live up to her promise "to avoid giving the least preference of one denomination above another," but there is no mistaking the centrality of Christianity in her explanations of Asian faiths. In her fourth edition, Confucius "lived about 500 years before our Savior" (56); a Hindu penitent hears a missionary preach the Gospel and declares, "*This is what I want*" (109n); and Tibetan Buddhists are compared to "Romanists" who tell beads and venerate the Dalai Lama, who is "nearly the same" as the Pope (290). Adams's *Dictionary*, then, shows just how fully American interest in Asia had shifted from the political to the theological by the beginning of the nineteenth century. And though a number of Asian faiths are presented in her book, Hinduism receives the greatest amount of attention.

The theological shift in her *Dictionary* is fully consonant with the religious attitude toward the Orient of the mythographers—mainly Maurice—whom Adams cites. And even though she includes reference to true scholars like Jones, the authority of the old mythography is paramount and completely unquestioned. By contrast, in his comic *History of New York*, Washington Irving calls that authority into question through parody and satire; significantly, mythographic accounts of India form part of Irving's parodic treatment of the kind of universal history that mythographers such as Maurice and Bryant evoked. Irving begins his history of New York at an absurdly high level of generality by accounting for the origins of the world itself and its motion around the sun. Among the various theories he rejects is one "the Brahmins assert, that the heavens rest upon the earth, and the sun and moon swim therein like fishes in the water, moving from east to west by day, and gliding along the edge of the horizon to their original stations during the night." Another is the cosmology of "the Pauranicas of India," which explains lunar eclipses as occasions when "a great dragon swallows up the moon."[71] The first "theory" is taken from the notes to an edition of Luiz Vaz de Camoens's *Lusiad*, an epic account of Vasco da Gama's voyage to India; the second comes from an essay by Sir William Jones. Such sources were highly respected, and by using them Irving lends an air of authority to his fanciful "history." The combination of real and mock scholarship is one of the things that makes Irving's *History* so amusing, as the opening of its chapter 2 shows: "Having thus briefly introduced my reader to the world, and given him some idea of its form and situation, he will naturally be curious to know from whence it came, and how it was created. And, indeed, the clearing up of these points is absolutely essential to my history, inasmuch as if this world had not been formed, it is more than probable, that this renowned island on which is situated the city of New York, would never have had an existence" (Irving, 26). Another Hindu creation myth, this one derived from John Holwell's *Gentoo Philosophy*, is put forward to explain the creation of the world, which would of course include the island of Manhattan: "Thus it is recorded by the Brahmins . . . that the angel Bistnoo [Vishnu], transforming himself into a great boar, plunged into the watery abyss, and brought up the earth on its tusks" (28). The "Brahmins" are included, along with the "negro philosophers of Congo" and "Mohawk philosophers," in a class of "ancient and outlandish" thinkers "whose deplorable ignorance . . . compelled them to write in languages which but few of my readers can understand" (28). The joke is made more interesting by the fact that Holwell was one of those Indologists who provided accounts of Hindu myths without understanding the language in which the myths were written.

No further references to India inform Irving's comic account of the founding of the city of New York, but he does employ the same mythographic strategy to explain the population of the American continent that other mythographers like Jacob Bryant and Thomas Maurice used to explain the Indians in India: he says Native Americans are all descendants of one of the sons of Noah. He is especially good at sending up Bryant, whose *New System; or, An Analysis of Ancient Mythology* relied almost exclusively on etymology to show that the names of pagan gods are merely corrupted forms of true names that appear in the Bible, whose historical veracity cannot be questioned. For example, Bryant claimed that "the history of the Patriarch" Noah is represented "by the ancients" under such "titles" as "Thoth, Hermes, Menes, Osiris, Zeuth, Atlas, Proroneus, [and] Prometheus."[72] Irving satirizes Bryant when he claims that the name Noah has its cognate in the Chaldean "Xisuthrus—a trivial alteration, which, to an historian skilled in etymologies, will appear wholly unimportant" (Irving, 32). The satire effectively calls into question the other identifications common to the mythographic tradition, such as the claim that Noah was known to "the Indians as Menu" (32). A couple of concluding points need to be made about Irving's satire of orientalism in *The History of New York*: one, that it shows a fairly complete awareness of the available scholarship on the Far East at the time; and two, that the earlier scholarship was unsatisfactory—because of the scholars' limited knowledge of Asian languages and their reliance on the outmoded assumptions of mythography.

Irving and Adams therefore both point, albeit in very different ways, to the next stage in the development of the American Orient. Hannah Adams, in her earnest way, thoroughly details the shift in interest from politics to theology, a shift that has its cognate in a migration of American curiosity about the East from China to India. Also, the successive editions of her dictionary reveal that Adams was alert to a profound shift in the way the meaning of Asiatic cultures was constructed, without a full understanding of the meaning itself. That is, she charts the changes that occurred as knowledge about the Orient became more scholarly and less reliant on the old mythographic methods that sought to do one of two things: either to use comparisons with other ancient religions to validate Christianity as the one true faith, as Maurice did; or to deploy those religions in an argument against the authority of Christianity, as Volney did, by suggesting its dependence on some prior antiquity, itself of dubious origins (sun worship, ancestor worship, and so on). Irving's satirical history likewise conflates modern scholarship and outmoded mythography but does it knowingly, and in order to realize the comic potential of such a conflation. Simply stated, Irving's satire shows that the mythographic method can no longer be taken seriously, and that negative estimates of the Asiatic world based solely on comparisons with Christianity have no value or validity whatsoever. Such comparisons are outmoded, however, only if Christianity is assumed to be the superior religion. A more tolerant comparison might construe Christianity as the theological equal of some Asiatic faith—which is precisely what occurred in the nineteenth century when American Unitarians experienced the Oriental Renaissance for themselves.

2

The Nineteenth Century

From Theology to Scholarship

JOHN ADAMS'S DISCOVERY of William Jones in 1817 and his distant relative Hannah Adams's publication of the fourth and final edition of her celebrated dictionary in the same year occur at a critical moment in the history of the American Orient. Both Adamses looked to the authority of mythographic scholarship to support their own presuppositions about the value of traditional Christianity. Their presuppositions could not have been more unlike, however, the elder Adams finding fodder in the mythographers for his conviction that the young nation he had helped create still faced threats from organized religion, the younger one finding—in the mythographic analyses of Jones, Maurice, and the rest—confirmation of both the singularity and the superiority of the Christian faith.

Only one year later, in 1818, the theological ground shifted when Unitarian leaders in New England began to learn more and more about the Hindu East, not only from books by British orientalists like Jones and his colleague Charles Wilkins but also from reports by missionaries in India who had firsthand contact with Brahmin intellectuals. These theological interests came to the fore as political meanings receded and the literary value of newly translated (or newly arrived) Hindu classics slowly began to be appreciated. Neither John nor Hannah Adams was particularly appreciative of, say, the *Bhagavad-Gita* as epic literature, nor, for that matter, were the Unitarian churchmen who succeeded them. Indeed, even the great figures of the American Renaissance who helped to establish a national literature, notably Emerson and Thoreau, did not really focus on the aesthetic import of the Asian texts they read so avidly, contenting themselves mainly with theological meanings.

The basic observation that Hinduism was valued for theological rather than literary reasons at the beginning of the nineteenth century is not so simple as it seems. After all, the interest that John Adams took in Hindu literature was likewise theological, but in Adams's case the mythographic tradition dictated that there was really no meaningful difference between literature and theology when it came to Hinduism: literature was nothing more than the allegorical husk that the mythographer stripped away to reveal the theological truth lying behind the epic poem or the tragic drama. And for the enlightened philosophe, theological truth was political falsity, nothing less than the means whereby priests and kings, whether Asiatic or European, maintained their power and constrained the rights of men. Once the Revolution restored and assured those rights in America, the mythographer's unmasking of the politics behind the theology no longer had so urgent a purpose. Hence, it is not surprising that the Hindu faith was regarded in a different light in the early decades of nineteenth-century New England. No longer could it be dismissed for political reasons, since those reasons no longer obtained. But to say that Hinduism was taken more seriously as a substantial theology is not to say that it was universally tolerated. On the contrary, the antiquity of the Hindu faith raised questions about the historical validity of certain biblical assertions, so much so that some New England divines felt an obligation to make reasoned arguments against the religion of India. Others, however, were sensitive to key theological universals that they shared with their Hindu brethren half a world away.

I

The growth of Unitarianism in New England runs parallel with emerging awareness of Indian religion. Time and again, the "religious intelligence" sections of Unitarian periodicals alert their readers to the possibility that rational religion has a counterpart in Hinduism or in other Eastern "sects."

As in so many other areas, the basis for this understanding lies in the work of Charles Wilkins and William Jones. Wilkins's translation of the *Bhagavad-Gita* (1785) frequently, and possibly intentionally, represents the Hindu faith in language that echoes the vocabulary of religious dissent in Great Britain. Dissent places a premium on the doctrine of salvation by faith, not works, since "works" include not only charitable Christian acts but also religious ceremonies presided over by priests. In his rendering of the *Gita*, Wilkins has Krishna tell Arjuna that "works affect not me, nor have I any expectations from the fruits of works. He who believeth me to be even so, is not bound by works."[1] And there is something of Puritan resolve in Krishna's assurance that "a man's own religion, though contrary to, is better than the faith of another, let it be ever so well followed. It is good to die in one's own faith, for another's faith beareth fear" (B-G, 48–49). The point here is that the language of Wilkins's *Gita* would sound familiar to Christian readers who had removed themselves from the established church in England. Moreover, there is some compelling evidence that this particular version of the Hindu classic would appeal to a specific variety of dissenting Christian faith that was as much in evidence in America as in Great Britain. In his introduction to the translation, Wilkins argues that the original purpose of the work "was to unite all the prevailing modes of worship of those days" and to promulgate "the unity of the Godhead, in opposition to idolatrous sacrifices, and the worship of images," thereby bringing about "the downfall of Polytheism." This must have been the ancient intent of the author of the *Gita*, Wilkins implies, because "the most learned *Brāhmāns* of the present times are Unitarians according to the doctrines of *Krĕĕshnă*" (B-G, 24).

Not only the Hindus but the Sikhs as well furnished Wilkins with material suggesting analogies between Indian and rational religion. In 1788 he published in the first volume of the *Asiatic Researches* a description of a Sikh ceremony which included an account of "a hymn in praise of the *unity,* the *omnipresence,* and *omnipotence* of the Deity."[2] The *Christian Disciple,* a Boston Unitarian journal, published this and other excerpts from Wilkins's essay in September 1814,[3] five years before William Ellery Channing's signal sermon on "Unitarian Christianity," widely regarded as the premier manifesto of American Unitarianism.[4] The *Disciple* singles out Wilkins's comment on "the sacred book, written by the founder of the sect," which "teaches that there is but one God, omnipotent and omnipresent; filling all space and pervading all matter; and that he is to be worshipped and invoked." The conclusion that ends the report is remarkable for its ecumenical openness: "The account we have of the principle doctrines of the Seeks, should excite our gratitude to the common Father of our race, that he has, in one way or another, diffused some correct ideas of himself, more generally than has been known or supposed by Christians" ("Important Documents," 269, 271).

In October 1814, the *Christian Disciple* followed up the account of the Sikhs as practitioners of a universal, enlightened faith with several "Remarkable Extracts" from Sir William Jones's mythographic essay "On the Gods of Greece, Italy, and India." Also published in the first volume of the *Asiatic Researches,* the essay implies that the "resemblance between the popular worship of the old *Greeks* and *Italians* and that of the *Hindus,*" as well as the equally "strange religions" of "*Egypt, China, Persia, Phrygia, Phoenice* [and] *Syria,*" results from the prior antiquity of Indian civilization. A key phrase in Jones's discourse is "popular worship," by which is meant polytheism; polytheism, in turn, is understood as a perversion of the true faith: even "the most distinguished inhabitants of the primitive world" are said to have "deviated . . . from the rational adoration of the only true GOD."[5] Jones's presentation of Hinduism is consistent with that of most eighteenth-century mythographers: the mass of worshipers are incapable of conceiving the sublime unity of the Godhead, so the priests manufacture a lower form of the faith that the unlettered can understand and practice in the form of ritual, rather than rational, adoration. Traditional Puritans who read such accounts were therefore free to understand Hinduism as an all-too-familiar form of orthodoxy: a complex, excessively ceremonial faith that perpetuated the power of the priesthood and denied the individual worshiper direct access to the one true God. But if the Trinitarian Congregationalist saw in the lower form of Hinduism a cognate to the Anglican or Roman Catholicism his ancestors had come to the New World to escape, the Unitarian could understand the higher Hinduism as an analogue to his own pursuit of an even purer religion than the one his Trinitarian contemporaries practiced. This much is suggested by the three passages that the editors of the *Christian Disciple* chose to print from Jones's celebrated discourse.

The first describes the paradox of "the triple divinity Vishnu, Siva, Brahma" residing within "only one Supreme Being, whom they [the learned Indians] call Brahma, or the GREAT ONE, in the neuter gender," thus distinguishing the Supreme Being from the male-gendered gods of the Hindu trinity. This "Deity is ever present in his work, and constantly supports a series of perceptions which in one sense" the learned Indians "call illusory, though they cannot but admit the reality of all created forms."[6]

The second extract points to the similarities of the Hindu trinity to the Christian one, and also to "that of *Plato* which he calls the Supreme Good, the Reason, and the Soul." Jones's comment on this triad of trinities takes account of the theological controversy that had followed him from Great Britain to Calcutta at the end of the eighteenth century and that would arrive in New England at the beginning of the nineteenth: the Indian and the Platonic trinities "are infinitely removed from the holiness and sublimity of the doctrine which pious *christians* have deduced from texts in the Gospel; though other Christians, as pious, openly profess their dissent from them. Each sect must be justified by its own faith and good intentions" ("Remarkable Extracts," 344).

The third passage from Jones's essay addresses the prospects of missionary work in India, or "the general extension of our pure faith in Hindustan." It anticipates problems with the "Musselmans" because the followers of Mohammad "consider our doctrine as perfect blasphemy." Not so the Hindus: they "would readily admit the truth of the gospel." An impediment to conversion, however, is the Hindu contention that the Christian gospel "is perfectly consistent with their Sastras." The extract ends with a truly remarkable comment that, in effect, dismisses the need for conversion; Hindus and Christians, it seems, worship the same God at different altars: "The Deity, they say, has appeared innumerable times, in many parts of this world, and of all worlds, for the salvation of his creatures; and though we adore him in one appearance, and they in others, yet we adore, they say, the same God; to whom our several worships, though different in form, are equally acceptable if they be sincere in substance" ("Remarkable Extracts," 344).

The editors of the *Christian Disciple* offer no direct comment on the excerpts from Jones's essay, except, perhaps, for the title "Remarkable Extracts." But an indirect comment appears to have been made through editorial placement, because the extracts are sandwiched between two articles on heresy: an account of the burning of Protestants for heresy in France during the reign of Francis I, and the views of one Dr. Doddridge on "the scriptural meaning of the word *heresy*."[7] The first article makes heresy heroic in the clear-cut case of Protestant dissent from the Church of Rome, which is "heresy" only from the Catholic perspective; the second investigates the difficulty of establishing precisely what heresy means within the Protestant context alone. The editorial choice to position the essay "On the Gods of Greece, Italy, and India" between two very different explorations of heresy seems quite calculated. In the high-toned prose of William Jones, the Hindus do not come across as heretical at all, either in the historical sense chronicled in the first essay or in the definitional sense articulated in the second. But even if they had, it is doubtful that the readers of the *Christian Disciple* would have found them objectionable on that account, anyway.

   Interest in Hinduism among New England divines continued to build
during the second decade of the nineteenth century. That interest received
particular emphasis from the writings and activities of Rammohun Roy
(1772–1833), a member of the Brahmin caste in India who became something of a cause célèbre among Boston Unitarians. Born into a family
that had for several generations amassed wealth in service to the Moghul
dynasty, Roy managed his father's property as a young man before becoming involved with the British East India Company in the late 1790s, when
he began lending money to lesser officials. He entered the service of the
company himself in 1803 and worked as a civil servant in various capacities until 1815. As a secular Brahmin he was ostracized by the pandits of
Calcutta, but the British Indologists H. T. Colebrooke (1765–1837) and
H. H. Wilson (1786–1860) sought out his opinions on the Vedas, even as
Roy entered into a series of theological controversies with the local pandits.
Hence Roy emerged as the preeminent native authority on Hindu theology
in the eyes of British orientalists and, later, American Unitarians. When Roy
died in 1833, William Ellery Channing, the founder of American Unitarianism, mourned the loss in a letter to the British Unitarian Lucy Aiken: "I
feel his loss deeply, I cannot name a stranger whom I so wished to see. Do
treasure up your recollections of him, and give them to me and the public.
I lived in hope that he was to visit this country, and now I can only know
him in the common country of all pure and noble spirits."[8]
   The American Unitarian connection with the noble Brahmin began to
form in March 1818, when the *North American Review and Miscellaneous
Journal,* edited by Edward T. Channing, William Ellery's brother, summarized the contents of three pamphlets by Roy: two English translations of
the Upanishads, with explanatory prefaces, and a polemical piece called *A
Defense of Hindu Theism.* Under the title "Theology of the Hindoos, as
taught by Ram Mohun Roy," the review details what had by 1818 become
a commonplace claim: that the Brahmins of India had "carefully concealed"
the true doctrines of the Hindu religion contained in the Sanskrit Vedas,
which only they could read, "and insisted on the barbarous sacrifices and
idol worship, which had been introduced and perpetuated by their order."[9]
No doubt because the claim was made by someone who was himself a
member of the Brahmin caste, and made in the spirit of religious reform,
the teachings of Roy were especially noteworthy. The author of the article
says that "considerable excitement has lately been produced in India by
the attempts of a very wealthy and learned native, named *Ram Mohun
Roy,* to restore the pure doctrines of the Vedas" (Roy, 387). The *Review*
describes these doctrines as belief in "the existence, the unity, the overruling
providence of a Supreme Being, and the propriety, if not the necessity, of

worshipping him as a being invisible and of pure intelligence" (386). The *Review* also quotes Roy's own description of this Being: "The Supreme Spirit is one and unchangeable. He overspreads all creatures; is merely spirit, without the form either of any minute body, or of an extended one, which is liable to impression or organization. He is pure, perfect, omniscient, the ruler of the intellect, omnipresent, and self existent" (389).

The excitement generated by Roy lies in his capacity to understand polytheism allegorically, just as the enlightened mythographers did. Thus Roy chides his less enlightened co-religionists, such as "the followers of Vishnu," for "mistaking the allegorical representations of the Sastras for relations of real facts" (Roy, 391). In the preface to his translation of the Cena Upanishad, Roy expresses some hope that his countrymen will soon "foresak[e] the superstition of idolatry" and "embrace the rational worship of the God of nature, as enjoined in the Veds [*sic*], and confirmed by the dictates of common sense" (392). The author of the *Review* article is prescient in concluding that the subject of Rammohun Roy's interests (which he calls "novel, at least in this country") "is likely hereafter to attract much attention" (398). The attention the author thinks is sure to come to Roy rests in his religion or, rather, in the potential for conversion that such a religion implies: "Ram Mohun Roy is not a christian, it is true, but the doctrine he inculcates differs very little from the christian doctrine respecting the nature and attributes of the Deity. It is the same in its spirits and objects. If he can introduce it among his countrymen, it will be a great step toward advancing the cause of christianity in the East" (398).

The notice in the *North American Review* was the first of no less than 180 articles mentioning Rammohun Roy to appear in American magazines from 1818 to 1833, the year of Roy's death (and close to 40 appeared after his death). The vast majority of these articles—some 136—were published in the *Christian Register,* starting with "Unitarian Christianity in India" in the premier issue of 20 April 1821. Produced by the American Unitarian Association, the magazine was the leading Unitarian weekly throughout the nineteenth century and well into the twentieth.[10] In the 1820s the *Christian Register* followed the career of Rammohun Roy closely and paid particular attention to a defining moment in that career subsequent to Roy's involvement with the Baptist Mission at Serampore, a Danish colony near Calcutta. Roy had already published *Abridgement of the Vedanta* (1816) simultaneously in English, Bengali, and Hindustani—as well as the English translations of selected Vedas and the *Defense of Hindu Theism* noted by the *North American Review*—when the Serampore mission encouraged him to print extracts from the Gospels in English, Sanskrit, and Bengali. The book was published by the Baptist Mission Press in 1820 as *The*

Precepts of Jesus: The Guide to Peace and Happiness, though without the translations into the two Indian languages.[11] The absence of the projected Bengali translation, especially, made the compilation useless for conversion purposes. Also, as the subtitle of the slim volume (eighty-eight pages) suggests, Roy was interested in the sayings of Jesus not as a means of salvation but as a basis for ethical conduct. As he wrote in 1817 to John Digby, the East India official for whom he worked as a private *munshi,* or clerk: "The consequence of my long and uninterrupted researches into religious truth has been that I have found the doctrines of Christ more conducive to moral principles, and better adapted for the use of rational beings, than any other which have come to my knowledge."[12] Because Roy had separated morality from mystery in *The Precepts of Jesus,* the Baptist missionaries attacked the book published by its own press. Roy countered the hostile reviews of his compilation with *An Appeal to the Christian Public in Defense of the "Precepts of Jesus"* (1820) by styling himself, anonymously, as "A Friend of Truth."[13]

Roy's redaction of the gospels as *The Precepts of Jesus* in 1820 compares to Thomas Jefferson's abridgement of the scriptures as *The Life and Morals of Jesus of Nazareth* in 1803, even though there is no evidence that Roy had any knowledge of the so-called "Jefferson Bible." Both editors used the King James translation as their source text, and both included many of the same passages, such as the Sermon on the Mount (indeed, Roy's *Precepts* begins with that sermon). But the two versions differ in that Jefferson's provides a full narrative account of the life of Jesus, whereas Roy's offers only the sermons and parables, along with the moral admonitions to the Pharisees and the spiritual instructions to the disciples. Neither version includes any mention of miraculous events, such as the virgin birth or the resurrection, nor any reference to the miracles that Jesus himself is reputed to have performed. Jefferson ends *The Life and Morals* with the death of Jesus, combining John 19:42 and Matthew 27:60: "There laid they Jesus: and rolled a great stone to the door of the sepulcher, and departed."[14] Roy concludes *The Precepts* with Jesus' commandment to his disciples "that ye love one another" (John 15:17).[15] The rapidly shifting theological fortunes of Rammohun Roy are nicely captured by the publication history of this little book: after the Baptist Mission Press brought out the first edition of *The Precepts of Jesus* in Calcutta, the Unitarian Society began to reprint it in London.

Meanwhile, even as Roy was defending the morality of Jesus against the attacks of one contingent of the Baptist mission, he was working closely with another contingent on a Bengali translation of the four Gospels from the original Greek. His collaborators were the Reverends William Yates and

William Adam. The translation hit a snag with the Greek word *dia* in the third verse of the opening chapter of the Gospel of John. The word may be translated either as "by," as in the King James version—"All things were made by Him"—or as "through." The three translators, with Roy leading the way, decided that a more faithful rendering of the original yielded a new reading with a very different meaning: "All things were made through him." As one commentator puts it, "In the context of Roy's Vedantic beliefs, the latter rendering almost amounted to asserting the Vedantic theory of creation by emanation and contradicted the Church doctrine of creation by God's command. The subsequent theological controversies separated Roy from the Trinitarian missionaries" (Rayapati, 78). The final irony of the situation is that, at Roy's urging, Rev. William Adam left the Serampore Mission altogether and established a Unitarian Church at Calcutta, earning the erstwhile Baptist the irreverent epithet by which he was sometimes known: "the second fallen Adam" (Singh, 255).

Among the Unitarian periodicals, the *Christian Register* devoted the most attention to the activities of Rammohun Roy. The premier issue of 20 April 1821 observed that the "very learned and opulent Bramin in Calcutta" had "distinguished himself by his writings and instructions on the doctrine of the divine unity," at the same time making the Unitarian mission aware that "the doctrine of the trinity" was the greatest obstacle to the conversion of the "native Hindoos."[16] In December the journal printed a front-page, six-column article on Roy that includes, among other items, the letter that "the celebrated Hindoo Unitarian Reformer" had written in 1817 upholding Christian doctrine for its morality and rationality. The article also contains a thorough account of the controversy subsequent to the publication of Roy's *Precepts of Jesus,* including the "Christian Missionary's remarks" attacking "the radically false supposition, that the moral sayings of Jesus, even if separated from the dogmas propounded by him, are able to 'guide us to peace and happiness.'" In Roy's high-toned response to his critics, he chides them for "applying the name of Heathen to one who takes the precepts of Jesus, as his principal guide in matters of religious and civil duties."[17] Even though questions are raised about whether Rammohun Roy is really a Christian, he emerges as a kind of Unitarian hero anyway because of his principled opposition to his Calvinist critics.

By May of 1822 the second fallen Adam, with Roy's urging, had renounced the doctrine of the Trinity, and the *Christian Register* gave its readers a full account of Adam's conversion to the Unitarian cause. What is most interesting about the account is the editors' observation that Adam was persuaded "by the arguments of the natives whom he was endeavoring to convert to his own faith—thus was he led to reject an important part of his own principles relative to the nature of God, and to embrace a faith in an important respect resembling the leading tenet of the native Hindoos; viz, the Unity of God; for if we are rightly informed, their many thousand inferior deities are only so many modifications of one Supreme Creator and Controller of the universe."[18] The argument was often made in the pages of the *Christian Register* and other Unitarian periodicals that the Hindus were ripe for conversion because of the monotheism underlying the superstition and idolatry of the vulgar version of their faith. But the story of Rammohun Roy and William Adam introduced a novel variation on that argument: now the Hindu could be regarded not as the object of conversion but as the means. The implications of this change were quite remarkable: by the middle of 1822 the Hindus and the Unitarians were on the same theological and philosophical side in the debate with traditional Christians.

II

In 1822 Ralph Waldo Emerson wrote to his Aunt Mary Moody to thank her for the material on Rammohun Roy that she had sent him. His reply reveals him to be a thoroughgoing Unitarian, the appropriate theological posture for a recent graduate of Harvard College: "I know not any more about your Hindu convert than I have seen in the *Christian Register*, and am truly rejoiced that the Unitarians have one trophy to build upon the plain where the zealous Trinitarians have builded thousands."[19] While the reference to Roy as a "Hindu convert" is unknowingly ironic in light of the Adam controversy, the comment does reveal at least a passing interest in a significant Hindu figure who was to preoccupy New England Unitarians for at least a decade. But his aunt's conveyance of information about Roy was not the first occasion for Emerson to direct his attention to the East. On 7 April 1821 he had written her to make sure she would be present for the reading of his poem "Indian Superstition" at the Harvard College Exhibition on 24 April.[20] So even as a Harvard undergraduate Emerson had already turned his attention to the Orient as a source of inspiration, one that he would draw on for his entire career.

This reliance does not mean, however, that Emerson's intellectual—or spiritual—development should be regarded as a simple issue of influence. As Russell B. Goodman puts it, "Emerson's philosophy, from his college days onward, *grew up* together with his knowledge of an interest in Hindu philosophical writing." Goodman also makes the point that Emerson's reading habits were directed by the sort of nonscholarly scholarship he describes in "The American Scholar" (1837). Not only did Emerson glean much of his knowledge of Hindu writing at second or third hand; he "was not even a good reader of the texts he had[;] the *Vishnu Purāna*, for example, contains much more—e.g., rules of sanitation, dynastic lists—than the idea of unity."[21] But for the American scholar as Emerson describes him, books "are for nothing but to inspire": "There is then creative reading as well as creative writing."[22] This attitude toward the sacred texts of the East combines with an element of outright error: in a letter of 17 June 1845, Emerson's grasp of Hinduism is shown to be a bit shaky, to say the least, when he calls "the 'Bhagvat-Geeta,' the much renowned book of Buddhism."[23] For all this, it is possible to track Emerson's growing interest in Asian philosophy over his long career, beginning with the "Indian Superstition" poem of 1821. More important, it is also possible to track the meaning that such philosophy had for him. Where his fellow Unitarians used Hinduism to enliven their faith, to maintain a spiritual element in a belief system that threatened to become too rationalistic, Emerson put Asiatic religion to work to maintain the moral element in a philosophical system that threatened to become too cultural. To put the matter in simple terms, India kept transcendentalism from becoming too German.

The same year Emerson wrote "Indian Superstition," he read Lord Teignmouth's *Memoirs of the Life, Writings, and Correspondence of William Jones.* Emerson also followed British assessments of Indian civilization as they appeared in the *Edinburgh Review,* which he read regularly. An 1818 issue included an essay, "The Religion and Character of the Hindoos," which caught Emerson's attention, as a journal entry of 1823 shows. These two works, together with the information about Rammohun Roy passed on to him by his aunt, were the principal orientalist sources that Emerson is known to have read in the 1820s. In the mid-1830s, however, his curiosity about "the mysterious east," as he termed it, entered a new phase with a reading of Sir William Jones's *Institutes of Hindu Law; or, The Ordinances of Menu,* "one of the most important books read in Concord."[24]

In 1840 he withdrew from the Boston Athenaeum the six-volume *Works* of Jones, which contain *The Ordinances of Menu,* "On the Gods of Greece, Italy, and India," and many other translations and scholarly essays. In 1842 he read Charles Wilkins's translation of *The Heetopades of Veeshnoo-Sarma* and excerpted axioms from it for publication as "ethical sayings" in the July issue of *The Dial.* Emerson secured his own copy of Wilkins's translation of the *Bhagavad-Gita* in 1845, but he already knew of the Hindu classic by way of Victor Cousin's *Cours de philosophie* (1828), which he read in 1831 (Goodman, 627). In 1845 he also read Horace Hyman Wilson's rendering of the *Vishnu Purana: A System of Hindu Mythology and Tradition* (1840), as well as Henry Thomas Colebrooke's *Miscellaneous Essays* (1837), a two-volume tome of 1,000 pages containing explanations of different Hindu schools of thought and translations of several Upanishads. Two years later Emerson went to the Harvard College library and borrowed William Ward's copious *View of the History, Literature, and Mythology of the Hindoos* (1818), another two-volume, 1,000-page work of exhaustive scholarship. Emerson obviously continued to come into contact with literature from the Indian tradition after this period, especially through his friendship with Henry David Thoreau, who shared Emerson's Oriental interests in the early years of their friendship. But the 1840s is the decade when Emerson's Asiatic enthusiasms seem to have been most intense.

Paradoxically, the period of these enthusiasms coincided with the moment of a significant shift in the history of American orientalism. The American Oriental Society was formed in 1842, the same year that Emerson excerpted passages from Wilkins's version of the *Hitopadesa* for *The Dial*. While it is true that the charter members of the society were mostly ministers and missionaries, its foundation marks the beginning of a shift from a theological to a scholarly orientation toward the Orient. In 1845 and 1847 Emerson was reading scholarly works—Colebrooke and Ward, for instance—but not for scholarly reasons. What he chose to quote from Colebrooke's *Miscellaneous Essays* and his own comment on the quotation makes the point: "He who eternally restrains this and the other world, and all beings therein; who, standing in the earth, is other than the earth; whom the earth knows not, whose body the earth is, who interiorly restrains the earth *the same is thy soul* [Emerson's emphasis], and the Internal Check immortal." Emerson's comment: "The internal check is the Supreme Being" (quoted in Christy, 288).

Hinduism may have helped Emerson in his "progression" from Unitarianism to transcendentalism, but that progression was retrograde in relation to the new direction of American orientalism toward scholarly understanding and, later, aesthetic appreciation. In 1843, around the time that Emerson was mining Hindu texts for theological, transcendental meanings, Edward E. Salisbury was appointed professor of Sanskrit and Arabic at Yale University, the first such appointment in the United States. Salisbury had studied Oriental languages in Berlin and was the first American to be able to actually read the celebrated works of Hinduism that so inspired Emerson, Thoreau, and others.[25] But the growing professionalization of Oriental studies evidently left no mark on Emerson at all. Besides, the remark about the "internal check" of the Supreme Being suggests a concern with homegrown Protestant morality which is hardly consonant with a scholarly understanding of Hinduism.

If Emerson lagged behind in the turning of American orientalism away from theology and toward scholarship, he was also a latecomer to the theological understanding of Asian thought, Hinduism especially. The relationship between Unitarianism and the higher Hinduism was well established by the time Emerson certified his break with rational religion in "The Divinity School Address" (1838). Curiously, the language of Hinduism helped Emerson to make the break, because by the time of the address the ancient Indian faith had come to be seen not as a variant of rational religion (as it was in 1818) but as a way of recovering a sense of spirituality that Unitarianism had largely lost. The Unitarian logic remains, but now Emerson has a new attitude toward that logic. In "The Divinity School Address" he understands "all religions [as] forms" of one "Supreme Wisdom" that allows men "to love God without mediator or veil."[26] The lecture takes this basic Protestant tenet and tricks it out in new Asiatic dress: "This thought dwelled always deepest in the minds of men in the devout and contemplative East; not alone in Palestine, where it reached its purest expression, but in Egypt, in Persia, in India, in China. Europe has always owed to oriental genius, its divine impulses" (78–79). This passage accomplishes two things that are typical of Emerson's orientalism: first, it collapses multiple cultures into a single, universal, and undifferentiated divinity; and, second, the unitary wisdom of the East serves to supplement, and sometimes correct, the transcendental strivings of the West.

East met West again in July 1842 when Emerson extracted passages from Wilkins's *Heetepades of Veeshnoo-Sarma* for publication in *The Dial*. Emerson had started the journal with Margaret Fuller to serve as a forum for transcendental ideas and to raise "one cheerful, rational voice amidst the din of mourners and polemics."[27] Sadly, he had himself joined the ranks of mourners when his son Waldo died of scarlet fever in January 1842, an event that may have informed his choice of several extracts from Wilkins's text. The very first axiom counsels abnegation: "Whatsoever cometh to pass, either good or evil, is the consequence of man's own actions, and descendeth from the power of the Supreme Ruler." The second identifies the role of human existence with spiritual values: "Our lives are for the purpose of religion, labor, love, and salvation. If these are destroyed, what is not lost? If these are preserved, what is not preserved?" Another reminds the reader of the irrelevance of mortality: "Why dost thou hesitate over this perishable body composed of flesh, bones, and excrements?" Further selections range from some fairly ordinary admonitions, such as the moral prohibition against eating meat, to paradoxical pronouncements such as the one that ends the extracts: "He, whose inclination turneth away from an object, may be said to have obtained it." The last axiom could not help but remind the Christian reader of certain New Testament paradoxes, such as Jesus' claim that "he that loseth his life for my sake shall find it" (Matthew 10:39).[28]

In fact, all the extracts need to be read in light of the rationale that Emerson provided for making the selections in the first place: "Each nation has its bible more or less pure; none has yet been willing or able in a wise and devout spirit to collate its own with those of the other nations, and sinking the civil-historical and the ritual portions to bring together the grand expressions of the moral sentiment in different ages and races, the rules for the guidance of life, the bursts of piety and of abandonment to the Invisible and Eternal; —a work inevitable sooner or later, and which we hope is to be done by religion and not by literature" (VS, 82). Here Emerson echoes the terms of his "Divinity School Address," where he sought to separate and elevate "the intuition of the moral sentiment" from the trappings of "historical Christianity," which, he says, "destroys the power of preaching, by withdrawing it from the exploration of the moral nature of man, where the sublime is, where are the resources of astonishment and power" (76, 86). Emerson's conflation of morality and sublimity here is crucial to the project he proposes, a project not unlike Rammohun Roy's *Precepts of Jesus,* except that Emerson would go further than Roy and redact extraneous dogma not just from the Hebrew and Christian scriptures but from the bibles of all nations. Emerson himself never got around to making such a collation in fact, but many passages of his essays and lectures assume the existence of Universal Scripture in theory.

The choice of the *Hitopadesa* as the source of inaugural entries for a projected universal bible reveals the same kind of ignorance as that which led Emerson to think that the *Bhagavad-Gita* was a renowned book of Buddhism. In fact, the *Hitopadesa* is a collection of animal fables, not unlike those of Æsop, to which William Jones compared the Sanskrit work.[29] As one scholar explains, the book "is not a piece of sacred literature" but "a manual of instruction in practical politics and economics." Originally intended for "the gullible and naïve sons of a king" who required such instruction, the work assumes the universal desire "for material possessions and physical pleasures." Those individuals who do have "a keen sense of moral responsibility . . . have to be educated to cope with their unscrupulous counterparts. The *Hitopadesa* serves this purpose. Its narratives dramatize the treachery, dishonesty, and selfishness that underlie the conduct of human affairs."[30] In short, the real character of the work is completely misrepresented and obscured by Emerson's transcendental treatment of it in *The Dial.* True, all the moral axioms that Emerson cites do appear in the *Hitopadesa,* but they are spoken by such characters as Chitra-greeva the pigeon, Hiranyaka the mouse, Durganta the lion, and many others. The first three axioms quoted above are taken from a fable titled "The traveler and the tiger" and the last from "The huntsman, the deer, the boar, the serpent and the jackal." Both fables provide instruction on "The Acquisition of a Friend," but contemporary readers of *The Dial* would have had no way of ascertaining this purpose. One can only wonder whether Emerson himself really understood not only the purpose but also the tone of the work he presented in such elevated—and misplaced—spiritual terms.

The same issue of *The Dial* that includes Emerson's excerpts of Wilkins's rendering of the *Hitopadesa* opens with a lecture that Emerson read at the Masonic Temple in Boston in early December 1841. "Lectures on the Times" offers evidence not only of its author's openness to new ideas but also of his readiness to assume a larger role in the promulgation of those ideas. The lecture advocates social reform in several areas, with the abolition of slavery foremost among them, but criticizes "the reforming movement" because its "benefactors hope to raise man by improving his circumstances," whereas what is needed are "new infusions . . . of the spirit by which he is made and directed."[31] Early on we are told that "the Times are the masquerade of the eternities" (153), so it follows that any action taken in time requires the direction of those "eternities," as this Platonic formulation shows: "The conscience of the Age demonstrates itself in this effort to raise the life of man by putting it in harmony with the Beautiful and the Just" (159). The true merit of the reform movement shall be known by "the books it reads and translates," a point that Emerson elaborates by claiming that the age is ripe for another renaissance:

> A great deal of the profoundest thinking of antiquity, which had become as good as obsolete for us, is now reappearing in extracts and allusions, and in twenty years will all get printed anew. See how daring is the reading, the speculation, the experimenting of the time. If now some genius shall arise who could unite these scattered rays! And always such a genius does embody the ideas of each time. Here is great variety and richness of mysticism, each part of which . . . , when it shall be taken up as the garniture of some profound and all-reconciling thinker, will appear the rich and appropriate decoration of his robes. (161)

Although neither this passage nor the lecture as a whole makes any reference to Hinduism, the fact that a sample of "the profoundest thinking of antiquity . . . reappear[s] in extracts" in the same issue as the lecture suggests that Emerson himself may be that genius who will unite "the scattered rays" of a rich and reforming mysticism. The idea, at least, is consistent with the notion of a universal bible collated from the scriptures of all nations.

Perhaps the best candidate for an "all-reconciling thinker," and one of Emerson's models in this regard, is Plato, or at least the Plato that appears in Emerson's *Representative Men* (1850). "Plato; or, the Philosopher" was early recognized as an essay crucial to an understanding of Emerson's syncretic orientalism. In 1885 the American Hegelian philosopher William T. Harris took Platonism as a key to Emerson's orientalism, noting that "what Emerson says of Plato we may easily and properly apply to himself."[32] The Plato of Emerson's essay is, above all, the philosopher most "capable of a larger synthesis."[33] And philosophy itself is defined by a capacity to comprehend the "two cardinal facts" that constitute human efforts to understand reality: unity and variety (Plato, 637). These two properties are, respectively, the special intellectual provinces of Asia and Europe. Despite the fact that, "in all nations, there are minds which incline to dwell in the conception of the fundamental Unity," the "tendency finds its highest expression in the religious writings of the East, and chiefly, in the Indian Scriptures, in the Vedas, the Bhagavat Gita, and the Vishnu Purana" (638). Europe, by contrast, is the domain not only of variety but of all the political and cultural institutions that variety implies; likewise, unity is a complex, generative principle: "These two principles reappear and interpenetrate all things, all thought; the one, the many. One is being; the other, intellect; one is necessity; the other, freedom; one, rest; the other, motion; one, power; the other, distribution; one, strength; the other, pleasure; one, consciousness; the other, definition; one, genius; the other, talent; one, earnestness; the other, knowledge; one, possession; the other, trade; one, caste; the other, culture; one, king; the other, democracy" (639).

As the last few pairings suggest, the contrast of unity and variety has some far-reaching social implications in their respective regions: "The country of unity, of immovable institutions, the seat of a philosophy delighting in abstractions, of men faithful in doctrine and in practice to the idea of a deaf, unimplorable, immense fate, is Asia; and it realizes that fate in the social institution of caste. On the other side, the genius of Europe is active and creative: it resists caste by culture; its philosophy was a discipline; it is a land of arts, inventions, trade, freedom. If the East loved infinity, the West delighted in boundaries" (Plato, 640). For all the rhetorical balance involved in Emerson's analysis here, his historical understanding is oddly asymmetrical, since the Asia of his imagination appears to be largely ancient, whereas his Europe is mostly modern; nor does Emerson take account of the politics of European empire that have helped to make Asia a place of "immovable institutions" with limited prospects of progress. In any event, the only way that Plato can emerge as the philosopher of synthesis is by making "eastern pilgrimages" to "imbib[e] the idea of one Deity, in which all things are absorbed." Hence, Plato is credited with joining "the unity of Asia, and the detail of Europe . . . to enhance the energy of each" (640).

This is the point at which critics are justified in inferring that the Plato of Emerson's essay is closer to Emerson himself than to the historical Plato, since "there is to this day no evidence that Plato either visited India or knew any Indian texts, philosophers or doctrines."[34] But the Plato essay does provide insight into Emerson's understanding of Hinduism, as Frederic Ives Carpenter shows in *Emerson and Asia* (1930), the first detailed account of Emerson's orientalism. Carpenter begins by saying that Emerson understood the word *Asia* as "a symbol for the unknown—for the other half of the world—for mystery, and romance, and poetry, and love, and religion."[35] Also, for Emerson the lines between Plato, Platonism, and Neoplatonism were far from clear: he "credited Plato with the doctrines that the Neoplatonists of Alexandria had deduced from his philosophy, and these doctrines bore a strong Oriental tinge" (Carpenter, 15). The reader of *Emerson and Asia* might be somewhat puzzled at first when he sees two chapters on Neoplatonism, but at the end of the day Carpenter seems to have gotten an essential element of Emerson's orientalism right: there is nothing specifically Asiatic about it; rather, Hinduism and the rest serve mainly to supplement ideas that are basically of West European origin. In this respect Emerson the transcendentalist follows in the footsteps of his Unitarian precursors, who looked to Indian religion for confirmation of their theology rather than to learn anything new from it.

That is certainly one way of understanding Emerson's orientalism: as a means of enriching transcendentalism so that the philosophy appeared more nearly all-encompassing and universal. But another element of Emerson's orientalism is really in conflict with transcendentalism, or at least one of the tendencies of transcendentalism traceable to the movement's roots in German culture. That tendency is culture itself or, rather, culture understood in the sense of self-culture or self-development. The conflict between this sort of culture and the transcendental movement was acutely felt by Margaret Fuller, who wrote in a letter, "I fear I am merely '*Germanico,*' and not 'transcendental.'" The conflict that Fuller describes is rooted in her embrace of Goethe as the prophet of self-culture. "Very early I knew that the only object in life was to grow," Fuller says, and her devotion to Goethe is borne out by the translations she did of his work and by the biography she began of the man. Of his friend and fellow editor at *The Dial*, Emerson said, "Nowhere did Goethe find a braver, more intelligent, or more sympathetic reader," adding that "the effect on Margaret was complete."[36]

If the comment sounds critical, the tone is consistent with Emerson's attitude toward Goethe, whom he criticized for subordinating morality to culture: "He has not worshipped at the highest unity; he is incapable of a self-surrender to the moral sentiment." Emerson also says that Goethe "can never be dear to men" because he was not devoted "to pure truth; but to truth for the sake of culture."[37] One of the things that Hinduism and other Asiatic faiths did for Emerson was prevent him from following too closely the European example of Goethe. Orientalism kept culture from taking over the self—after all, in the Plato essay, Asiatic caste is the antithesis of European culture. Emerson does acknowledge the appeal of culture, but he is quick to say that self-development must be kept in check: "In this aim of culture, which is the genius of [Goethe's] works, is there power. The idea of absolute, eternal truth, without reference to my own enlargement by it, is higher" (760). Self-development, then, has its dangers, but Hinduism and other Asiatic faiths represent, for Emerson, higher means of "enlargement" which do not risk sacrificing morality to culture. Some such notion might explain the ease with which Hindus "become" Unitarians or transcendentalists: they are beyond culture. What is clear is that a belief in the integrity and growth of the self cannot coexist with selflessness, or the merging of individual ego with universal consciousness, which is typical of transcendentalism in general and of Emerson in particular.

III

Thoreau's orientalism differs from Emerson's in several respects. For one thing, as his selections for the "Ethical Scriptures" series in *The Dial* indicate, his Asian interests were not dominated exclusively by Hinduism. At Emerson's request, and after Emerson himself had selected passages from Wilkins's rendering of the *Hitopadesa,* Thoreau kept to the Hindu tradition by choosing excerpts from Jones's translation of *The Laws of Manu* for the January 1843 issue of *The Dial.* But Thoreau broadened the scope of New England orientalism in subsequent issues, selecting "Sayings of Confucius" for the April number and "Chinese Four Books" for October. Thoreau's selections contrast markedly with the remaining "Ethical Scriptures" attributed to Emerson: "Extracts of the Desatir," a collection of sayings from Persian prophets first translated into English in 1818, and two samplings of esoteric philosophy that were already part of an older tradition of orientalism: extracts from a 1650 translation of the *Divine Pimander* of Hermes Trismegistus (January 1844) and "Chaldean Oracles" (April 1844), translated by Thomas Taylor, the British Neoplatonist.[38] Emerson's Persian, hermetic, and Neoplatonic selections help to make a key point that sets him apart from Thoreau. Whereas Emerson collapsed all Asian religions— Hinduism principal among them—into one vast, syncretic, "perennial" philosophy, Thoreau appears to have accepted the Asian faiths on their own terms and tried to incorporate elements of them into his own life.

This was the conclusion Christy came to in 1932, when he wrote that Thoreau applied "Orientalism to [his] individual conduct of life" (187). More recently, Alan D. Hodder has observed that Thoreau, whether in his journals or in the work he published, marshals his "Asian materials . . . in the service of some ulterior personal quest."[39] As a result he sometimes sounds like a convert and is far from timid in stating his preference for Eastern religions over Christianity, as when, in *A Week on the Concord and Merrimack Rivers,* he acknowledges "that some will have hard thoughts of me, when they hear their Christ named beside my Buddha."[40] Such passages prompted James Russell Lowell to ask, quite reasonably, "What . . . have Concord and Merrimack to do with Boodh?"[41] But Thoreau clearly was not a convert to another religion, however much he may have incorporated an Eastern sensibility into his native Concord consciousness. Besides, Thoreau himself seemed to think that his Oriental interests followed from some innate predisposition toward them, as he noted in a journal entry of 1 September 1841: "One may discover the root of a Hindoo religion in his own private history, when, in the silent intervals of the day or night, he does sometimes inflict on himself like austerities with a stern satisfaction."[42]

The orientalist introduction provided by Emerson in the early 1840s combined with Thoreau's increasingly independent explorations of Asian materials for *The Dial* put him in a good position to adapt the literature of the East to his own writing, which he began in earnest when he retired to the cabin at Walden Pond on Independence Day, 1845. The solitary life in the woods that he led there sometimes justifies the identification of the man as a kind of Yankee yogi, a conception that Thoreau himself entertained. In 1849, he wrote to his friend and occasional protégé Harrison Blake, a schoolteacher from Worcester, Massachusetts, and a former Unitarian minister: "Depend upon it that, rude and careless as I am, I would fain practice the yoga faithfully. . . . To some extent, and at rare intervals, even I am a yogi."[43] No wonder Blake "came to look upon Thoreau as a kind of spiritual counselor" (Hodder, 6). Still, it is hard to say what Thoreau might have meant by "practice the yoga," since he could not have had any technical knowledge of such practice.[44] A number of passages from *Walden,* such as one near the beginning of the "Sounds" chapter, suggest a fairly simple identification of yoga with quiet contemplation: Thoreau describes himself sitting "in my sunny doorway from sunrise to noon, rapt in revery," and realizes "what the Orientals meant by contemplation and the forsaking of works."[45] This and many other passages from *Walden* show a Thoreau who has assimilated Eastern thinking in a profoundly personal way, sometimes to a point where he is able to generate an orientalism of his own, as in the famous "artist of Kouru" section in the last chapter of Walden—an Asian fable that appears to be wholly original with Thoreau. But it is largely because East and West are melded so well in *Walden* that Thoreau's first book forms a more interesting episode in the history of the American Orient: in *A Week on the Concord and Merrimack Rivers* the seams show between the two traditions in a way that they do not in *Walden*. In *A Week*, the sense of contrast and critique is stronger, as the East is employed not solely for the purpose of individual enlightenment but also to suggest social and religious alternatives to the West. At the same time, Eastern wisdom has its limitations, and Thoreau does not hesitate to point them out.

The book begins with "Saturday," but "Sunday," appropriately enough, is the day in *A Week* that Thoreau reserves for his most explicit criticism of Christianity. He calls the Christian God "the almighty mortal" and remarks, in comic disbelief, that "the Christian fable" of Jesus has been added "to the mythology of mankind" (*Week*, 65, 66). The force of the fable based on "the humble life of a Jewish peasant" is measured by its ability, after "eighteen hundred years," to still have the capacity "to make a New York bishop so bigoted" (67). The reference to "my Buddha" follows, but Thoreau shifts the tone and allows that a Christian may love Christ as much as or more than Thoreau loves Buddha, "for love is the main thing, and I like him too" (67). But the preference is still for the lovable Buddha over the merely likable Christ, and a few pages later the New Testament comes in second to an assortment of Oriental texts: "The reading which I love best is the scriptures of the several nations, though it happens that I am better acquainted with those of the Hindoos, the Chinese, and the Persians, than that of the Hebrews, which I have come to last. Give me one of these Bibles, and you have silenced me for a while" (72). This sense of competing traditions points to what may be Thoreau's strongest critique of Christianity, which must be quoted at length:

> Yet the New Testament treats of man and man's so-called spiritual affairs too exclusively, and is too constantly moral and personal, to alone content me, who am not interested solely in man's religious or moral nature, or in man even. . . . Christ was a sublime actor on the stage of the world. He knew what he was thinking of when he said, "Heaven and earth shall pass away, but my words shall not pass away." I draw near to him at such a time. Yet he taught mankind but imperfectly how to live; his thoughts were all directed toward another world. There is another kind of success than his. Even here we have a sort of living to get, and must buffet it somewhat longer. There are various tough problems yet to solve, and we must make shift to live, betwixt spirit and matter, such a human life as we can. (*Week*, 73–74)

The necessity of living, and not just believing, is what sets Thoreau off from Emerson, but this passage says much more than that. A life lived "betwixt spirit and matter" goes a long way toward explaining the double life that Thoreau himself lived, as private thinker and public lecturer, poet and activist, hermit and abolitionist, and so on. But to call this life a double one is to miss the point, since Thoreau's meaning seems to be that the spiritual life must inform material existence just as—and this formulation is surprising and new—material existence must inform the spiritual life.

The idea that the contemplative man is at the meeting point of two worlds finds its way into *The Week* again and again. It appears early on in the "Sunday" chapter when Thoreau describes actual reflections on the water as the perfect invitation to reflect, philosophically, while rowing on the water, about the water:

> It required some rudeness to disturb with our boat the mirror-like surface of the water, in which every twig and blade of grass was so faithfully reflected. . . . The shallowest still water is unfathomable. Wherever the trees and skies are reflected there is more than Atlantic depth, and no danger of fancy running aground. We noticed that it required a separate intention of the eye, a more free and abstracted vision, to see the reflected trees and the sky, than to see the river bottom merely; and so are there manifold visions in the direction of every object, and even the most opaque reflect the heavens from their surface. Some men have their eyes naturally intended to the one, and some to the other object. (48)

The implication here is that Thoreau is one of those rare men capable of intending his eyes to both objects, living "betwixt spirit and matter."

Thoreau's sense of the interrelatedness of spirit and matter, and his recognition of the need to live as "human [a] life as we can," might point toward those Confucian texts so readily dismissed by earlier critics, such as Christy, who saw too much political conformism in them for the philosopher of civil disobedience.[46] But the Confucian influence becomes more likely when we look at the passages that Thoreau chose as examples of "Ethical Scriptures" in *The Dial*. His selections from Joshua Marshman's 1809 translation of Confucius's *Lun yu* (now familiarly known as *The Analects*) is remarkable for the omission of political axioms in favor of such aphorisms as "Have no friend unlike yourself" and "Silence is absolutely necessary to the wise man."[47] The first of these is used in expanded form in the great paean to friendship in the "Wednesday" chapter of *The Week*; the second is fundamental to Thoreau's thinking, especially in *Walden*.[48] Thoreau's second set of Confucian sayings for *The Dial* was drawn from David Collie's 1828 version of *The Chinese Classical Work Commonly Called the Four Books,* which included the *Da xue* and *Lun yu* attributed to Confucius and two additional texts by the neo-Confucian Mencius, namely the *Meng zi* and *Zhong yong*. A passage that seems directly relevant to the idea of a human life situated between spirit and matter is this one: "Wherever the superior man passes, renovation takes place. The divine spirit which he cherishes above and below, flows on equal in extent and influence with heaven and earth." Another passage says something close to Thoreau's comment about men who direct their vision solely to one object or another: "The men of the present day cultivate divine nobility in order that they may obtain human nobility; and when they once get human nobility, they throw away divine nobility. This is the height of delusion, and must end in the loss of both."[49]

The elevated language of the Mencius passage obscures the point somewhat, since the notion of nobility seems foreign to *A Week on the Concord and Merrimack Rivers*. But the idea of the river journey or, rather, of the surface of the river itself as a trope for some necessary, intermediate border between matter and spirit has far-reaching implications. Thoreau is careful to keep the reader mindful that his narrative is at once ordinary and extraordinary, mundane and elevated. From the start, he places the lowly Concord in the context of the mythic rivers of antiquity, notably the streams that flow upon Parnassus and Helicon, the mountains of the Muses. The Mississippi, the Ganges, and the Nile are added to the associations that enlarge the meaning of "our muddy but much abused Concord river." The ordinary Concord thereby acquires the properties of the great rivers of the world, which invite "the dwellers on their banks" to engage in one of two mutually exclusive activities: to "accompany their currents to the lowlands of the globe, or explore at their invitation the interior of continents" (*Week*, 12). The paradox, in Thoreau's case, is that he accomplishes both, riding the river into the interior not of the continent but of himself. The retrospective river journey that Thoreau takes with his brother turns them both into inverted, spiritual versions of Lewis and Clark, metaphorically drifting down the Mississippi and up the Ganges. But the double voyage here, as elsewhere, serves the purpose of affirming humanity, a destination not to be attained by some single means alone, whether material Mississippi or spiritual Ganges.

The "Monday" chapter of *A Week* contains Thoreau's most sustained contrast of East and West, analogous to Emerson's comparison in the Plato essay from *Representative Men*. But where Emerson divides Asia and Europe into the respective regions of unity and variety, caste and culture, and the rest, Thoreau makes political values paramount: "The wisest conservatism is that of the Hindoos," while "Christianity, on the other hand, is humane, practical, and, in a large sense, radical" (*Week*, 136). At first, the "Monday" comparisons of Hinduism and Christianity seem to contradict those in the "Sunday" section. There, the New Testament is said to be "too constantly moral" and Christ's teachings "all directed toward another world" (73), which hardly sounds practical or radical. And if the New Testament is "too constantly moral," how different can it be from the *Bhagavad-Gita*, which counsels "an everlasting moral drudgery" (*Week*, 136)? The contradictions between "Sunday" and "Monday" begin to be resolved somewhat as the contrasts between Hinduism and Christianity are explained more fully. But the prior antiquity of the Hindus is preserved when Thoreau describes Jesus as a kind of western Asiatic novelty never imagined by "those eastern sages": "a youth, wholly unforetold by them,— not being absorbed into Brahm, but bringing Brahm down to earth and mankind; in whom Brahm had awaked from his long sleep, and exerted himself, and the day began,—a new avatar. The Brahman has never thought to be a brother of mankind as well as a child of God" (136–37). The New Testament, then, provides its followers with "practical texts" and "good sense": "It never *reflects*, but it *repents*" (137).

This last formulation is the key to the distinction between the two faiths, and helps to clarify the seeming contradiction that posits a Christianity "too constantly moral" and a Hinduism marked by "everlasting moral drudgery." There are simply two types of morality: one insists on action and the other requires obedience. The constant morality of Christianity involves the kind of action that leads to individual repentance and social reform; the moral drudgery of Hinduism—that is, obedience to the rites and rituals of the faith—obviates the need for action and leads to individual reflection and social conservatism. The Brahmin's faith allows him to get past morality and into contemplation, while the Christian's beliefs locate him, necessarily, in the practical realm of morality: "The New Testament is remarkable for its pure morality; the best of Hindoo scripture, for its pure intellectuality" (*Week*, 137). The Eastern sages may be "infinitely stagnant," but they are also "infinitely wise," and no "Western philosophers have . . . conceived of the significance of Contemplation in their sense" (136, 137).

Thoreau explores the relation between action and contemplation by quoting extensively from the *Bhagavad-Gita*, the dialogue between the warrior Arjuna and Krishna, an avatar of the god Vishnu. As Thoreau puts it, the god advises "the irresolute soldier who fears to slay his friends" that the end of all action "is an immense consolation; eternal absorption in Brahma" (*Week*, 135–36). The sense that all actions have the same result is indeed "a sublime conservatism," yet the realization of "the inevitability and unchangeableness of laws" has its attractions. "What after all does the practicalness of life amount to?" Thoreau asks, and what is action beside contemplation: "The most glorious fact in my experience is not any thing that I have done or may hope to do, but a transient thought, or vision, or dream, which I have had. I would give all the wealth of the world, and all the deeds of all the heroes, for one true vision" (140). Having accepted and even endorsed the counsel that Krishna offers Arjuna, and argued the benefits of the sublime conservatism of the Hindus, Thoreau makes one of those rhetorical turns that takes the reader by surprise: "But how can I communicate with the gods who am a pencil-maker on the earth, and not be insane?" (140).

Thoreau then recasts the contrast between East and West in new terms that are more immediately relevant to the practicalities of pencil-making and other, more pressing actions. The teachings of the *Bhagavad-Gita* "are not always sound sense in practice. The Brahman never proposes coura-geously to assault evil, but patiently to starve it out" (*Week*, 140). And as for Krishna's argument, praised only a few pages prior for "a sublimity of conception, reasoning, and diction, almost unequaled,"[50] Thoreau now says flatly that it is "defective": "No sufficient reason is given why Arjoon should fight. Arjoon may be convinced, but the reader is not, for his judg-ment is *not* 'formed upon the speculative doctrine of the *Sankhya Sastra*'" (140). In other words, Thoreau now takes account of context and asks whether the wisdom of the ancient Hindu text can still speak "to a western mind" (140). Here the contrast between East and West becomes explicitly political, even as the terms *east* and *west* acquire metaphorical meanings that describe a profound conflict not between nations but within them:

> Behold the difference between the oriental and the occidental. The former has nothing to do in this world; the latter is full of activity. The one looks in the sun till his eyes are put out; the other follows him prone in his westward course. There is such a thing as cast, even in the West; but it is comparatively faint. It is conservatism here. It says forsake not your calling, outrage no insti-tution, use no violence, rend no bonds, the State is thy parent. . . . There is a struggle between the oriental and the occidental in every nation. (*Week*, 141)

And in every individual as well, Thoreau seems to imply. But despite the turn at the end which takes account of the different roles that action and contemplation can play in the world, Thoreau hardly ends up promoting the practical life alone. This book, and his next one, are dedicated to the integration of action and contemplation, nature and spirit, in the achieve-ment of a human life.

The double sense of spirituality and naturalism is also captured in "Saturday," the first day of the journey, when the brothers happen upon a man fishing in the river who triggers a memory of another fisherman, "an old brown-coated man who was the Walton of this stream" (*Week*, 24).

The man has been dead so long that "nobody else remembers him now": "His fishing was not a sport, nor solely a means of subsistence, but a sort of solemn sacrament and withdrawal from the world, just as the aged read their bibles" (25). The fisherman, it is clear, has much in common with the naturalist, for just as fishing involves the sort of serene withdrawal the old man embodies, so "the fruit of the naturalist's observations is not in new genera or species, but in new contemplations still, and science is only a more contemplative man's recreation" (25). A few pages on appears the extensive description of various fish, complete with scientific names, but also with playful side comments, implying that combination of observation and recreation which forms the naturalist's attitude, as Thoreau understands it. A good example of this sort of naturalism is the description of "the Horned Pout, *Pimelodus nebulosus*, sometimes called Minister, from the peculiar squeaking noise it makes when drawn out of the water" (31).

The comic observation helps to set up, in a playful way, the criticism of institutionalized Christianity that follows in the "Sunday" chapter. But juxtaposition of the naturalist who knows the Latin name of the homely Pout and the fisherman for whom fishing was a "solemn sacrament" captures the naturalistic and spiritual polarities of the book, which, by the end, merge into the vision of the poet-naturalist, suggesting that Thoreau himself provides the model for a new type of man to replace the one who "nowhere, east or west," knows how to live "a *natural* life." The new kind of man that Thoreau imagines is one who "needs not only to be spiritualized, but also *naturalized,* on the soil of the earth" (379). The sentence seems to say that the soil of the earth is the ground not only of the natural life, which is understandable enough, but of the spiritual life as well. Earlier in this last chapter Thoreau claims that "the eye which can appreciate the naked and absolute beauty of a scientific truth is far more rare than that which is attracted by a moral one" (361).

The comment confirms the common critical assessment that "the older Thoreau got, the more interested he became in science."[51] The appreciation of scientific truth expressed in the final chapter of *A Week on the Concord and Merrimack Rivers* also looks forward to Thoreau's last book, *Cape Cod*, in which he leaves the orientalism of his first book far behind. The only reference to any Asian text in *Cape Cod* is a line from the *Rig-Veda-Sanhitá* in the H. H. Wilson translation: "As the Veda says, 'there is nothing to give support, nothing to rest upon, nothing to cling to'" (96). The passage is used to describe the forbidding "immensity of the ocean," but the sea is pretty clearly here a metaphor for an inhuman world that Thoreau wants no part of, as he says, "I felt that I was a land animal" (96). Thoreau's sense of himself as a land animal follows from his discovery of Darwin, whose *Journal of the Voyage of the H.M.S. Beagle* he quotes at least twice. But even when Darwin is not quoted directly, his great argument makes itself felt. Since Thoreau was working on *Cape Cod* until his death in 1862, it is probable that his thinking was shaped not only by his reading of the *Voyage of the Beagle* but also by the *Origin of Species* itself. Thoreau was one of the earliest American readers of Darwin's *Origin,* having acquired a copy no later than March 1860, when he expressed to F. B. Sanborn his favorable opinion of evolutionary theory.[52]

One passage from *Cape Cod* seems especially inspired by Darwin: on one of his beach walks somewhere between Truro and Provincetown, Thoreau comments on the spare, North Atlantic strand as "a sort of neutral ground, a most advantageous point from which to contemplate this world. It is even a trivial place," by which Thoreau appears to mean that there is nothing sublime about the experience of nature, which is, after all, "neutral ground." The passage continues in such as way as to make Thoreau's "trivial" experience of the Atlantic strand profoundly Darwinian: "The waves forever rolling to the land are too far-traveled and untamable to be familiar. Creeping along the endless beach amid the sun-squawl and the foam, it occurs to us that we, too, are the product of sea slime" (*Cape Cod,* 147). The rhetoric here seems to capture conservative criticism of Darwin and turn it back on itself. Surely more than one Congregationalist churchman in the wake of Darwin's discovery must have offered assurances to his parishioners that the origins of mankind were actually divine, and that humanity was much more than "the product of sea slime."

So the transcendental sensibility recedes in this last book, and sometimes vanishes altogether, as in a powerful passage where Thoreau describes the remains of a human body, some victim of shipwreck, washed up on the beach:

> Close at hand they were simply some bones with a little flesh adhering to them, in fact, only a slight inequality in the sweep of the shore. There was nothing at all remarkable about them, and they were singularly inoffensive both to the senses and the imagination. But as I stood there they became more and more imposing. They were alone with the beach and the sea, whose hollow roar seemed addressed to them, and I was impressed as if there was an understanding between them and the ocean which necessarily left me out, with my snivelling sympathies. That dead body had taken possession of the shore, and reigned over it as no living one could, in the name of a certain majesty which belonged to it. (*Cape Cod,* 84–85).

This great passage compares with Mathew Arnold's poem "Dover Beach" (1867) as an expression of the profound sense of human limitation that followed from Darwin's discoveries, except that Thoreau seems to accept the fact more readily and more completely than Arnold does.[53] Indeed, as the metaphorical "sea of faith" withdraws in Arnold's poem, what is left behind is not so much the neutral fact or the trivial reality of human existence as something that is neither better nor worse than other forms of life but, rather, an anguished recognition that the miseries of existence are suddenly without the protections of a beneficent God. But the poet quickly substitutes one type of illusion for another, replacing the assurances of faith with the comforts of romance: "Ah, love, let us be true / To one another!" Arnold says the world "Hath really neither joy, nor love, nor light, / Nor certitude, nor peace, nor help for pain."[54] Thoreau, in effect, asks, "Why should it?"

Thoreau's transformation from Brahmin to Darwinist does not mean that the theological dimensions of the American Orient will cease to have meaning in the years after Thoreau. On the contrary, spiritual meanings proliferate as Hinduism, Buddhism, and other Eastern religions are woven into the fabric of American culture. It may very well be that the Darwinian reality Thoreau faced actually makes Eastern religions more acceptable, paradoxically, to the would-be believer, since the nineteenth-century contest between faith and science was played out solely in Christian terms and in Christian nations. After all, the Hindus did not posit an earth only 6,000 years old, as fundamentalist Christians did, but one somewhere in the neighborhood of two billion (the creation is dated 1,972,947,101 BCE),[55] a span of time much more amenable to Darwinian chronology and a good deal easier to accord with the archaeological record than the traditional Christian one. Thoreau, however, does not quibble over such details, and he is certainly not out to "reconcile" religion and science. Quite the contrary, in fact: surely the blind power of the natural world that Thoreau acknowledges in *Cape Cod* cannot help but dissipate the energy of all religions, so that orientalists after him can never look at Hinduism, Buddhism, or any other Eastern faith in quite the same way again.

IV

The difference between Emerson's and Thoreau's treatment of the Orient shows that the younger man was more in tune with changing attitudes, with the desire on the part of some Americans to become better acquainted with the facts of the Far East: the languages, the history, the geography, and so on. Thoreau's specificity emerges as a more salient and useful approach than Emerson's syncretism, and although Thoreau was not exactly an orientalist in the scholarly sense, he seems to have kept up with contemporary cultural and professional developments in a way that Emerson did not. Emerson was content to select extracts from the *Divine Pimander* of Hermes Trismegistus from a late seventeenth-century translation and print them in *The Dial* as "Ethical Scriptures." By contrast, the treatment of Buddhism in *A Week on the Concord and Merrimack Rivers* shows that Thoreau was alert to the recent publication of Eugene Burnouf's *Introduction à l'histoire du buddhisme indien* (1844) and to emerging interest in Buddhism generally. No doubt it is because of his sensitivity to Buddhism that for more than a century Thoreau was thought to be the translator of the passages from *The Lotus Sutra,* taken from Burnouf, that had appeared in *The Dial* as "The Preaching of Buddha." In fact the translation was done by Elizabeth Peabody (1804–1894), the educational reformer who established the first English-speaking kindergarten in the United States. Like her friend Margaret Fuller, Peabody was a charter member of the Transcendental Club; unlike Fuller, she was drawn to both Buddhism and Hinduism during a period of religious curiosity and uncertainty, when she also annotated some of the fables from Vishnu-Sarma's *Hitopadesa.*[56] Peabody's treatment of Burnouf in the January 1844 issue of *The Dial* occurred in advance of Edward E. Salisbury's "Memoir on the History of Buddhism," presented before the American Oriental Society in May, not to mention Salisbury's review of Burnouf in the first volume of the society's journal.

Thoreau's early interest in Buddhism puts him, along with Peabody and Salisbury, among the first Americans to take that particular Asian tradition seriously. He was also in the vanguard of a renewed interest in Confucianism, a curiosity about the Chinese classics not seen since the eighteenth century when Benjamin Franklin, mainly, mined them for moral and political meanings. The revival may be said to have begun with the new translations of Confucius by James Legge which began to appear in 1861. This is the edition Emerson was perusing in 1863, when he wrote in his journal, "I am reading a better Pascal."[57] That comment, incidentally, shows again that Emerson always read with a syncretic eye and was ever alert for points of connection between Eastern and Western philosophy. Thoreau died before he got a chance to look at Legge, but he had earlier rejected the older translations by the French Jesuit Philippe Couplet (Paris, 1687) and by the Protestant missionaries Joshua Marshman (Serampore: Mission Press, 1809) and David Collie (Malacca: Mission Press, 1828). Even though he had relied on Marshman and Collie for the Confucian selections that appeared in the April and October 1843 issues of *The Dial,* he turned to the French version by Guillaume Pauthier (Paris, 1841) for all nine of the quotations from Confucius sprinkled throughout *Walden.* The reason for the latter choice is obvious: Collie's and Marshman's translations were suspect because they had been made under the aegis of Christian evangelicalism (Collie, for example, alleged that Confucius was subject to "the destructive influence of the most gross and dangerous ignorance, viz., Ignorance of his Creator"), whereas Pauthier was a true scholar, one of the most celebrated sinologists of his time.[58] For all of Thoreau's scholarly inclinations, however, he began to lose interest in the Orient even as greater opportunities to study it presented themselves. In 1855 he received a gift of forty-four volumes of Oriental works from his English friend Thomas Cholmondely, but by that time his interests had shifted. As Ellery Channing put it, "After he had ceased to read these works, he received a collection of them, as a present, from England."[59]

Meanwhile, as Thoreau turned to botanical studies inspired by Darwin and contemplated a long work on seed dispersion and "The Succession of Forest Trees" (the title of his last essay), the American Oriental Society and the universities in New York, New Haven, and Boston began to transform orientalism into a professional discipline. Even before the society was founded in 1842, Isaac Nordheimer (1809–1842) had begun teaching Sanskrit at the City University of New York, offering a course in 1836 on Wednesday and Friday evenings. Born in Bavaria, Nordheimer studied philology at the University of Munich, concentrating in Sanskrit, Greek, Latin, and Hebrew. He is known today principally as a Hebrew scholar and grammarian;[60] though his involvement with Sanskrit is noteworthy, he can hardly be called a Sanskrit scholar. That distinction belongs to Edward E. Salisbury (1812–1901), who was appointed chair of Arabic and Sanskrit at Yale University in 1841, the first such post in the United States. Salisbury, like Nordheimer, was trained in the German system, having studied in Berlin with Franz Bopp, the celebrated professor of Sanskrit and comparative philology. Salisbury delayed acceptance of the Yale position until he had completed additional European study in Sanskrit, mainly in Paris and Bonn (where August Wilhelm Schlegel held the first Sanskrit chair in a German university). In 1843 he began teaching his Yale courses in Sanskrit and Arabic while also becoming extremely active in the American Oriental Society. In 1854 he turned over his Sanskrit duties to his student William Dwight Whitney (1827–1894), making Whitney the first American to hold a separate chair in the language.[61]

Whitney went on to become one of the most distinguished Indologists of the period. His clear-eyed, scholarly approach to the Sanskrit materials he studied helped to dispel, at least temporarily, the old stereotype of "Indian spirituality." A recent South Asian critic claims that Whitney remains "one of the very few American scholars to notice the element of strenuous materialism and vigorous naturalism in Vedic Hindu thought." This same critic makes the valuable point that Whitney and later Indologists, such as

Charles Lanman—T. S. Eliot's Sanskrit teacher at Harvard—pursued their discipline not for the sake of antiquarianism but to learn more about their own Aryan ancestry. The Vedas were meaningful, Whitney said, because they contained "the language and the religion of our own earliest·traceable ancestors."[62]

Whitney's comment about language and religion captures the dual concerns of the American Oriental Society, at least in its early years. The historian Carl T. Jackson estimates that approximately half the articles in the society's journal were philological in nature, an approach consistent with the kind of training that Salisbury and others had received in Europe. He also observes that "the typical member seems to have been a minister, theologian, or missionary."[63] In fact, the constitution of the society changed over the years, evolving from an organization with a predominantly missionary interest to one whose focus was mostly philological. The early members of the Society were hardly orientalists in the same sense that, say, the first members of the British Asiatic Society were. Almost all the founding members were Congregationalist churchmen, and only one had any claim to philological expertise outside of Hebrew, Latin, and Greek. The act of incorporation of the society names John Pickering (1777–1846), William Jenks (1778–1866), and John J. Dixwell as the founding officers. Pickering was the first president; Jenks, Moses Stuart (1780–1852), and Edward Robinson (1794–1863) were vice presidents; Dixwell served as treasurer.[64] Among these men, Pickering, an attorney by trade, and Dixwell, president of the Massachusetts Bank, were the only ones without a theological background. Pickering did have some claim to philological knowledge, although he seems to have been more of an amateur than a scholar; he is said to have "acquired" most of "the principal European and Semitic languages" and had some acquaintance with Chinese (DAB, 8:565). Jenks was a Congregationalist clergyman who compiled a six-volume commentary on the Bible; the idea of the Society is supposed to have originated with him (DAB, 5:54). Stuart was likewise a clergyman and a biblical scholar with a thorough knowledge of Hebrew and German; a professor at Andover College and the author of some forty books and brochures, he had a substantial reputation abroad among the theologically minded (DAB, 9:175). Robinson was one of Stuart's students at Andover, where he later taught as well, before moving on to chair the department of biblical literature at Union Theological Seminary in New York City (DAB, 8:40).

The Congregationalist makeup of the American Oriental Society perhaps accounts for the relative paucity of articles about Hindu India in the first volume of its journal, which covers the years 1842–1849. There are two substantial articles about China—one dealing with paper money and

another on trade and treaty possibilities—and a rather long, highly technical treatise on Arab music. Possibly, the emphasis on the non-Hindu Orient
is reflective of the founders' Congregationalist identity, since the Unitarians
had fairly cornered the market on Hinduism by the 1840s.

The missionary intent of the society at the time of its formation is implied
by Article II of its constitution, which sets out the three primary "objects" of
the organization: "1. The cultivation of learning in the Asiatic, African, and
Polynesian languages. 2. The publication of Memoirs, Translations, Vocab-
ularies, and other works relating to the Asiatic, African, and Polynesian languages. 3. The collection of a Library" (*JAOS*, 1:vi). The inclusion of Africa
might, at first, seem consistent with the usual notions of nineteenth-century
orientalism, which necessarily included Egypt and Ethiopia in its scholarly
orbit of interest. But the American inclusion of Africa as one of the areas
in which the society meant to cultivate learning, as well as the emphasis on
translations, really relates to missionary work. The intent becomes clear
from the first volume of the journal, which includes several reports from
the American Board of Commissioners for Foreign Missions, the American
Baptist Board of Foreign Missions, and other missionary organizations.
Such reports relayed information about "philological" advances in Asian
countries: "At *Bangkok* . . . Mr. J. T. Jones has translated the whole New
Testament into Siamese" (*JAOS*, 1:63). One report lists all the languages
in which "printing has been executed" (meaning the printing of Christian
literature), including "Mahratta, Goojooratee, Hindoostanee," Tamil, Chinese, and Japanese, as well as Cherokee, Choctaw, Seneca and other Native
American Languages (*JAOS*, 1:61). These types of reports appeared less
frequently as the society became more concerned with professional developments in comparative philology, though a notice about "New Testament
translations in the languages of Alaska" does appear in the proceedings of
1876 (*JAOS*, 10:122). How Alaskan and other Native American languages
qualify as Oriental is not clear, unless "Oriental" is understood to mean
something like "unconverted." That meaning would seem to cover people
on the eastern coast of Africa as well: the first volume of the journal presents "Three Chapters of Genesis translated into the Sooahelee [Swahili]
Language," by the Rev. Dr. J. L. Krapf (*JAOS*, 1:259–74).

The index to the first twenty volumes of the *Journal of the American
Oriental Society* (covering the years 1842–1899) lists numerous articles
about the translation of the Bible or parts of it into a half-dozen different languages (Arabic, Chinese, Turkish, Mongolian, and more than one
Syriac language). But it is not altogether clear from the early reports of the
society's activities whether scholarly knowledge of Oriental languages has
value because it advances the work of missionaries in Asia, or whether the

work of the missionaries has value because it advances the knowledge of Oriental languages. In 1842, Rev. Rufus Andersen is pleased to observe that "there are about one hundred American missionaries east and west of the Ganges" who have command of almost a dozen Indian languages (*JAOS*, 1:xliv), a propitious situation for both missionary work and philological investigation: "Thus in the wisdom of Providence has it happened, that, while the propagation of Christianity, on the one hand, is opening to us new sources of information in different languages—which are the essential instruments of all knowledge—on the other hand the progressive acquisition of those languages is constantly placing at our hands new means of disseminating religious instruction." The "field of inquiry" is said to be "of almost boundless extent—the history, languages, literature, and general characteristics of the various people, both civilized and barbarous, who are usually classed under the somewhat indefinite name of *Oriental* nations" (*JAOS*, 1:2, 1:5). The history of the American Oriental Society makes clear that the balance and interdependency of missionary work and philological knowledge was not long sustained. By the end of the nineteenth century the society's focus was almost exclusively philological.

In the dual context of religion and philology, the work of Edward E. Salisbury truly stands out, not so much for its philological qualities as for its open and objective attitude toward Eastern religion. His "Memoir on the History of Buddhism," read at the annual meeting of the society on 28 May 1844, is a landmark in the history of the American Orient. The essay anticipates the serious and respectful treatment accorded to Buddhism later in the century, when the faith was often praised as the moral equal of Christianity. Salisbury was the first to identify the essence of Buddhism as "a quickening of moral feeling," which he saw as a reaction "against the Pantheism of the Brahmans" (*JAOS*, 1:84). He was also the first American to emphasize the canonical texts of Buddhism, including "the Mahâvanso, a book of history, which bears strong internal marks of authenticity, composed on the island of Ceylon, in the Pâli language" (*JAOS*, 1:83). And, possibly most important, Salisbury was the first to have conveyed the meaning of nirvana to American readers with a sense of nuanced understanding:

> All action, purpose, feeling, thought, having been abstracted from the idea of Deity, the highest attainment which human beings can propose to themselves, is of course a similar sublimation of existence above all qualities. This is the Nirvâna of the Buddhists; and because the only proper criterion of virtue, with them, is negation of all predicates, it follows, that to pursue any certain course of conduct, to cherish emotions of any sort, . . . has, according to their system, no intrinsic merit or demerit. As the means of arriving at that highest state

of absolute quiescence, Buddhism directs to the acquisition of knowledge of the illusive nature of all created things, by studious application of mind, and moral discipline. (*JAOS*, 1:85)

The high moral status of Buddhism is opposed to the lower forms of Hinduism when Salisbury observes that "the images of Buddha are not monstrous, but seem to portray real humanity," in contrast to the "absurdly inhuman" representations of Hindu deities (*JAOS*, 1:87). He also poses questions about the historical Buddha, the growth of the faith in India, and the introduction of that faith into Ceylon by Buddhist missionaries (*JAOS*, 1:106). For the most part, Salisbury succeeds in advancing scholarly understanding, but at times he falls back on outworn mythographical ideas that are strange to contemplate today, such as the notion that Buddhism exercised some "influence . . . upon the Scandinavian mythology, and upon the civilization of the Indian [i.e., Native American] races in the central part of our own country." To his credit, he does say that such ideas are "as yet too visionary [i.e., speculative] to receive any more than this passing notice" (*JAOS*, 1:131). Later, in reviewing Burnouf's *Introduction à l'histoire du buddhisme indien*, Salisbury performs a valuable introductory function of his own by providing generous quotations from the book, in English, together with extensive commentary. He maintains the tolerant and respectful tone throughout, even when he introduces a formulation that will be repeated in a less respectful way later in the century—that the Buddha preached atheism: "It would seem, that while he spread principles of atheism which tended to the abolishment of all religious worship, he yet prudently provided for the toleration and ultimate triumph of his doctrine, by not making a direct attack upon the established worship of the deities of his country" (*JAOS*, 1:297).

Not least because of his pioneering work in Buddhism, Salisbury remained the scholarly mainstay of the *Journal of the American Oriental Society* during the first decade of its existence, contributing some twenty articles to the three volumes that appeared between 1842 and 1852. Most of these were reviews, catalogues of manuscripts, translations, and reports on the proceedings of the society itself: that is, they were fairly traditional, nontechnical papers that, with the exception of the articles on Buddhism, hardly broke new scholarly ground (and even in the case of Buddhism, he was mainly reporting on the work of others). Significantly, Salisbury's final publication in the third volume of the journal (1852) is a brief notice of the "Text of the Atharva-Veda; announcement of Whitney's collations" (*JAOS*, 3:501–2). The notice amounts to the passing of the torch, not only from Salisbury to Whitney as the dominant voice of the society but also from an older style of academic antiquarianism to a more rigorous, scientific approach consistent with the principles of nineteenth-century positivism. Salisbury continued to contribute to the journal after 1852, but as one of his very last articles shows, he was hardly in step with the times: "On some of the relations of Islamism to Christianity" (*JAOS*, 10:76–77), published in 1873, is categorically removed from something like "On the so-called vowel increment, with special reference to the views of Mr. J. Peile" (*JAOS*, 10:67–68), which Whitney published in the same year. From 1852 on, Whitney contributed a steady stream of specialized technical notes and articles that sometimes touched on religious issues (e.g., "The Vedic doctrine of a future life") but more often than not explored complex philological topics (e.g., "The teachings of the Vedic Prâtiçâkhyas, with respect to the theory of accent, and the pronunciation of groups of consonants"). All told, Whitney published more than ninety articles in the *Journal* between 1852 and 1894, the year of his death. His brand of exacting Sanskrit analysis and Indological investigation was continued by his students Charles Rockwell Lanman, who first published in the *Journal* in 1877, and Maurice Bloomfield, who contributed dozens of articles, beginning in 1878.

Lanman's and Bloomfield's specialized contributions made the *Journal of the American Oriental Society* a respected organ for the burgeoning field of Sanskrit studies. Lanman's prestige was furthered by the *Sanskrit Reader* he published in 1884, a book used by generations of students. Bloomfield was perhaps the greatest Vedic scholar in America, having translated the *Atharva Veda* in 1899 for Max Müller's *Sacred Books of the East*. He is also celebrated for his *Life and Stories of the Jaina Savior Pārçvanātha* (1919), the first monograph by an American scholar on Jainism, which, along with Buddhism and Hinduism, is one of the three indigenous faiths of India grounded in the ancient texts written in either Sanskrit or Pali. Paradoxically, while Lanman, Bloomfield, and other academicians were doing pioneering work in Sanskrit, it was the old-fashioned Salisbury who first took note of the next big thing in Oriental studies. In 1853 he published a brief article, "United States Expedition to Japan," in which he expressed the hope that Commodore Perry's naval squadron would succeed in its mission to establish "friendly commercial intercourse" between the two countries (as President Millard Fillmore put it) and "enlarge our knowledge of that great Empire." Salisbury was especially pleased that the expedition included one of the society's own members, Rev. George Jones, U.S.N., "who accompanies the Commodore as chaplain," adding that "the Society will hereafter receive important communications from him in answer to a series of inquiries addressed to him by a committee appointed for the purpose, previous to his departure" (*JAOS*, 3:493, 494). As it turns out, no notices of any kind appear in the *Journal* with the Reverend Mr. Jones as author, but the editors did print a number of articles about Japanese language and culture.

Topics related to "Japan, Japanese" take up less than one column in the index to the first twenty volumes of the *Journal*, whereas indexed entries headed "India" take up three pages; "Sanskrit" and "Sanskrit Grammar," four; "Upanishad," "Veda," and "Veda, Mythology," three. Using this rough estimate, the society devoted about twenty times as much scholarly attention to Indian and Sanskrit subjects as it did to Japanese topics. Remarkably, a "Note on Japanese Syllabaries" appears in the second volume of the *Journal*, published in 1851, surely the first reasonably accurate account of the Japanese writing system to appear in America. Even though the note includes some curious misinformation—such as the notion that the *katakana* script "is appropriate to men, and the hira-kana to women" (*JAOS*, 2:58; in fact, *katakana* is used to write foreign words and *hiragana* to write native words)—it provides a great deal of accurate linguistic information that must have been of great interest to American philologists. The note was written by Samuel Wells Williams, who ran a missionary press in Hong Kong, where he used a set of Chinese fonts to publish missionary literature. His explanation of Japanese syllabaries in the *Journal* includes the full list of *katakana* graphs, printed from a set of fonts "which is in the possession of the Corresponding Secretary of the Society" (*JAOS*, 2:55). The corresponding secretary at the time was the ubiquitous Edward E. Salisbury. Aside from a one-page "Review of Japanese Botany," published in 1855, Salisbury chose not to pursue the opportunity he had helped create to study the language and literature of Japan. Instead, as the pages of the *Journal* over the last quarter of the nineteenth century amply illustrate, thanks to Whitney, Lanman, Bloomfield, and others the ancient Sanskrit Orient crowded out almost all the others to a remarkable degree.

The dominance of Sanskrit study can be attributed to the philological advances of the Germans, who, following the lead of Sir William Jones, convincingly demonstrated the importance of the language to reconstructions of the protolanguage called "Aryan" or "Indo-European," from which most Indian and European languages had descended. But there are at least two other possible reasons for the obsessive interest in Sanskrit on the part of fin-de-siècle scholars in America. One is suggested by Whitney's remarks about the Vedic origins of "the language and religion of our own earliest traceable ancestors." The assertion of an ancestral relationship to an ancient cultural tradition added meaning and prestige to a scholarly enterprise taking place in a nation barely 100 years removed from its origins. Also, at a time of increasing American chauvinism and xenophobia, much of it directed against Asian immigrants and expressed through exclusionary legislation, treating Asian antiquity as the locus of Aryan origins had a certain paradoxical logic. After all, the study of Sanskrit involved the language and culture of a people who, strictly speaking, no longer existed. The explanation for the elevation of ancient India to a position of such intense scholarly interest is likely more complex than either pride of origin or fear of foreignness, but one thing is clear: while the majority of scholars looked backward to ancient India, a few looked forward to modern Japan, as the meaning of the American Orient shifted yet again and a new aesthetic world opened up to the West.

3

The Fin de Siècle

From Scholarship to Aesthetics

DURING THE last third of the nineteenth century, with the demise of the last shogunate in 1867, Japan broke with its feudal past and began to join the community of modern nations. When the Meiji dynasty was restored the following year, it undertook a systematic program of modernization, encouraging scientists and educators from the West to come to Japan and share their knowledge. Around the same time that American scholars began investigating Eastern culture in earnest, the Japanese established Western-style universities to encourage scholarship of a different stripe. Among the Americans who came to Japan as official guests of the empire were Edward Morse and Ernest Fenollosa, Morse to teach evolutionary biology and Fenollosa to teach philosophy, specifically the social Darwinism of Herbert Spencer. In addition to these two key figures, both of whom occupied official positions, several other important Americans came to Japan mainly through the influence and agency of Morse, who invited his friend William Sturgis Bigelow; Bigelow, in turn, persuaded his friends Percival Lowell, Henry Adams, and John La Farge to make the trip across the Pacific.

Each of these men came to Japan for a different reason, but all of them left Japan with a common interest in the Japanese, intrigued either by their religion and philosophy or by the way their religion and philosophy were expressed in art. The New Englanders were largely responsible for starting the collections of Japanese art now housed in American museums. What makes this group so different from the American philosophes who looked to Confucian China in the eighteenth century or the Unitarians and transcendentalists who found inspiration in Hindu India early in the nineteenth is the actual journey to the East that they undertook and their physical encounter with the culture itself. No longer was the American Orient limited to texts of dubious provenance and uncertain translation. Now Americans encountered the East firsthand, learned the language, and, in some cases, converted to an Asian faith. Lafcadio Hearn, a longtime resident of the United States if not a citizen, even changed his name, to Yakumo Koizumi.

Japan's exposure to the West began in 1549, when the Jesuit priest Francis Xavier arrived and established a missionary post. His success in converting the population was impressive, with some 300,000 new Christians professing belief by 1600, despite a proscription against the religion issued by the military leader Hideyoshi in 1587. When Tokugawa Ieyasu (1543–1616) came to power in 1598, however, he rapidly purged the country of Christians and closed Japan to the West, with the lone exception of Dutch trading ships, which were allowed to dock at Nagasaki (but at no other port). The Tokugawa shogunate, the last in Japanese history, continued until 1867. During this period, the Japanese people were forbidden to leave; those who did so were executed upon their return; and any foreigners who happened upon the country's shores, even by shipwreck, were put to death.[1]

Small wonder, then, that in *Moby Dick* Herman Melville evoked the island nation to suggest something almost as mysterious and enigmatic as the great white whale itself, describing a Pacific of "unknown Archipelagoes and impenetrable Japans."[2] The final undoing of Tokugawa Japan began when Commodore Perry arrived in Edo Bay in 1853, starting the process that resulted in a treaty between the United States and the shogunate which was signed the following year. American interest in Japan began in earnest in the summer of 1860, when a Japanese diplomatic mission visited the United States to formally ratify the Perry treaty. The delegation toured several cities, including New York, and were honored by parades and other public festivities. On 26 June the *New York Times* reported that the parade occasioned by the Japanese visit was "decidedly the most magnificent display our city ha[s] ever seen."[3]

The way for the modernization of Japan was opened by the Meiji restoration of 1868, which reestablished the imperial court. The desire on the part of the Japanese "to escape from the 'shameful inferiority' to the West" led to a systematic program to "learn from the West the secrets of its strength." But "there was a paradox in this. As in some European countries, a nationalism rooted in a conservative view of society was to dissolve much of the tradition it was developed to defend."[4] The simultaneous desire for imperial power and Western modernization came into conflict in 1895, when Western powers forced Japan to accept a peace treaty with China at variance with the terms originally negotiated, which included Korean independence (Roberts, 847). The treaty spurred a reaction against the West and brought an effective end to the Meiji modernization. Hence, the Americans were welcome in Japan for roughly thirty-five years (1860–1895). During this period they learned a great deal about Japanese art, literature, and religion and disseminated that knowledge upon their return to the United States in lectures, books, and, perhaps most significantly, the medium of material culture: the pottery, paintings, and other artifacts they had collected in Japan.

I

One of the first Americans to go to Japan was the geologist-adventurer Raphael Pumpelly, who had already traveled widely in Europe, gone to school in Freiberg, and fought Indians in the Arizona territory. Through a commercial agent by the name of C. W. Brooks, the Tokugawa shogunate engaged Pumpelly to teach the Japanese the techniques of modern mining. He left San Francisco on a clipper ship in November 1861 and arrived the following February, an unusually long crossing. After a series of bureaucratic delays he began his official duties in May 1862.[5] Pumpelly's *Reminiscences* of the period (published in 1918) reveal a man eager to understand and adapt to Japanese culture. He is surely one of the first Americans to have learned the Japanese language. While awaiting his orders in Yokohama, he began study with a monolingual teacher, having already taught himself the *katakana* "alphabet." Pumpelly did not understand that *katakana* is the syllabary reserved for writing foreign words alone and so "was quite taken aback on finding that no books were printed in that character."[6] Despite these difficulties, he endeavored to learn the *hiragana* syllabary as well, and even some Chinese characters, while continuing to work on the spoken language, in which he was truly immersed. Astonishing as it sounds, after only six months or so Pumpelly claims that he "was able to speak the common dialect fairly well" (*R,* 1:336–37). During the winter of 1862–63 he lectured on mining and metallurgy, and because his audience "had learned much . . . about minerals and rocks" while working with him in the field, "there was thus a common ground on which to build"; hence, "hardly any foreign words were used." Rather than falling back on English terms, Pumpelly says, "sketches largely took their place" (*R,* 1:337). Applied linguists today would call what Pumpelly did in his lectures the direct method.

Pumpelly brought the same respect for tradition that he demonstrated in his use of language to the protocols of politeness so critical to social interactions in Japan. He writes of arriving at a village where the behavior of the residents suggested "that no foreigners had visited this place before." Careful to follow Japanese customs, Pumpelly and his companions "removed our shoes and entered the neatly matted rooms." A few paragraphs later he observes that conflicts in Japan are more effectively resolved by "persuasive politeness" than by "force" (*AA&A,* 105–106). The most extensive evidence of Pumpelly's capacity for assimilation is the account of a meeting with a district magistrate who has never met with Westerners before and knows nothing of the "compromise between foreign and Japanese etiquette"—bowing *and* shaking hands, for example—usually adopted. Once it becomes clear that the meeting with the magistrate will have to "conform to the complicated Japanese ceremonial," Pumpelly performs it successfully and to the full satisfaction of his official host:

> Accordingly we ranged ourselves and the officers of our escort in a row, squatting upon our marrow bones, while our visitor and his attendants faced us in another row, exactly five feet distant. This done, using our knees as pivots, every man threw his body forward, with the palms of his hands resting on the mat, and regarding his vis-à-vis for an instant, lowered the head till the forehead rested on the floor. In this position, each side murmured in a low tone the customary formula, and then raised the head just far enough to see that the other side was being equally polite. Another lowering of the head, and another formula, and the ceremony was ended. (*AA&A,* 176)

Such passages show an appreciation for Japanese culture that could hardly have been widespread in America during the Civil War period, to say the least.

Like the Americans who would follow him in the next decade—Morse, Fenollosa, Bigelow, Lowell, Adams, and La Farge—Pumpelly left Japan with a deep regard for Japanese aesthetics, even though he did not leave with a great number of aesthetic artifacts (as Morse, Fenollosa, and Lowell assuredly did). Pumpelly was particularly struck by the care of the Japanese to integrate the built environment with the natural one: "The works of man, fields, gardens, hamlets, castles, grand or humble abodes and solemn temples, all blend . . . into a harmony of form and color" (R, 1:284). Elsewhere in his *Reminiscences* Pumpelly shows himself an acute observer of Japanese religious ritual, whether Buddhist or Shinto, and he is deeply aware of the political unrest during the shogunate period leading up to the Meiji revolution. As a result, his sense of the Japanese aesthetic sensibility is not divorced from religious and political contexts: "This close sympathy with nature was really only the reflection of a spiritual harmony, whose outward expression was loyalty, loyalty to self, to feudal lord, and to ideals. The artist, the craftsman, even the laborer, sought to express beauty in his work and the evidence of his love of doing" (R, 1:284). This sense of the integration of political, spiritual, and aesthetic values is something new in the American Orient. Moreover, one should not assume that Pumpelly retrospectively adjusted his impressions of Tokugawa Japan circa 1860 for his 1918 autobiography in the light of subsequent understanding, because his 1870 account of Japan is even more remarkable for its enlightened comprehension of the feudal country just beginning its rapid transformation into a modern state.

In a chapter titled "Politics" from *Across America and Asia*, Pumpelly urges Western nations to adopt "a thorough change in its policy toward orientals" (AA&A, 126). His position is so forceful and so contrary to the colonial policies of European nations that it must be quoted at length:

> When an Englishman, or an American, or a Frenchman—starting from the firm belief that all orientals are infinitely beneath his own race—assumes that they have no rights he is bound to respect; ignores the fact that, as a stranger, he is tolerated in their land by courtesy or necessity, and forcibly attempts to assert that superiority; he should be taught that he does so at his own risk. As with the individual, so with the nation. The representatives of the Western governments are clothed with almost sovereign power; and are only too often also imbued with the prejudice of race. That which they would not dream of doing in the face of an European power, they often do not hesitate to practice toward a weaker oriental nation—constantly violating international law at the same time that they demand of them an observance of it. (AA&A, 125)

Although Pumpelly was a scientist and not an artist, his refusal to regard the Japanese as an inferior people anticipates the aesthetic attitude of Americans who traveled to Japan in the decades after Pumpelly, once the Meiji empire was established.

Pumpelly did not really build on his status as a pioneer in American-Japanese relations. His influence was limited for the very good reason that the civil disturbances beginning shortly after his arrival soon constrained foreign travel. As Pumpelly observed, the Edo government was accused "of throwing the resources of the country open to foreign spies" and "forced to suspend many of its liberal schemes." Caught in the middle of the revolution, Pumpelly was told in February 1863 to end his efforts to educate the Japanese in the techniques of modern mining (*AA&A*, 191). Unlike the Americans who followed him near the end of the next decade, he evidently had no interest in popularizing Japan. When he returned to the United States, he took part in a geological survey of Michigan and worked briefly as the state geologist of Missouri. Although he lectured at Harvard (on ore deposits) in 1869 and took a home in Boston in 1875, as a man of science with a career in geology he was well removed from both the older Brahmin circles and the younger generation of Bostonians who would make their mark in the New Japan (*DAB*, 8:265). Besides, both Morse and Fenollosa were from Salem, not Boston, and it was Morse and Fenollosa whose influence extended furthest among the American artists and intellectuals who next turned their attention to the Japanese Orient.

II

Edward Sylvester Morse (1838–1925) was not the first American after Pumpelly to make the trip to Japan, but he became the most significant because of his wide influence. Originally from Maine, he launched his scientific career at Harvard University when he became a special student of Louis Agassiz (1807–1873), studying the evolution of brachiopods. His work on Atlantic coast brachiopods attracted the attention of Darwin himself, and it was as a Darwinist that Morse was invited to lecture at the University of Tokyo in 1877. His friend William Sturgis Bigelow (1850–1926), a fellow scientist holding a medical degree from Harvard, became interested in Japan after attending a series of lectures given by Morse at the Lowell Institute in Boston. Like Morse, Bigelow possessed impeccable scientific credentials, having studied in Europe after receiving his medical degree, first in the clinics of Vienna and then in the laboratory of Pasteur, where he spent a year studying bacteriology. What is striking about the two scientists is how different their responses to Japan were: Morse maintained an attitude of scientific detachment and was content simply to record in brief verbal and pictorial sketches (he was a gifted draftsman) what he saw of Japan; Bigelow, by contrast, became so interested in Mahayana Buddhism that he converted to the faith. When he died, he was buried in the robes of a Buddhist priest, and some of his ashes were sent back to Japan to rest in a Buddhist temple.[7] But he remained a man of science till the end. In fact, Bigelow's lone published work on Japan, *Buddhism and Immortality*, attempts to reconcile religion and science.[8]

Morse did not see the need for any such reconciliation. Indeed, one of the things that pleased him when he gave the first of three lectures in Japan on "Evolution" (a term that Morse always capitalizes) was the absence of religious objection: "It was delightful to explain the Darwinian theory without running up against theological prejudices as I did at home."[9] This observation is recorded in *Japan Day by Day,* the book Morse wrote in 1917 at Bigelow's prompting. Morse had written Bigelow that he was looking forward to "a long leave of absence" from the Peabody Museum of Salem and the Boston Museum of Fine Arts (he was almost single-handedly responsible for supplying those museums with their collections of Japanese ceramics and had curatorial responsibilities at both) "in order to finish a number of studies on Mollusks and Brachiopods." Bigelow responded with a kind of admonition: "You are still frittering away your valuable time on the lower forms of animal life, which anybody can attend to, instead of devoting it to the highest, about the manners and customs of which no one is so well qualified to speak as you. Honestly, now, isn't a Japanese a higher organism than a worm? Drop your damned Brachiopods" (quoted in *JDD,* ix–x). Morse followed Bigelow's advice and began to turn the 3,500-page journal of his Japanese experiences of forty years earlier into a book. He first thought of organizing the material into a series of topics similar to the ones he had lectured on at the Lowell Institute after his Tokyo teaching stint; eventually, however, he settled on a form much closer to the original journal, as reflected in the title: a record of day-by-day experiences and observations. The result is surprisingly fresh, and Morse generally succeeds in capturing the sense of immediacy he must have felt when he encountered the sights and smells of Japan firsthand, and for the first time. For example, his record of the conventions of Japanese theater includes a remarkable moment in the act of putting down that record: "The prompter, instead of being concealed, as with us, walked about deliberately on the stage, coming up behind each actor in turn (my table has just been shaken by an earthquake, June 25, 1877, —another shock, and still another), crouching down as if he were hiding, and prompting in a voice loud enough to be plainly heard" (*JDD,* 1:30).

One of the most valuable things about Morse's book is the information it provides about the educational policies of the Meiji government. He notes that Japan was spending roughly one-third of its annual budget on education at a time when Russia was spending "a half of one percent"

(*JDD*, 1:282). At the University of Tokyo, different academic fields were the province of different groups of foreign nationals, selected, presumably, on the basis of reputation and prestige. "The Medical College is officered by the Germans," Morse says, whereas the branch of the university where he taught zoology included "four or five Englishmen, eight or nine Americans, a Frenchman, two Germans, and a number of Japanese assistant professors" (*JDD*, 1:281). Morse lectured in English, all students being required to attend a preparatory school in the language prior to admission to the university (though some students also received instruction in other languages, such as German in the medical school) (*JDD*, 1:15, 2:221). He found his students extraordinarily attentive—"all greedy to learn. . . . [T]heir courtesy, and their respectful demeanor is an inspiration"—and thus the perfect audience for his favorite scientific topic: "Most of them are rationalists and a few are Buddhists, so with these conditions I anticipate a delightful experience in presenting Darwinism pure and simple" (*JDD*, 1:284).

Near the end of his first term of teaching, and after giving "a strong lecture on Evolution," his classes "expresse[d] a strong desire to have a course on the subject." He put off a full course until after his leave of absence, but he did deliver three lectures on evolution. The first, on 6 October 1877, was a great success: "A number of professors and their wives and from five hundred to six hundred students were present, and nearly all of them were taking notes. It was an interesting and inspiring sight" (*JDD*, 1:315, 339). He was later told that his was "the first lecture ever given in Japan on Darwinism or Evolution" (*JDD*, 1:340). Morse's biographer speculates that his Japanese audiences were responsive to Darwin for cultural rather than scientific reasons: "In disclosing the scientific and philosophic doctrine of evolution, Morse, all unconsciously, reconciled for the Japanese the acceptance of Western civilization and the concept of loyalty to ancestors. Evolution was the endorsement of ancestor-veneration. Evolution taught the continuity of the life of the past with the life of the future on earth."[10]

Morse also gave public lectures at the invitation of a group of Japanese professors who had visited the United States and returned with an admiration for the American "system of lecture courses as a means of public instruction." The lecture he gave was something of an experiment for the Japanese, the first ever delivered by a foreigner "under conditions of an organized course of lectures" (*JDD*, 1:413, 415). Morse chose archaeology as his topic, another field in which he had considerable expertise, having recently discovered and excavated at Omori some shell mounds containing ancient artifacts that became the foundation of his extensive ceramics collection. After Morse published his findings in *Shell Mounds of Omori*

(1879), Darwin wrote to him commending "the progress of Japan, in which you have been aiding," as "about the most wonderful in the world."[11] The great scientist's endorsement heightened Morse's appeal as a lecturer, which was already considerable. One account calls him "an ideal popular lecturer, spontaneous, dramatic, witty, and always well informed." He also illustrated his talks with blackboard sketches and evidently had the ability to draw with both hands simultaneously (*DAB*, 7:242). Morse could hardly have been as spontaneous and witty before audiences of the Japanese public, because his remarks had to be translated sentence by sentence as he went. But his archaeological talk was so well received that the organization asked him to give more speeches, which he agreed to do once he returned from his American tour: "The subject will be Darwinism," he said (*JDD*, 1:415).

The following fall Morse was one of several distinguished lecturers at a series sponsored by an organization called the New Kodankai, styled after the American system (admission was charged). The lectures, scheduled for alternate Sundays from 21 September 1878 through 5 January 1879, "were given in a large hall, and the audience averaged from 600 to 800 and showed no diminution near the end."[12] What Morse means is that the entire audience stayed for the full duration of the lectures, which he finds remarkable: "The intellectual character of the audience may be judged by the fact that it sat patiently through a session of four or five one-hour lectures with only a slight intermission between them. What lecture audience in America, or in any other country, could stand such an ordeal as that!" (*JDD*, 2:427, 430). The "ordeal" of each night's lecture lineup involved a mixture of Japanese and American speakers. Besides Morse—who gave four lectures on Darwinism as well as talks on "Insect Life," "The Glacial Theory," and "Laws of Growth in Animals"—the American speakers were Ernest Fenollosa and the physicist Thomas C. Mendenhall. The latter's contribution is recorded only as an "introductory address." Fenollosa gave a series of three lectures titled "The Evolution of Religions," which, as might be expected, drew fire from Christian missionaries, who worried in print that Morse's activities threatened "to raze all that the missionaries are building." One of their leaders, Dr. H. P. Faulds, carried on a public debate with Morse and "argued against the evolutionary theory as by no means proven. But other [Japanese] Christians found the drift of the theory to be irresistible, and changed their logic, claiming theism to be consistent with evolution." They also offered to pray for Professor Morse.[13]

The list of lectures by Japanese professors in the Kodankai series provides an index of intellectual concerns during the Meiji period, as does Morse's summation of books by Western authors translated into English. The Japanese lecturers were "professors of the Imperial University, officials

of Government departments, editors, a Buddhist priest, and other prominent men" (*JDD*, 2:427). They spoke on political, scientific, and philosophical topics of obvious importance to the modernization effort. Mr. Kawazu,
a government official, lectured on "Advantages and Disadvantages of a
Representative Assembly" and "The Absurdity of Socialism"; Mr. Kikuchi,
a professor of mathematics, addressed "The Evolution of the Solar System"
and "Evolution in General"; Mr. Sugi, chair of the statistical department,
gave two lectures titled "Moral Statistics," no doubt influenced by the
philosophy of Herbert Spencer (*JDD*, 2:428–29, 430). Spencer appears
to dominate the list of books translated into Japanese, a list conveyed
to Morse, from memory, by one of his university associates, Professor
Toyama. It includes "Darwin's 'Descent of Man,' and 'Origin of Species';
Spencer's 'Education' (of which thousands were sold); Montesquieu's
'Spirit of Law'; Rousseau's 'Social Contract'; Mill's 'On Liberty,' 'Three
Essays on Religion,' and 'Utilitarianism'; Bentham's 'Legislation'; Lieber's
'Civil Liberty and Self-Government'; Spencer's 'Social Statics,' 'Principles
of Sociology,' 'Representative Government,' and 'Legislation'; Paine's 'Age
of Reason,' and Burke's 'Old Whig and the New'" (*JDD*, 2:317–18).[14] The
mix of nineteenth-century science and eighteenth-century enlightenment
titles makes sense in view of the crash course on modernity that the Meiji
government had set itself.

Morse was deeply impressed by how dedicated the Japanese were to
the program of education on which they had embarked. He was gratified
that so many students and professors had put themselves in the position of
learning what he had to teach. But he seems not to have been terribly interested in learning a great deal about the Japanese. Unlike Raphael Pumpelly,
Morse made no effort to learn more than a few words of their language,
and he indicated little curiosity about the country's traditions of art and
literature. His biographer Dorothy Wayman remarks that although Morse
was "privileged to visit a land only ten years removed from actual medieval
feudalism, he overlooked the poetry and romance," adding that "anything
beyond the evidence of Morse's senses was beyond his interest."[15] Hence,
he ignored "politics, religion, and philosophy" to focus "his studies in three
areas: the country's sea life, homes, and ceramics" (Jackson, 203). The study
of ceramics—which became an obsession—would seem to belie the claim
that the aesthetic sensibility of the Japanese was simply outside the orbit
of Morse's interests, but the ceramics obsession was spurred by the chance
discovery of a small saucer in a china shop "that was an exact replica of a
pecten shell."[16] Morse began collecting ordinary pieces of pottery because
of their similitude to shells, then graduated to a more sophisticated level of

collecting when his Japanese friends introduced him to connoisseurs who were more expert than he "in identifying rare specimens." Morse perceived that the practice "was nothing more nor less than an exact science, a classification of objects according to certain physical criteria."[17] It is as a naturalist, then, that Morse approaches the delicate art of Japanese ceramics. His narrow focus notwithstanding, he is fully aware that the Japanese have achieved a high level of civilization, one "marked by extreme simplicity and exquisite refinement" (*JDD*, 2:205); he just happens not to be terribly curious about it. When he visits Kyoto, he knows that the city has a reputation as an "artistic center," yet he is not drawn to fine art on this visit. Instead, he pays attention to "fences, roof-tops, window-openings, sliding screens and the devices for sliding them, trellises, balcony rails," and even "advertisements"—"art and refinement are everywhere" (*JDD*, 2:258–59). When Morse attends a concert at the university, he finds some parts of the performance "ludicrous" and concludes that "from our standpoint I should not call it music" (*JDD*, 1:400). Such examples could be multiplied at length: Morse always judges Japanese culture "from our standpoint."

The cultural contrast between East and West becomes, for Morse, a matter not simply of difference but of outright inversion, something that he comments on at length:

> Among the earlier features in this country noticed by foreigners is the fact that in many operations we do just the reverse of the Japanese, and this feature has been commented on a thousand times; nevertheless, I cannot help recalling it. The Japanese plane and saw toward them instead of away from them as we do; they begin a book on what we should call the last page, and at the upper right-hand corner and read down; the last page of our books would be the first page of theirs; their boats have the mast near the stern and the sailor sculls from the side; in the sequence of courses at dinner candy and cake are offered first; they drink hot water instead of cold and back their horses into the stall. (*JDD*, 1:25)

When he attempts Japanese archery, he finds "the bow very awkward, as their method of release with the arrow on the right of the bow is so different from our method of shooting" (*JDD*, 2:211–12). Of course, Morse is simply making observations, which is what a scientist does, and many of the inversions he observes are in fact the case. But he is content to let the observations sit, without coming to any larger cultural conclusions. Bigelow, Lowell, and Fenollosa will make similar observations about the "reverse" nature of Japanese culture, but they will go on to formulate elaborate theories about the meaning of the inverse relationship of East and West.

William Sturgis Bigelow's comment to Morse in 1917—that "a Japanese is a higher organism than a worm"—was a humorous way of chiding his friend on his failure to write up his memoirs of his Japanese experiences. But it also captures something of Morse's perspective on certain aspects of Japanese culture, notably religion. In Kyoto, from his hotel near several Buddhist temples, he says of the devotions of the priests that "the sounds [they] emit in their prayers can with difficulty be distinguished from the hum of insects." He also confuses a priest's bell with the sound made by a type of insect he has observed elsewhere in Japan (*JDD*, 2:259–60). The remark seems to be made without humorous intent: like the fine art of Japanese ceramics, the Buddhist faith is regarded exclusively from the perspective of the naturalist.

Curiously, the sense of disjunction between empiricism and religion expressed by Morse was something that Bigelow tried to overcome. His efforts to reconcile science and religion can also be seen as a struggle to resolve an inner conflict between the "masculine" drive for success in Victorian-era America and a post–Civil War reaction to that ethos which sought to cultivate "feminine" ideals of spirituality. As the historian T. J. Jackson Lears puts it, "Bigelow's idealist paean to Nirvana sanctioned his repudiation of the achievement ethos; it also merged with the mystical wave in the urban Northeast. Despite his reputation as an idiosyncratic dilettante, Bigelow was actually in the tide of an important popular movement."[18] That movement was really a double one, emphasizing not only the "Eastern mysticism" Lears identifies but also the "scientific" foundations of Eastern faiths—Buddhism especially—as the Asian delegations to the World's Parliament of Religions in Chicago show (see chapter 5).

Bigelow's scientific credentials were certainly the equal of Morse's, yet Bigelow turned to Buddhism not as an escape from empiricism but, strangely, as a complement to it. In 1908 he followed such luminaries as William James (1897) and Josiah Royce (1899) in delivering one of the Ingersoll lectures, the series "The Immortality of Man," established in 1893 in honor of George Goldthwait Ingersoll by his daughter Caroline. In his lecture, published in 1908 as *Buddhism and Immortality,* Bigelow averred that "consciousness is continuous and universal. Matter is separate and particular. But we habitually think in terms of matter. In short, we live in terms of matter. It is only on those terms that we live at all."[19] Arguing from the evidence of matter is familiar enough in the Western tradition; arguing from the evidence of the soul is something new, but that was essentially Bigelow's task in the lecture. As Beongcheon Yu put it in a paraphrase of Bigelow's argument, "Only when purified of matter, which is finite, can we realize this universal consciousness, the origin and end of all existence, where alone peace reigns."[20] Bigelow identifies this peace as something "that the material world cannot give,—the peace that passeth understanding trained on material things,—infinite and eternal peace,—the peace of limited consciousness unified with limitless will. That peace is NIRVANA" (Bigelow, 75). Despite such mystical asseverations, Bigelow goes to considerable lengths to reconcile Western science and Eastern religion. For example, he equates the Darwinian idea of descent with modification with the Buddhist doctrine of reincarnation, citing "the fact of the resemblance of offspring to parents" (Bigelow, 50). For him, the West's habit of regarding the body "as the determinant factor" in heredity and the East's tendency to understand "the collection of qualities familiarly expressed by the term 'soul' as dominant" is a trivial difference, mere haggling over terms: "There is no disagreement in regard to the facts" (Bigelow, 51, 50). The claim is key to his larger effort to harmonize Darwinism and Buddhism, to show, in short, that souls evolve.

Bigelow evokes both Darwin and Mendel in the service of the new doctrine of evolutionary reincarnation. He remarks on "the very close resemblance" of one particular child to a grandparent in cases of numerous grandchildren and makes the astonishing claim that "heredity by physical transmission offers no explanation"; it seems that in these cases "the single resemblance is the natural result of the rebirth of a single soul" (Bigelow, 54–55). He finds in such soul-rebirth confirmation of "Mendel's law." But he also believes, with Darwin, that "'those characteristics are most sure to be transmitted which have been longest transmitted'"; thus what is transmitted from grandparent to grandchild has to be "the oldest thing . . . about the individual organism," which would be, "according to Darwin," character (Bigelow, 55–56). Hereditary transmission of genetic traits and reincarnation, then, are simply two different ways of explaining the same facts.

But what of the ultimate goal of Buddhism, the eventual "evolution" away from character and out of self altogether? Once again, the theory of evolution is used to explain how humanity might eventually progress to what Bigelow calls "universal consciousness"—"what all existence started from and is returning to." Depending on the place of an "organized being" in the "scale of evolution," the state of universal consciousness is more or less possible of attainment. A fish is further from the state than a dog, and a dog is not so close to universal consciousness as a human being. But human beings resemble dogs insofar as they are removed from the sublime state of universal consciousness, not having yet evolved into "higher beings" (Bigelow, 61).

Bigelow is careful to point out that the kind of higher being he has in mind is not the glorified body in a state of bliss. Even though "such glorified celestial existence is the final goal of most religions," the celestial state, celebrated in Christian theology, is nothing more than "an intermediate step in normal evolution between the human consciousness and infinite consciousness," in the case of northern or Mahayana Buddhism. Somehow, the use of Darwin and the fleeting mention of Mendel seem less relevant to Bigelow's explanation of "the facts as they appear from the Buddhist stand-point" than his citation of Emerson, which comes fairly late in the lecture. He reports the great man's response to someone from an obscure sect who says, "Mr. Emerson, do you know the world is going to be destroyed in ten days?" Emerson's reply is said to be "good Buddhist doctrine": "Well, I don't see but we shall get along just as well without it" (Bigelow, 66–67). The evocation of the great transcendentalist helps to show just how odd Bigelow's lecture is, especially when one recalls that Thoreau's discovery of evolutionary theory helped him put Emerson and the East behind him. In other words, Darwin eventually took Thoreau out of the American Orient, but he seems to have led Bigelow toward it.

III

By the time John La Farge (1835–1910) journeyed to Japan in 1886 with his friend Henry Adams, he was a well-known artist, respected on both sides of the Atlantic. Thirty years earlier he had gone to Paris to study painting with Thomas Couture, best known for his allegorical canvas *The Romans of the Decadence* (1848), a pictorial comment on what the artist perceived to be the failings of France in his own times. He was also the master of Manet, but that great artist had long since left Couture's studio when La Farge arrived in 1856. So although the American no doubt learned something about technique from Couture, his studio could hardly have been a hotbed of new artistic ideas. But La Farge was a cousin of Paul Saint-Victor, the man who introduced the Goncourt brothers to Japanese art in 1861. The artist lived with Saint-Victor during his Paris sojourn of 1856–1858 and evidently came to share his cousin's orientalist enthusi-asms. In a letter of 1878, La Farge reflected on this period of his life by stressing the seminal importance of Japanese art to the development of his own: "Part of my want of success was owing to the fact that I admired Japanese art which no artists but one or two would look at. Ask yourself who in 1858 either here or in England was to say what they would today. I was merely a quarter century ahead of the boys of today." Art historians have finally confirmed that La Farge's *japonisme* did in fact anticipate that of his more celebrated contemporaries, including James Abbott McNeil Whistler (whose first "Japanese" paintings date from 1864).[21]

After Paris, La Farge returned to New York to read law, which he had been doing before the European trip, but he showed no enthusiasm for the profession. His career as an artist began in earnest when he went to Newport in 1860 to study with William Morris Hunt (1824–1879), who had also started out as one of Couture's pupils but later became an American practitioner of the Barbizon School of landscape painting. Under Hunt's influence, La Farge painted *Paradise Valley* in the late 1860s, a canvas that provided evidence of an artistic approach quite similar to the one eventually labeled impressionist in France. In fact, he might even have anticipated that movement, as his remarks of the time suggest: "I wished to apply principles of light and color of which I had learned a little. I wished my studies of nature to indicate something of this, to be free from *recipes*, as far as possible, and to indicate very carefully in every part, the exact time of day and circumstance of light."[22] While studying with Hunt in Newport, La Farge fell in love with Margaret Perry, grandniece of the commodore whose Black Ships had opened Japan to the West only a few years before. After marriage to Margaret in 1860, La Farge tried to form a trading company with his wife's brother Thomas and another Newport resident to import Japanese prints and bric-a-brac into the United States, but this plan collapsed with the outbreak of the Civil War.[23] As his family grew, La Farge divided his time between Newport and New York, where he kept his studio and where he could be more involved in the intellectual and artistic life of the times. It was in New York in 1867, at the Century Club, that he met Raphael Pumpelly, who had returned from Japan "with hundreds of old Japanese prints." Pumpelly had acquired the prints "without any expert knowledge" and was "greatly pleased" by La Farge's critical approval of the collection (R, 2:582). Shortly thereafter, Pumpelly asked La Farge to write the chapter on Japanese art for his 1870 book, *Across America and Asia*. The "Essay on Japanese Art" distinguishes La Farge as the first American artist to make a serious, systematic attempt to understand the aesthetics of the Japanese pictorial tradition.

Like so many progressive artists of the nineteenth century, La Farge was originally inspired by the writings of John Ruskin, then reacted against them as artists moved in new directions. In his essay on Japanese art, La Farge begins by measuring the meaning of Ruskin's reaction: "Interest in Japanese art must have much increased, to have made Mr. Ruskin fear some malign influence upon his artists coming from this heathen source; and it is true that many artists are in the habit of looking to it for advice and confirmation of their previous tendencies and efforts in art."[24] The comment obviously conveys an awareness of the rise of *japonisme* in the latter half of the nineteenth century, but La Farge is quick to point out the limits of that kind of interest. Far from being "the objects of a vulgar curiosity" to be collected, Japanese works "furnish a test, if ever there was one, for discernment in art" (195). What La Farge discerns in Japanese art is "a sobriety, a simplicity, a love of subdued harmonies and imperceptible gradations, and what may be called an intellectual refinement akin to something in the Western mind"; in other words, Westerners are equipped to appreciate the Japanese because of something shared or universal. This quality, whatever it is, is analogous to "the treasures of form left to us by the Greeks." When he speaks of "subdued harmonies" and "imperceptible gradations," La Farge refers to color, and his point seems to be that the Japanese have done for color what the Greeks did for form. And just as the rediscovery of the Greeks led to the Renaissance, so might the discovery of Japanese art aid in the recovery of something "put aside by Western knowledge" that "recall[s] the very arrangements of Nature," no less (196). The comment suggests the prospect of a new Oriental Renaissance in Western art in the late nineteenth century, a renaissance that most art historians would now agree did, in fact, occur.

La Farge is careful to clarify that the appeal of Japanese art does not lie solely with its refinements of color; its artists are also masters of composition, even though the composition evident in Japanese art is different from that of the Western tradition. Because "great beauty of color is apt to obscure the structure on which it rests," La Farge turns to drawings and woodcuts in black and white to "gauge [Japanese] power of design." Here he discerns an essential difference between Japanese and Western composition, with the latter's strong reliance on perspective—a judgment borne out by countless critics since. What La Farge notices most in Japanese design is "a balancing of equal gravities, not of equal surfaces. A Western designer, in ornamenting a given surface, would look for some fixed points from which to start, and would mark the places where his mind had rested by exact and symmetrical divisions. These would be supposed by a Japanese, and his mind would float over them, while they, though invisible, would be felt beneath. Thus a few ornaments—a bird, a flower—on one side of this page would be made by an almost intellectual influence to balance the large unadorned space remaining" (197). Here in La Farge's 1870 essay is the first clear articulation by an American artist of a new set of aesthetic principles based on an understanding of the Japanese tradition. His ideas do not differ appreciably from those disseminated a generation later by Arthur Wesley Dow (1857–1922), the arts educator whose classes at the Pratt Institute, the Art Students League, and Columbia University promulgated the theories set down in his influential *Composition: A Series of*

Exercises Selected from a New System of Art Education (1899). That book was inspired by the Japanese prints Dow had studied while working as a curator of Japanese art at the Museum of Fine Arts in Boston, whose Oriental collections were largely due to the efforts of the Americans considered in this chapter, Fenollosa especially. La Farge is therefore in the vanguard of the American movement that led, through Dow, to photographers such as Alvin Langdon Coburn and Gertrude Käsebier, and to painters such as Max Weber and Georgia O'Keeffe.[25]

Although La Farge repeatedly refers to Japanese art as "decoration" or "ornamentation," he does not construe the Japanese tradition as *simply* decorative; quite to the contrary, he writes, the Japanese have managed to unify "decoration and pictorial art," whereas the West has separated them. He brings out the advantage of the Japanese approach by a comparison with Chinese art, "often ridiculed for its complete absence of perspective":

> The Japanese have improved upon the usual Chinese manner, and have invented an interesting compromise, in which certain rules of linear or iso-metric perspective are used with a deep feeling for the actual appearance of nature: and by the use of high horizons, so that the different planes shall come one above the other, they manage to frame large compositions within quite an illusive effect. It is owing to this bird's-eye view that they are able to represent crowds and masses of people with enviable felicity, and give the feeling of open air and expanse to their smallest landscapes. (200)

The understanding of Japanese art that La Farge conveys here certainly seems sophisticated for the time, but even he knows that such understanding is limited to two-dimensional art, mainly prints and drawings, and to photographs of architecture and sculpture. An example of the latter is the frontispiece to Pumpelly's book, a photograph of the colossal statue of the Buddha at Kamakura. In "its serene ideal of contemplation," La Farge finds "a surmise of some of the things that might have been in Japan" (201).

When La Farge went to Japan with Henry Adams in 1886, he sought out the great statue for himself, sketched it in watercolor, and then executed at least two versions of it (also in watercolor) when he returned to New York.[26] The Japanese trip also helped La Farge work through the problems posed by a major commission: a mural depicting the ascension of Christ in the Church of the Ascension in New York City. He had begun work on the design before he left for Japan but felt stymied by the convention of representing an event of universal importance in the local landscape of Judea. In Japan he found "an atmosphere not inimical, as ours is, to what we call the miraculous" and was especially inspired by the sight of Mount

Fuji. He made a sketch of the mountain on the spot and experienced the breakthrough he needed to execute the final design of *The Ascension*, in which a modified version of Mount Fuji serves as background.[27]

La Farge's Japanese trip began at the instigation of Adams, who contacted the artist early in 1886 and offered to pay all expenses. Adams's wife Marian, nicknamed Clover, had committed suicide on 6 December 1885, after thirteen years of marriage. The couple evidently had considered a trip to Japan only a few months earlier, a sojourn that could have taken advantage of William Sturgis Bigelow's presence there, since he was Clover's cousin on her mother's side.[28] In April, Adams wrote to his friend Charles Milnes Gaskell that he had "decided to get myself quite out of the way" but had ruled out Europe because "it is full of ghosts."[29] Whether the journey to Japan was also haunted by the ghost of his dead wife is hard to say, but it seems unlikely that the sardonic Adams would have undertaken any kind of spiritual journey whatsoever. Midway across the continent to the embarkation port of San Francisco, Adams and La Farge were asked by a reporter in Omaha why they were heading for Japan. When La Farge said they were going to "seek Nirvana," the reporter opined that he thought "Nirvana was out of season." The joke would likely have pleased Adams, even though once he was aboard ship in mid-Pacific he did describe himself and La Farge as "two woe-begone Pagans, searching [for] Nirvana."[30]

When the two pagan pilgrims arrived in Yokohama, they were welcomed by Bigelow, who took them to Nikko and installed them in what Adams called "a little Japanese toy-house."[31] Adams was grateful for the cleanliness and comfort of the household, run by the Fenollosas, who were Bigelow's neighbors in Nikko, but he found little to like in Japan. His letters to friends back home comment more than once on his own laziness and on the country's conduciveness to indolence: "Japan has the single advantage of being a lazy place. One feels no impulse to exert oneself; and Buddhist contemplation of the infinite seems the only natural mode of life."[32] Though he never says so, Adams's perspective must have been colored by deep depression over his wife's recent suicide.

La Farge, by contrast, was delighted with the opportunity to encounter firsthand a culture that he had formerly known only from prints and books. In 1897 he published an account of the 1886 trip in book form as *An Artist's Letters from Japan* (installments had appeared in the *Century Magazine* at regular intervals since 1890). The book is dedicated to Okakura Kakuzo (1862–1913), one of the most important cultural figures of the Meiji period, who, with his former teacher Ernest Fenollosa, helped to affirm the cultural value of Japanese art as a means of establishing a national identity. The dedication is presented in Japanese script with an

English translation: "I wish to put your name before these notes . . . because the memory of your talks are connected with my liking of your country and its story, and because for a time you were Japan to me."[33] The form of address La Farge uses for the dedication is "Okakura San," appropriate Japanese usage among friends and equals. Years later, Okakura returned the favor when he dedicated *The Book of Tea* (1906) to La Farge, only instead of *san* he used the honorific *sensei,* the form of address reserved for teachers or masters (La Farge was Okakura's elder by almost thirty years).[34] Both men, then, recognized that each had learned something of value from the other. And both men were, in different ways, involved in the discovery or rediscovery of Japanese art. By the time they met in 1886, the twenty-four-year-old Okakura, who had been employed by the Ministry of Education since his graduation from Tokyo Imperial University in 1880, had teamed up with Fenollosa and established himself as an authority on the long-neglected art of Old Japan. More important, he had begun to insist on the importance of that art to the revival of the New.[35]

Both Okakura and La Farge, then, regarded Japanese art as the means to a kind of renaissance. La Farge, however, was interested in the art of Old Japan less as the vehicle for a renaissance in Japan itself than as a means of reviving the Western tradition. As in the chapter he wrote for Pumpelly's 1870 book, in *An Artist's Letters from Japan* La Farge invokes the by now familiar notion of an Oriental Renaissance: he stands before "ancient religious paintings of Buddhist divinities" and recalls "what I had once felt at the first sight of old Italian art" (*ALJ,* 14). Although La Farge had Ruskinian doubts about the value of the actual Renaissance, he clearly sees in Japanese art a necessary corrective to the art of his own times. Indeed, on this subject La Farge frequently sounds the pessimistic tone associated with his friend Adams. At one point he expresses concern not only that the lesson of Japanese art will fail to impress itself on the West but that the West will influence Japan for the worse: "[The] apparent want of comprehension of the first principles of the plastic arts in our poor work, and in a vast proportion of our best, . . . makes any reasonable man a pessimist as to our near future. Every poor element of our civilization is against it, and our influences are now deteriorating the art of Japan." This threatened deterioration is all the more alarming given La Farge's view that Chinese culture has already been so corrupted by foreign influence that it has "practically disappeared" (*ALJ,* 130). In fact, the value of Japanese culture is twofold: not only is it of value in itself; it is also indispensable to an understanding "of what ancient China was" (*ALJ,* 130).

Japanese preservation of the ancient "Chinese prototype" (*ALJ,* 130) would seem to be at odds with another of La Farge's ideas, one that would have an afterlife in the writings of Ezra Pound some twenty years later: namely, the notion that "artists are the antennae of the race."[36] La Farge formulates the notion thus: "The work of art is often a contradiction of the period, or a step in advance; . . . the moods of feeling of the future are as often reflected by art as the habits of the present" (*ALJ*, 149). But in the end, the idea of Japanese art as the ancient preserver of cultural verities is not contradicted by the capacity of contemporary art to capture future sensibilities. The avant-garde position harmonizes with the ancient Japanese tradition (which preserves the greater antiquity of China) for the simple reason that the aesthetic values of Japanese art are precisely what the (Western) art of the future *needs*. Time and again, La Farge compares the Japanese way with the Western and inevitably finds the latter lacking: "The Japanese sensitiveness to the beauties of the outside world is something much more delicate and complex and contemplative, and at the same time more natural, than ours has ever been" (*ALJ,* 30). A favorite formulation figures Americans and Europeans as barbarians: during the period when Japan was closed to all but Dutch traders, the artifacts that found their way to the West included "odds and ends of real art, . . . along with all the poor stuff that would naturally be made for us barbarians" (*ALJ,* 148). The strongest expression of this sentiment comes at the end of La Farge's chapter—or "letter"—on Japanese architecture. The author is struck by the austerity of Japanese domestic spaces: "There is nothing, apparently, but what is necessary, and refinement in disposing of that." This "idea of doing with little" holds great appeal for La Farge, as it did for Thoreau, who would certainly have assented to the artist's unease with the bric-a-brac of modern life: "It is possible that when I return I shall feel still more distaste for the barbarous accumulations in our houses, and recall the far more civilized emptiness persisted in by the more aesthetic race" (*ALJ,* 127).

La Farge's awareness of the value of emptiness shows that he was one of the first Americans to gain a meaningful understanding of Taoism. True, Hannah Adams had provided a rough account of "the followers of *Laokium*" (i.e., Lao-tzu) as early as 1801.[37] Later, Bronson Alcott was reputed to have been "the only member of the Concord group who ever read the *Tao Tê Ching*," yet he did not number Lao-tzu among the other Eastern luminaries, such as "Vishnu, Gotama, Confucius, [and] Mencius," whose teachings would constitute the "Bible of Mankind" that he and Emerson contemplated compiling.[38] La Farge's interest in Taoism is much more personal and detailed than that of any other American before him, most likely as a result of his close relationship with Okakura (whose *Book of Tea* includes a chapter titled "Taoism and Zennism"). But the artist also made an effort to read some of the Taoist texts on his own, evidently in

Latin, since his interests preceded the English translations done by Herbert Giles in 1889 and by James Legge in 1891.[39] In *An Artist's Letters from Japan,* La Farge devotes a full chapter to "Tao: The Way," in which he reveals a deep appreciation for the temple architecture at Nikko from the Tokugawa period. La Farge applies the lesson of the Tao to art and architecture by saying that, just as Lao-tzu "neither preached nor discussed" but taught "by parables and side glimpses and innuendoes[,] illuminated by that light which exists in the natural heart of man," the artist (or the architect) should not impose his will on nature by following set forms or conventions but, instead, "try the freshness of the springs, to see if new impressions come as they once did in childhood" (*ALJ,* 117).

It is not clear whether La Farge actually read the *Tao-te-Ching* or not, but there can be no doubt that, through whatever means, he managed to enter the conceptual universe of Taoism, as the conclusion to the chapter shows: "I have become as a blank to be filled. I employ my mind as a mirror; it grasps nothing; it refuses nothing; it receives, but does not keep. And thus I can triumph over things without injury to myself—I am safe in Tao" (*ALJ,* 118). The passage compares to any number of verses from the *Tao-te-Ching,* such as this one (in James Legge's 1891 translation): "The Tâo is (like) the emptiness of a vessel; and in our employment of it we must be on our guard against all fullness."[40] Eastern emptiness—or its close cognates lightness and fragility—impresses La Farge so much that he comes to question the entire aesthetic basis of Western art and architecture. He says of one Tokugawa temple at Nikko that it "has more details of beauty than all our architects now living, all together, could dream of accomplishing in the longest life." Then comes a stunning criticism of Western tradition: "When I began to reflect how this wood and plaster had more of the dignity of art and of its accessible beauty than all that we have at home, if melted together, would result in; that these frail materials conveyed to the mind more of the eternal than our granite, it seemed to me that something was absolutely wrong with us" (*ALJ,* 100).

As this passage shows, La Farge follows Fenollosa and Lowell in thinking of the Japanese as the antithesis of the Americans and the Europeans. He calls Japan "this land of inversion" (*ALJ,* 189), an epithet that implies, given all the talk of Western barbarism, that the values of the West are the ones that need to be adjusted. The Japanese may be on the other side of the world, but it is the Americans who have turned the world upside down. La Farge possibly goes further in his thinking about the relation of East and West than either Lowell or Fenollosa, both of whom came to understand East and West as complementary, true to the neo-Hegelian thinking of the time. Open and open-minded relations between Japan and America, then, might lead one day to a new synthesis, a new order, a new civilization that would combine the best of both cultures. But La Farge, with all his talk about the barbarism of the West, leaves little doubt that the way forward, if there is one, does not involve synthesis at all. Rather, Americans should become more Japanese and less American.

In a way, La Farge's views reflect those of both of his two friends Okakura and Adams, who could not have been more different from one another. Like Okakura, La Farge suggests that the cultural synthesis predicted by the neo-Hegelians has already occurred—in Japan. Later, Okakura would make the synthetic argument in *The Awakening of Japan* (1904), seeing his country as the product not of neo-Hegelianism but of neo-Confucianism, a tradition "rich in creative efforts both in art and literature" which "aimed at a synthesis of Taoist, Buddhist, and Confucian thought" and which, moreover, "marks the result of a brilliant effort to mirror the whole of Asiatic consciousness."[41] At the same time, when La Farge measures Western materialism against the culture of the Far East, he evokes the sense of American decadence so often expressed by his friend Adams. Although Adams does not mention his trip to Japan in his highly ironic, third-person biography, *The Education of Henry Adams,* that work does provide insight into its author's attitude toward the relationship of East and West. In it, he describes a trip to the Near East in which he hoped to find evidence to refute his brother Brooks's contention "that the relation between civilizations was that of trade." He seems to come close to finding "a city of thought along the great highways of exchange" in Constantinople, but the satisfaction of the quest is less important than the terms that Adams uses to define it: the East in this case is the antithesis of materialism. Elsewhere, the East connotes escape: not so much the antithesis of Western values as the negation of them. The Paris Exposition of 1889 left him feeling "nothing in common with the world as it promised to be. He was ready to quit it, and the easiest path led back to the east."[42]

Adams expressed the same sentiment at the end of his trip to Japan. The search for "Nirvana," in his case, seems to have been little more than a desire to escape not only from the American tradition but also from the Adams lineage. As he wrote to John Hay from San Francisco immediately upon his return from Japan, what he had "learned" from the trip with La Farge was that he needed to end his life in China:

> Another nugget of golden learning acquired by me, is the certainty that Japan
> and its art are only a sort of antechamber to China, and that China is the only
> mystery left to penetrate. I have henceforward a future. As soon as I can get
> rid of history and the present, I mean to start for China, and stay there. You
> will hear of me then only as of a false pig-tail pendant over eighteen colored

suits of clothes; which, I am told, is the swell winter dress of a Chinese gentle-
man. In China I will find bronzes or break all the crockery. Five years hence, I
expect to enter the celestial kingdom by that road, if not sooner by a shorter
one, as seems more likely to judge from the ways of most of my acquaintances
at home.[43]

It is not hard to hear Adams contemplating the prospect of suicide in that
last sentence, nor is it hard to hear that his experiences of the Far East have
left him with a feeling of emptiness completely unlike the Taoist one La
Farge came to cultivate in Japan. Perhaps most remarkable of all is how far
Adams's view of China is from the one his great-grandfather maintained
in his political writings and in his correspondence with Thomas Jefferson.
But it is also well removed from the vision of the Orient that was emerging
among his contemporaries, none of whom was more dedicated to articulating that vision than Ernest Fenollosa.

IV

Ernest Fenollosa was the son of a Spanish-American immigrant who settled
in Salem, Massachusetts, to teach music at a time when that city was the
most important port for the maritime trade with the East Indies. Prior to
Perry's opening of the treaty ports in the late 1850s, the Dutch East Indies
would have been the conduit for curios from Japan and other countries of
the East. And while most of the porcelain and lacquer work would have
been sold in the more fashionable markets of New York and Boston, the
Fenollosa household would have had its share. The point here is not so
much to explain Ernest Fenollosa's later orientalism as the product of the
material culture to which he was exposed as a young man but to suggest
a certain saturation of Eastern objects and ideas in New England life not
limited to the transcendental circles of Concord. If the philosophes of the
eighteenth century represent the first wave of New England orientalism,
and the Unitarians and transcendentalists of the nineteenth century the
second, then Morse, Bigelow, Lowell, La Farge, and Fenollosa belong to the
third wave. In Fenollosa's case, the temptation is to say that he responded
to the heritage of New England orientalism by reacting to the element
of falseness in it. Unitarian interpretation of Hinduism was not authentic
Eastern religion; Oriental bric-a-brac was not art.

But Fenollosa did not go to Japan to find the authentic Orient that the
American Orient obscured, at least initially. He went to teach the Japanese
modern philosophy, having been recruited to do so by his Salem neighbor
Edward S. Morse. When Morse left Japan to honor his American lecture
obligations in early 1878, he resolved to return with a physicist and a

philosopher. Thomas C. Mendenhall of the Ohio Agricultural and Mechanical College accepted the physics post when Morse made the offer after a lecture in Columbus. The offer to Fenollosa, whom Morse did not know beforehand, was more roundabout: he made inquiries of associates at Harvard, and Fenollosa came with the strongest recommendations, including those of President Charles W. Eliot and Professor Charles Eliot Norton. Fenollosa must have appealed to Morse for other reasons as well: as a staunch Darwinist, Morse must have been pleased that Fenollosa had abandoned Divinity School to study art after taking his undergraduate degree. And as an undergraduate, Fenollosa had been responsible for forming the Spencer Club at Harvard. Spencer's *Social Statics* had already been translated into Japanese, so a young American proponent of social Darwinism and other Spencerian ideas made for a perfect fit. Morse offered Fenollosa the job, and he accepted; together they sailed for Japan and arrived in Yokohama in August 1878.[44]

In Japan, Fenollosa followed Morse's lead and gave public lectures on Sundays in addition to teaching his university classes. He also began a personal odyssey that took him, philosophically, from positivism to idealism and, aesthetically, from fin-de-siècle *japonisme* to modernism. For the Japanese, it is hard to say whether Fenollosa's greatest importance lay with his philosophical or with his aesthetic enthusiasms. He taught them Spencer when they had a hunger to learn the ways of Western economic individualism, a difficult lesson for a people so recently removed from feudalism but hardly removed at all from the social protocols of class and clan. To be sure, Spencer was not the only avenue to individualism. G. B. Sansom notes that Samuel Smiles's *Self-Help* was translated into Japanese in 1870 and went through numerous editions subsequently. He also says that Defoe's *Robinson Crusoe* was read as an allegory of Japanese modernization, with one translator arguing in his preface, "If men . . . read it carefully they will see that it shows how by stubborn determination an island can be developed."[45] Nonetheless, together with his colleague Shoichi Toyama, a literature professor who went to the University of Michigan to study Spencer, Fenollosa has been credited "with making a lasting impression on Japanese thinking."[46] The comment refers to Japan's embrace of capitalism, but it could just as well point to the nation's acceptance of its own artistic traditions, which Fenollosa did so much to foster.

Fenollosa's advocacy of Spencerianism is hard to square with his promotion of Japanese art, but Spencer was not the only philosopher who appealed to him. At Harvard, he took up the study of Hegel when he enrolled in the Divinity School and was especially impressed with the philosopher's theory of history. Like other educated Americans of his generation, Fenollosa was in a position to appreciate the importance of Hegel in the context of the United States. In his *Lectures on the Philosophy of History* (1837), Hegel claimed that "America is . . . the land of the future, where, in the ages that lie before us, the burden of the World's History shall reveal itself." The philosopher suggested that the dialectical process of history would culminate in a New World synthesis when America got around to leaving "the historical lumber-room of Old Europe" and "abandon[ing] the ground on which hitherto the History of the World has developed itself."[47] Fenollosa would also have read that "the History of the World travels from East to West, for Europe is absolutely the end of history, Asia the beginning" (*Lectures*, 109). Hegel further averred that the New World offered "only an echo of the Old World," an attitude that needed to be abandoned if America hoped to measure up to the progressive ideal of history, "for America is . . . the land of the future" (*Lectures*, 90). Fenollosa eventually took Hegel's formulations to mean that history, which had ended in Europe, could be renewed in America by returning to the site of history's beginning and realizing a synthesis of East and West.[48]

American Hegelianism already had a long history by the time Fenollosa took up philosophy with the Harvard professor Charles Carroll Everett, who had studied in Germany and authored a book of Hegelian philosophy himself, *The Science of Thought: A System of Logic* (1869).[49] Around the same time that Everett published his book, William Torey Harris, a former shorthand instructor, and Henry C. Brokmeyer, an iron-molder from Germany, tried to "make Hegel talk English" at meetings of the St. Louis philosophical society and in the pages of the *Journal of Speculative Philosophy*, which began publication in 1867. The year 1865 had seen the publication of J. H. Stirling's *The Secret of Hegel*, "a widely read general guide" to the philosopher which influenced both Emerson and Whitman.[50] Emerson, of course, had experienced some version of Hegel still earlier, when the German immigrant writer Frederick Augustus Rauch introduced the philosopher to the transcendentalists in *Psychology: A View of the Human Soul* (1840), said to be the first Hegel-inspired book published in the United States. But the New England Hegelians were rather different from those in the heartland cities of St. Louis and Cincinnati, who were intent on "transcending transcendentalism" (Goetzmann, 5, 15). Many of them eventually found their way to Marxism, whereas Fenollosa adhered more closely to the version of Hegel he was taught at Harvard.

The basic Hegelian notion of history as "a progressive unfolding or revelation of the mind of God in concrete experience" has been explained as "a kind of Manifest Destiny of the mind, aiming always towards the formation of a greater community" (Goetzmann, 14, 16). Hence, Fenollosa's

East-West fusion would be the culmination of the dialectical process Hegel envisioned, since there could be no greater community than the world at large. While some contemporary Hegelians were turning the philosopher on his head to pursue dialectical materialism, Fenollosa remained steadfastly "spiritual," in the sense that he sought an even higher synthesis than the one Hegel imagined, which was limited to America as "the land of the future." Fenollosa found an antithesis to the American thesis in Japan and saw the fusion of the two cultures as the highest synthesis of all. This great synthesis could be achieved through aesthetics, if only the West could come to understand what was essential about Eastern art. At Tokyo University, Fenollosa was largely relieved of his Spencerian duties in 1884 when other professors were recruited for the task, and he was free to work out his Hegelian ideas in the classroom: "The courses which Fenollosa presented in 1884 to each of his undergraduate classes indicate the direction his thinking was taking: Freshman—Synthetic Logic; Sophomore—History of Modern Philosophy to Hegel; Junior—Hegel with Side Glances at Spencer; Senior—Ethics, Aesthetics, and the Philosophy of Religion."[51]

As the title of the senior course indicates, Fenollosa construed art in a larger cultural context. The student of Japanese aesthetics was necessarily a student of Japanese religion as well, a seemingly obvious fact in a country filled with Buddhist art. At the time, however, the Japanese did not understand the images and objects they saw in their temples as works of art, the way Europeans understood the Christian icons and artifacts in their cathedrals. Moreover, the Japanese had come to regard their own artistic traditions as inferior to those of the West. As part of the modernization program, the Italian artist Fontanesi was invited to Tokyo to teach the Japanese how to see and how to represent what they saw correctly, using Renaissance perspective, modeling, shadowing, anatomy, and the rest. Around the same time that the Japanese were being taught to imitate Western traditions, Fenollosa was beginning to question them. The year before he left for Japan he had abandoned his graduate training in philosophy to work at the Massachusetts Normal Art School while studying painting at the Boston Museum of Fine Arts. He may have left Harvard, but he did not leave Hegel, who helped him to understand the aesthetic importance of expression over imitation. In 1882, Fenollosa lectured on Japanese art to a group of influential aristocrats, telling them that "Japanese art is really far superior to modern cheap western art that describes any object at hand mechanically, forgetting the most important point, expression of Idea." He had been led to this view not only by his earlier reading of Hegel and his art studies in Boston but also by a careful study begun in 1879 of original works by Sesshu, Motonobu, and other Japanese masters. The 1882 speech

helped to catalyze skepticism of Westernization and urged the Meiji government to change its approach toward Japanese art: thereafter, Western-
style art instruction ceased, and systematic inventories of art works housed
in temples began. Since Fenollosa was at the center of these changes, he
was appointed to a special commission charged with touring the world to
observe the art schools and academies of other nations; the commission's
recommendations would be used in establishing a School of Fine Arts and
in articulating a national policy of art education.[52]

Fenollosa's ambitious plans to reinvigorate the art of Japan by making
the Japanese more aware of their own artistic traditions would not have
been possible without the support and assistance of his Japanese hosts,
since Fenollosa's command of the language was extremely limited. As his
interests shifted from philosophy to art, he was fortunately able to take
advantage of a group of educated Japanese whose English was excellent:
his own students at Tokyo Imperial University. Of these, the two most
important figures were Ariga Nagao (1860–1921), who would go on to
become a scholar of international law, and Okakura Kakuzo, seemingly
ubiquitous in American circles during the Meiji era. In 1884 they helped
Fenollosa found the Kangakai (Painting Appreciation Society), which gave
him the opportunity to promulgate his ideas among artists, not just academics. In fact, around this time Fenollosa left the university altogether and
joined Okakura at the Ministry of Education, where his former student
had been employed since 1880 and where he had special responsibilities
in the division of the ministry overseeing art education. These two venues
allowed Fenollosa, with the assistance of Ariga and Okakura, to wield considerable sway over the direction of Japanese culture. But his influence was
profoundly paradoxical: on the one hand, his interest in Japanese artistic
tradition, its relation to Chinese antiquity, its relevance to contemporary
artmaking, and so on, all reflected a genuine effort to understand Eastern
art on its own terms; on the other hand, his insistence that art had to be
understood as an expression of national character was completely Western.
As Victoria Weston explains, "Fenollosa, like many Westerners, believed
in art as a necessary adjunct to the project of nation-building. In speeches
made during the 1880s, Fenollosa urged the Japanese government to create a national art infrastructure: national museums, national art education,
and juried exhibitions. Great nations needed great 'national art' to compete
in world commodity markets and to project the appropriate aura of high
culture."[53] Thanks to Fenollosa, then, the revival of an Eastern tradition
occurred in the context of a Western ideological paradigm. Okakura, for
one, bought into the Fenollosa program wholeheartedly, accompanying
him on his tour of American and European art schools to ascertain the

most progressive methods of art education. La Farge, by contrast, expressed skepticism about the project, seeing "vague visions of distorted values" and fearing that "commercial authorities" would be "looked upon as artistic" (*ALJ*, 221). The supremely confident Fenollosa (Adams called him "a tyrant" on matters of art)[54] naturally had no doubts whatsoever about his mission. After all, when he left Japan with Okakura, Adams, and La Farge in 1886, he did so as an imperial commissioner of the Japanese government.

But Fenollosa hardly needed to be commissioned to advocate for the Japanese. Once back in the United States, in addition to his official duties as an analyst of Western methods of art education, he began to promote his own theories of culture. In lectures and magazine articles—as well as in a long poem—he argued that the synthesis of East and West would give rise to a new world culture that would mark a fresh stage in human progress. Fenollosa was not alone in thinking of the Far East as the antithesis of Western industrialized democracy. Percival Lowell, with whom Fenollosa worked closely in Japan, published *The Soul of the Far East* in 1888, a book that puts forth the idea of the "Far Oriental" (a term encompassing the Japanese, Chinese, and Koreans) as a literal antithesis of Western man. With the Japanese, especially, "the world stands reversed," so that when "we gaze at them," we seem to be "viewing our own humanity in some mirth-provoking mirror of the mind."[55] Lowell also anticipates Fenollosa in suggesting that East-West opposition will ultimately lead to some kind of larger synthesis, since the worldview of the Far Oriental might be used "stereoptically" in combination with that of the Near Occidental: "For his mind-photograph of the world can be placed side by side with ours, and the two pictures combined will yield results beyond what either alone could possibly have afforded. Thus harmonized, they will help us realize humanity" (*Soul*, 4).

The prospect of a larger synthesis, however, is never explored in Lowell's book, because he finds "the power to fuse . . . wanting" as a result of Oriental backwardness: the Eastern races have not evolved at the same rate as the Western. The retarding factor is impersonality, which turns out to be the "soul" invoked in Lowell's title: "If with us the *I* seems to be of the very essence of the soul, then the soul of the Far East may be said to be Impersonality" (*Soul*, 15). In his final chapter, Lowell employs Darwinian—or pseudo-Darwinian—language to provide scientific support for his central claim: that any future fusion of East and West will have to wait because the Far Oriental simply isn't ready to take so momentous a step. Indeed, so strong is the Eastern impulse toward impersonality (evidenced in the language of the Japanese through the absence of personal pronouns and in their religion through the self-annihilating state of nirvana) that the very race risks extinction. This is so because the instinct of self-preservation depends on the instinct of individuality, which the Far Oriental lacks (*Soul*, 197). But the Darwinian argument is more complex than this, since evolution "shows . . . that individuality bears the same relationship to the devel- ' opment of mind that the differentiation of species does to the evolution of organic life: *that the degree of individuation of a people is the self-recorded measure of its place in the great march of mind*" (*Soul*, 195). Clearly, the Far Oriental is out of step in this great march: "Just as surely as morning passes into afternoon, so surely are these races of the Far East, if unchanged, destined to disappear before the advancing nations of the West" (*Soul*, 226). Hence, Lowell ends his book without suggesting anything like the larger harmony "that will help us realize humanity" with which he began it.

Lowell's emphasis on the backward nature of the Japanese and their inability to "fuse" made *The Soul of the Far East* of limited use to the neo-Hegelian Fenollosa. At the same time, Lowell's claim that the Far Oriental was "destined to disappear" in the face of Western modernity struck a highly responsive chord in the mind of the neo-romantic writer Lafcadio Hearn. Hearn and Fenollosa were almost exact contemporaries (Hearn was born in 1850, Fenollosa in 1853), but the two men could not have been further apart in their attitudes toward Japanese culture. Indeed, Hearn emerges as a kind of anti-Fenollosa because of his deep skepticism about the value of the modernity Fenollosa and other American employees of the Meiji regime advocated. The peripatetic Hearn arrived in Japan in 1890, his interest in the island nation having been inspired chiefly by Lowell's *Soul of the Far East* (which he called "an astounding book—a godlike book") and by the Japanese exhibit at the World's Industrial and Cotton Centennial Exposition, held in New Orleans in December 1884.[56] Hearn went to the exposition as a reporter for the *New Orleans Times-Democrat* and filed dispatches about the Japanese exhibit that downplayed the material progress of the New Japan, celebrating the aesthetic culture of the Old instead.

Hearn's obsessive interest in Old Japan eventually resulted in a contract with Harper's for a travel book, *Glimpses of Unfamiliar Japan* (1894). The curious title signaled Hearn's intent to acquaint readers with traditional elements of Japanese life that had been obscured by the Meiji modernization. In his preface to the volume Hearn claimed that "the Occidentalized Japanese of to-day stands almost on the intellectual plane of the cultivated Parisian or Bostonian." He sought out "the rare charm of Japanese life . . . ' not to be found in its Europeanized circles" but "among the great common people."[57] Hearn's exploration of Old Japan was fortuitous in its timing:

his reaction against the "Occidentalized Japanese" in his books coincided with the re-affirmation of Japanese tradition and the anti-Western sentiment that emerged in 1895 when Russia, France, and Germany intervened in the treaty negotiations between China and Japan in the aftermath of the first Sino-Japanese War. The growing resentment against the West is captured in "A Conservative," a story from Hearn's 1896 collection *Kokoro: Hints and Echoes of Japanese Inner Life* (*kokoro*, Hearn explains, means "the heart of things").[58] This story, like Hearn's Japanese work generally, makes for a stark contrast with Fenollosa's Hegelian fantasies of East-West fusion.[59]

"A Conservative" is a narrative of the maturation and education of a young man of the samurai class who comes of age during the great transition from the feudal period of the shogunate to the modern era of the Meiji. Except for its length (forty pages), "A Conservative" might fairly be called a *Bildungsroman*: indeed, the narrative captures not only the growth of an individual consciousness but also the emergence of a broader social sensibility during the Meiji period. The young man in Hearn's story grows up steeled in the samurai code, considering "duty the guiding motive of life, self-control the first requisite of conduct, pain and death matters of no consequence in the selfish sense" (*K*, 171). He is "scarcely more than a boy" when the feudal nation is "startled by the coming of the Black Ships" (*K*, 176). Soon thereafter he is witness to rapid social upheavals, as the government mandates "that Western knowledge . . . be taught in all schools; that the study of English . . . be made an important branch of public education; and that public education itself . . . be remodeled upon Occidental lines" (*K*, 178). Although the young samurai accords his Western teachers the public respect due any *sensei,* privately he regards them as less than human, "as more closely allied to animals than to mankind" (*K*, 180). The youth dutifully submits to the new order, not because he is cowed into obedience but because he understands the patriotic necessity of doing so, "to prepare himself to play the man in the drama of the future" (*K*, 185).

Somewhat surprisingly, the samurai student converts to Christianity, partly because he recognizes in the Western religion certain ethical precepts already familiar to him from studying the Confucian classics, and partly because he believes that the foreigners' faith is the source of their awesome power: "If the superior force of Western civilization really indicated the superior character of Western ethics, was it not the plain duty of every patriot to follow that higher faith?" The narrator offers a correction to this view which the young samurai is not yet in a position to appreciate—that the "material progress" of the West has been achieved "chiefly through a merciless competition out of all harmony with Christian idealism" (*K*, 189). Hearn expands this argument into a polemic against the effectiveness of Christianity in a Buddhist nation and avers that "the more intelligent the pupil, the briefer the term of that pupil's Christianity," concluding that "a Buddhism fortified by Western science will meet the future needs of the race" (*K*, 193). Hearn was right about the confluence of Buddhism and science, as the Japanese delegates to the World's Parliament of Religions made clear in Chicago in 1893 (see chapter 5). In "A Conservative," the scientific, secular conversion soon displaces the Christian one, when the samurai student rejects the church because "its tenets are not based on true reason or fact" (*K*, 194).

At this point the young man embarks for Europe and America to further explore the relation of Western religion to Western power, having become a "freethinker" in political as well as religious terms (*K*, 196). His exposure to Western culture—"the theatres, the opera"—lead him to wonder "why the Western conception of the worth of life differed so little from the Far-Eastern conception of folly and of effeminacy" (*K*, 199). He finds the West ethically inferior to the East but remains impressed by the intellectual "sublimities" of Western science, "whose logic he knew to be irrefutable." He also knows that the Japanese must become masters of this logic, or "perish utterly" (*K*, 204, 205). When he finally returns from his long exile, as his fellow passengers aboard the steamer strain for a sight of Mount Fuji, the samurai has a different vision: "He saw neither Fuji above, nor the nearing hills below, changing their vapory blue to green; nor the crowding of the ships in the bay; nor anything of the modern Japan; he saw the Old" (*K*, 208).

In a way, the conclusion of "A Conservative" suggests the resolution of a dialectical process, but one different from the sort that Fenollosa imagined. The synthesis that the samurai has worked out for himself is a fusion of Buddhist ethics and Western science. For Hearn, this is where the synthesis stops; for Fenollosa, the Japanese capacity to fuse Eastern religion with Western intellect produces a new thesis that begs for further merger with the Western counterthesis in an ongoing dialectical process that will lead to a new world culture. In retrospect, the "romantic" Hearn was a realist after all, at least by comparison with Fenollosa, for he was, in a way, on the right side of history, however wrong that history turned out to be: the samurai scientist he imagines in his story is a prototype of the techno-fascist of the twentieth century.

Fenollosa, by contrast, maintained his Hegelian faith in the higher synthesis and saw that synthesis embodied to an extraordinary degree in the Japanese people. In an 1892 article for the *Atlantic Monthly,* he argued that

Japan's rapid modernization offered evidence for a new kind of synthetic civilization because the country not only adapted to Western ways but also reacted to them, made adjustments, and preserved a set of venerable and indispensable Asian traditions. Japan, he wrote, is "our most alert pioneer" in the process that will lead to "the fusion of Eastern and Western types": "Through her temperament, her individuality, her deeper insight into the secrets of the East, her ready divining of the powers of the West, and, more than all, through the fact that hers, the spiritual factor of the problem, must hold the master key to its solution, it may be decreed in the secret council chambers of Destiny that on her shores shall be first created that new latter-day type of civilized man which shall prevail throughout the world for the next thousand years."[60] The millennialist thinking is of a piece with the perception, widespread in Boston artistic circles in the early 1890s, that the world had entered an era of decline. In fact, Fenollosa also aired his theories in *The Knight Errant*, whose editors were convinced of the decadence of American society and eagerly awaited the collapse of democracy.[61] Fenollosa may not have been as reactionary as most of the authors who published in that magazine, but he shares with them the sense of social decline and the wish for renewal from without, a classic decadent formulation.

What made the Japanese so strong a candidate for cultural renewal was their individuality, a term that had a special meaning for Fenollosa, one very different from the notion put forward by Lowell, who, again, thought that the Japanese were doomed to extinction because of an insufficient "degree of individuation." In the *Atlantic Monthly* essay "Chinese and Japanese Traits," Fenollosa explains that individuality is "the power to produce freshly from within, to adapt and act under rapid change of environment. It transcends institution, custom, love of approbation, fear of disapproval, all slowly acting forces of sheer mass. It is spontaneous origination, the salt of social life, the last hope of a race." Individuality, then, is a kind of organic capacity for change, a capacity that is countered by what Fenollosa calls "formalism," which seems to have won the day in China. Where China once possessed sufficient "individualistic illumination . . . to fuse together the three great religions of Taoism, Confucianism, and Buddhism," in the "days of her decadence" China has allowed "babbling Confucians of the narrowest commentating school" to dim "the glow of native genius with such a crust of literary formalism that intelligence has been stunted and government itself petrified" ("Traits," 770–71). The Japanese have of course borrowed from the Chinese, but their individuality has kept the forms (of religion, of art, of government) from falling into formalism.

The Japanese, it seems, represent a synthesis of individualism and formalism, and it is this capacity that has allowed them to "solve the problems of self-evolutionary reconstruction," by which Fenollosa means an ability to adapt. Spencer and Hegel both sound through Fenollosa's "scientific" explanation of Japanese adaptability: "The very scientific idea of life is perpetual power of readaptation; and the highest life is reached when this readaptation implies a synthesis of all the organs and faculties through a free presiding intelligence" ("Traits," 772). The next stage in the synthesis, after the Japanese fusion of individuality and formalism, would be the fusion of East and West.

In the year following the appearance of the *Atlantic* essay Fenollosa produced a collection of poems, the centerpiece of which is "East and West," an epic in theme if not in length. Although published in 1893, the poem dates from June 1892, when Fenollosa read it before the Phi Beta Kappa society at Harvard University. The original audience did not have the benefit of the preface to the poem, which helps to make sense of the grand theme of "East and West," involving a double antithesis. Just as the predominantly "masculine" values of the West are countered by the "softening" influence of Christianity—"the feminine faith of love, renunciation, obedience, salvation from without"—so the "feminine" refinement of the East has been balanced by "her martial faith of spiritual knighthood, self-reliance, salvation from within." "This stupendous double antithesis," Fenollosa adds, "seems to me the most significant fact in all history." The coming fusion is figured as "a twofold marriage" that will combine "Scientific Analysis and Spiritual Wisdom," thereby wedding "for eternity the blended grace of Æsthetic Synthesis and Spiritual Love."[62]

The workings of this "stupendous" synthesis are described in the five parts of the poem: "The First Meeting of East and West" (the ancient, original "fusion" wrought by Alexander the Great after he conquered Persia); "The Separated East" (the feminine isolation of quiescent Buddhism and refined art, mainly in Japan); "The Separated West" (the masculine conquests of Western imperial powers, however tempered by Christianity); "The Present Meeting of East and West" (the Meiji modernization); and "The Future Union of East and West" (the eventual harmony of masculinity and femininity that will bring forth the "Model of millennial man"). The last two sections merit the greatest attention because they represent, respectively, versified versions of Fenollosa's recent experience in Japan and the philosophy he extrapolated from that experience.

"The Present Meeting of East and West" offers ample criticism not only of the West's economic exploitation of Japan but also of Japan's failure to recognize the value of her own cultural patrimony. Fenollosa decries "the great trade of this mad masquerade" in language that, possibly, is deliberately contrived to illustrate the West's lack of artistic refinement:

> O you West in the East like the slime of a beast,
> Why must you devour that exquisite flower?
> Why poison the peace of the Far Japanese?
> Is there no one to tell of the birthright they sell?
>
> (EW, 39)

The last rhetorical question is amply answered by the poet himself as he recounts in verse form the kind of art education that he witnessed in Japan and that inspired him to encourage native artistic practices: "And here come art students with honors! / They graduate strictly in marble madonnas" (EW, 41). Nonetheless, the present meeting of East and West is a harbinger of the eventual union of the hemispheres through music, for "music predicts our native power to compass a profounder integration," as Fenollosa puts it in his preface (EW, vi). How the Western capacity to appreciate Beethoven and Brahms (the only two composers mentioned in the poem) might lead to the fusion of East and West is not completely clear, yet that is what the poem says: "such . . . powers / E'en now are dimly ours; Foretaste of human bliss / In tuneful synthesis!" (EW, 44–45). It is hard to tell whether Fenollosa means that music is simply a metaphor for the coming synthesis, or that the synthesis will actually make some kind of music because the East-West "harmony" he contemplates is so powerful.

The "music of the hemispheres" is sounded in the final section in ecstatic language that celebrates the formation, through East-West fusion, of "the self-hood unconscious of self!" (EW, 48). The "world's twin soul," the aforementioned "Model of millennial man," is supposed to harmonize masculine force and feminine forms: "Then shall art with beauty rife / Melt into the Art of Life" (EW, 49, 50, 51). Two points about this East-West utopia call for special emphasis: one, it is aesthetic; and, two, it is Christian. Presumably, the West takes aesthetic refinement from the East, even as the East takes in Christianity, which the East is evidently prepared to do because it is especially well-disposed toward feminine forms, of which Christianity is one. But Fenollosa's message is hardly missionary; Christianity is simply necessary to the "stupendous double antithesis" the Hegelian poet has worked out for himself:

> If true harmony is prized,
> Man is self-decentralized;
> Christ's impersonality
> World-absorbed and emphasized!
>
> (EW, 51)

The "twofold marriage" promised in the preface appears near the end of the poem, which certainly seems climactic, as the dominant masculinity of the West is married to the dominant femininity of the East, along with their respective antinomies—that is, the greater masculinity of the West is wedded to the lesser of the East, even as the greater femininity of the East is married to the lesser of the West:

> Thus may knighthood of defiance
> Consecrate the arm of science;
> Twin-joined vigor of the ages,
> Corner-stone of God's reliance.
>
> Thus may Christlike Mercy render
> Holiest warmth to Beauty tender;
> Twin-joined womanhood of races,
> Sunlike heart of God's own splendor.
>
> Corner-stone and sunlike heart!
> Strife in Wisdom, Love in Art!
> Thou art joined in twofold marriage,
> Links which time can never part!
>
> (EW, 53)

When the twofold marriage is consummated (the union is highly spiritual, to say the least), a "dim uncertain form divine" is born ("O love, thy soul and mine"), but it soon "fades in formless light / Too exquisite for human sight." The newly born synthetic soul is then transported

> Out of this mortal world,
> This temple transitory
> For nature's unemancipated priest,
> Into the silence of Nirwana's [sic] glory,
> Where there is no more West and no more East.
>
> ·(EW, 55)

In addition to a preface, Fenollosa provided a set of notes to explain some of the more recondite allusions in the poem. Most of these clarify references to Japan, but one explains an aspect of the Hegelian infrastructure of the poem that is useful to Fenollosa's further explanation of his fusion theory. In the third section, "The Separated West," the masculine soul of the imperialistic West is described as an "expansive self-willed personality," and Fenollosa explains what he means in a note: "It will be perceived that I oppose personality, the self-centered and self-originated will of an incarnate man, to individuality, the unconscious strength and freedom of an intelligence immersed in the divinity of its work" (EW, 212). The Hegelian "clarification" between personality and individuality would come into play in yet another exposition of Fenollosa's theory of East-West synthesis a few years later.

By the time he got around to articulating the theory in magazine format again, in the December 1898 issue of *Harper's,* America's position in the world had changed. "The Coming Fusion of East and West" appears between a doggerel poem celebrating Dewey's victory in Manila Bay and the report of the rescue in the Philippines of one American gunboat by another; the latter was written by the naval lieutenant who was a first-hand witness to the action.[63] At first glance the juxtaposition seems to suggest that Fenollosa is out of step with his times, speaking of fusion in the midst, literally, of confrontation. But Fenollosa understands the Spanish-American War as actual evidence of the dialectical process of history he seeks to explain: "The forcing together of the two halves of our race by the Spanish war, and the unfolding, if only for a glimpse, of a common, unheard-of destiny in the East, are like the very voice of Time suddenly made audible."[64] Where Fenollosa *is* out of step with many Americans at the end of the nineteenth century is in his liberal understanding of race relations. Far from being a jingoistic cheerleader for the racial superiority of the Anglo-Saxons, he holds the view that the future of humanity requires a mingling of the races. Part of his argument is that modern Europe had its origins in an earlier East-West fusion—"that former contact . . . resulted in a union of cultures"—when Alexander extended his empire into India. The opportunity for a new "race union" is especially critical: indeed, the longed-for fusion of East and West represents humanity's last chance, "for there is no new blood, no outlying culture-germ for subsequent infusion. Such as we make it now, it must remain till the end. This is man's final experiment" ("Fusion," 116–117). The formulation is a little different from the decadent desire for fresh barbarian blood, since Fenollosa's fusion involves two different types of civilization in place of the usual union of barbarism and excessive civilization. "Each has the privilege to supply what the other lacks," he says ("Fusion," 122).

But Fenollosa's argument for the fusion of East and West is not based solely on some abstract doctrine of contraries. He has a keen sense of history and makes some startling criticisms (of the British, especially) that demonstrate what we would now call "global awareness." He is particularly concerned that Russia may take possession of "that golden key" of economic development "where it is really hidden—in the capitalization of Chinese industry." The Anglo-Saxon, whether British or American, "deserves to pass from the world" if he fails to join "his superb business methods" with "Japanese aptitude" to exploit the economic potential of

China. Should he do so, "before the end of the next century Shanghai should become the metropolis of the globe, with a commerce rivaling New York and London's" ("Fusion," 121). The comment is prescient, excepting the removal of "Japanese aptitude" from the eventual emergence of China as a world economic power. Fenollosa understands the Japanese as "the only possible mediators between Asiatic thought and the thought of the West" ("Fusion," 120), and he sees evidence in his own time that Japan is the only nation capable of rejuvenating China by providing a model for modernization.[65] By the same token, the nation best equipped to partner with Japan in the larger rejuvenation of the human race and in the production of "a new world-type" ("Fusion," 116) is America.

Once again, the Spanish-American War was testament to America's readiness to assume the leadership role in the coming fusion. Somehow, Fenollosa either ignored or saw beyond the chauvinism on his own shores to imagine an eagerness on the part of Americans to engage in a level of racial understanding that was gainsaid by their ugly attitude toward the immigrant populations, Asian in particular. Strangely, Fenollosa celebrated the new age of American imperialism ushered in by the war as a sure sign of the fusion to come: "This morning we have waked to find ourselves citizens of a new world, full of Drakes, and Sydneys, and Phillips, and Armadas; rich in immeasurable colonies, investments, adventures; of an unlimited mind-expansion; of a race-sympathy new in human annals." In the years to come, Fenollosa's ideal history did not fare so well against the actual history of the twentieth century: the Russo-Japanese War, the years of Japanese militarism and isolationism, Pearl Harbor, World War II, and the internment camps full of Japanese American citizens were hardly the stuff of "race-sympathy." It is hard to say whether Fenollosa would have understood the historical upheavals of the twentieth century as somehow necessary to the Hegelian dialectic leading to the new synthesis of world culture, but that is certainly how he saw those of the past. "Columbus and his discovery are but a four-century-old stepping stone" to the coming fusion of East and West, he says, "for we were obstacles in his western path that had to be first mastered. Today we enter literally into his dream and carry the Aryan banner of his caravels where he aimed to plant it—on the heights of an awakened East" ("Fusion," 122). That is how Fenollosa ends his essay, with a prophecy that the end of history will accomplish what Columbus originally set out to do.

Ernest Fenollosa's strange career can be characterized in mock-Hegelian terms as a failed synthesis of matter and spirit. His importance in the history of art is undeniable: he was among the first, in either the West or the East, to recognize Japanese art as the equal of any that the West had produced. Not only did he recognize its importance; he also categorized it and historicized it, understood it in the necessarily concrete terms of dates and places, masters and apprentices, and so on. But reality alone was not sufficient: the art that Fenollosa discovered had to have a meaning beyond the culture that produced it. Even as he worked out the material details of the tradition he had discovered, he blurred those details by subjecting them to an impossibly high level of abstraction which, in retrospect, looks a bit like the work of a crank. Today, it is safe to say that Fenollosa's place in posterity is not the product of his neo-Hegelian dreams or of the doggerel poetry he wrote to celebrate those dreams. Likewise, Fenollosa's considerable influence on modernist literature is itself based not on the original literature he produced but on his "ideogramic" translations of Japanese and Chinese works, another area where his cultural impact is real and lasting. His mistaken theories about the Chinese writing system were also—belatedly, and thanks to Ezra Pound's discovery of them—a major impetus to the imagist revolution in poetry which occurred in the second decade of the twentieth century. Fenollosa's influence, then, involves little of that which was most important to Fenollosa himself: namely, the higher synthesis that he believed would form the basis of an entirely new civilization, once the fusion of East and West had been achieved. For Fenollosa believed, in short, that the American Orient was something real, or one day would be, once Destiny had done its work.

4

The Twentieth Century I
From Aesthetics to Modernism

THE YANKEE experience in Japan repeats the presuppositions of the fin de siècle and the aesthetic school but with significant variations: yes, beauty exists for the sake of beauty, and art is mostly an end in itself; at the same time, however, the aesthetic sphere has the potential to affect the world at large—not in an immediate social sense but in some obscure, protracted, abstract fashion. Ernest Fenollosa, John La Farge, and Percival Lowell were men of their time who found in the Japanese an intensity of aesthetic experience they had rarely encountered before. But they had, in fact, encountered it before; otherwise they would never have been able to recognize the recrudescence of such a highly developed aesthetic society as the one they saw in Japan. Whether in earlier synthetic cultures like Byzantium, where the Roman West met the Orthodox East, or Venice, where Europe fused with the Islamic world, Americans in Japan found precedent for a society where art was a part of daily life. In the late nineteenth century,

Fenollosa, especially, felt himself witness to a second Oriental Renaissance in the Far East that matched the first awakening of the West to the Hindu culture of South Asia in the late eighteenth century. But Fenollosa is a transitional figure insofar as he did not understand the East solely in "renaissance" terms as a recovery of aesthetic energies that had existed at other places and at other times in the past; he also understood the Orient as an opportunity to move forward, as the means to a higher cultural synthesis with the West which would produce a new kind of culture altogether. This forward-looking sensibility was part of Fenollosa's appeal to the modernists of the early twentieth century. For Ezra Pound, especially, the Japanese and Chinese traditions that Fenollosa introduced to the West were among the means of making American literature anew.

But the aesthetic appeal of Asian traditions to the artistic avant-garde in the early twentieth century is only part of the story. Fenollosa's Hegelian dream of the fusion of East and West also had a racial element that became horribly disfigured as the modernist era unfolded. In this regard, Fenollosa was not simply idealist; he was idealistic: his vision of a world culture where a new "race-sympathy" would bridge differences between East and West was an illusion. In fact, the modernization of Japan that Fenollosa was enlisted to support had results that he could hardly have imagined. Far from pursuing policies of synthesis and fusion, the powerful nations of the twentieth century asserted the superiority of their own national cultures at the expense of the weak. What became of Asiatic cultures during the age of modernism is in some wise paradoxical: avant-garde authors did not look to the future as Fenollosa did—they looked to the past. The role of tradition in modernist culture is a complex one anyway, but the orientalist element in modernism complicates the meaning of tradition even further. Like their nineteenth-century precursors in Japan, American modernists were mostly antimodern, the break with tradition largely limited to aesthetics alone. The combination of advanced aesthetics and regressive politics is a well-known element of modernist culture, especially as exemplified by such figures as Ezra Pound, T. S. Eliot, and Amy Lowell. But what is perhaps less evident is the extent to which those authors and others enlisted Eastern culture to perpetuate Western traditions and Western ideologies.

I

The permutations of Ezra Pound's understanding and misunderstanding of Asian culture is a story in American letters that has been told many times. The usual arc of that story takes Pound from aesthetics to politics, from imagism to fascism, as his poetic career traveled from *japonisme* to Confucianism. Hence, Pound's "Oriental" career appears to have fallen into at least three phases: first, an early Japanese period that was concerned solely with poetics (the relationship between haiku and imagism, or Nō drama and vorticism—in the latter case the idea being to use some central image as the basis for a longer work); second, a near-simultaneous Chinese period that was likewise aesthetic but had a transitional dimension in that it got Pound thinking about the relationship between language and reality; and third, a later phase in which fascism and Jeffersonianism were amalgamated with Confucianism. In truth, the relationship between aesthetics and politics in the Pound narrative is complex and nonlinear, mainly because of the critical influence of the late work of Fenollosa, whose aesthetic theories were freighted with Hegelian formulations that made the relationship of East and West richly dialectical, a matter of the utmost historical and political importance. Upon Fenollosa's death in 1908, Pound acquired the manuscripts he left from his widow Mary, who was in London and met with Pound there in late 1913. Mary Fenollosa's choice of Pound as her husband's literary executor may have been based on an antipathy that she and Pound shared toward stodgy academics and old-fashioned scholarship.[1] In any event, Pound received from her a treasure trove of Japanese and Chinese materials that he reworked into two books of pure literature: *Cathay* (1915), a collection of poems translated from the Chinese; and *Certain Noble Plays of Japan,* reprinted as *"Noh," or Accomplishment* (1917). Pound also published *The Chinese Written Character as a Medium for Poetry* (1920), from the Fenollosa manuscript that had the farthest-reaching consequences for Pound's career.

Pound's openness to Mrs. Fenollosa's offer of her husband's papers is not surprising, given the opportunities for contact with Asian culture that he must have had prior to meeting her in 1913. Like other Americans of his generation, Pound was the beneficiary of a more widespread dissemination of Asian culture into American life than earlier generations had known. The Philadelphia Centennial Exposition of 1876 featured both a Chinese and a Japanese pavilion, and the incorporation of these exhibitions into the celebration of the nation's founding did much to encourage the spread of the American Orient through the mechanism of material culture. But even before the Philadelphia exposition, and well before the Pound family moved to that city in 1889, Philadelphia was known for its connection to China. Because Beijing happened to be on the same line of latitude (40 degrees) as Philadelphia, as Benjamin Franklin had observed, enterprising types had tried to cultivate silkworms and grow Chinese tea there. Around the same time (1828), a giant pagoda, known locally as "The Temple of Confucius," was built in Fairmont Park. In successive decades two different museums devoted to Chinese artifacts drew large crowds to Philadelphia. The first was built in 1839 by Nathan Dunn, a celebrated merchant, to house the collection of 1,200 or so objects that he had acquired when living in China for over a decade; the second opened in 1847 and was run by John Peters, who had assembled an even larger collection. The Peters museum was still in operation during Pound's time in the city.[2]

Though it is hard to gauge the importance of "Philadelphia Orientalism" to Pound's development, there can be no question that he found inspiration in American authors such as Emerson and Whitman, both of whom had made Eastern traditions seminal to their own work. One critic speculates that Pound "would likely have been pleased to learn that selections from Confucius were read at Whitman's funeral,"[3] and he may well have been, but his published comments on Whitman say little about the older poet's orientalism. In 1909, Pound honored Whitman as "a forebear of whom I ought to be proud" and acknowledged that "the vital part of my message, taken from the sap and fibre of America, is the same as his."[4] Then, in a 1913 essay, Pound certified Whitman as an American touchstone, one who, especially for the poet in exile, made it impossible "to forget one's birth-right." The point is that an American artist abroad is no less American for it: "If a man's work require him to live in exile, let him suffer, or enjoy, his exile gladly. But it would be about as easy for an American to become a Chinaman or a Hindoo as for him to acquire an Englishness or a Frenchness, or a European-ness that is more than half a skin deep" (*SP*, 124). The remark about "Chinamen" and "Hindoos" can be used to make a vital point about both Whitman and Pound: that different cultures, whether European or Asiatic, are not to be imitated for their own sake, or celebrated for their difference, but exploited as an artistic means to a specifically American end. In Pound's case, there was probably no better vehicle for the expression of a uniquely American consciousness, especially political consciousness, than the Confucian classics.

Like T. S. Eliot, whose study of Hinduism and Indian Buddhism at Harvard University ran parallel with Pound's Chinese and Japanese investigations, Pound continued the New England tradition of American orientalism. Unlike Eliot, however, he had no interest in the religious ramifications of Asian literature, focusing instead on the aesthetic import of Japanese haiku and Nō drama and on the poetical possibilities implied by an unusual (and erroneous) understanding of the logographic writing system used for the Chinese languages. The importance of the Fenollosa materials cannot be overstated, since they led to Pound's Nō translations, the *Cathay* collection, and the long-standing obsession with Chinese characters. But Pound's Oriental interests preceded the Fenollosa influence, as the imitation of

Japanese haiku shows, with "In a Station of the Metro" (published June 1913 but written earlier) being the most celebrated example of the form (Stock, 186–87). The biographer Noel Stock says that Pound "had read a little Confucius as early as July 1907" as a result of his parents' interest in a Christian mission in China (176). Around the time Pound met with Mary Fenollosa in late 1913, he was reading the French translation by Guillaume Pauthier of the Confucian Four Books. His Chinese interests were heightened by the discovery of Fenollosa's manuscript on the Chinese written character, which by any measure has to be regarded as a seminal text in Pound's career. But although *The Chinese Written Character as a Medium for Poetry* may have been indispensable to Pound's avant-gardism, it also offers evidence of how firmly rooted Pound's orientalism was in the New England tradition, especially as represented by Ralph Waldo Emerson.

At first glance, Emerson seems too far removed from the modernist orbit of Pound to matter. The relevance is real, however, and specific to the theory of language that Pound promoted, and which he found abundantly represented in Fenollosa's essay on the Chinese written character. The theory is simply that language is a medium for representing reality directly, rather than an arbitrary system of signs used to communicate meaning through a set of cultural conventions. In Emerson, signs do constitute language, but they are natural, not arbitrary. In the chapter "Language" from *Nature* (1836), Emerson says, "Words are signs of natural facts."[5] He understands the natural world in Swedenborgian fashion as a site of signs, or a "forest of symbols," as the Swedenborgian Baudelaire put it some years later. Things in nature speak to us, and that language is best which most transparently captures the conversation between man and things. Moreover, such language is at base "picturesque"—that is to say, words picture reality: "Every appearance in nature corresponds to some state of the mind, and that state of the mind can only be described by presenting that natural appearance as its picture" (*N*, 20). The formulation anticipates Fenollosa's thinking in *The Chinese Written Character as a Medium for Poetry,* as does Emerson's claim that picturesque language is also poetic: "As we go back in history, language becomes more picturesque, until its infancy, when it is all poetry; or all spiritual facts are represented by natural symbols" (*N*, 22). During the period of his second residency in Japan (1896–1900), Fenollosa took up the study of Chinese characters at the same time that he was teaching Emerson's work to his advanced classes. He also met with students at his home, where "he combined readings of classic Chinese poems with discussions of Emerson" and was delighted to find "hieroglyphs of nature" in the language of both East and West.[6] Hence, it is fair to say that *The Chinese Written Character as a Medium for Poetry* embraces Emerson's ideas about language and poetry and finds expression of those ideas realized in Chinese "ideograms."

Not surprisingly, Pound has little to say about Emerson in his published essays, but many of Emerson's ideas about language sound through them nonetheless. In "Language," Emerson provides a definition of imagism *avant la lettre* that can stand beside many of Pound's pronouncements, notwithstanding Emerson's nineteenth-century diction. Commenting on the debasement of language, Emerson employs the kind of monetary metaphor favored by Pound, circa 1935: "Old words are perverted to stand for things which are not; a paper currency is employed, when there is no bullion in the vaults" (N, 22). Then follows the definition of "imagism":

> But wise men pierce this rotten diction and fasten words again to visible things; so that picturesque language is at once a commanding certificate that he who employs it, is a man in alliance with truth and God. The moment our discourse rises above the ground line of familiar facts, and is inflamed with passion or exalted by thought, it clothes itself in images. A man conversing in earnest, if he watch his intellectual processes, will find that a material image, more or less luminous, arises in his mind, contemporaneous with every thought, which furnishes the vestment of the thought. (N, 23)

Granted, there is no evocation of orientalism in Emerson's formulations here, but that connection is made by Fenollosa and then transmitted to Pound, knowingly or not. Pound is part and parcel of this tradition when he announces to Harriet Monroe that "language is made out of concrete things."[7] The Chinese character, understood "ideographically," makes the connection of words to things even more concrete in a kind of apotheosis of the ideal transparency that Emerson urged as the goal of poetic language. As the critic Ira Nadel puts it, "Chinese for Pound meant the recovery or reinvention of Adamic speech, 'in which words contain the essence of the things they name,' a return to the world Emerson had outlined."[8] Actually, Emerson does much more than outline the transparent relationship of language and nature: he fills in the details for all to see.

Fenollosa's *Chinese Written Character* contains several passages that are largely paraphrased from Emerson's *Nature*. Perhaps the clearest of these is the one in which Fenollosa contends that all speech is substantially "built upon substrata of metaphor."[9] In *Nature*, Emerson claims that any abstract term "used to express a moral or intellectual fact, if traced to its root, is found to be borrowed from some material appearance. *Right* means *straight*; *wrong* means *twisted*; *transgression*, the crossing of a line; *supercilious*, the *raising of an eyebrow*" (N, 20). Likewise, Fenollosa believes that "abstract terms, pressed by etymology, reveal their

ancient roots, imbedded in direct action" (*CWC*, 22). When this Emersonian notion is applied to Chinese, supplemented by two gross errors
(one social, the other linguistic), the Chinese written character becomes
the ideal "medium for poetry." The first error, also committed by Percival
Lowell, is thinking that the people of the Far East are representatives of
an aesthetic race: Fenollosa says that because of his "years in close relation with Orientals, I could not but breathe in something of the poetry
incarnate in their lives" (*CWC*, 5). The second error is thinking that the
Chinese writing system is pictographic rather than phonographic. Even
though it is true that a small percentage of Chinese characters have their
origins in pictograms, all of the characters, including the "pictographic"
ones, represent the sounds of the various Chinese languages (and represent
them in different ways, of course; just as English and French share the
same alphabetic writing system, so the distinct languages Mandarin and
Cantonese share the same logosyllabic system). Only Western students of
Chinese, like Fenollosa and Pound, "see" the meaning in the characters
instead of hearing it.

But linguistic correctness is beside the point here: what matters is Fenollosa's belief that the Chinese were a poetic people and that they had the
good fortune to write their language using a system that would allow them
to bring out "the poetry incarnate in their lives." For Fenollosa and Pound,
the meaning of the Chinese character is always "borrowed from some
material appearance," as Emerson puts it. Hence, Fenollosa thinks that
"in reading Chinese we do not seem to be juggling mental counters, but
to be watching *things* work out their own fate" (*CWC*, 9). This is the very
logic that informs Pound's reading of Chinese characters throughout his
career, beginning with his glosses and translations of the poems at the end
of the Fenollosa essay. There, Pound's attempts at "ideographic" readings
of a number of characters suggest the belief that a character is a compact,
imagistic poem in itself, a little image composed of smaller images. Such
readings are sometimes "etymologically" correct, as with the character for
the word *xìn*, which Pound glosses as "truth" or "sincere": "man and word,
man standing by his word" (*CWC*, 40–41). But they are more often than
not wildly conjectural, as with the reading of the character Pound takes to
mean "star," in which he sees the pictographic element "fire over moving
legs of a man" (*CWC*, 35). In fact, he has misread the character *hùang*,
"sway," for *xīng*, "star," and so misconstrues the line of poetry he means to
translate. Also, Pound appears to have had no understanding of the basic
fact that many characters include sound elements derived from other characters as clues to pronunciation, and that the sound element is unrelated to
the meaning of the character to which it has been added.

The extent to which Fenollosa stands as an aesthetic precursor of Pound cannot be overstated. To the sense of language as concrete and imagistic that he found in Emerson's writing and transferred to Chinese characters, Fenollosa added a sense of dynamic synthesis derived from Hegel. In his 1896 essay "The Nature of Fine Art," he once again anticipated Pound's ideas:

> Synthetic thinking demands a pregnant language; rich, juicy, significant, full words, charged with intense meaning at the center, like a nucleus, and then radiating out toward infinity, like a great nebula. This is poetry, the making a word stand for as much thought and feeling as possible, and that through the mutual modifications of the successive words. No literary production which does not have this synthesis in its meanings, principle, and illustration, fact and ideal, the organic fibre of the world, all packed away together in its lightest phrases, plays a part in the sphere of literature as a fine art.[10]

In 1915, Pound tried to clarify the meaning of "Imagisme" in language remarkably similar to Fenollosa's. The older writer's "intense meaning at the center" seems to echo through Pound's claim that "intense emotion causes a pattern to arise in the mind," and certainly "synthetic thinking" is implied when Pound says that "the Image is more than an idea. It is a vortex or cluster of fused ideas and is endowed with energy" (SP, 374, 375). As this language shows, by 1915 Pound had already moved on from imagism to vorticism, in collaboration with Wyndham Lewis in Blast Magazine, but vorticism no less than imagism has partial roots in Fenollosa's orientalism. Indeed, when Pound reworked the Fenollosa manuscripts, he found in Nō drama a means of extending the aesthetic of imagism into larger works. Moreover, the dynamic conception of poetry conveyed in Fenollosa's 1896 essay, with "full words charged with intense meaning at the center, like a nucleus, and then radiating out toward infinity, like a great nebula," is not unlike Pound's expanded notion of the image as "a radiant node or cluster; . . . a VORTEX, from which, and through which, and into which, ideas are constantly rushing."[11]

Fenollosa's influence on Pound is not only literary or aesthetic but also political, insofar as Fenollosa believed that aesthetic culture could have political effect. In his 1892 analysis, "Chinese and Japanese Traits," Fenollosa had argued for a relationship between governance and aesthetics. An overconventionalized Confucianism "of the narrowest . . . school" is supposed to have "covered the glow of native genius with such a crust of literary formalism that intelligence has become stunted and government itself petrified."[12] Pound, likewise, thinks that imprecise language leads to imprecise thinking, and thence to sloppy policy and bad government. And

he finds the corrective to the problem in Chinese antiquity, citing again and
again "the Confucian answer when asked about the first act of government:
'call things by their right names'" (*SP*, 84). Hence, one of the many virtues
Pound finds in Thomas Jefferson is the capacity to use language clearly
and effectively: "Has any statesman since Jefferson shaken himself free of
clichés, or helped free others in greater degree?" Jefferson was politically
effective because he "used verbal formulations as tools."[13] But Pound also
thinks of good government and good verse as having certain things in
common:

> My next analogy is very technical. The real life in regular verse is an irregular
> movement underlying. Jefferson thought the formal features of the American
> system would work, and they did work till the time of general Grant but the
> condition of their working was that inside them there should be a *de facto*
> government composed of sincere men willing the national good. When the
> men of their understanding, and when the nucleus of the national mind hasn't
> the moral force to translate knowledge into action I don't believe it matters
> a damn what legal forms or what administrative forms there are in a govern-
> ment. The nation will get the staggers. (*JM*, 94–95)

A good government, then, has the same deep structure as a good poem, at
least in some abstract sense. Fenollosa does not go so far as to contemplate
versification as a model for government, but he does share with Pound
the idea that lifeless language can drain the effectiveness out of political
judgment.

Pound published Fenollosa's essay twice, first in 1920 as part of *Insti-
gations*, and then again in 1936 as a separate pamphlet. The 1936 edition includes a headnote dated 1918 and a "Terminal Note" dated 1935.
The dating of the essay highlights the importance that it held for Pound
at two critical periods of his career: the first during the teens when he
was deeply involved in the poetic avant-garde movements imagism and
voticism; the second during the late thirties when he became personally
involved in authoritarian politics. As noted, the periodization of Pound's
career into an early aesthetic stage and a later political phase is one of the
conventions of Pound scholarship, a convention called into question by the
text of the Fenollosa essay itself. Although *The Chinese Written Character*
is often characterized as an aesthetic manifesto, Fenollosa's aesthetics are
always bound up in his ideas of an East-West cultural synthesis, ideas that
have enormous political ramifications. Indeed, the opening paragraph of
the essay predicts the synthesis that Fenollosa had been urging since the
early 1890s: "This twentieth century not only turns a new page in this
history of the world, but opens another and a startling chapter. Vistas of

strange futures unfold for man, of world embracing cultures half-weaned from Europe, of hitherto undreamed responsibilities for nations and races" (*CWC, 3*). The reader unschooled in Fenollosa's Hegelian theory might be baffled by the overheated rhetoric at the outset, but that theory is a subtext of the aesthetic that surfaces only occasionally, as when Fenollosa comments on the similitude of Chinese and English syntax, word order which is supposed to convey "the *natural order*—that is, the order of cause and effect" (*CWC*, 13). The East-West synthesis implied here is perhaps weighted more heavily toward the Chinese side, for Fenollosa clearly has in mind the importance of the East in the rise of the world culture he envisioned. Near the end of the essay he speculates that the presumed "ideographic" nature of Chinese might have world-historical consequences: "Such a pictorial method, whether the Chinese exemplified it or not, would be the ideal language of the world" (*CWC*, 31). Chinese, then, is not a model solely for poetry—in the sense that the kind of clarity, precision, and concreteness allegedly conveyed by the Chinese written character should be the goal of all language—because what is at stake in language is nothing less than truth itself: "All truth has to be expressed in sentences because all truth is the *transference of power*" (*CWC*, 12). Pound undoubtedly understood such passages aesthetically when he first read the Fenollosa manuscript in 1912, but when he published it again in 1936, he had to be much more aware of the essay's relevance to his own political thought, after that thought had taken a pronounced "Confucian" turn.

Pound was reading Confucius in the French translation of Pauthier around the time he met with Mary Fenollosa in 1913. Fifteen years later he translated part of the Pauthier text into English as *Ta Hio* (1928), the title Pauthier used for the *Da xue*, conventionally known as *The Great Learning*. In the 1930s Pound experienced a "conversion" to Confucianism, as Feng Lan puts it, and responded to T. S. Eliot's question about his beliefs by saying, "I believe the *Ta Hio*."[14] The belief, however, is thoroughly political, not theological, for what most distinguishes Pound's orientalism during this phase of his career is a return to the political values that colored the American philosophes' understanding of Confucius. This does not mean that Pound attaches the same political values to the writings of Confucius that Franklin and Jefferson did but, rather, that the focus of his interests is political instead of theological or aesthetic (although aesthetic values are often bound up with political values in Pound's mind). But the political is paramount: Thomas Jefferson and Benito Mussolini are both illustrative of values that Pound finds in Confucius, and that he thinks are critical to the operations of modern society.

One of the best illustrations of Pound's "belief" in the sociopolitical relevance of the *Da xue* is an essay he published in the *Aryan Path*. This theosophical journal was edited in Bombay by B. P. Wadia, a convert to theosophy who toured the United States from 1922 to 1928, working for the United Lodge of Theosophists before returning to India in 1929 and founding a lodge in Bombay.[15] In the late 1930s, Wadia's magazine was evidently known for its anti-Nazi editorial policy, which probably explains Pound's choice to publish several essays there, including "The Immediate Need of Confucius" in the August 1937 number. As the title suggests, the essay argues for "the Western need of Confucius, and specifically of the *Ta Hio,* and more specifically of the first chapter of the *Ta Hio*" (*SP,* 77). One of Pound's more interesting points is that modern society is less precise in its thinking than medieval society because of the development of science: "When the experimental method came into material science giving a *defined* knowledge in realms whereto verbal distinctions had not then penetrated, and where they probably never will penetrate, the Occident lost the habit of verbal definition." Knowledge has developed at a pace that has outstripped the verbal capacity to distinguish it with precision, and science has alienated the one Western institution known for its definitional prowess, the Catholic Church in the age of Scholasticism: "Catholicism led Europe as long as Erigena, Grosseteste and their fellows struggled for definitions of words" (*SP,* 76). But since scholastic logic is not adequate to describe the modern world that science has revealed, some other method is needed to convey meaning in precise, concrete terms; that method is "ideogramic": "Ernest Fenollosa emphasized a difference between the approach of logic and that of science. Confucius left his record in ideogram. . . . Fenollosa accented the Western need of ideogramic thinking. Get your 'red' down to rose, rust, cherry, if you want to know what you are talking about. We have too much of this talk about vibrations and infinites" (*SP,* 78). To think ideogramically is to understand something in concrete terms ("rose, rust, cherry"), not in abstract terms ("vibrations, infinites"). For Pound, the political implications of this method are indeed staggering: "Men suffer malnutrition by millions because their overlords dare not read the *Ta Hio*" (*SP,* 80).

The connection between precise language and the kind of governance that might save millions from malnutrition is not exactly spelled out in "The Immediate Need of Confucius." But in his tract titled *Jefferson and/ or Mussolini* (1935), Pound makes this relationship explicit by constructing an "ideogram" of good government composed of the three "radicals" Jefferson, Mussolini, and Confucius. More than once in this strange text (written in 1933), Pound invokes the Confucian dictum that an ability to distinguish causes and effects is the basis for right action: "Things have roots and branches; affairs have scopes and beginnings. To know what precedes and what follows, is nearly as good as having a head and feet."[16] The Confucian capacity "to distinguish the root from the branch" lies behind Jefferson's freedom from cliché and Mussolini's "emphasis on having a government strong enough to get . . . justice. That is to say taking first the 'government' in our text and proceeding at reasonable pace toward the 'which governs least.'" Pound's argument for authoritarian government here also includes a reference to "the Noh programme" in which "the Shura or battle play precedes the Kazura or drama of mysterious calm drama" (*JM*, 45). The Confucian "sense of the 'root and the branch'" is invoked again when Pound favorably compares Mussolini to Jefferson with respect to the Italian leader's "readiness to scrap the lesser thing for the thing of major importance, indifference to mechanism as weighed against the main purpose" (*JM*, 64). Authoritarian power, in Pound's view, is welcome so long as it is based on an understanding that the root gives rise to the branch, the purpose dictates the mechanism, or—in language more traditionally associated with the Italian peninsula but which Pound does not use—the end justifies the means.

Pound's choice of Confucius rather than Machiavelli as the means whereby he recommends fascist politics might be one way of making authoritarian ideology "new" or, at least, making it seem new. Newness, one of Pound's aesthetic values ("Literature is news that STAYS news"),[17] is invoked as a political value near the end of *Jefferson and/or Mussolini* in a chapter titled "Kung": "Make it new, make it new as the young grass shoot." In this chapter Pound makes what only a few years later he would call the "Immediate Need of Confucius" as clear as he can by summarizing "the doctrine of Confucius" in a few sentences:

> That you bring order into your surroundings by bringing it first into yourself; by knowing the motives of your acts.
> That you can bring about better world government by amelioration of the internal government of your nation.
> That private gain is not prosperity, but that the treasure of a nation is its equity.
> That hoarding is not prosperity and that people should employ their resources.
> One should respect intelligence, "the luminous principle of reason," the faculties of others, one should look to a constant renovation. (*JM*, 112)

The "Kung" chapter concludes with four logograms constituting a highly symmetrical sentence which amounts to a graphic representation of the stability and order that Pound urges on the nation-states of Europe elsewhere in the tract:

新 日 日 新

In his translation of the *Da xue,* these logograms appear alongside "Tseng's Comment" on Confucius and are translated thus: "As the sun makes it new / Day by day make it new / Yet again make it new" (C, 36). The inscription is supposed to have appeared in gold letters on King T'ang's bathtub as a daily (or at least frequent) reminder of one of the principles of governance. Pound's commentary in the translation, originally done in 1928, is simply: "This is the second chapter of the comment containing and getting the grist of the phrase: Renew the people. Ideogram: axe, tree and wood-pile" (C, 39). By 1935, in *Jefferson and/or Mussolini,* Pound has manufactured a fuller, more ideologically charged comment on the characters: "The first ideogram (on the right) shows the fascist axe for the clearing away of rubbish (left half) the tree, organic vegetable renewal. The second ideograph is the sun sign, day, 'renovate, day by day renew.'" Confucius, in short, is enlisted in support of "La rivoluzione continua" (*JM,* 113).

The Westernization of the Confucian classics could not be clearer: Pound's reading of Confucius depends on his eccentric combination of enlightenment and authoritarian values, as the title *Jefferson and/or Mussolini* implies. But the Westernization runs deeper than a simple ideological reinterpretation of Confucius. As several critics have shown, Pound was predisposed to read Chinese characters in an idiosyncratic way because of his exposure to the libertarian strain in American politics which received particular reinforcement from anarchist quarters during the fin de siècle and in the early years of the twentieth century. Like James Joyce and other modernist figures, Pound was attracted to an extreme form of libertarian philosophy known as Egoism—originally promulgated by the German philosopher Max Stirner—the target of an extended critique by Karl Marx in *The German Ideology.* The seminal work that drew fire from Marx is Stirner's *Der Einzige und sein Eigentum* (1844), translated as *The Ego and His Own* by the American intellectual anarchist Steven Byington (1868–1958) and published in 1907 by Benjamin Tucker (1854–1939), another American anarchist of some renown. In Pound's case, the American connection to Egoism is probably less important than the feminist connection. In 1913, Pound became the poetry editor of Dora Marsden and Harriet Shaw Weaver's *New Freewoman,* a magazine that was initially supportive of the suffragist movement but shifted in the direction of a more broadly defined libertarianism, as its change of name to *The Egoist* indicates. Even before the name change the journal was subtitled *An Individualist Review,* and it is worth noting that Pound identified himself as an "individualist" at a time when that term was a near synonym of "egoist" or "anarchist."[18] The larger point here is that the kind of libertarian politics with which Pound involved himself is hard to square with Confucian tradition.

As strange as it seems, Pound manages to "reconcile" individualism and authoritarianism in his translation of Confucius's *Lun yu.* According to Feng Lan, Pound's translation manages to recover "a suppressed reading without knowing of its previous existence."[19] The reading at issue hinges on the ambiguity of certain Chinese characters that Pound translates as "Support oneself," whereas earlier translators (and Confucian commentators) had settled on the contrary meaning, "Subdue oneself." Pound's translation of the opening section of book 12 of the *Analects* is "Support oneself and return to the rites, that makes a man" (C, 243). By contrast, Legge's classic translation runs: "To subdue one's self and return to propriety, is perfect virtue."[20] The latter meaning is much more traditional, but as Lan explains, an ambiguity in the Chinese text centered on the verb *kè* has led to centuries of exegetical scrutiny. The verb can mean either "overcome" or "enable," so the phrase in which it appears can be read either as "to overcome the self in order to restore the rites" or "to enable the self in order to revitalize the rites" (Lan, 86–87). Unknowingly, Pound's "Support oneself" taps into the ambiguity but only on one side of it. Most likely, he imagined he was "correcting" Legge's translation because of some additional meaning that he "saw" in the characters. But regardless of whether the self is supported or subdued, the purpose is to enhance the empire, to contribute to political stability and endurance. Lan concludes that "Pound utilized Confucian doctrines in a rather 'opportunistic' manner that characterizes his overall dealings with Confucianism," and that he "initially saw Confucianism as a liberal discourse supporting the rights of the individual" (Lan, 91). Support for this assertion can be found in the 1914 essay "The Words of Ming Mao," where Pound claims that "dependence on self is the core of Confucian philosophy."[21] And in 1917, in "Provincialism the Enemy," he writes that "Confucius' constant emphasis is on the value of personality, on the outlines of personality, on the man's right to preserve the outlines of his personality, and of his duty not to interfere with the personalities of others" (SP, 193). In 1920, Pound says of Remy de Gourmont that the French author's recognition of "the right of individuals to *feel* differently" is "Confucian" (LE, 340). The evidence is overwhelmingly in favor of Lan's position that Pound viewed Confucianism as a form of "libertarian discourse" which supported the rights of autonomous individuals (Lan, 96). Pound's

Confucianism, then, is a clear case of the pattern wherein the East awakens Western values in the alienated American. Confucius complements and even advances the liberal values Pound saw in Jefferson and the libertarian values he found in Stirner.

Hence, Pound emerges as possibly the clearest exemplar of the American Orient, understood in dynamic terms as a set of intellectual and cultural contradictions that validate Western values by finding a purer form of those values in Eastern philosophy and art. Pound's orientalizing of Western ideologies as different as libertarianism and authoritarianism is something he shares with those American philosophes he so admired. And while Benjamin Franklin does not occupy so elevated a place in Pound's political pantheon as John Adams or Thomas Jefferson, he really has more in common with Franklin, who, like Pound, saw confirmation of authoritarian ideology in the Confucian tradition. Pound's return to the Confucian classics recapitulates the earliest manifestations of the American Orient.

Similarly, Pound's protégé T. S. Eliot and his rival Amy Lowell recapitulate key moments in the later history of American orientalism. Eliot's Indic studies at Harvard University stimulated interests in Hinduism and Buddhism which he first put to philosophic purpose but which also had considerable relevance to some of the greatest poetry of the twentieth century. But regardless of whether the topic is Eliot's almost forgotten dissertation on the philosophy of F. H. Bradley or the Sanskrit allusions in *The Waste Land,* theological meanings appear much more salient than anything political or aesthetic. And just as Eliot follows the track of early nineteenth-century Americans in recognizing the relevance of Hindu thought to Christian theology, so Lowell follows the aesthetic inclinations of those late nineteenth-century Americans who discovered new artistic values in Old Japan. But Pound's Confucian politics, Eliot's Indic theology, and Lowell's Japanese aesthetics do more than merely recapitulate the history of the American Orient up to the modernist era. These three modernist figures were, after all, contemporaries, so the fact that their Oriental interests differed so much one from the other shows just how deeply Asian thought, whether political, theological, or aesthetic, had entered into American cultural life by the early twentieth century.

II

One of T. S. Eliot's first encounters with Eastern thought came through the medium of popular culture, when he read Sir Edwin Arnold's *The Light of Asia* (1879) as a boy in St. Louis.[22] In later life Eliot worked a reference to Arnold's poem into a 1944 lecture on the question of minor poetry and confessed an enduring fondness for a work that had surely been forgotten by the middle of the twentieth century. He said he felt "a warm affection" for this "long epic poem on the life of Gautama Buddha: I must have had a latent sympathy for the subject-matter, for I read it through with gusto, and more than once."[23] Also, Eliot's early biography reveals a rebellion against the plainness of Unitarianism which has an analogue in Emerson's life story.[24] So it is not surprising that, like Emerson, Eliot should have found something in Eastern tradition to supplement the Western. His orientalism may have begun with a popular response and a theological reaction to Eastern culture, but the real impetus that impelled his career forward was scholarly, confined to the same university that had educated generations of orientalists before him, from Emerson to Fenellosa.

When Eliot began master's work at Harvard University, he took courses with Irving Babbitt, one of the first to take a comparative East-West approach to religion and philosophy. Babbitt is known today as one of the apologists for the New Humanism, the central tenet of which is that modern man exists in a state of dissociated sensibility in which scientific naturalism (typified by Bacon) wars with romantic naturalism (typified by Rousseau); the corrective is a return to true humanism—not the errone-ous Renaissance variety but rather "the balanced belief of the Greeks."[25] Babbitt also developed his argument through reference to Eastern figures: "A part of my own method," he said, was "to put Confucius behind Aris-totle and Buddha behind Christ."[26] Although this statement comes from a book published well after Eliot left Harvard, it captures the kind of broad, ecumenical approach Babbitt represented. Indeed, the East-West compari-son was necessary to Babbitt's claims about the need for balance and har-mony. Like Fenollosa, he saw the two cultures as complementary: "What is wanted is neither Oriental quietism, nor again the inhuman strenuousness of a certain type of Occidental; neither pure action nor pure repose, but a blending of the two that will occupy all the space between them,—that activity in repose which has been defined as the humanistic ideal."[27] This formulation is taken from a book published in 1908, the same year that William Sturgis Bigelow delivered his Ingersoll lecture, "Buddhism and Immortality," in which he too tried to harmonize the quietism of Eastern religion and the strenuousness of Western science. Babbitt and Bigelow may very well have influenced Harvard administrators to make a special plea for the scholarly study of Buddhism in an addendum to the college catalogue of 1912: "It is of the utmost practical and political importance that the West should understand the East. To open the way to such an understanding is the work of trained scholars. Buddhism is perhaps the most important single element among all those that make the East what it is."[28] Eliot's years at Harvard (1906–1910, 1911–1914), then, were notable for the interest in Asian thought, especially Buddhism, on the part of his teachers and fellow students.

But it was as a doctoral student in philosophy that Eliot moved from passing familiarity with Asian thought to the beginnings of its deep and abiding influence. His Indic studies at Harvard recapitulate the history of Hinduism in the nineteenth century, insofar as they are directed toward either the disruption or the enlivening of an existing tradition. In the nineteenth century, Hinduism was useful to Unitarian theology contra Trinitarian Christianity; in the twentieth century, Eliot found Hinduism (and Indian Buddhism) useful to overturning the assumptions of Western philosophy. His Indic studies eventually led him in a theological direction, and the aesthetic deployment of that theology served to show the limitations of modernity. Much of Eliot's modernism is directed toward that end: to reveal the shortcomings of the Enlightenment when man is confronted with modernity and experiences some kind of spiritual need that cannot be satisfied by philosophy.

Although Eliot's doctoral dissertation, *Knowledge and Experience in the Philosophy of F. H. Bradley,* makes no mention of Asian religion, his Indic studies seem to have complemented the conclusions he reached in his thesis, as Jeffrey M. Perl and Andrew P. Tuck have shown in their analysis of Eliot's graduate education. They point out that "approximately one-third of Eliot's graduate program was devoted to courses in Asian philosophy and philology" and that the notes he took on these subjects reveal a significant turn in his intellectual development: "As one reads through them, it becomes apparent that his Orientalist interests, both Buddhist and Hindu, reflected his dissatisfaction with the modes and methods of Western philosophical discourse."[29] A specific example of this dissatisfaction is expressed in one of Eliot's notebooks: "The world in which we live lokadhātu is the result of our common dhātus and efforts. (This is neglected in Western philosophy)."[30] The word *dhātus* "can mean parts, essential parts, elements, [or] constituent substances," so the sense of the comment seems to be that totality or community ("the world in which we live") is the aggregate of the elements that constitute it: "Eliot thought that this was worth saying because so much of Western philosophy had been dedicated to demonstrating the opposite, that the Real World is something utterly apart from the shared world of human experience."[31]

The problem of shared experience is precisely the one taken up by Eliot in his dissertation on Bradley: how do we know that our individual experience of the world is the same as that of everyone else? The partial answer is that we must assume that all individuals experience the world alike;

otherwise there could be no collectivity of any kind, no community, no sense of tradition. In his dissertation, Eliot uses a special term, "finite centre," to designate individual consciousness or subjectivity and tries to work through the problem of how it is that finite centres construe a shared world of objective reality when all each individual finite centre can know for certain is the phenomenal appearance or "presentation" of that world: "The real world is real because and in so far as it appears to a finite centre, and yet it has in each appearance to mean to be more—to be real, that is, only so far as it is not an appearance to a finite centre."[32] An object is an object only in the context of subjectivity, of being experienced by someone, by a "finite centre"; by the same token, a subject is a subject only in the presence of objects. So even the "I" is a product of experience, which explains why Eliot prefers not to use terms like *I*, *self*, or *individual consciousness*. But Eliot is not Bishop Berkeley, and the world does not disappear when it ceases to be perceived—quite the contrary, in fact. Eliot claims that the object "is none the less *real* when I am not attending to it, but it is no longer an object" (*KE*, 158). What happens to the subject when it is not in the presence of objects? Does it cease to be real? For Eliot, these questions have no meaning: "Again and again," writes one critic, "he emphasizes the fact that, while in our daily practical life we assume that there is quite brutally a distinction between real and unreal, self and world, subject and object, in theory the distinction can nowhere be drawn."[33] Eliot concludes that "there is no 'objective' criterion for reality in the sense of an external solid world to which our individual presentations should conform" (*KE*, 140).

In the absence of an objective criterion for reality, Eliot falls back on the subjective criteria of "presentations": if two or more "finite centres" agree on an interpretation of reality based on individual presentations of it, then reality may very well exist, which is not quite the same as saying that it *must* exist:

> I have tried to show that there can be no truth or error without a presentation and discrimination of two points of view; that the external world is a construction by the selection and combination of various presentations to various viewpoints: and that the selection which makes reality is in turn made possible by the belief in reality: unless we assumed the existence of a world of truth we could not explain the genesis of error, and unless we had presentations of error as well as of truth we could not make that construction which is the real world. (*KE*, 142)

This passage merits emphasis because its tenor is more theological than philosophical, as the use of the word *belief* suggests. The duality of truth

and error at first seems to imply the pre-Augustinian tradition of Mani-
chaeism, except that the Western formulation does not allow for the necessary nature of the relationship of truth and error: the dependency of one
upon the other.

The line of thinking here is much closer to a specific variety of East
Asian Buddhism that Eliot encountered at Harvard when he took the course
"Schools of Religious and Philosophical Thought in Japan" with Masaharu
Anesaki, a world-renowned expert in the field.[34] Eliot's notes on this course
show that Professor Anesaki emphasized the South Asian basis of Japanese Buddhism in the Indian school of Madhyamika ("Middle Way"). The
founder of this school was the second-century Buddhist Nagarjuna, whose
goal was "to show the self-contradictory nature of every concept and doctrine about reality" and, further, "to show that nothing positive or negative
can be asserted of reality." According to Perl, "Mādhyamika is known as the
'doctrine of emptiness' because Nāgārjuna held that *everything* is provisional
and contingent (empty). . . . Still, it is only because things exist in relations
to other things that they may be said to exist at all."[35] The "belief in reality"
that Eliot constructs through the interplay of truth and error certainly seems
to rely, at least in part, on the knowledge of Nagarjuna's teachings that he
gained from Professor Anesaki. And the larger idea—that skepticism, far
from excluding belief, is a necessary condition for it—was to remain a part
of Eliot's thinking, in both poetry and prose, throughout his literary career.
Indeed, the interdependence of skepticism and belief seems to be an instance
of a still larger concept, which Eliot explains in his dissertation: "Every experience is a paradox in that it means to be absolute, and yet is relative; in that
it always goes beyond itself and never escapes itself" (*KE*, 166).

This last formulation reappears in Eliot's criticism of great authors such
as Dante and Goethe, who have some kind of identity that is uniquely their
own but who also have universal appeal. In Dante's case, "the localization
('Florentine' speech) seems if anything to emphasize the universality."[36]
Eliot's Dante and Goethe essays are singled out here because in both the
measure of the two authors is taken in part through a comparison with
Indic literature, notably the *Bhagavad-Gita*. The Indian epic is invoked in
"Dante" (1929) and "Goethe as the Sage" (1955) when Eliot tries to work
through the problems of, respectively, belief and wisdom. In "Dante," he
distinguishes "between philosophical *belief* and *assent*" to make the point
that the reader need not share the poet's worldview in order to appreciate
and understand the poetry through which that worldview is rendered: "If
you can read poetry as poetry, you will 'believe' in Dante's theology exactly
as you believe in the physical reality of his journey; that is, you suspend both
belief and disbelief" (*SE*, 219). Eliot emphasizes this point further through

the negative example of Goethe and the positive example of the *Bhagavad-Gita*: "With Goethe . . . I often feel too acutely 'this is what Goethe the man believed,' instead of merely entering into a world which Goethe has created; with Lucretius also, less with the *Bhagavad-Gita*, which is the next greatest philosophical poem to the *Divine Comedy* within my experience" (*SE*, 219). Some twenty-five years later Eliot revised his estimation of Goethe and discovered that the German poet had something in common with the *Bhagavad-Gita* after all. That something was wisdom.

Eliot's reconciliation with Goethe is complex and paradoxical. Unlike Emerson, who was critical of both Goethe's self-cultivation and the self-cultivation he inspired in others, Eliot accepts the cultural paradigm Goethe encouraged and puts it into practice in his effort to come to terms with the German poet: "The effort to reconcile myself to Goethe" is undertaken "because I should otherwise have neglected some opportunity of self-development" (*OPP*, 244). Goethe joins Shakespeare and Dante in the triad of European poets whose greatness is based on their "*Permanence* and *Universality*" (*OPP*, 245), criteria that Eliot is able to define in fairly clear terms. But then he introduces a final criterion that he cannot define but only describe, "for it is simply the word *Wisdom*. There is no word, however, more impossible to define, and no word more difficult to understand" (*OPP*, 256).

Eliot treats Dante, Shakespeare, and Goethe as philosophical poets, at the same time maintaining the distinction between poetry and philosophy. That distinction, in turn, hinges on the difference between "the *philosophy* of a poet and his *wisdom*," a point elaborated using the same examples as those cited in the earlier essay on Dante: "the *Bhagavadgita, De Rerum natura* of Lucretius, and the *Divine Comedy*." Because the *Bhagavad-Gita* "is the most remote from me in language and culture," the appeal of the poem cannot lie in philosophical understanding or in religious belief but in something else. The three European poets, likewise, require appreciation of something other than philosophical ideas: "Whether the 'philosophy' or the religious faith of Dante or Shakespeare or Goethe is acceptable to us or not . . . there is the Wisdom that we can all accept" (*OPP*, 261–62, 263). Wisdom must be "the same for all men everywhere"; otherwise, "what profit could a European gain from the Upanishads, or the Buddhist Nikayas?" The question hints at the elusive meaning of wisdom and also implies Goethe's special relevance to that meaning, since wisdom involves self-development: "The wisdom of a great poet is concealed in his work; but in becoming aware of it we become ourselves more wise" (*OPP*, 264). Eliot implies that an effort of understanding similar to that required for the *Bhagavad-Gita* is required for Goethe because he is culturally more remote than the English Shakespeare or the broadly European Dante. Because the wisdom is more "concealed" in the case of the *Gita* and Goethe, the effort to get at it results in a higher degree of self-development; the reader becomes "more wise" in the process.

The poetic process that seeks to conceal wisdom in the work is pretty clearly one that Eliot sought to emulate in his own work, especially in devotional poems such as *Ash Wednesday* (1930) and in the highly philosophical *Four Quartets* (1943), not to mention *The Waste Land* (1922). The critic Cleo McNelly Kearns distinguishes between metaphysical complexity and philosophical simplicity, and allies Eliot's Indic studies with the latter: "The emergence of this wisdom voice is almost inconceivable in Eliot's work without the continuing influence of Indic traditions" (Kearns, 20). The former "dislocates" language and renders a complex meaning; the latter simplifies and makes meaning acceptable even if it cannot be understood, perhaps especially if it cannot be understood. In the Goethe essay, Eliot says that "all language is inadequate, but probably the language of poetry is the language most capable of communicating wisdom" (*OPP*, 264). In *The Waste Land,* however, philosophical simplicity is secondary to metaphysical complexity, which raises questions about how closely Eliot's "wisdom voice" is allied with Indic tradition, since this poem no less than the later, more overtly philosophical ones in the Eliot canon draws on the languages and myths of India.

There appear to be two schools of thought regarding Eliot's use of Eastern language and culture in *The Waste Land*. The first holds that he was truly able to get inside Vedic or Pali tradition and speak with an informed voice from within those traditions. Kearns, for instance, claims that "Eliot demonstrated . . . an almost uncanny ear for nuances and idioms of Indian thought," a claim supported by "many Indian readers"—one of whom is C. D. Narasimhaiah, who sees in Eliot's use of the word "Ganga" something more authentic than "the corrupt prosaic Ganges" (Kearns, 26, 219 n12). By contrast, the second school of thought sees Eliot as "one of the last Orientalists" whose perspective on India is tainted by the colonial context in which that orientalism emerged; this perspective is reflected through his use of Sanskrit, which Harish Trivedi finds "distinctly fastidious, precious, and pedantic."[37] Trivedi holds that Eliot's Indic references are always presented from the perspective of a cultural outsider, not because of some failure of effort to honestly understand Eastern thought but because that thought is always overlaid by Christian tradition. Lyndall Gordon, likewise, maintains that Eliot stays well outside Hindu spirituality, as illustrated by the way the Sanskrit word "Shantih" is used at the end of *The Waste Land*: it is there merely "for its novelty," because Eliot's "explanatory note shows that he thinks in traditional Christian terms: 'And the peace of God, which passeth all understanding, shall keep your hearts and minds through Christ Jesus.'"[38] In fact, Gordon's observation would have been more forceful had she cited Eliot's actual note: "'The peace which passeth understanding' is *our* equivalent to this word" (emphasis added).[39] His note makes clear that Eliot speaks from within the Christian tradition and is simply using Indic tradition to supplement his own, which is not quite the same thing as saying that he is subordinating Indic religion to Christianity. Eliot's position vis-à-vis the American Orient would seem to be not so different from Emerson's, except that where Emerson supplemented West with East through aphoristic conviction, Eliot's Asiatic allusiveness is carried out in a more circumspect way. The method seems to support the idea that Eastern religion was somehow helpful to Eliot in his own drama of skepticism and belief, in his private dance of doubt and vision.

Eliot's use of Sanskrit in *The Waste Land* can help to make this point, even though the Sanskrit is problematic at a basic level. Trivedi has analyzed the six Sanskrit words deployed in the poem—"Ganga," "Himavant," "*Datta*," "*Dayadhvam*," "*Damyata*," and "*Shantih*"—and found Eliot's usage wanting in various ways. There is nothing particularly nuanced or idiomatic about the word *Ganga*; that is simply what the river Ganges is called in India. "Ganga was sunken" (*CP*, 68) shows Eliot "going out of his way to use a form which has always been virtually the only form used in India but is for that very reason the far less familiar and more exotic form for his Western readers" (Trivedi, 123, 125). Trivedi cites this usage as another instance of the kind of linguistic novelty Gordon sees in *Shantih*. "Himavant" (*CP*, 68) is also an exotic novelty in comparison with the more familiar and expected *Himalaya*, usually anglicized as "the Himalayas." *Himavanta* is the older Sanskrit word for the mountain range; used in the *Rigveda*, it appears in one of the creation hymns from that work which was reproduced in the basic *Sanskrit Reader* edited by Charles Lanman, Eliot's teacher. So Eliot probably selected "Himavant" "not simply because it was the rarer form but also because . . . it came from 'one of the abysmally ancient Vedic hymns'" (Trivedi, 125).[40] "Himavant," then, is a "pedantic conceit," the kind of thing that might be expected from one of "the last Orientalists" (Trivedi, 125, 68).

But for all the scholarly precision, the two words in the context of the poem end up saying something that is, from the Indian perspective, quite imprecise:

> Ganga was sunken, and the limp leaves
> Waited for rain, while the black clouds
> Gathered far distant, over Himavant.
>
> (*CP*, 68)

Trivedi makes the point that "it is even more unlikely for Ganga ever to be sunken than it is for the Sweet Thames not to flow softly" (135). The critic is speaking not in literal but in metaphorical terms: a sunken Ganges is counter to centuries of mythological tradition, for the river is always representative of a life-giving and purifying power that is divine in origin. Trivedi's rather damning interpretation of the imagery is that "Hinduism and the much vaunted Indian spirituality . . . are seen as sunken against the abiding and exclusive truths of Christianity" (135). It is certainly understandable how this meaning might come across to an Indian reader, but Eliot may be guilty of nothing more than mistaken universalism, of assuming that the Christian trope of the waste land might be some kind of "archetype" rather than what it is: a local (i.e., European) myth. But there is no doubt that Eliot has Christianized his Indian image to conform to other, more overtly Christian images in the poem, just as he has Christianized the meaning of the Sanskrit *shantih*.

Are the three admonitory imperatives *Datta, Dayadhvam, Damyata* likewise Christianized? Here the case is more complicated, in part because Eliot, at least in the notes he added to the poem in December 1922, seems to be aware that his use of Sanskrit is pedantic and exotic. His own gloss on the three words suggests a measure of self-parody and no small degree of pranksterism: "'Datta, dayadhvam, damyata' (Give, sympathise, control). The fable of the meaning of the Thunder is found in the *Brihadaranyaka–Upanishad*, 5, I. A translation is found in Deussen's *Sechzig Upanishads des Veda*, p. 489" (CP, 75). The relevant section actually follows the one Eliot indicates, and of course the translation he so helpfully invites the English reader to peruse renders the Sanskrit into German. More important, and this point relates more to the poem itself than to the note, the three words that expand on the root *da* in the *Brihadaranyaka* are presented in a different order and with meanings slightly different from the ones Eliot assigns. In the Indic text, the narrative involves the three types of beings—gods, humans, and demons—that the creator Prajapati has fathered. The three groups come to him separately to seek enlightenment, and he instructs them all by speaking the syllable *da* and then asking, "Have you understood?" The gods interpret *da* to mean *damyata*, "control yourselves"; the humans understand *da* as *datta*, "give"; and the demons construe the syllable as *dayadhvam*, "be compassionate." Prajapati assures each group that they have indeed understood his instructions, and the different beings go their separate ways.[41] In *The Waste Land*, "DA" is expanded first to mean "give," then "sympathize," and finally "control," at least according to the notes. In contrast to the *Brihadaranyaka*, the thunder does not appear to address three distinct groups; rather, the audience for each of the three injunctions seems homogeneously human, which has the effect of suggesting that the voice of the thunder, despite the Sanskrit, speaks with a Judeo-Christian accent. Perhaps the thunder speaks to suffering humanity here as God spoke to Job, "out of the whirlwind," but with a voice that "thundereth marvelously" (Job 37:5, 38:1; see Trivedi, 134). Also, the response to each injunction in Eliot is completely different from its counterpart than in the *Brihadaranyaka*: *datta* evokes guilt ("What have we given?"); *dayadhvam* calls forth images of isolation rather than sympathy ("each in his prison"); and *damyata* implies not self-control but obedience to others ("beating obedient / To controlling hands" [CP 68–69]).

    The last Sanskrit instruction in Eliot, which is first in the Indic text, calls for special comment. One of the things implied in the *Brihadaranyaka* by having the gods interpret *da* as "control yourselves" is that the gods understand they have the obligation to exercise care in their relations with human beings. Eliot's nautical image involves an analogy: just as an expert sailor can control a boat, so one person may control another, provided the other person is sufficiently compliant: "your heart would have responded / Gaily, when invited, beating obedient / To controlling hands" (CP 69). Sexual meanings are evoked here because of the similarity in diction to the clerk-typist scene earlier in the poem: "Exploring hands encounter no defense" (CP, 62). The sexual reference is probably itself a metaphor, part of a long religious tradition that figures the obedient soul as the bride of Christ. But even without this interpretation, the meaning of the Sanskrit *damyata* is virtually reversed from its original meaning in the *Brihadaranyaka*, with the substitution of self-control for submission. Eliot, in other words, works the Sanskrit injunction into an allegory of Christian obedience. The question remains as to the degree to which Eliot knowingly realigned the meanings of Sanskrit words to conform to Christian tradition. His explanation of *shantih* as "the peace which passeth understanding" is a case in point. As Trivedi explains, the word "does not mean peace, but when thrice invoked as benediction as at the end of the Upanishads, it assumes a special meaning as the dictionary explains: 'may the three kinds of pain [i.e., *daihika, daivika* and *bhautika*: bodily, spiritual, and material] be averted'" (134).[42] Does Eliot simply get the Sanskrit meanings wrong, or does he know more about Sanskrit than he lets on in the notes? That is, does he deliberately mislead his readers in the notes so as to direct those readers toward a more overtly Christian interpretation of the poem than the strictly Indic meanings of the Sanskrit would allow? These questions cannot really be answered, nor need they be. Whether the notes are in truth "the remarkable exposition of bogus scholarship" that Eliot said they were in 1956

(*OPP*, 121) or a sincere but sometimes mistaken attempt to elucidate the poem, their effect is the same: the inculcation of Christian meanings by Indic means.

Not all of Eliot's work belongs to the canon of "wisdom poetry" that he tried to describe in the Goethe essay, but *Four Quartets* clearly does. Beginning with "Burnt Norton" in 1935 and ending with "Little Gidding" in 1942, the four poems (collectively published in 1943) show Eliot trying to "participat[e] in that 'Wisdom that we can all accept' (*SE*, 263), quite apart from any 'ideas' we may find in it or to which we must assent" (Kearns, 231). The seriousness of the poems reflects the seriousness of the times: all but "Burnt Norton" were written during World War II, and two of them—"The Dry Salvages" and "Little Gidding"—were composed, all or in part, during the London blitz (September 1940–May 1941). In *The Idea of a Christian Society* (1939), Eliot called the Munich pact of 1938 a sociopolitical trauma from which "one does not recover" because it creates doubts about the very "validity of a civilization." What the times demanded, for Eliot, was "an act of personal contrition, of humility, repentance, and amendment."[43]

Eliot's response to the outbreak of war, then, was a redoubling of religious values, a fact that cannot be ignored in assessing the meaning of *Four Quartets*. But the reality of the war came home for Eliot when the blitz began on 7 September 1940. In "The Dry Salvages" (published February 1941) when the poet asks, "Where is there an end of it, the soundless wailing," a sense of wartime anxiety comes through, though the wail of the air raid sirens Eliot heard could hardly be called "soundless." Likewise, "Little Gidding" (begun early in 1941) evokes the immediate aftermath of a London bombing in these lines: "Dust in the air suspended / Marks the place where a story ended. / Dust inbreathed was a house" (*CP*, 193, 202). These two later poems have a retrospective effect on the earliest, "Burnt Norton," the title of which refers to a house in Gloucestershire built on the site of another house destroyed by fire in the seventeenth century.[44] That is, the uncertainty and anxiety that Eliot experienced in wartime London can be felt in the earlier poem as well. And although such lines as "The black cloud carries the sun away" (*CP*, 179) were not meant to evoke the wartime world when they were written, the decision to include the earlier poem in an eventual collection of four was made in late 1940 (Ackroyd, 362), a particularly intense period of British engagement with Axis forces. Even if this connection is discounted, it is still true that the four poems are grounded in their own times in a way that is not generally acknowledged. Indeed, Eliot himself appears to have encouraged a reading removed from immediate context when he wrote in a draft of "The Three Voices of Poetry" that the last three quartets were "patriotic poems" and then canceled the remark (Ackroyd, 264). He may have been at pains to establish the universality of *Four Quartets* by downplaying the contemporary relevance of the individual poems, thereby ensuring the "wisdom" of the overall work. In any event, the wartime context of the poems underscores the thematic emphasis on impermanence and suffering which runs through them, and also heightens the need for a religious response.

That response, and the strongest guarantee of wisdom in *Four Quartets,* lies in Eliot's imitation of the two poems that he most often invoked whenever he tried to explain or describe the greatness of poetry: *The Divine Comedy* and the *Bhagavad-Gita.* Part II of "Little Gidding" includes a long section modeled on canto 15 of the *Inferno* in which Dante the pilgrim describes a meeting with his old master, Brunetto Latini, in the circle of the sodomites. Part III of "The Dry Salvages" imagines a new colloquy between Krishna and Arjuna which takes place not on the field of the Kurus but in modern London. The temporal dislocation of these two wisdom voices from the past is something the two passages have in common, since the Dante passage from "Little Gidding" is also set in the modern city. Eliot's orchestration of these ancient voices through modern personae is of a piece with his earlier philosophical speculations in his dissertation, *Knowledge and Experience*, on the nature of reality. That is, the personae are devices for mimicking the different perspectives on reality that are normally possible through only one "finite centre" at one time and in one place. By imagining, poetically, his own experience of wartime London from the perspective of Dante and the poet of the *Bhagavad-Gita*, Eliot validates those experiences, creating a sense of community and shared values with people of other places and times. Of course, this sense of community, relationship, or tradition is made possible solely by the "belief" that other people's experiences are qualitatively the same as one's own. In Eliot's case, that imaginative leap was surely helped by Dante's own experiences of political betrayal and appeasement, and by Krishna's counsel to Arjuna that the great war he faces calls for a spiritual response.

Eliot himself provides a key to reading the work in terms of multiple temporal and geographical perspectives (illustrated by *The Divine Comedy* and the *Bhagavad-Gita*) in these lines from "The Dry Salvages":

> I have said before
> That the past experience revived in the meaning
> Is not the experience of one life only
> But of many generations.

(CP, 194)

In this connection the critic Kearns notes that "if *Four Quartets* is a Christian poem at heart, it is not a devotional poem in the conventional sense, and the primary Christian coloration is refreshed, examined, made new by the presence of other voices and points of view" (Kearns, 231). This is a claim for which there is substantial critical consensus. Narsingh Srivastava, in his study of the relations of the *Gita* to *Four Quartets,* says that the poems present "a multisided perception of reality, as though through a prism in which each side reveals the whole of the prism."[45] Kristian Smidt comments that the outlook of *Four Quartets* "comprehends considerably more than the Christian view," adding that "there is nothing very dogmatic about the *Quartets.*"[46] But Eliot himself offers the best comment on the relationship of Christian belief to other forms of worship and wisdom in his introduction to *Thoughts for Meditation* (1951), an anthology of religious texts edited by the Indian scholar Nagendranath Gangulee:

> There are some readers who . . . regard Asiatic literature as the sole repository of religious understanding; there are others who . . . refuse to venture further than a narrow Christian tradition. For both kinds of reader, it is salutary to learn that the Truth . . . is not wholly confined to their own religious tradition, or on the other hand to an alien culture and religion. . . . I am aware also that there are readers who persuade themselves that there is an "essence" in all religions which is the same, and that this essence can be conveniently distilled and preserved. . . . Such readers may perhaps be reminded that no man has ever climbed to the higher stages of the spiritual life, who has not been a believer in a particular religion or at least a particular philosophy. . . . It was only in relation to his own religion that the insights of any one of these men has its significance to him, and what they say can only reveal its meaning to the reader who has his own religion of dogma and doctrine in which he believes.[47]

Eliot's position, then, is that neither the Asiatic nor the Christian traditions have a monopoly on truth; at the same time, whatever commonalities they share do not add up to anything uniform or archetypal. Rather, the insights of one tradition can be appreciated and understood only from the perspective of the other. And this pretty much describes the placement of the reader of *Four Quartets*. Even if that reader is not "a believer of a particular religion or . . . a particular philosophy," he or she is put in the position of one who is, and experiences something like belief for the duration of the poem: "you are the music / While the music lasts" (*CP,* 199). The devotional "music," in turn, depends on the counterpoint of Eastern and Western traditions.

The *Gita* passage from "The Dry Salvages" and the Dante passage from "Little Gidding" have a number of things in common. First, they both modernize the settings of the ancient poems to which they refer: Krishna speaks to passengers on the British rail system and to voyagers aboard a modern ocean liner; similarly, the Dantesque colloquy takes place in modern London, with dead leaves blowing about "Over the asphalt" in "the urban dawn" (*CP*, 203). Second, both passages relate, either directly or indirectly, to the wartime conditions that are so deeply woven into *Four Quartets*. The *Gita* passage alludes to war outright: "So Krishna, as when he admonished Arjuna / On the field of battle" (*CP*, 197). In the Dante passage, the reference to war involves some effort of interpretation, but not much. The speaker of the section encounters his interlocutor "Between three districts where the smoke arose" in the early morning hours "Near the ending of interminable night" (*CP*, 202–3), so it is easy to imagine the setting of wartime London as a modern inferno. This interpretation is helped by Eliot's reference to the circle of the sodomites, not because of any suggestion of the sin for which Brunetto Latini is punished there but because of the punishment itself: fire raining down from the sky.

The allusion to Dante's master points to another connection as well between the *Inferno* passage and the *Gita* passage, this one somewhat more complicated than the rest. In "The Dry Salvages," Eliot contemplates the effect of past and future on individual identity and finds that identity is so inconstant (the "I," after all, is a construct of experience, and experience changes) that the train passengers who leave one station can hardly be said to be the same as those who arrive at the next: "You are not the same people who left that station / Or who will arrive at any terminus, / While the narrowing rails slide behind you" (*CP*, 196). The meaning here, or at least one likely meaning, is that one does not have to die and be reborn again and again to experience the condition of reincarnation that Krishna describes in the *Bhagavad-Gita*. The vast rounds of existence from the Hindu epic are recast as the cyclical routines of daily life in the modern city. If anything, the idea of reincarnation is even stronger in the *Inferno* passage, for Eliot himself is recast as the pilgrim Dante encountering his old master Brunetto, whereupon Eliot translates Dante exactly: "What! are *you* here?"

As for Brunetto himself, he is probably a composite figure, the reincarnation of more than one "dead master"; after all, Eliot calls him "a familiar compound ghost / Both intimate and unidentifiable" (*CP*, 203). It would probably be too constrained a reading to suggest that the figure is a "reincarnation" of Ezra Pound, whom Eliot had referred to as "*il miglior fabbro*" ("the better craftsman"), Dante's epithet for Arnaut Daniel in canto 26 of the *Purgatorio*. That said, the figure does convey a Pound-like sense

of disillusion near the end of the section, when he discloses the last of "the
gifts reserved for age":

> And last, the rending pain of re-enactment
> > Of all that you have done, and been; the shame
> > Of motives late revealed, and the awareness
> Of things ill done and done to others' harm
> > Which once you took for exercise of virtue.
>
> > > (CP, 204)

The "rending pain of re-enactment" is a pretty fair description of the kind
of karma that Krishna counsels Arjuna about. Indeed, the ancient Hindu
and the medieval Catholic voices cross and combine here, as the "Brunetto"
figure says things that one would be more likely to find in the *Bhagavad-
Gita* than in the *Divine Comedy*.

And this, finally, is the point: by bringing together two religious perspectives, Eliot is able to intensify meanings that they have in common, for the
purpose, as he said, not of suggesting some kind of shared "essence" but
of conveying the depth and mystery of the religious experience, regardless
of *how* it is experienced. Near the end of Part III of "The Dry Salvages,"
Eliot works an actual translation of the *Bhagavad-Gita* into his poetic recreation of the voice of Krishna in modern times:

> At the moment which is not of action or of inaction
> You can receive this: "on whatever sphere of being
> The mind of a man may be intent
> At the time of death"—that is the one action
> (And the time of death is every moment)
> Which shall fructify in the lives of others:
> And do not think of the fruit of action.
> Fare forward.
>
> > > (CP, 197)

One of the interesting things about this passage is that it seems to balance against "Brunetto's" consciousness of the (often unintended) effects
of human action. The two passages appear to say rather different things,
but they are really complementary: the *Gita* passage, like the *Gita* itself,
urges action without anxiety over the fruits of action, while the Dante passage comments on the law of unintended consequences. But it is precisely
because the consequences of actions cannot always be foreseen that Krishna
urges resolution in the performance of those actions, since their ultimate
results are out of human hands. Action and inaction are two "sphere[s] of
being" that are impossibly combined. Eliot alludes to the Krishna passage

at the end of "The Dry Salvages" when he describes the "impossible union" of various "spheres of existence":

> Here the impossible union
> Of spheres of existence is actual,
> Here the past and future
> Are conquered, and reconciled,
> Where action were otherwise movement
> Of that which is only moved
> And has in it no source of movement—
> Driven by demonic, chthonic
> Powers. And right action is freedom
> From past and future also.
>
> (CP, 199)

The last two lines here quoted could well have come from the *Bhagavad-Gita,* even though the ostensible subject under discussion is "Incarnation," meaning the incarnation of Christ. The "impossible union" of which Eliot speaks has different meanings in different religious traditions, but the experience of those different meanings is equally valid for those holding the beliefs that make the experience possible. This claim—that impossible unions of spheres of existence are nonetheless actual—may be the central meaning of *Four Quartets* as a whole. That is, after all, the meaning that closes the poem, as Eliot contemplates a state of existence "Between two waves of the sea" where "the fire and the rose are one" (*CP,* 209).

The impossible union of fire and rose that concludes *Four Quartets* has spiritual meaning consistent with the religious imagery used throughout the suite of poems. But fire and rose also suggest the physical elements of classical, medieval, and renaissance tradition. Indeed, fire, earth, water, and air form a major structural motif of *Four Quartets* (Ackroyd, 262), a motif that helps to bring the poem into the orbit of classical philosophy. The motif of the four elements suggests a further reference to Lucretius's *De Rerum Natura,* the poem that Eliot always invokes, along with *The Divine Comedy* and *The Bhagavad-Gita,* whenever he tries to elaborate the meaning of "wisdom poetry." Although he does not allude to *De Rerum Natura* outright in *Four Quartets* as he does to *The Divine Comedy* and *The Bhagavad-Gita,* the philosophical dimension of the poem leads one to ask how the kind of philosophical voice represented by Lucretius is supposed to relate to the Christian voice of Dante and the Hindu voice of Krishna in the broader conception of the wisdom voice. Lucretius, after all, was an Epicurean, and his epic poem on the nature of things is written from a perspective long recognized as frankly atheist. This aspect of Lucretius is not something Eliot chose to emphasize, or even mention, in those essays in which he tried to describe the elusive nature of wisdom poetry. In a 1924 essay on Paul Valéry, however, Eliot expresses admiration for Lucretius as a model for the impersonal method, a method that would seem to be indispensable to the broader purpose of writing wisdom poetry. He describes Lucretius's capacity for impersonality as "the passionate act by which he annihilates himself in a system and unites himself with it, gaining something greater than himself. Such a surrender requires great concentration."[48] Surrender and self-annihilation in Eliot's world are simultaneously religious and aesthetic values, and it may be that Lucretius enters Eliot's triad of wisdom poets by virtue of impersonality (Dante is also invoked in the Valéry essay, and although the *Bhagavad-Gita* is not, Eliot names the Upanishads as well as "the Red Slayer," a reference to Emerson's "Brahma," thereby completing the Classical-Christian-Hindu triad).[49]

But it may also be that wisdom, or the wisdom voice, requires the same kind of interplay of various perspectives that Eliot described in his dissertation as the means whereby the "existence of the world of truth" emerges (*KE*, 142). Philosophy alone is not sufficient for the experience of wisdom, but neither is religion, whether Christian or Hindu. Philosophy, however, can be supplemented by religion, so long as the religious perspective is not limited to a single set of beliefs. The kinds of "local" worlds represented by *De Rerum Natura, The Divine Comedy,* and *The Bhagavad-Gita* condition one another in such a way that something universal is experienced. Eliot's critical writing makes clear that wisdom is not the sole province of the Christian tradition; on the contrary, focus on a single tradition necessitates belief, and belief is, paradoxically, remote from wisdom. Hence, Eastern traditions are employed in *Four Quartets* to activate the Western, to take it out of the realm of dogma by shifting the reader out of belief and into wisdom, since wisdom is something that religious traditions as different as Christianity and Hinduism have in common. In the end, *Four Quartets* works as wisdom poetry not because it inculcates belief in a particular system but because it doesn't. Instead, the poem allows the reader to experience what it feels like to believe, at least as long as the reading lasts.

III

T. S. Eliot and Ezra Pound are not the only American modernists who managed an aesthetic revision of Western tradition by means of Eastern culture. Following the publication of Pound's *Cathay* in 1915, William Carlos Williams began incorporating Chinese motifs into his poetry, notable examples from the early 1920s being "To the Shade of Po Chü-i" and a section of

"Portrait of the Author" which alludes to the Tang dynasty courtesan Yang Guifei (719–756). Williams, like Pound, took musty Oriental material from the Victorian sinologist Herbert Giles and made it new. And even before Pound's *Cathay* or his "In a Station of the Metro," Wallace Stevens intuited a relationship between his own artistic impulses and those that gave rise to Chinese landscape painting, a relationship evidently borne out by "Thirteen Ways of Looking at a Blackbird" (1917). That poem is usually allied with traditions as divergent as cubism and pragmatism but might just as easily be construed as a suite of haiku. Marianne Moore, like Stevens, appears to have come to poetic terms with Eastern culture first by way of painting, as suggested by her "Nine Nectarines and Other Porcelain" (1935), which pictures nectarines "Fuzzless through slender crescent leaves / of green or blue or / both in the Chinese style."[50] Lesser poets on the margins of modernism whose work reveals an interest in Eastern aesthetics include Adelaide Crapsey (1878–1914) and Sara Teasdale (1884–1933). Crapsey has a secure place in literary history because of her invention of the cinquain, a five-line syllabic form comparable to the Japanese tanka; and Teasdale, though it would be wrong to identify her too closely with modernist orientalism, actually anticipated the *japonisme* of her better-known contemporaries with "To Japanese Incense," published in 1907. The closing lines of that poem capture the cultural position of the early modernists who tried to revive their own traditions through those of China and Japan, "seek[ing] an ancient Eastern god / Thro' Western air."[51] Eliot and Pound, then, do not lack for company in their avant-garde explorations of oriental themes, forms, and imagery.

One name that does not come up as often as it should in the roll call of American modernists who cultivated an Eastern aesthetic is Amy Lowell. Her connection to the American Orient is probably more secure, and certainly more personal, than that of any of the aforementioned authors, including her great rival Ezra Pound. Largely because of her brother Percival, Lowell developed an interest in the Far East well in advance of her expatriate contemporaries. Indeed, Percival began to send Amy packages from Japan in 1883, when she was nine years old, so it might be said that Amy Lowell and American *japonisme* grew up together. The experience included not only the prints, fans, and bric-a-brac that her brother mailed to her from Japan but also the occasional return to the Lowell home in Brookline, Massachusetts (the estate was called "Sevenels": i.e., seven L's, because of seven generations of Lowells), by the brother himself, sometimes accompanied by his Japanese translator, Miyaoka Tsunejiro.[52] Amy developed a warm relationship with Miyaoka in her childhood and sustained it well into her maturity. In 1921 the two exchanged gifts in the form of books. Amy sent Miyaoka a copy of *Can Grande's Castle* (1918), which includes "Guns as Keys: And the Great Gate Swings," a long, contrapuntal poem about Commodore Perry's mission to Japan. Her description of the poem in the letter to Miyaoka accompanying the book leaves no doubt about her Eastern enthusiasms:

> I wrote the poem out of a sort of atavism and after much reading of Japanese literature, of which, it is needless to say, I am an ardent admirer. The prints and picture books like the little one you have just given me, and which my brother Percival used to send across the Atlantic [*sic*] all through my childhood, made Japan so vivid to my imagination that I cannot realize that I have never been there. Certainly it imbued me with a love for the country and the people, which the games we used to have together strengthened so much that I shall always feel a bond drawing me to your country.[53]

The bond was also strengthened by her brother's several books about Japan, the most important among them *The Soul of the Far East* (1888), which Amy read as a teenager.

All these influences help to make the case that American authors hardly needed to wait for Pound to realize the aesthetic potential of the Far East. The impact of *The Soul of the Far East,* in particular, is generally overlooked as a modernist influence, mainly because Lafcadio Hearn was so taken with that book, and Hearn operated in a cultural sphere remote from modernism. The neoromantic Hearn, however, helped to keep the spiritual and aesthetic values of Old Japan alive in the face of the philosophical and scientific programs of the New. The Lowell-Hearn path to Oriental modernism is evident not only in the case of Amy Lowell but also in the career of her friend and fellow poet John Gould Fletcher (1886–1950). Fletcher acknowledged the impact *Cathay* had on him, but he also numbered Hearn and the Oriental Wing of the Boston Museum of Fine Arts among the influences that so affected him when he was an undergraduate at Harvard University (1902–1907).[54] And who is to say that this strain of American orientalism did not come into play in the career of Pound himself when he remade Fenollosa, whose work would otherwise be remembered mainly for its dogmatic tone and doggerel style?

Amy Lowell was no stranger to doggerel verse herself, as her first collection of poetry shows. In 1910 she sent a sheaf of poems to the *Atlantic Monthly* after a notice in the society pages of a Boston paper announced that a childhood friend was marrying the editor of the magazine. Two years later *A Dome of Many-Coloured Glass* appeared under the Houghton Mifflin imprint. The title of the collection alludes to "Adonais," Percy Shelley's romantic elegy on the death of John Keats, who was the dominant influence on Lowell at the time. (Thanks in part to the earlier efforts of the poet Louise Imogen Guiney and the pictorialist photographer F. Holland Day, literary Boston had experienced a Keats revival not long before Lowell came on the cultural scene.)[55] Most of the poems are conventional and forgettable, including "To John Keats," a sonnet that concludes the main section of the book. It begins by praising Keats as a "Great master!" and ends by asking the master to "Forget thy empurpled state . . . / Of greatness, and be merciful and near": "so may we / Faint throbbings of thy music overhear."[56] The inflated, archaic diction and the inverted syntax in this short sample are well represented elsewhere in the collection; such elements are precisely those that the modernist-imagist revolution meant to remove from poetry, and the discovery of Japanese and Chinese literature helped that revolution along. Curiously, one of the better poems in the collection is "A Japanese Wood-Carving"—better not because the poet deploys any of the tonal or formal devices of Japanese poetry but because the subject matter makes Keatsian diction and imagery inappropriate. The wood-carving of the title pictures "the untamed sea" in a summer wind, "which whips the blue / And breaks it into gleams and sparks of light" (19). The idea behind the piece is the artist's ability to transform nature: the first part of the poem imagines the prior life of the seascape as a tree in the forest before "the patient, careful knife" of the Japanese woodcarver crafted the vivid scene. And it is vivid: one passage describes diving seabirds, "Their dripping feathers shining in the sun / While the wet drops like little glints of light / Fall pattering backward to the parent sea" (19). The larger model for the poem is still Keats, whose "Ode on a Graecian Urn" likewise takes a scene on a static object and sets it in imagined motion. But by transposing the idea, culturally, from a classical to an Asian context, Lowell achieves a measure of freshness just shy of the modernist newness shortly to arrive from London and Chicago.

"A Japanese Wood-Carving" was one of the poems that had appeared in the *Atlantic* prior to its publication in book form. After Harriet Monroe read that poem and others in the magazine, she wrote to Lowell asking her to contribute to *Poetry: A Magazine of Verse,* the journal she planned to publish out of Chicago. Lowell responded with a check for twenty-five dollars and a promise to submit some new poems in the near future.[57] The first issue of *Poetry* was published in September 1912, but it was not until Lowell read Ezra Pound's manifesto of imagism in the March 1913 issue that she had the epiphany that was to change her life. Pound's "A Few Dont's [*sic*] by an Imagiste" and "Imagisme" (attributed to F. S. Flint), as well as the poems by "H. D. Imagiste" that had appeared in the preceding issue, combined to make Lowell declare, "Why, I, too, am an Imagiste!"[58] That summer she steamed off to London and insinuated herself into the imagist scene. At first, Pound was receptive, accepting her poem "In the Garden" for publication in the *New Freewoman* and later including the same poem in *Des Imagistes* (1914), the landmark imagist anthology he edited, which featured work by Hilda Doolittle, Richard Aldington, William Carlos Williams, Ford Madox Ford (then Ford Madox Heuffer), James Joyce, and others, including, of course, Pound himself. Lowell's contribution describes the sights and sounds of fountains in a garden at night ("It falls, the water, / And the air is throbbing with it") and concludes with a mildly erotic evocation of female desire: "And I wished for the night and you. / I wanted to see you in the swimming pool, / White and shining in the silver-flecked water."[59] By the time Lowell visited London again in the summer of 1914, Pound had moved on to vorticism and resented the literary initiative displayed by a woman whom he regarded, condescendingly, as an easily manipulated protégée ("When I get through with that girl," Pound once boasted to Robert Frost, "she'll think she was born in free verse.")[60] Lowell, however, was not done with imagism, and she and Pound clashed over publication plans for another imagist volume; the dispute included disagreement over "who was entitled to the name imagist."[61] In the end, Lowell took over the imagist brand, though Pound insisted on devaluing her management of the movement as "Amygism," a term reflective of a somewhat "competitive and adolescent reaction" on Pound's part.[62]

The direction of imagism under Lowell's stewardship did not at first maintain the Eastern emphasis that Pound established in *Des Imagistes*. After all, four of the six poems he contributed to that anthology are derived from Chinese models ("After Ch'u Yuan," "Liu Ch'e," "The Fan-Piece, for Her Imperial Lord," and "T'sai Chi'h"); he also included "Scented Leaves from a Chinese Jar," by Allen Upward. The review of *Des Imagistes* in *Poetry* emphasized the importance of Eastern aesthetics, even though, oddly, it focused on Japanese rather than Chinese poetry. After observing that "imagism is essentially a graphic art," the reviewer claimed that "a great many of the classical poems of the Japanese are also graphic in the sense in which I use it here," meaning that an intense visual awareness often informs the verbal artifact.[63] Lowell would not get around to literary *japonisme* until the third volume of *Some Imagist Poets,* as she renamed (or translated) the title that Pound had given the original collection. Lowell also relaxed the editorial policy the dictatorial Pound had instituted by allowing each poet "to represent himself by the work he considers best." Of the six poets who contributed to the 1915 anthology, only John Gould

Fletcher opted for Asian imagery, and then only in "The Blue Symphony" (e.g., "O old pagodas of my soul, how you glittered across green trees!"). The preface to the 1916 anthology tries to distinguish between "Oriental" (presumably Chinese) and Japanese prosody, the former based on repetition and the latter on precise syllable count, but the point is made only to argue that English meter is not the only cadence available.[64] Indeed, none of the poems by any of the poets (the same six comprised by the first volume: Richard Aldington, H. D., Fletcher, F. S. Flint, D. H. Lawrence, and Lowell) are remotely Oriental. The third and final anthology (1917), however, is a different story. Where the other poets wrote mostly of the Great War, Lowell (who had treated that topic, badly, in the 1916 volume) opted for the Oriental with a long suite of twenty poems under the general title "Lacquer Prints."

Almost all the poems in this series adopt the personae of Japanese men and women (more women than men) who make close observations about daily life in Japan. This "Japan," of course, is an aesthetic fantasy worked up from Lowell's reading, art collecting, and other vicarious experiences. That said, the poems are an obvious step forward, artistically, and the maturation of Lowell's style in "Lacquer Prints" is an individual instance of a larger truth: that, in poetry at least, orientalism played as important and constitutive a role in the development of American modernism as did, say, French symbolism. By the time she published "Lacquer Prints" in book form as *Pictures of the Floating World* (1919), their number had increased to fifty-nine. The book contains another Eastern-themed section titled "Chinoiseries," consisting of seven poems, longer and less concentrated, imagistically, than those called "Lacquer Prints."

The title of the 1919 volume translates the Japanese term *ukiyo-e*, used to describe the woodblock prints of the eighteenth century. As Mari Yoshihari explains, such prints "were created by artists and craftsmen of plebian or low samurai background, and depicted scenes from everyday life and entertainment of the urban classes. Originally associated with a Buddhist world view, the phrase 'floating world' subsequently came to suggest a hedonistic preoccupation with the present, with the latest fashions, pursuits, and lifestyles of urban cultures, and implied a certain chicness."[65] In addition to actual *ukiyo-e* prints, Lowell probably took inspiration from her brother's description of Japanese painting in *The Soul of the Far East*: "A Japanese painting is a poem rather than a picture. It portrays an emotion called up by the scene, and not the scene itself in all its elaborated complexity. It undertakes to give only so much of it as is vital to that particular feeling, and intentionally omits all irrelevant details."[66] The description

reads like a manifesto of imagism well in advance of Pound's pronouncements and helps to explain why Lowell was so quick to identify herself as
an imagist in March 1913: she had already encountered, many years before,
the aesthetic that Pound described at that time.

A number of the poems in the "Lacquer Prints" section of *Pictures of
the Floating World* have specific origins in Japanese cultural tradition. Several recount legends about famous Japanese figures: "Document" relates
an episode in the later life of the master printmaker Hokusai Katsushika
(1760–1849), when he summoned "the courage to draw those ancient
heroes / Who have been the models of glory" in an age of peace; "Disillusion" tells the story of a scholar who, "Weary of erecting the fragile tower
of words," hurls himself into a volcano; "The Emperor's Garden" repeats
the legend of the shogun Ashikaga Yoshimitsu (1358–1404), who ordered
"the miniature mountains in his garden / To be covered with white silk" on
a hot summer day to remind him of snow.[67]

Two poems are reworkings of classical Japanese literature, one possibly
adapted from *A Hundred Verses from Old Japan* (1909) by William N.
Porter, the other inspired by Arthur Davidson Ficke's *Chats on Japanese
Prints* (1915). Porter's book is a British translation of the *Hyakunin Isshu*,
or "Single Verses by a Hundred People," collected in 1235 by Fujiwara
Sadaie (1162–1241); Lowell flags "Temple Ceremony" as an adaptation
of a tanka by Henjo Sojo (816–890), a courtier who became a Buddhist
priest. Regardless of whether the Lowell version derives from Porter's or
from some other source, a comparison of the two translations speaks volumes about the imagist revolution. Porter changed the syllable count of the
tanka (5, 7, 5, 7, 7) by rearranging the line order, adding an extra syllable
to each line (the better to accommodate English meter), and rhyming the
second, fourth, and fifth lines to make "the sound more familiar to English
readers."[68] The result is predictably metronomic:

> Oh stormy winds, bring up the clouds,
> And paint the heavens gray;
> Lest these fair maids of form divine
> Should angel wings display,
> And fly far far away.[69]

Lowell's version retains only the five-line form (not the syllable count) of
the tanka and departs from the meaning of the Japanese original, written
just before Henjo Sojo entered the priesthood: he is supposed to have seen
a group of court dancers of such angelic beauty as to occasion the poet's
petition to the wind to keep them earthbound. Lowell, by contrast, wishes

the wind away so that the beauty of the dancers or, rather, of a single dancer may be seen more clearly:

> Blow softly,
> O Wind!
> And let no clouds cover the moon
> Which lights the posturing steps
> Of the most beautiful of dancers.
>
> (*Pictures*, 23–24)

The concentration on a single image and the abandonment of the iamb make the piece an exemplary exercise in the New Poetry, especially in contrast to the ponderous Porter.

The first poem in the "Lacquer Prints" section is also an exemplary imagist work, not only because of the concision of language and image but also because it illustrates the role that adaptation played in the development of modernist literature. Pound had Fenollosa to rework, Williams had Giles, and Lowell, likewise, had her sources. Here first is "Streets," which Lowell says is "adapted from the poet Yakura Sanjin, 1769":

> As I wandered through the eight hundred and eight
>   streets of the city,
> I saw nothing so beautiful
> As the women of the Green Houses,
> With their girdles of spun gold,
> And their long-sleeved dresses,
> Coloured like the graining of wood.
> As they walk,
> The hems of their outer garments flutter open,
> And the blood-red linings glow like sharp-toothed
>   maple leaves
> In Autumn.
>
> (*Pictures*, 3)

The original of the poem, as Lowell acknowledged, is in Arthur Davidson Ficke's *Chats on Japanese Prints*, a rather unfortunate title (one of many such titles in a series called "Books for Collectors"), since the book is in fact a thorough, well-illustrated history of the Japanese print.[70] In the chapter "The Early Polychrome Masters," Ficke refers to "a contemporary record that throws light on the temper of the people and the artists of this time."[71] The record is "The Story of the Honey-Sweetmeat Vendor, Dohei," reputedly written by the poet Yakura Sanjin (and illustrated by the printmaster Suzuki Harunobu), which Ficke translated from a German book by Dr. Julius Kurth.[72] Here is the relevant passage in Ficke from which Lowell made her adaptation: "Ladies with girdles of spun gold and long-sleeved girlish dresses sway their hips; and their garments, coloured like the graining of wood, flow as do torrents of Spring. . . . And as they wander along, the hems of their robes flutter open, and the blood-red silk linings gleam like maple foliage—though it is not yet Autumn!" (Ficke, 131). One of the remarkable things about the end product of this game of literary telephone (Sanjin to Kurth to Ficke to Lowell) is how fresh and original the poem sounds. True, Lowell has lifted whole phrases from Ficke ("girdles of spun gold," "coloured like the graining of wood"), but she has made all the right modernist choices in suppressing superfluous, "literary" language ("flow as do torrents of Spring"), in selecting the simplest, most direct verb ("walk" instead of "wander along," "glow" instead of "gleam"), and in intensifying the image ("sharp-toothed maple leaves" instead of "maple foliage"). The Japanese source, however compromised and derivative, evidently made it easier for Lowell to avoid the conventional meter and diction that she had learned all too well from the "great master" John Keats.

Adaptations such as "Streets" and poems derived from legend (e.g., "Desolation") form only a small part of the "Lacquer Prints" series; by far the greatest number of poems are those inspired by specific prints. Lowell's Easternizing of the tradition of *ut pictura poesis* also has precedent in Ficke's book: his so-called "chats" include a number of poems that dramatize or describe the subject of this or that print in verse form. Now largely forgotten, Ficke was once a well-known poet. Originally from Chicago, he was a regular contributor to Margaret Anderson's *Little Review* (in fact, four of the poems reprinted in *Chats on Japanese Prints* originally appeared in that journal). Like Anderson, he migrated to Greenwich Village, where he associated with Edna St. Vincent Millay and the socialist bohemian Floyd Dell. Though contemporary with the modernist movement, Ficke was a traditionalist who was deeply suspicious of the literary avant-garde. Together with his friend Witter Bynner (who was likewise an orientalist of some note), Ficke carried off a literary hoax by inventing a poetic movement called "spectrism" and publishing a book called *Spectra*. Bynner wrote under the pseudonym "Emanuel Morgan," while Ficke became "Anne Knish."

The theory of spectrism claimed that "the theme of a poem is to be regarded as a prism," among other things.[73] One of its targets was imagism, which at the time was identified much more closely with Lowell than with Pound in the United States. Lowell, however, was not deceived, nor was she especially insulted: she forgave her two genial antagonists, with whom she had a competitive but cordial relationship. In a letter to Bynner she takes note of Ficke's gift of a Japanese print, inscribed "With the admiration of the enemy," and she thanks Bynner for his defense of her "Guns as Keys" before the Chicago Poetry Society.[74] *Japonisme,* in other words, was neutral territory for these literary antagonists. Ficke evidently gave Lowell a copy of *Chats on Japanese Prints* in March 1916 when she lunched with him and Edgar Lee Masters in Chicago before lecturing at the Fine Arts Building on "The New Poetry, with Special Reference to Imagism." In April she wrote to Ficke thanking him again for the book, adding that she had "taken the liberty of making a poem from one of your translations of the Japanese poets, moving it round a bit and changing parts of it for my own benefit, and called it an adaptation of the poet in question" (i.e., Yakura Sanjin). In the same letter Lowell told Ficke his book had inspired her "to write a number of little 'Hokku' poems."[75] *Chats on Japanese Prints,* then, has to be numbered among the native influences that appear to have been much more important to Lowell's literary orientalism than the exilic influence of Pound, whose interests, it must be noted, lay more with Chinese than with Japanese tradition.

As with Porter, whose singsong tanka reveals the sorry state of poetry prior to imagism, so Ficke's labored verses show how well Lowell succeeded in the orientalist mode. Most of the poems sprinkled throughout Ficke's *Chats* are conventional in the extreme, and many evoke the English romantic tradition to convey the author's sense of Japanese *ukiyo-e.* In diction even more Keatsian than the language Lowell had used in 1912 for her first book of poetry, a poem titled "Shuncho" celebrates the printmaker:

> Your lovely ladies shall not fade
> Though Yedo's moated walls be laid
> Level with dust, and night-owls brood
> Over the city's solitude.
>
> (Ficke, 237)

Ficke maintains this style throughout: his poem on Hiroshige's print *The Bow Moon* alludes to Samuel Taylor Coleridge outright by comparing the moon in the print to "some lonely bride" wandering "through the halls of Kubla Khan" (Ficke, 380).

Lowell at least attempted to emulate Japanese literary convention and avoided overt reference to Western tradition in "Lacquer Prints." As she wrote to Ficke, his book inspired her to attempt "a number of little 'Hokku' poems," such as the one titled "Nuance": "Even the iris bends / When a butterfly lights upon it" (*Pictures,* 16). The title, unfortunately, Westernizes the poem by providing an abstract meaning in advance of the poem itself, but other haiku-like imitations seem truer to the form. In "Passing the Bamboo Fence," the title effectively functions simply as the first line of the poem proper: "What fell upon my open umbrella? / A plum-blossom?" (22). Neither of these pieces seems to have been inspired by a specific print, but many of the poems in the collection certainly were. The clearest example is "One of the 'Hundred Views of Fuji' by Hokusai":

> Being thirsty,
> I filled a cup with water,
> And behold! Fuji-yama lay upon the water
> Like a dropped leaf!
>
> (*Pictures*, 11)

The basis of the poem is Hokusai's woodblock print showing a much-amused man pointing to the reflection of the sacred mountain floating in the cup. Kodama takes Lowell to task for failing to notice that the cup, or saucer, actually holds sake (the title of the print is *Haichu no Fuji*, "Fuji in a Cup of Sake"), which adds to the humorous incongruity Hokusai has depicted.[76] But the error is an honest one: the introductory material about the print in the Hokusai book Lowell owned identified the liquid as water, not sake.[77] Another identifiable *ukiyo-e* is Hokusai's *Five Nightingales and Pale Red Plum*, which Lowell renders into quasi-haiku form: "Under the plum blossoms are nightingales; / But the sea is hidden in an egg-white mist, / and they are silent" (*Pictures*, 6). The effect of this poem, like that of "Nuance," is reduced by its interpretive title, "Desolation." Despite such lapses, her "Lacquer Prints" solidly established Lowell as a literary orientalist whose poetic output exceeded that of any other modernist writer who looked to the Far East for inspiration.

Lowell wrote "Lacquer Prints" off and on over a period of four years, beginning in 1915. She held off book publication of the series until 1919 because her publishers wanted something "more timely," meaning war poetry. But when the war ended the way was clear for *Pictures of the Floating World*.[78] In the interim Lowell had published *Can Grande's Castle* (1918), a collection of four lengthy poems written in "polyphonic prose," a form styled after "the long, flowing cadence of oratorical prose"—basically *vers libre* in paragraph form with frequent internal rhymes thrown in for good measure.[79] The title of the book refers less to Dante's patron Cangrande della Scalla than to the "remote events" surrounding him which may be experienced vicariously in the pages of a book. Such events, Lowell says, have been intensified and brought to life by the contemporary reality of the Great War: "Living now, in the midst of events greater than these, the books have become reality to me in a way they could never have become before, and the stories I have dug out of dusty volumes seem as actual as my own experience" (*Castle*, vii, ix–x).

The particular story that Lowell excavates and animates in "Guns as Keys: And the Great Gate Swings," the second poem in the collection, is the opening of Japan to the West in 1853. The poem first appeared in the August 1917 issue of *Seven Arts,* the pacifist-socialist journal edited by James Oppenheim and Waldo Frank which struggled to articulate the basis for a distinctively American culture.[80] Lowell had been inspired by an essay in the April issue of the magazine: "Young Japan," by Naruse Seichi, "author of plays and stories expressive of the new spirit in Japan."[81] Naruse describes the Meiji period as a time of revolutionary chaos and loss of identity, when the Japanese subordinated their own traditions to Western values. The resulting pessimism was intensified in 1903, when a young philosophy student named Fujimura Misao leaped to his death from the top of the Kegon waterfall after carving this message on a tree trunk: "How mightily and steadily go Heaven and Earth! How infinite the duration of Past and Present! Try to measure this vastness with five feet? A word explains the Truth of the whole Universe—*unknowable.* To cure my agony, I have decided to die. Now, as I stand on the crest of this rock no uneasiness is left in me. For the first time I know that extreme pessimism and extreme optimism are one" (Naruse, 620). The essay ends with the claim that the new Japan has moved out of its pessimistic stage, has reasserted traditional values, and is now ideally positioned "to bring about [a] marriage of Occidental and Oriental cultures" (Naruse, 625).

Lowell focuses not on Naruse's Fenollosa-like penchant for synthesis but on the story of the 1903 suicide, which furnishes her with material for the first section of the two-part "Postlude" to "Guns as Keys." In the preface to *Can Grande's Castle,* Lowell thanks Naruse "for his beautiful rendering of the original Japanese" of the suicide note, which she reproduces word for word in "Postlude." She also says in the preface that she intends no "discourtesy toward Japan" in the poem; rather, her purpose is "to place in juxtaposition the delicacy and artistic clarity of Japan and the artistic ignorance and gallant self-confidence of America" (*Castle*, xv, xvi). Apparently, she was concerned that the jingoism expressed in the American sections of the poem might be attributed to Amy Lowell herself rather than to the mostly masculine personae who give voice to that jingoism.

The poem begins by contrasting the "artistic clarity of Japan and the gallant self-confidence of America" through spare *vers libre* and verbose polyphonic prose. The initial juxtaposition sets the paddle-wheel steamer

Mississippi, one of Commodore Perry's ships, against a quaint, premodern scene from Old Japan:

> My! How she throws the water off from her bows, and how those paddle-wheels churn her along at the rate of seven good knots! You are a proud lady, Mrs. *Mississippi,* curtseying down Chesapeake Bay, all a-flutter with red white and blue ribbons.
>
>> At Mishima in the province of Kai,
>> Three men are trying to measure a pine tree
>> By the length of their outstretched arms.
>
> (Castle, 51)

The polyphonic prose segments are replete with specific, quantifiable details indicative of American modernity: the speed of the ship is clocked at "seven good knots"; it burns coal "at the rate of twenty-six tons per diem," takes on "ten thousand gallons of water" (*Castle,* 52, 53), and so on. Hence, it is significant that the first glimpse of Japanese life involves a primitive, rudimentary method of measurement that does not, in the end, succeed: "The men reach about the pine tree / But their hands break apart" (52). As the *Mississippi* steams around the globe in the direction of Mishima, various shipboard scenes suggest what is in store for the ancient feudal nation once the Black Ships arrive. The sailors urge "Blackey" to dance and sing "'Suwannee River' to show those dagoes what a tune is" (54). Meanwhile, Japan is pictured as a place of idyllic, aesthetic simplicity:

> The road is hilly
> Outside the Tiger Gate,
> And striped with shadows from a bow moon,
> Slowly sinking to the horizon.
>
> (Castle, 54)

Such passages led a Japanese American by the name of Paul Hisada to write to Lowell expressing admiration for "the vivid way in which she described Japanese scenery."[82] Lowell, of course, had never seen Japan; in the passage quoted above she was describing the frontispiece to Ficke's *Chats on Japanese Prints*: Hiroshige's *The Bow Moon.*

Most of the Japanese "scenes" that Lowell imagines do indeed resemble the "Lacquer Prints" that she had begun to write prior to "Guns as Keys." And several suggest a Japan that may fairly be called "feminine," either because they feature images of geishas and courtesans or because they suggest a degree of aesthetic delicacy that seems all the more refined in contrast to the crass masculine life of the American ships. The following juxtaposition, for example, could not be more extreme:

"Oh, shut up, Jack, you make me sick! Those pigs are like worms eating a
corpse. Bah!"

> The ladies,
> Wisteria Blossom, Cloth-of-Silk, and Deep Snow,
> With their ten attendants,
> Are come to Asakusa
> To gaze at peonies.
>
> (*Castle*, 61)

When the commodore's ships are finally at anchor in Edo Bay, the feminine imagery of the Japanese passages gives way to a masculine, but still
aesthetic, description of a highly ritualized execution. The condemned man
and his executioner were once "master and pupil," so the execution itself
becomes "an act of honourable devotion" (*Castle*, 73). After the pupil
strikes his master dead, he wipes his sword, "And his face is calm and
frozen / As a stone statue on a Winter night / Above a temple gateway"
(74–75). The execution at the end of the first section balances the suicide
at the end of the poem. More important, both deaths make the same allegorical comment on the coming of the Americans: their arrival means the
end of a centuries-old way of life, with all its stoic ceremony and aesthetic
refinement.

Once the Americans enter Japan, the polyphonic prose of the first section
is transformed, and the free-verse set pieces disappear: the second section
manifests, stylistically, the central theme of the poem, which, speaking of
the two-part Postlude only, Lowell described as a basic exchange of commerce for aesthetics: "What I meant to give in both those postludes was
the effect that each country had upon the other. In the Japanese section,
how difficult it was for the Oriental to assimilate the Occidental habits of
thought, how he broke in the effort; in the American part, how, in con-
quering Japan for our commerce, as we thought, we had ourselves been
conquered on the aesthetic plane, and our habits of thought insensibly
modified by contact with the Japanese."[83]

The aestheticizing of the polyphonic prose in the second section is obvious in such passages as this one, which reads like a description of a Whistler
nocturne: "Rockets rise from the forts and their trails of sparks glitter
faintly now, and their bombs break in faded colours as the sun goes down"
(*Castle*, 78). The evocation of Whistler is quite deliberate, for he, more
than anyone else, symbolizes for Lowell the culmination of the process
she describes in the poem: "A locomotive in pay for a Whistler; telegraph
wires buying a revolution; weights and measures and Audubon's birds in
exchange for fear. Yellow monkey-men leaping out of Pandora's box, shak-

ing the rocks of the Western coastline. Golden California bartering panic for prints. The dressing-gowns of a continent won at the cost of security. Artists and philosophers lost in the hour-glass sand pouring through an open Gate" (*Castle*, 94). In Lowell's reading of history, the Japanese come out on the short end of the deal: by exchanging tradition for modernity and aesthetics for progress, they cease to be themselves. The Americans, on the other hand, are the beneficiaries, because they have added to their own tradition without trading anything away. This meaning comes through with the final juxtaposition of the two cultures in the paired postludes to the poem: first the suicide of the Japanese student, then a description of a Whistler exhibition—both dated 1903, fifty years after the Perry expedition. In fact, the Whistler memorial exhibition that Lowell describes and that she attended was held between 23 February and 28 March 1904 at Copley Hall in Boston.[84] The American postlude ends the poem:

> "Nocturne — Blue and Silver — Battersea Bridge.
> Nocturne — Grey and Silver — Chelsea Embankment.
> Variations in Violet and Green."
> Pictures in a glass-roofed gallery, and all day long the throng of
> people is so great that one can scarcely see them. Debits —
> Credits? Flux and flow through a wide gateway. Occident —
> Orient — after fifty years.
>
> (*Castle*, 97)

The three paintings that Lowell describes (all in the Freer Gallery in Washington, D.C., today) were completed over the period 1868–1879 and are therefore illustrative of Whistler's mature style, after he had assimilated Japanese aesthetic principles into his work.[85]

The third painting Lowell names (or misnames), *Variations in Green and Violet,* was most likely the work that Ernest Fenollosa had in mind in an essay published in the December 1903 issue of *The Lotus,* only two months before the exhibition. In seeking to assess "The Place in History of Mr. Whistler's Art," Fenollosa claims that Whistler "is the first great master who comes after the union of East and West, the first who creates naturally and without affectation in their mingled terms."[86] *Variations in Green and Violet* is a rapidly executed oil sketch of two robed female figures in which the strokes of the brush suggest the draperies of the robes the women wear. The Fenollosa essay goes on to explain Whistler's status as the great master of East-West union in such a way as to suggest the painting Lowell mentions: "In his grandest figure work, where his broad brush has given us instantaneous sweeps of massy drapery line, we are driven, in spite of the alien material, to trace a parallel to the sculptures of the Parthenon.

His broadest color impressions are quite Greek in rhythm. But at the very next moment we are reminded of the broad blunt line of the great Japanese fifteenth-century master, Sesshu" (16).

Critics argue that Lowell chose to name the *Variations in Green and Violet* precisely because of Fenollosa's claim that Whistler had achieved a synthesis of East and West. Later, in the foreword to *Pictures of the Floating World,* Lowell asserted that "the march of peoples is always toward the West, wherefore the earth being round, in time the West must be East again."[87] But her formulation here, and in "Guns as Keys" as well, is not really the same as Fenollosa's, because Lowell believes, again, that the "synthesis" is one-sided: the West's gain is the East's loss. The curious thing about her antimodern attitude is that it is contrary not only to Fenollosa but also to Naruse, who, in his 1917 *Seven Arts* essay, made the same argument that Fenollosa had made two decades earlier, namely, that the Japanese were ready to consummate the marriage of East and West.

Lowell's insistence on maintaining the Oriental removal from modernity continued with *Fir-Flower Tablets* (1921), a book of translations from the Chinese done in collaboration with a childhood friend named Florence Ayscough (née Wheelock). Ayscough was born in Shanghai but attended school in Boston, where her mother was born. After her schooling and coming-out, she married and returned to Shanghai, where she served as librarian of the North China section of the Royal Asiatic Society. In November 1917 she visited Lowell at Sevenels and showed her hostess a collection of Chinese poem-paintings.[88] Ayscough planned to lecture on these "Written Pictures" and had done some translations of them but asked her friend to "put them into poetic shape." Lowell "was fascinated by the poems" and "realized that here was a field in which we should like to work."[89] Even though Ayscough had to return to China, the two agreed to a long-distance collaboration, which also involved Ayscough's Chinese teacher, Mr. Nung Chu, who spoke no English but provided scholarly information and details about the semantics of Chinese characters. In her preface, Lowell claims that all the existing translations of Chinese poetry are unsatisfactory, at least to her, and that the method she and Ayscough employed will introduce the reader "to a new and magnificent literature, not through the medium of the usual more or less accurate translation, but directly, as one might burrow it out for one's self with the aid of a dictionary." Lowell's own ignorance of Chinese is not an impediment to this "direct" understanding, given the division of labor involved in the project: "A sinologue has no time to learn how to write poetry; a poet has no time to learn how to read Chinese." Working together, however, the sinologue and the poet, "augmenting" each other's strengths, will produce hitherto unrealized results (*Tablets*, v).

Clearly, one of things Lowell means to do is out-Pound Pound. When she submitted the translations to *Poetry,* she tried to overcome Harriet Monroe's reservations by explaining that no one before her had made so extensive a study of the cadence of Chinese poetry: "Even Ezra has felt and announced his convictions, rather than tabulated, measured, and proved."[90] In "Guns as Keys," the Western preoccupation with precise measurement was presented as something inimical to Asian tradition, so, in a way, Lowell's censure of Pound would seem to ally him more closely with that tradition than with those who would tabulate and measure it.

Since Lowell intended *Fir-Flower Tablets* as the last, best word in Chinese translation, it is instructive to compare her renderings of classic Chinese poetry with those of others, including Pound. Herbert Giles, a former British consul stationed at Ningbo, China, who became professor of Chinese at Cambridge University in 1897, is possibly the most influential of the premodernist translators.[91] Pound and Williams both read Chinese poetry first in Giles's translations, and no doubt one source of Pound's excitement about the Fenollosa materials in late 1913 was his encounter with Giles earlier in the year. That is, the thoroughly Victorian Giles, with his polished, Tennysonian diction, provided the background against which modernist innovation, through Fenollosa, might occur: Giles revealed the need; Fenollosa the means. Here, for example, is Giles's version of Liu Che's poem "record[ing] the loss of a favourite concubine,"[92] from *Chinese Poetry in English Verse* (1898):

> The sound of rustling silk is stilled,
> With dust the marble courtyard filled;
> No footfalls echo on the floor,
> Fallen leaves in heaps block up the door. . . .
> For she, my pride, my lovely one is lost,
>
> (Giles, 18)

In case some reader might miss the point, Giles titled the poem "Gone." Pound retitled it with the name of the poet "Liu Ch'e" (better known as the Han Dynasty Emperor Wu [156–87 BCE]) when his version appeared in *Des Imagistes* (1914):

> The rustling of the silk is discontinued,
> Dust drifts over the court-yard,
> There is no sound of foot-fall, and the leaves
> Scurry into heaps and lie still,
> And she the rejoicer of the heart is beneath them:
>
> A wet leaf that clings to the threshold.[93]

The poem is not a reworking of anything in the Fenollosa materials but a straight adaptation of Giles's earlier version. Pound has turned the piece into an imagist poem by moving Giles's fourth line to the end and changing the number of the leaves from plural to singular (so that the effect is not dissimilar to the last line of his "In a Station of the Metro," written a few years before). That last line condenses the feeling of grief and loss that Giles spreads out over his closing, histrionic couplet. The awful ending aside, one could argue that some of Giles's individual lines are equal and even superior to Pound's (the first line, for instance), and it is telling that Pound has retained most of the key details that suggest, but do not say, what the circumstances of the poem are. The "rustling of the silk" means the subject of the poem is a courtesan; the "marble courtyard" fixes a palace as the scene; the silent "dust" that "fill[s]" the courtyard replaces the sound of the lady's "footfalls"; and the "fallen leaves" announce the state of despair and mourning.[94] All of this suggestive, imagistic material is in the poem before Pound gets to it, but there is no doubt that he has improved upon what he has found.

Pound's improvements result from his insistence on the indirect, suggestive mode throughout. He allows the images to speak on their own without lapsing into direct discourse, as Giles does, and as Arthur Waley also does in a translation contemporary with Pound's and Lowell's. Waley (1889–1966) operated on the fringes of the Bloomsbury group in London before making a name for himself as a sinologue and translator. After Pound's *Cathay* appeared, he translated some of the same poems "to show Pound a few things."[95] His translation of the Liu Che poem, done in 1919, takes the title "Li Fu-Jen," which is the name of the dead courtesan:

> The sound of her silk skirt has stopped.
> On the marble pavement dust grows.
> Her empty room is cold and still.
> Fallen leaves are piled against the doors.
>   Longing for that lovely lady
> How can I bring my aching heart to rest?[96]

The translation makes clear that the two sinologists, Giles and Waley, are intent on conveying the distress of the emperor at the end of the poem, but they are both so lacking in anything like artistic sensitivity that they fall back on clichés, however "accurate" the translations. The same straining after accuracy is evident in the title of the Lowell-Ayscough translation, which also names the author of the poem correctly: "To the Air: 'The Fallen Leaves and the Plaintive Cicada,' by the emperor Wu of Han" (*Tablets*, 139). According to Zhaoming Qian, *Luò yè āi chán qū*, the original title of the poem, literally translates as "Cicada's Elegy for a Fallen Leaf,"[97] which helps to explain the imagery in the poem itself:

> There is no rustle of silken sleeves,
> Dust gathers in the Jade Courtyard.
> The empty houses are cold, still, without sound.
> The leaves fall and lie upon the bars of doorway after doorway.
> I long for the Most Beautiful One; how can I attain my desire?
> Pain bursts my heart. There is no peace.
>
> *(Tablets, 139)*

Elsewhere in the collection, Lowell and Ayscough translate Chinese names into equivalent English epithets, a practice that probably explains "Most Beautiful One" as the English alternative to Li Fu-Jen. Also, the phrase "bars of doorway after doorway" means to render a detail of the original, which is something like "doubled outer door-bar."[98] The Lowell-Ayscough version may be an improvement on Waley's translation but has much in common with it, principally the fact of translation itself. Lowell and Waley were both out to surpass Pound, and the reason they failed to do so is obvious: Pound was not making translations, and they were. In the case of the Liu Che poem, all the sinologists were obligated to translate the last two lines of the poem, whereas Pound was free to devise his own ending, consistent with whatever he felt the tone of the poem to be.

Lowell and Waley, in short, both meant to employ professional sinology to put the amateur Pound in his place. Lowell's was the more uncertain operation, since, as she admitted, she knew no Chinese; moreover, she sought not only to unseat Pound but also to gain the approval of Waley. Hence, *Fir-Flower Tablets* is as much a book of scholarship as it is a book of poetry, or nearly so: the poems occupy about 170 pages, while roughly 140 are given over to maps, a table of Chinese historical periods, and a plan of a "typical Chinese house," in addition to Ayscough's lengthy introduction and copious notes—the sort of material one would expect from a Giles or a Waley. Ayscough's introduction makes a point of singling out Waley's "admirable work" as the only worthwhile "English renderings," the others (which would include Pound's) having "usually failed to convey the flavour of the originals" (*Tablets*, xx). She illustrates the difficulty of conveying this "flavour" by imagining the problems a Chinese translator would have making one of Amy Lowell's poems accessible to a Chinese reader. Her point is a good one: "The great stumbling block which confronts the translator . . . is that the words he would naturally use often bring before the mind of the Occidental reader an entirely different scene to that actually described by the Oriental poet" (xxi).

The problem Ayscough addresses we would now describe as the difficulty of communicating details of acquired culture (language, social mores, and so on) through learned means. In fact, all the scholarly apparatus in *Fir-Flower Tablets* is intended as an Occidental substitute for the Oriental culture that a Chinese person would simply know, without any awareness of having learned it (because she didn't: she acquired it). The purpose of the introduction, then, and the notes as well, is "to give as much background of this Chinese poetry as seems to me important," so that the English reader may apprehend "the [cultural] conditions it portrays" (*Tablets*, xxiii). For example, the first poem from Li T'ai-Po's series "Songs of the Marches" (a seventeen-line poem) is supported by three notes. One explains that "the Fifth Month" refers to June "(See Introduction)" and "the Heaven-high hills" to "the T'ien Shan Mountains, which run across the Northern part of central Asia and in places attain a height of 20,000 feet. (See map.)" A second note explains an allusion to "The Snapped Willow" as "the name of an old song suggesting homesickness." The third identifies "the Barbarians" as "the tribes of Central Asia, known by the generic name of Hsiung Nu," whose persistent invasions inspired the building of the Great Wall (*Tablets*, 175 nn1–3). The notes are much more extensive and detailed than this summary of the first three suggests, and, together with all the cross-referencing to introduction, map, table, and the like, they succeed (if that is the word) in building up the impression of sinological authority. At the same time, the impression is equally strong that, despite the claim of collaboration, the poems and the scholarly apparatus supporting them are oddly disjointed, belonging to two different worlds.

This impression follows from Lowell's evident intent to make the collection authoritative, at the same time putting herself in the position of overruling the authorities she assembled. As Mari Yoshihara points out, Lowell demanded that Ayscough produce "mountains of translations, cribs, ponies, glossaries, etymologies, and commentaries" while maintaining her own hold on all the "decision-making authority."[99] That authority extended over the "native" informant Nung Chu as well. When Nung suggested that his two collaborators include in the collection some poems written by women, Lowell wrote to Ayscough rejecting the suggestion outright and reminding her of the necessity of control: "Be firm with your teacher, hold him strongly between your finger and your thumb, and keep him to classics. Never mind his chivalrous affection for the ladies. The ladies—and I hate to have to say so—are seldom worth bothering with."[100] Lowell's denigration of "the ladies" not only expresses her need to maintain control over her collaborators but also provides a key to the poet's relation to Chinese poetry and to Asian culture generally. As "Guns as Keys" shows, she imagines the

Japanese as having been far better off in the days of the shogunate, before the Meiji regime opened the nation to the West. *Fir-Flower Tablets* likewise conveys a world before modernity, when aesthetic delicacy was presumed to be the order of the day. But the premodern Orient that Lowell explored through her books of poetry also harmonized with her own paradoxical acceptance of the patriarchal society into which she was born.

Given her unorthodox, liberated lifestyle (she had a close—probably lesbian—relationship with a woman, Ada Dwyer, who lived with her at her Sevenels estate in Brookline, Massachusetts, from 1915 on), it comes as something of a surprise that Lowell had no interest in the suffragist and other women's movements of her day.[101] Though supporting female suffrage at an abstract level, she would not lend her celebrity or wealth to the cause. She wrote to the Boston Equal Suffrage Association for Good Government that she found the typical suffragist "childishly silly," incapable of "calm judgment," and guilty of the charge of acting "just like a woman."[102] She thought advocates of birth control "tasteless" and condemned their actions with respect to the "ignorant proletariat." Although admitting that "a sane kind of birth control" might be "often necessary," she believed that "we really need large families more than we need birth control."[103] The Lowell family was nothing if not large, and that same family embodied the traditions of patriarchal New England society as few others could. The social order into which Amy Lowell was born served her purposes very well indeed. Without question, her activities, social and artistic, appeared more daring and individualistic against the background of her patriarchal heritage than they would have within a more contemporary, radical context. Had she joined her New England sisters in their suffrage and birth control movements, she would have been just another New Woman. Instead, she chose to uphold the patriarchal conventions and traditions she inherited and, moreover, reified them in her Oriental poetry.

The point can be made by yet another comparison with Ezra Pound. "The River Merchant's Wife: A Letter" is perhaps the most celebrated of the poems that constitute his *Cathay*. Lowell and Ayscough translated the same poem as "Ch'ang Kan" (the name of the village Pound calls "Chōkan"), and the differences in the two versions show how fully the female collaborators express the patriarchal structure of ancient Chinese society. The opening line of Pound's version reads: "While my hair was still cut straight across my forehead / I played about the front gate, pulling flowers" (*Personæ*, 130). Lowell and Ayscough's poem opens: "When the hair of your Unworthy One first began to cover her forehead / She picked flowers and played in front of the door" (*Tablets*, 28). Clearly, Lowell and Ayscough's decision to translate an epithet in the original as "your Unworthy One" and their use of the third person pronoun *she* where Pound uses *I* emphasize the subordination of women and their dependency on patriarchal institutions. Lowell's version does not employ the first person until the couple marry—"At fourteen, I became the wife of my Lord" (28)—implying that the young woman does not become fully herself until she has a husband. In the same line, Pound likewise employs the epithet "My Lord," but he also uses novel syntax to personalize the relationship—"At fourteen I married My Lord you"—and next characterizes the fourteen-year-old bride's behavior around her new husband as simple shyness: "I never laughed, being bashful. / Lowering my head, I looked at the wall" (*Personæ*, 130). The reaction of the young bride in Lowell's account is freighted with culture-specific meaning that Pound's version ignores: "I could not yet lay aside my face of shame. / I hung my head, facing the dark wall" (*Tablets*, 28). Ayscough glosses these lines with a note that makes the cultural meaning clear: "In China, little girls are supposed to hide their faces at the suggestion of marriage" (*Tablets*, 189–90 n43). Near the end of the poem, the yellow butterflies of autumn signal the pain of separation that increases with the passage of time. In Pound, the wife's sorrowful reaction to the butterflies is simple and succinct: "They hurt me. I grow older" (*Personæ*, 131). Lowell and Ayscough use the image not only to express grief but also to remind the reader of the patriarchal position the woman occupies by reprising the opening epithet: "Seeing them, my heart is bitter with grief, they wound the heart of the Unworthy One" (*Personæ*, 29). In short, Pound's "The River Merchant's Wife: A Letter" expresses the growth and deepening of a love relationship over many years; Lowell and Ayscough's "Chang K'an" also gives expression to that basic theme but does so within a cultural context that insists on an extreme subordination of women to the patriarchal order.

Lowell's orientalism, then, functions in the service of institutions and traditions with which she had considerable experience on her native New England ground. It is not too much to say that many of her Oriental poems fantasize as foreign the social structures with which she was thoroughly familiar. The best example of this broad category of poetry is her aptly titled "Free Fantasia on Japanese Themes," from *Pictures of the Floating World*. That poem begins with the author fantasizing at her writing desk, "Avid of adventure," longing to "experience new emotions— / Submit to strange enchantments" and "to influences, / Bizarre, exotic" (*Pictures*, 105–6). An Oriental fantasy follows, or rather a series of fantasies: "I would climb a sacred mountain"; "I would recline upon a balcony"; "I would sit in a covered boat," and so on (106–7). The balcony fantasy merits emphasis because here the poet imagines herself in a classic feminine role, as a geisha subordinate to her samurai lord:

I would recline upon a balcony
In purple curving folds of silk,
And my dress should be silvered with a pattern
Of butterflies and swallows,
And the black band of my *obi*
Should flash with gold, circular threads,
And glitter when I moved.
I would lean against a railing
While you sang to me of wars—
Past, and to come—
Sang and played the *samisen.*
Perhaps I would beat a little hand drum
In time to your singing;
Perhaps I would only watch the play of light
On the hilts of your two swords.

There is something poignant, and perhaps a bit amusing, in the idea of the stocky, mannish Lowell (whose weight resulted from a glandular disorder) imagining herself as a dainty geisha. In fact, the end of the poem suggests a deep sense of dissatisfaction in the life that she chose for herself as an independent woman of letters:

I would anything
Rather than this cold paper,
With, outside, the quiet sun on the sides of burgeoning branches,
    And inside, only my books.

(*Pictures,* 106–8)

The ending includes an irony—the fantasy would not have been possible without the "cold paper" and the books that brought it into being—but it also expresses a real desire to belong to a society where women are secure and content in their subordinate, domestic roles, while the men maintain the order of things in the larger world. Such a society was precisely the one into which she was born but could not fully participate in, as a woman, except by means of an Oriental fantasy of a floating world at once aesthetic and aristocratic.

The Orient affirmed, for Lowell, the social structures of her native New England. She used Japan the way Pound used China and Eliot, India. But where Pound employed Confucius to validate authoritarian politics and Eliot turned to Buddha and Krishna to enliven Christian tradition, Lowell found in the floating world of *ukioy-e,* haiku, and other Japanese aesthetic forms a way to resist the threat that modernity posed to the patriarchal, aristocratic assumptions of her social class. In the end, she probably had more in common with her adversary Pound than with the onetime, would-be Bostonian Eliot. After all, Pound's interest in Japanese Nō drama hinged on its aristocratic appeal: "These plays," he says in his introduction to *"Noh," or Accomplishment,* "were made only for the few; for the noble; for those trained to catch the allusion."[104] But for Pound and Lowell the cultivation of a literary elite was the least of it: both of them responded favorably to Mussolini's March on Rome in October 1922—Pound because he thought that, eventually, Mussolini would make the world safer for intellectual aristocrats like himself; Lowell because she hoped the kind of politics Mussolini practiced would lessen the chances of the world's becoming more dangerous for the social aristocracy to which she belonged.[105]

Pound and Lowell also point, paradoxically, to the most considerable development in the history of American involvement in Asian thought: the transformation of that thought through the medium of mass culture. Neither had any direct role in this transformation, but both anticipated it by urging mass acceptance of their orientalist enthusiasms, Pound through his polemical writings and Lowell through her public lectures. Ironically, Pound's wish that Confucianism might be experienced by the masses has, in a way, come about, though not through the medium he imagined: namely, the mass politics of the 1930s. During that period, the eventual triumph of individualist over collectivist ideology could hardly have been foreseen, nor could the eventual displacement of modernism by mass culture have been predicted. But both have come to pass: capitalism is triumphant, both ideologically and culturally. The mixture of political, social, and aesthetic formulations that Lowell employed in the 1910s and 1920s and that Pound explored in the 1930s cannot be used to characterize the American Orient in the decades since, nor can T. S. Eliot's combination of scholarly and theological approaches. Times have changed, and the meaning of the American Orient has changed with them. But it is also true that the exploitation of the Far East in mass culture after World War II had considerable precedent in the nineteenth century. Indeed, the cultural elevation of the Far East by the modernists Pound, Eliot, and Lowell was at least partly a response to the popularization of Asiatic traditions through mass-culture media in the nineteenth century, as shown by Eliot's reaction to Sir Edwin Arnold's *The Light of Asia,* Pound's exposure to Oriental exhibits in popular museums, and Amy Lowell's *ukiyo-e* print-collecting. But regardless of their conflicted and complicated relation to prior expressions of the Far East in American culture, the modernists employed the Orient to fix that culture securely within the political, religious, and social traditions of the West.

5

The Twentieth Century II

From Modernism to Mass Culture

ONE OF THE paradoxes of American literary modernism which orientalism helps to illuminate is the conflicted attitude that modernists have about modernity. Conservative political values, even reactionary political values, can coexist with the most advanced forms of aesthetic innovations. The expression of the American Orient in popular culture is likewise beset with paradoxes, but the conflict of advanced aesthetics and reactionary ideology is not among them. At the same time, the medium of popular culture is no guarantee of democratic values or of social progress. But since popular culture by definition involves media and institutions that, for commercial reasons, are designed to appeal to as wide an audience as possible, the congruence of cultural accessibility and democratic ideals often yields results that are hardly as antimodern as the work of American high modernists like Eliot and Pound. One has only to contrast Eliot's political conversion to royalism with Rabindranath Tagore's enlightened internationalism, promoted on his first American lecture tour (1916–1917) to overflow audiences. Or contrast Pound's conception of China with Pearl S. Buck's: the modernist poet's orientalism is fraught with reactionary ideology that one would be hard put to locate in *The Good Earth*. Since all these figures are contemporary with one another, the conclusion that orientalism has one meaning for the modernists and another for the masses is inevitable.

No doubt future historians will one day designate the limits of the "long twentieth century" and specify the decade in the nineteenth century that marks its origin, as well as the decade or even the day (4 November 2008?) that marks its terminus in the twenty-first. But what is already clear is that the proliferation of popular culture in the twentieth century had partial origins in the nineteenth. Even as Emerson and the transcendentalists were contemplating the Orient, the great impresario P. T. Barnum was planning the most profitable means of exhibiting it. The American success of Edwin Arnold's *The Light of Asia* (1879) was not only concurrent with the emerging study of Buddhism in the United States but may have actually spurred it on. The question of what is scholarly and what is popular is especially fraught with the American section of the Theosophical Society, whose ambitions to become a mass movement were bound up with the analysis of extremely complicated, esoteric ideas couched in erudite "Oriental" language. Theosophy also had something in common with modernism, and it lies in the background of one strain of modernist thought that emerged around the second decade of the twentieth century—a kind of middle-brow modernism that tried to popularize the avant-garde by collapsing distinctions between art and life. On more than one occasion, some Wise Man from the East was enlisted to proselytize for the progressive, yet spiritual, lifestyle.

The notion is consistent with earlier claims that scientific progress finds a complement in Eastern religion, as maintained by many of the Asian delegates to the World's Parliament of Religions in 1893, an event with some truly far-reaching effects on popular manifestations of the American Orient. The transition from modernism to mass culture in the twentieth century cannot be considered without a glance backward at certain nineteenth-century developments in popular culture, such as P. T. Barnum's "Ethnological Congress" and Arnold's *The Light of Asia,* as well as the more serious, well-meaning explorations of Eastern thought exemplified by the Theosophical Society and the Parliament of Religions. No discussion of this aspect of the American Orient can be complete, however, without an examination of the two most powerful forms of popular culture that emerged as the twentieth century progressed: the commercial novel and the commercial film. Happily, Pearl S. Buck's *The Good Earth* (1931) illustrates both: the best-selling novel and the Hollywood version of it can be considered together to illuminate what are possibly the most far-reaching manifestations of the American Orient in mass culture.

I

The starting points for any discussion of mass awareness of the Orient in American life have to be P. T. Barnum, the man who practically invented popular culture, and Edwin Arnold, whose *Light of Asia* cast the life of the Buddha in a poetic form that made the esoteric accessible to Victorian audiences. At first glance, these two practitioners of the popular would seem to be utterly different from each other, and certainly the forms in which they worked are radically different. But Barnum and Arnold are alike insofar as they both sought to appeal to a genteel, Victorian audience by manufacturing moral values for material otherwise considered ethically and ethnically suspect. Barnum's task was probably the more difficult of the two, since public entertainment in the nineteenth century was almost universally viewed as morally suspect and socially vulgar. But Arnold too was in a difficult position: how could the life of an Oriental pagan be made to appeal to the Christian reader? His two-pronged solution emphasized the parallels between the Bible story of Jesus and the legend of Gautama, while also suppressing or altering certain doctrines, such as nirvana, which led some to allege that Buddhism was nothing more than Asiatic atheism. For his part Barnum cast the most extravagant entertainments in the guise of history or science to educate and elevate members of all classes. In both cases, making the genteel Christian feel comfortable was key. That both Barnum and Arnold experienced their greatest Oriental successes in America during the decade that saw the first of several federally mandated restrictions on Asian immigration is another thing these extremely disparate figures have in common. The perfect occasion for the manufacture of Oriental fantasies was the moment when American anxieties over actual Asians was especially intense.

    P. T. Barnum had tried for some time to transform the alleged exoticism of the Orient into commercial spectacle with mass appeal. The great showman exploited Western fantasies of the East as early as the 1840s by exhibiting Bedouin tribesmen in his American Museum in New York City. In 1850 he added "the celebrated Chinese Collection" to the museum and exhibited "the 'Chinese family,' consisting of two men, two 'small-footed' women, and two children."[1] This family was evidently not one of Barnum's early hoaxes (like the famous "Fejee Mermaid") but a real group of Chinese people, since the impresario had to engage an interpreter to make sure they would "behave themselves" when he sent them on tour.[2] In 1851 Barnum recruited a Singhalese "chief" to accompany a herd of elephants in his Asiatic Caravan, Museum, and Menagerie.[3] But these were mere token efforts on the way to Barnum's larger ambition of putting together an exhibition featuring "specimens" of "every accessible people, civilized and barbarous, on the face of the globe."[4] The design was finally realized in two distinct forms that treated the civilized and the barbarous separately: the "Congress of Nations," a pageant that opened the Great Roman Hippodrome of 1874–1875, and the "Ethnological Congress," an exhibition that was part of the Barnum & London Circus of 1884. The first congress featured the "ANCIENT AND MODERN MONARCHS" of the "CIVILIZED NATIONS"; the second displayed "100 UNCIVILIZED, SUPERSTITIOUS AND SAVAGE PEOPLE." More important, the "civilized" congress relied on white performers dressed in exotic costumes to depict Oriental potentates such as Tippoo Sahib and Muhammad Ali, whereas the "uncivilized" one employed actual representatives of Asian races and cultures, "specimens" from around the globe.[5] The first congress pretended to be historical, whereas the second aspired to scientific status, as the use of the fairly new word *ethnological* implies: "The ethnologist finds gathered together for his leisurely inspection representatives of notable and peculiar tribes, . . . types which otherwise he would never see, as they can only be sought in their native countries."[6] The exhibition included Burmese priests, "High Caste Hindoos," and "short-headed, broad-skulled, . . . flat-faced" Buddhists. The racialist language is important to the depiction of the Orientals as "savage" and "barbarian," useful rhetoric in Barnum's campaign to court the Christian patron, whose moral objections to public amusements had to be overcome if the show were to succeed.[7]

    The Christian spectator of the Oriental spectacle, then, was put in a position of both moral and racial superiority when Barnum presented his Ethnological Congress. This formula seems to have come into focus as America's attitude toward its immigrant populations began to shift in the 1880s. The Chinese Exclusion Act of 1882, which curtailed Chinese immigration, was one indication of how threatening the Asian population had become to the American way of life. Barnum's presentation of that population in his Ethnological Congress seems, at first, to have been somewhat compromised by the star of the show, the famous Chinese giant Chang Yu Sing. Barnum persuaded Chang to leave a London show for New York by offering him the exorbitant salary of $500 a month. He arrived in December 1880, more than a year before the Exclusion Act went into effect, and, at a height close to eight feet, was soon being billed as the "Chinese Mastodon." The animal epithet notwithstanding, Chang impressed New Yorkers as "the urbane Chinese giant," according to one newspaper account, and as a man of culture, smoking cigars and playing chess.[8] In 1881, one of Barnum's ads described him as "the Chinese Giant, not the ogre of Fairy Tales, but a Gentleman, Scholar, and Linguist—the tallest man in the world."[9] Clearly, Chang was presented differently from most of the Oriental "specimens," not because he was civilized but because he *had been* civilized or, better, colonized. After all, when he was exhibited, he wore the two-and-a-half pound pocket watch with the nine-foot chain that had been given to him by Queen Victoria.[10] The more sinister species of "Chinaman" was represented by Che Mah Che Sang, less than three feet tall but still a Yellow Peril all by himself. Che Mah was reputed to be a clever rebel with so much power over his fellow Chinese that the emperor had to organize an army against him and drive him into Siberia. In reality he was a Jewish dwarf from London.[11]

Barnum's mixture of sensationalism and moralism meant that spectators of his versions of the American Orient could feel not only entertained but improved, simultaneously diverted from the reality of their lives and assured of the superiority of their own cultural values. A similar mixture likely lies behind the enormous popularity of Edwin Arnold's *The Light of Asia,* a versified biography of the Buddha published in 1879 which had gone through more than eighty American editions by the end of the century. The work is said to have done "more than any other single book to popularize Buddhism in the West." It may have sold as many as a million copies in the United States, making it the equal in popularity of such American best sellers as Frances Hodgson Burnett's *Little Lord Fauntleroy,* Helen Hunt Jackson's *Ramona,* and possibly even Mark Twain's *Huckleberry Finn.*[12] In 1884 the showman Adam Forepaugh, one of Barnum's competitors, capitalized on the popularity of Arnold's epic by exhibiting a "sacred" white elephant (covered with a coat of plaster, actually) named the "Light of Asia." The same year a New Jersey entrepreneur used the name for a giant wooden elephant with a tin skin that he built on the Cape May boardwalk to house shops and concessions.[13] These examples aside, in most cases the American public's response to *The Light of Asia* was a good deal more complicated than its reactions to Barnum's Oriental spectacles. On the one hand, the Christian reader was bound to be enthralled by the exotic narrative of the Buddha's elevated teachings and could feel good about herself for reading it; on the other hand, the book might well raise doubts about the assumed superiority of Christian values. The many parallels between

the life of Jesus and the life of Buddha that Arnold so obviously incorporated suggested that Christianity was hardly unique; moreover, the spiritual and moral values of Buddhism may actually have anticipated those
of Christianity. Was Buddha simply a precursor of Jesus, or was Jesus an
actual follower of Buddha?

Arnold's poem took the question of historical influence out of the academy and into the parlor. In a review of *The Light of Asia* in the *International
Review*, Oliver Wendell Holmes teased his readers by asking the identity of
someone whose birth had been heralded by angels, whose youthful wisdom
surpassed that of his elders, and whose doctrines of peace and love were so
powerful that they attracted numerous disciples. Would not anyone "say at
once that this must be another version of the story of the One who came
upon our earth in a Syrian village, during the reign of Augustus Caesar,
and died during the reign of Tiberius?" Then, after Holmes had revealed
that the answer was not the obvious one, he praised the tone of Arnold's
poem as "so lofty that there is nothing with which to compare it but the
New Testament." [14] Similarly, W. C. Brownell, writing in *The Nation*, called
the poem "the gospel of Buddha in verse according to Edwin Arnold,"
and wondered whether it "would have ever been written if Mr. Arnold . . .
had never read the New Testament." [15] To be sure, the appeal of the poem
was not exclusively religious: the *Boston Evening Transcript* commented
on "the marvelous richness of its imagery . . . and purity of diction" that
complemented its "profundity of thought." The *New York Evening Post*
also pointed to the double appeal of *The Light of Asia*: "It is as a poem
first, and afterward as a fine ethical study, that the work demands attention,
and in both of these characters it is a work of an unusually high order." [16]

Arnold's high ethical purpose is clear from his preface, where he observes
that the personality of the Buddha "cannot but appear the highest, gen-
tlest, holiest, and most beneficent, with one exception, in the history of
Thought." [17] That comment, making Buddha second to the exceptional
Christ, was likely necessitated by the presentation in the poem itself, which
begins by telling readers that what they are about to read is "The Scripture of the Saviour of the World" (Arnold, 1). Thereafter, the analogues to
the New Testament come thick and fast: Siddârta's mother Queen Maya
experiences something akin to the Virgin Birth, dreaming "that a star from
heaven . . . / Shot through the void; and, shining into her, / Entered her
womb upon the right" (2). Later, young Siddârta resolves to "teach compassion unto men" (12) and begins to prepare himself for this task by
sitting beneath "the jambu-tree" and meditating on "this deep disease of
life" (14). The gospel analogy is complete when angelic figures observe the

future Buddha beneath the jambu-tree and take "good news to the Gods" (15). Biblical language is also sounded when King Suddhôdana, Siddârta's father, predicts that his son will be "a King of kings" (17), even though his meaning is secular, not spiritual.

The gospel echoes are less pronounced in the second book of the poem, when the father seeks to distract his son from spiritual inclinations by encouraging courtship. The king sets the boy up as judge of a beauty contest, and, sure enough, Siddârta falls in love with Yasôdhara, not so much because she is beautiful as because the two have known each other in a prior life (20). After their marriage, and after Yasôdhara has a prophetic dream, Siddârta wonders what would happen if someone such as himself "Gave all, laying it down for love of men, / And thenceforth spent himself to search for truth." He concludes that millions will be "Saved by this sacrifice I offer now" (64), as Arnold resumes the New Testament analogy.

The analogy is probably strongest in the sixth book, in which Siddârta sits beneath the Bohdi-tree and experiences something very like Christ's temptation in the wilderness. A series of "fiends who war with Wisdom and the Light," led by "the Prince of Darkness, Mara," struggle mightily "to keep the Truth from Buddh" (Arnold, 103). Among the more intriguing tempters is the sorceress Sîlabbat-paramâsa, a personification of institutionalized religion, "who gives dark creeds their power." She appears as "lowly Faith, / But ever juggling souls with rites and prayers; / The keeper of those keys which lock up Hells / And open Heavens." She asks the Buddha if he will "dare . . . / Put by our sacred books, dethrone our gods, / Unpeople all the temples, shaking down / That law which feeds the priests and props the realms?" The Buddha answers: "What thou bidd'st me keep / Is form which passes, but the free Truth stands; / Get thee unto thy darkness" (105). The exchange suggests a Buddha who is a kind of sublime Protestant, as does Arnold's identification of the subject of his poem as "that noble hero and reformer" (vii). Indeed, the implicit comparison of Buddhism and Protestantism that Arnold makes in the poem prompted widespread discussion among numerous denominations in nineteenth-century America. Two of the most extreme examples of Protestant reaction are the book-length repudiations of *The Light of Asia* by Samuel Henry Kellogg (1839–1899), a Presbyterian clergyman from Allegheny, Pennsylvania, and William Cleaver Wilkinson (1833–1920), a Baptist preacher who spent most of his life in and around Rochester, New York.[18]

Of the two, Kellogg's is the more reasoned and authoritative book. His title alone conveys the secondary nature of Buddha in relation to Jesus— *The Light of Asia and the Light of the World* (1885)—but Kellogg goes to some pains to make his critique professional and scholarly. He offers an impressive list of sources at the outset to support the claim that "the present work is based upon a study of . . . Buddhist authorities": "the *Pàtimokka,* translated by professor Oldenberg and T. W. Rhys Davids . . . ; the *Mahàvagga,* translated by the same, . . . the *Cullavagga,*" and many more works from the Buddhist canon translated from Pali or Sanskrit, most in Max Müller's *Sacred Books of the East* series.[19] Armed thus with orientalist authority, Kellogg proceeds with his systematic comparison of the two religions, as these chapter titles show: "The Legend of the Buddha and the Story of Christ"; "The Doctrine of the Buddha and the Doctrine of Christ"; "Buddhist Ethics and the Ethics of the Gospel." Where Arnold and many of his contemporaries saw analogies between Buddha and Jesus, Kellogg mostly sees contrasts: "Christ was born in poverty; the Buddha in riches, in the palace of a king. The Buddha is represented, even in the legend, as born *in* marriage; the Christ as born supernaturally of a pure virgin, *before* marriage. The Buddha is represented as having himself been in need of salvation, and for a long time ignorant how to gain it; the Christ, never" (63). Kellogg concludes his book by observing that Christianity can pass the test of historical investigation, whereas Buddhism cannot: "It appeals to no historical facts in any of its stupendous assertions" (370).

By contrast, the Baptist churchman Wilkinson saw no need to appeal to history or scholarship as Kellogg did, since for him, Buddhism was quite simply the work of the devil; Arnold, therefore, had done the devil's work, and anyone who admired *The Light of Asia* did so "unwisely."[20] Wilkinson does allow that Buddhism has its appeal, but as a man of God he is all too familiar with the source of that appeal: "I can only judge the devil by what is taught of him in the Bible. There . . . he is represented to be a compound of malicious cunning and malicious power. I am quite clear that if I myself were such a being as this, I should go about my object of defeating Jesus in His attempt to save the world, very much as the devil has in fact gone about that object, if we are at liberty to suppose that the devil has been largely the author of Buddhism" (97). This assessment comes after Wilkinson's attack on the literary value of *The Light of Asia,* so it is not surprising to hear the minister conclude that "whether as literature . . . or as an exposition of Buddhist doctrine and life, the 'Light of Asia' must be pronounced unworthy to survive" (177).

The last two books of Arnold's poem make a number of moral arguments that help to show why Kellogg and Wilkinson felt compelled to speak out against the story of the "Indian Messiah," as Oliver Wendell Holmes termed it.[21] In book 7 the Buddha delivers a moral message that might seem a bit too secular for some Christians:

. . . he taught the Five [Rules]
Showing how birth and death should be destroyed,
And how man hath no fate except past deeds,
No Hell but what he makes, no Heaven too high
For those to reach whose passion sleep subdued.

(Arnold, 123)

The doctrine of karma expressed here is obviously at odds with the Cal-vinist doctrine of election as taught by Congregationalists and Presbyte-rians. At the same time, the relegation of heaven and hell to the realm of human responsibility suggests the allegorical readings that Unitarians gave to Christ's message or, for that matter, the words of Jesus Himself, who did allege that "the kingdom of God is within you" (Luke 17:21).

In the last of the eight books Arnold abandons the blank verse form and casts the language of Buddha in rhyming quatrains that continue to assert the sentiments of an extremely liberal theology:

Pray not! the darkness will not brighten! Ask
    Naught from the Silence, for it cannot speak!
Vex not your mournful minds with pious pains!
    Ah! Brothers, Sisters! seek

Naught from the helpless gods by gift and hymn,
    Nor bribe with blood, nor feed with fruits and cakes;
Within yourselves deliverance must be sought;
    Each man his prison makes.

(Arnold, 139)

Later in the Buddha's sermon the Five Rules are explained in couplets that nonetheless manage to echo the language of the Ten Commandments in the King James version: "Bear not false witness, slander not, nor lie; / Truth is the speech of inward purity." This admonition is followed by a couplet worthy of the Temperance League: "Shun drugs and drinks which work the wit abuse; / Clear minds, clean bodies need no Soma juice" (Arnold, 155). The larger point here is that the teachings of the Buddha in Arnold's telling range over such a wide field of Victorian morality that the liberal Christian reader could feel elevated by the sentiments they express. And that same reader could also feel informed by the presentation of exotic beliefs, such as karma and nirvana, outside the Christian system.

The widespread acceptance of Arnold's poem by the liberal Christian reader may have been prepared, in part, by Charles D. B. Mills's *The Indian Saint,* published in 1876, only three years before the appearance of *The Light of Asia.* Mills (1821–1900) was a Unitarian Universalist minister from Syracuse, New York, and a student of Arabic and other Oriental languages.

He was also a freethinker of some importance who was extremely active in the abolitionist, suffragist, and temperance movements. Susan B. Anthony spoke at his funeral, and Elizabeth Cady Stanton wrote his obituary for the *Free Thought Magazine*. In it, she mentions his authorship of *Buddha and Buddhism* (as *The Indian Saint* is subtitled) and adds that Mills "was a great lover of Emerson and had a keen sympathy with Oriental thought and literature."[22] Stanton is accurate in her assessment of Mills as a Buddhist sympathizer, since *The Indian Saint* understands Buddhism as one of the more important faiths in the universal "church of Humanity" that is in the process of unfolding as proof of "the divine in history."[23] The sympathetic treatment of Buddhism is also quite systematic, grounded in the work of such notable scholars as Eugène Burnouf and Max Müller. Using these authorities and many others, the book provides a thorough overview of the Buddha's life and influence, as well as a generous sampling of "Sentences from Scripture" (chapter 4), meaning the Buddhist canon, and an exploration of "The Doctrine" (chapter 5). In the latter chapter Mills addresses, for example, the common criticism that the Buddha preached atheism, and refutes the charge thus: the Buddha perhaps "forebore . . . from making any impersonation of God," but he remained "a deep, emphatic believer" in "Truth or the Law" (133). Mills concludes with a chapter titled "The Fine Problem," which describes a Buddha who grappled with the same difficulty that confronted freethinkers in the last quarter of the nineteenth century: namely, "the one problem of human life," which is how to "correlat[e] time with the eternal, [o]uter and inner, corporeal and ethereal" (163, 164). Hence, this first book on Buddhism written by an American presents not only a sympathetic portrait of the Buddha but also a Buddha who is himself sympathetic to the concerns of the progressive Christian, since both have to come to terms with the same existential problems.

An ambiguous, all-purpose theology, alternately familiar and exotic, is certainly one of the things that Mills's *The Indian Saint* and Arnold's *The Light of Asia* have in common. Another is the promotion of cultural values consistent with those that arose in the United States in the aftermath of the Civil War. Granted, these values are closely intertwined with the theology, but there is nonetheless something strongly democratic in the Buddha's message, as in these lines from *The Light of Asia* denouncing systems of caste and class:

> Pity and need
> Make all flesh kind. There is no caste in blood,
> Which runneth of one hue, nor caste in tears,
> Which trickle salt with all.
>
> (Arnold, 94)

Such lines harmonize with the renewed sense of union that emerged out of the shared suffering of the war. More important, disenchantment with the martial ideals of the war years led many Americans to cultivate a more genteel, spiritual identity.[24] And this general pattern is recapitulated in *The Light of Asia*. The early books of the poem show a Siddârta who is a rather heroic figure, on track to become a great warrior and king, which is what his father wants him to be. A memorable moment comes when Siddârta, recalling the actions of Odysseus near the end of Homer's epic, strings a great bow that the other suitors for Yasôdhara's hand cannot manage, twanging the cord as Odysseus does (Arnold, 23). But Siddârta renounces heroism for the spiritual life, which is initially a cause of great disappointment to his father. Indeed, the father's initial outrage when his prodigal son returns as an impoverished holy man suggests a conflict between the "achievement ethos" and the reaction to that ethos on the part of young men who chose to pursue spiritual or aesthetic lives.[25] Arnold's Buddha is not William Sturgis Bigelow or Henry Adams exactly, but a late nineteenth-century American weary of manly accomplishment could certainly see a family resemblance. The spiritualizing of the heroic ethos that Arnold captures in *The Light of Asia* was something that the first reviewers of the poem noticed. One called it "'an Idyll of the King' with Gautama instead of Arthur for its hero, and Nirvâna instead of the Christian ideal and the Holy Graal as his aim."[26]

Arnold's poem performed yet another function in late nineteenth-century America. Because of the parallel lives of Jesus and Buddha, and because Arnold makes Siddârta such a heroic, sympathetic figure, the Christian reader might reasonably question Arnold's depiction of the religious leader and desire more authentic, scholarly information—either to assuage doubts about Christianity or to confirm them (depending on the reader). In other words, *The Light of Asia* might be read in such a way as to spur curiosity about Buddhism. Such a reading informs an 1884 review of Max Müller's *Sacred Books of the East,* in which the writer commends Müller's scholarly series for providing the facts to counter Arnold's probable misrepresentation: "Recent writings, especially those of Edwin Arnold, have invested Buddha with a species of interest which should make readers desirous of studying him and his teachings more at first hand. The life of Buddha included in the collection we are describing is of value in that respect." First-hand study is necessary because of the misleading comparisons of Christ and Buddha that the poem encourages: "The conception of [Buddha] in such poems as 'The Light of Asia,' and in the writings of those who would gladly disparage Christianity by comparing it with Buddhism, should be tested by the actual facts of his career. . . . How little of title Buddha can have to be compared to Jesus, or his religion with Christianity, will then appear."[27] The reviewer does not seem to know that Arnold himself maintained a scholarly, even scientific, attitude toward Buddhism not wholly belied by his popularization of it. Arnold was in the vanguard of those liberal scholars and theologians at the end of the century who argued that Buddhism, unlike Christianity, could be reconciled with Darwin's theory of evolution. As Arnold put it, "Between Buddhism and modern science there exists a close intellectual bond."[28]

The Light of Asia therefore took hold in America during the last quarter of the nineteenth century for more than one reason. Because of the parallels between the Buddha and Jesus, the poem appealed to the genteel Christian reader. Those same parallels, however, ignited controversies in two groups: conservative Christians who challenged Arnold's account for theological reasons, and skeptical intellectuals who questioned it for scholarly reasons. But regardless of whether Arnold's representation of the Buddha was theologically or historically correct, it harmonized with a broader longing in American life for spiritual alternatives to material success or heroic achievement. It was therefore the forerunner of two other important popularizations of Buddhism, neither of which would likely have enjoyed the success they achieved without Arnold's example: Henry Steel Olcott's *Buddhist Catechism* (1881) and Paul Carus's *The Gospel of Buddha* (1894). Olcott's *Catechism* went through forty editions before he died in 1907; Carus's *Gospel* is still in print, with millions of copies sold.[29] Carus was a rationalist who followed Arnold in his understanding of Buddhism as a theology compatible with modern science, whereas Olcott was a mystic who did not follow Arnold at all, except as a popularizer of Eastern culture. Olcott and his eccentric accomplice Helena Petrovna Blavatsky follow Emerson, if anyone, in attempting to syncretize esoteric systems and Asiatic beliefs. The product of their joint efforts to meld the Orient with the occult they called theosophy, a movement that probably has more in common with P. T. Barnum's sense of showmanship than with Edwin Arnold's gift of making the exotic accessible.

II

The origins of theosophy lie in the strange confluence of spiritualism and science in the mid-nineteenth century. From 1848 on, when the famous Fox sisters (Margaret, Leah, and Catharine) of Hydesville, New York, near Rochester, started communicating with the spirit world by means of mysterious raps and knocks, the hitherto immaterial world of the beyond seemingly began to be revealed through physical phenomena. Naturally, these phenomena had to be investigated in a systematic fashion, using scientific methods: such was the mandate, for example, of the Society for Psychical Research, founded in London in 1882. The Theosophical Society also had a scientific mandate to complement its religious mission, as Henry Steel Olcott (1832–1907) explained in 1875 when he gave his inaugural address as president of the society: "To the Protestant and Catholic sectaries we have to show the origin of many of their most sacred idols and most cherished dogmas; to the liberal minds in science, the profound scientific attainments of the ancient magi."

Olcott's partner in executing this dual mission was the celebrated medium Helena Petrovna Blavatsky, who in 1877 published the first of the two foundational texts of the theosophical movement, *Isis Unveiled;* the second was *The Secret Doctrine,* published in 1888. These massive tomes were said to comprise the ancient wisdom communicated to Blavatsky by Mahatmas or Masters occupying a spiritual plane but originating in the Orient of India and Tibet. *The Secret Doctrine* is by far the more "Oriental" of the two books, since *Isis Unveiled* draws mainly on an occult, hermetic tradition that had been circulating in the West for centuries; indeed, the title of the work suggests the Egyptian obscurities claimed by the Masonic Brotherhood in the eighteenth century. The Eastern emphasis of *The Secret Doctrine* is largely due to the relocation of Olcott and Blavatsky in 1878 to India, where they set up their theosophical shop in Adyar, in Madras. Also, the Oriental flavor of Blavatsky's second opus may have been partly necessitated by the scandal of 1884, when her housekeeper revealed the fraudulent basis of phenomena Blavatsky had presented to paying audiences as proof of the Masters' existence. An investigator from the Society for Psychical Research rendered the final scientific judgment on Madame Blavatsky: that she would be forever remembered "as one of the most accomplished, ingenious, and interesting impostors of history."[30]

The revelations of Blavatsky's impostures understandably weakened her support in Great Britain and America, but not in India. Because the attacks on her credibility came from the British and from Christian missionaries, Blavatsky and theosophy came to be identified more strongly with Hindu and Buddhist culture, despite the fact that Asian faiths were deemed inferior to and derivative of theosophy.[31] As W. Michael Ashcraft puts it, "Many argue that Blavatsky used Hindu and Buddhist concepts to articulate Theosophy. Theosophists, of course, argue the reverse: that Hindus and Buddhists inherited the wisdom of Theosophy millennia ago." Despite the elements in theosophy evidently derived from Blavatsky's reading of the Vedas and the Upanishads—"universal but impersonal oneness, a divine spark in each human being, measuring time in cycles rather than linearly, and the justification of ethical behavior based on karma and reincarnation"—the core of her teaching remains occult or hermetic. Although she and Olcott began calling themselves Buddhists in 1880, that maneuver amounted to little more than an incident in the larger project whereby Blavatsky, especially, "orientalized Western esotericism."[32] Ironically, while the "Theosophical Twins" Blavatsky and Olcott were busy exploiting the actual Orient in the name of the occult, members of the American branch of the Theosophical Society were pursuing Eastern ideas with greater respect for the texts and traditions that had produced them. Whereas Olcott "theosophized" Buddhist doctrine by writing his *Buddhist Catechism* (1881), the head of the American section, William Q. Judge, took a more scholarly approach: in practically every issue of *The Path,* the theosophical journal he edited out of New York City, Judge included long essays explaining Eastern beliefs, reviews of recent translations of Eastern texts, and the like. Where Olcott and Blavatsky used theosophy to legitimate Asian traditions, Judge found parallels in those traditions to legitimate theosophy.

This distinction becomes obvious when Blavatsky's *Secret Doctrine* is compared to the treatment of Oriental knowledge in Judge's *The Path.* Early on, Blavatsky claims that the "teachings" in the *Secret Doctrine* "antedate the Vedas," adding in a note that the statement is "based on the knowledge of facts. Every century an attempt is being made to show the world that Occultism is no vain superstition."[33] The subordination of Vedic to theosophical knowledge could not be clearer. Likewise, Blavatsky maintains a distinction between "*orthodox* Buddhism" and "*esoteric* Budhism [*sic*]," the latter spelling based on "the Sanskrit root 'Budh,' *to know.*" The distinction is important because the Buddha is supposed to have taught "a philosophy built upon the ground-work of the true esoteric knowledge," having given "to the world only its *outward* material body and kept its *soul* for his Elect" (*SD*, xxvii, xxv, xxvii). In other words, all that the Buddha taught and all that developed out of his teachings—Buddhism, in short—is inferior to the esoteric knowledge of "Budhism" that theosophy has discovered. Even though "the profane Orientalist" may know something about orthodox Buddhism or orthodox Hinduism, that knowledge is as nothing beside "the book of Dzyan (or 'Dzan')," which "is utterly unknown to our philologists," even though it "is found scattered throughout hundreds and thousands of Sanskrit MSS" (*SD*, xxvii–xxviii).

The Path also presented Buddhism under two aspects, but unlike Blavatsky, the author of the essay "The Nature and Office of Buddha's Religion" had a more understanding attitude toward the relationship of orthodox teachings and esoteric meanings: "A religion, as such, must for the most part propound what is not generally seen and felt in the nature of sentient beings. It must also proclaim the 'ways and means' by which the good of the world is attained. These *teachings* are essential to a religion or it would, at best, become only a system of philosophy or a science of nature. We find these two essentials fully treated in the religion of Buddha."[34] Likewise, a more generous attitude toward the kind of scholar Blavatsky called "the profane Orientalist" emerges in the lead article of the second issue of *The Path*, "Studies in the Upanishads." Its author refers to Max Müller's *Sacred Books of the East* and commends the great orientalist as someone "to whom all western students must ever remain grateful." More important, Hinduism is presented in a way that seems to supplement theosophy. The word *Upanishad* is said to mean "secret charm" or "philosophical doctrine," meanings that come into play in an explanation of the nature of "sacrifice": "the sacrifice which a man performs with knowledge, with faith, and with the Upanishad, *i.e.*, with an understanding of the secret charm, or underlying principles and effects, is more powerful than when with faith, the only knowledge possessed is of the rites themselves, their origin and regularity. The sacrifice referred to is, not only the one offered on the altar in the temple, but that daily sacrifice which every breath and every thought, brings about in ourselves" (*Path*, 1.2 [May 1886]: 34). That these kinds of remarks were being made *before* Blavatsky's *Secret Doctrine* was published supports two points: one, that the Americans did not require the example of Blavatsky to incorporate Asiatic faiths into their discussions of theosophy; and, two, that the American discussion was more sympathetic to traditional Oriental scholarship.

The Path also provides evidence that the American branch of the Theosophical Society under Judge's supervision remained true to the three "Objects" of the founders:

1. To form a nucleus of the Universal Brotherhood of Humanity, without distinction of race, creed, sex, caste or colour.
2. To encourage the study of Comparative Religion, Philosophy, and Science.
3. To investigate unexplained laws of Nature, and the powers latent in man.[35]

The second object, especially, is amply represented in the pages of the magazine during its first year (April 1886–March 1887). A good example of theosophical comparatism is the four-part series "Hindu Symbolism," by Isaac Myer, which ran in the October, November, February, and March issues. The discussion of symbolism is based on four illustrations taken from a German study by Niklas Müller, *Glauben, Wissen und Kunst der alten Hindus,* published in 1822. Myer says his capacity to interpret the symbolism of the images was greatly aided by "our study of the Kabbalah" (*Path*, 1.7 [October 1886]: 220), as his analysis of an androgynous figure shows:

> This symbol, the divine type of the first male and female, which can be compared with the terrestrial Adam before the final separation of Eve, is really in consonance with this Adam's perfect ideal, the Adam Kadmon or Heavenly Adam of the Kabbalah. The Brahma-half is on the right side, the good side, man's, the Maya-half is on the left, the evil side, the woman's. So according to the Hebrew sacred writings, through Eve the woman, evil was brought into the world. Compare this with the Greek myth of Pandora. (*Path*, 1.9 [November 1886]: 251–52)

The description of the patriarchal myth of the origins of evil gives more or less equal weight to the Hindu, Hebrew, and Greek versions, but by the end of the series the author has concluded that the "Aryan or Hindu system . . . is believed to contain in germ all the others which have since arisen, as: the Hermetic, the Jewish, the Christian, and others" (*Path*, 1.12 [March 1887]: 372). However amateurish and simplistic, Myer's understanding of the origins of other world religions in Hinduism is based on comparative analysis. Blavatsky, by contrast, always insisted that all religion, including Hinduism, developed out of the secret doctrine that theosophists had discovered.

Considered from one perspective, theosophy was clearly a mass movement. That perspective has been admirably described by Peter Washington in his book about Madame Blavatsky and the many converts and followers who found that *Isis Unveiled* "answered to deep needs at a time when religious doubt was fueled by the first great age of mass education." Washington characterizes Blavatsky's nineteenth-century audience as a collection of "passionate amateurs and spiritual autodidacts" pursuing self-improvement in the middlebrow milieu of "evening classes, public lectures, workers' educational institutes, debating unions, libraries of popular classics, socialist societies and art clubs—that bustling, earnest world where the readers of Ruskin and Edward Carpenter could improve themselves, where middle-class idealists could help them to do so, and where nudism and dietary reform linked arms with universal brotherhood and occult wisdom."[36] From another perspective, however, theosophy was an elite society devoted to the scholarly pursuit of esoteric knowledge. Actually, these two perspectives capture divergent aspects of the movement's historical development: the more insistently spiritualist approach of Blavatsky and Olcott belongs to the early stages of theosophy's history in America; the more intellectual, scholarly approach of Judge characterizes the later phases of that history, after Blavatsky and Olcott made the movement international by setting up headquarters in India and by establishing branches in Europe. As Carl T. Jackson points out, the American branch of the theosophical movement headed by Judge put far more focus on Oriental religion: "Indeed, no contemporary Western group spent more energy explaining and encouraging the adoption of Eastern conceptions."[37]

The orientalist emphasis and the scholarly spirit that Judge brought to theosophy made the movement a prototype of the middlebrow modernism that developed in the early twentieth century, as strange as this seems. Indeed, the relation between theosophy and early modernism is far from simple, despite the interest that such figures as William Butler Yeats, Oscar Wilde, and H. G. Wells showed in the movement. The relation is not exactly the familiar one between high culture and popular culture: after all, modernism is not quite the high culture movement it has largely been represented to be, and theosophy obviously aimed for the heights.[38] As modernism developed, its middlebrow advocates imagined the movement as something that could actually be lived. The middlebrow modernists accepted the avant-garde art of Stravinsky, Picasso, Joyce, and other high modernists not only for its aesthetic value but also for its revolutionary implications in areas other than the aesthetic: modern art was evidence of modern life, proof that some paradigm had shifted and that life had to be lived differently. Theosophy was not, like modernism, an aesthetic movement, however closely it may have been associated with aesthetes and decadents during the fin de siècle. But under Judge's stewardship, theosophy was similar to modernism in being both recondite and revolutionary, an elite movement with ambitions for mass acceptance. Not everyone could understand it, at least at first, but once they did, they would see that it was a philosophy of life keyed to modern times.

III

Barnum, Buddhism, and Blavatsky: all three of these elements in the movement of the American Orient into mass culture were evident in one way or another at the World's Parliament of Religions, held in Chicago in 1893 in conjunction with the Columbian Exposition. Although Barnum had died in 1891, Barnumism was still very much alive at the world's fair, as contemporary commentators made clear. The *New York Times* called the midway the "Greatest Show on Earth," adding that "the late P. T. Barnum should have lived to see this day."[39] The sense of spectacle associated with the Orient in Barnum's over-the-top exploitation of Chinese, Hindus, and other "primitive" peoples had a kind of higher correlative in the Parliament of Religions, which included delegates from India, Japan, and other Asian nations, all of whom made compelling presentations. The Buddhist delegates, especially, presented the greatest challenge to the organizer's assumptions about the meaning and merits of Asiatic faiths. These delegates included the Singhalese Buddhist Anagarika Dharmapala, who had toured Japan with William Henry Olcott[40]—only one of several connections between Buddhism and theosophy manifested in Chicago in 1893. The theosophists held their own congress to coincide with the Parliament of Religions and invited Dharmapala to speak.[41] Elements of the exotic and the esoteric combined with the spectacle of the fair itself to bring the Orient into the orbit of American popular culture as never before.

The exposition of which the parliament was part commemorated much more than the quadricentennial anniversary of Columbus's discovery of America: it also celebrated the city of Chicago's elevated status as the equal in progress and culture of New York and Boston, Paris and London. Moreover, the exposition offered evidence, through its many exhibits of arts and manufactures, that America had taken a place of special significance in the Western march of power across the globe, initiated by the voyage of Columbus. The destiny of the nation was made manifest in the material form of the exposition's White City itself, which, like the Capitol in Washington, employed neoclassical architecture to emphasize connections between American values and the cultural legacy of Greece and Rome, the latter an especially pertinent model for a country with emerging imperial ambitions. Also manifest was the sense of America as the apotheosis of the Christian mission, which had moved westward with Columbus from the Old World to the New, and then westward with the frontier until it reached the Pacific. Fittingly, the Columbian oration on Dedication Day in October 1892 was delivered by Chaucey Depew, president of the New York Central Railroad. Depew claimed that "the spirit of equality of all men under God and law" had traveled "westward with Columbus to America's shores," then moved farther westward from the East Coast to the West, just as the railroad had. Depew concluded his oration by saying that the White City "condenses and displays the power and fruitage of this transcendent miracle."[42] How this miracle related to the Eastern faiths that the West had, presumably, transcended was not a topic taken up by the railroad magnate on this occasion.

But the question of the relationship of Oriental religion to the triumphalist version of Christianity voiced by so many at the exposition was taken up at the World's Parliament of Religions that ran for over two weeks in September 1893. It was organized by John Henry Barrows, a Presbyterian so ecumenical in his thinking that he created the impression the parliament was motivated by Unitarian impulses.[43] In fact, his published remarks evaluating the assembly a year after he convened it suggest an odd mixture of missionary and universalist thinking. The ecumenical spirit is sounded as Barrows explains the mixture of faiths on hand when the parliament opened on 11 September: "It was indeed a meeting of brotherhood, 'where the Brahmin forgot his caste and the Catholic was chiefly conscious of his catholicity'; and where, in the audience, 'the variety of interests, faiths, ranks, and races, was as great as that found on the platform.'" He follows this paean to variety and catholicity, however, with the observation that such expressions of universalism are solidly grounded in Christianity: "As the representatives of China, Russia, Germany, Hindustan, Sweden and Norway, Greece, France, Africa, the United States, and the all-clasping Empire of Great Britain, from England to New Zealand, uttered their thoughts and feelings, multitudes entered anew into the spirit of the Nazarene Prophet, who seemed always to include the whole world in His purpose and affection."[44] The notion that religions remote from the Christian orbit are nonetheless expressions of universal Christian truths seems particularly pronounced in the case of Asiatic faiths. Barrows proudly lists the number of speakers for different Oriental religions—"more than a dozen" Buddhists, seven apologists for Chinese beliefs, two Shintoists—but reminds the reader that "much that passed for Oriental religion was a reflection of Christian truth and European philosophy." Still, he allows that "the Oriental speakers were, on the whole, fairly representative of the higher ideals of their own faiths, if not of the popular religions" ("Results," 134). Most remarkable of all, Barrows takes the view that non-Christian religions are simply imperfect because they have not yet progressed to the level of wisdom and sublimity embodied by Christ: "As Judaism and Christianity were reconciled in the Epistle to the Hebrews, so Buddhism and Christianity, Hinduism and Christianity, Confucianism and Christianity, Islâm and Christianity, are yet to be reconciled by some supreme minds, who shall show to India, China, Japan, Arabia, that in Christ all that is good and true in these faiths has been embodied and completed by a special revelation" ("Results," 142). In many respects, Barrows's attitude toward religion is consistent with the larger ideology represented by the Columbian Exposition itself: namely, that American modernity had reconciled Anglo-Protestant religion with the progressive ideals of the European Enlightenment.[45] The evidence was there for all to see in the great classical facades and in technological marvels such as the Ferris wheel.

Barrows's unease over the Oriental religions and his condescending assurance that they would one day be "completed" by Christian revelation are especially noteworthy, given the presentations made by two delegations in particular, the Buddhist and the Hindu. What made these delegations different was the way their representatives presented their religions in a manner supposedly reserved for Christianity alone—as the fulfillment of the enlightenment paradigm of progress. Shaku Soen from Japan and Anagarika Dharmapala from Ceylon (now Sri Lanka) presented Buddhism as a philosophical system that allowed its practitioners to adapt to the complexities of the modern world. Swami Vivekananda lectured on Hinduism as a progressive faith based on spiritual laws, analogous to the natural laws of modern science: "Just as the law of gravitation existed before its discovery, and would exist if all humanity forgot it, so with the laws that govern the spiritual world."[46] Vivekananda's interpretation of these spiritual laws reveals that he, no less than his America contemporaries, misunderstood Darwin's scientific paradigm as a process of amelioration rather than modification; of progression rather than adaptation: "Man is to become divine, realizing the divine, and, therefore, idol or temple or church or books, are only the supports, the helps of his spiritual childhood, but on and on he must progress" (WPR, 2:976). The Hindu swami's sketch of a universal religion derived from Vedic "laws" was the last thing the parliament's organizers wanted from its delegates, as Barrows wrote in his summary: "The idea of evolving a cosmic or universal faith out of the Parliament was not present in the minds of its chief promoters. They believed that the elements of such a religion were already contained in the Christian ideal and the Christian scriptures."[47] Moreover, Buddhism, Hinduism, and the other non-Christian faiths represented at the congress performed the useful function of illustrating just how universal Christianity really was, because "certain truths of Christianity find their prophecy or adumbrations in some of the ethnic faiths." Barrows said the parliament's organizers "had no thought of attempting to formulate a universal creed" because there was no need to do so, given the laws of spiritual evolution: "The best religion must come to the front, and the best religion will ultimately survive, because it will contain all that is true in all the faiths" (WPR, 2:1572).

A strong challenge to the promoters' notion that the universal faith was already fully evolved and manifest in the Christian ideal came from the Buddhists, especially the Japanese, who used the congress to further the modernization agenda of the Meiji Empire. Even though their presence at the parliament was not officially sanctioned by the Meiji government, the six delegates who represented several different Buddhist sects were unified in their support of Japanese modernization and intent on exploiting Western perceptions that Buddhism was fully compatible with science. Even Edwin Arnold, author of The Light of Asia, construed "the doctrine of karma as a[n] account of the transformation of species" and called Buddhism "anticipatory Asiatic Darwinism."[48]

The scientific nature of Buddhism was explained by Shaku Soen (1859–1919), whom Barrows called "the Buddhist bishop" (in fact he was chief abbot of one of the Renzai Zen temples in Japan).[49] In "The Law of Cause and Effect as Taught by the Buddha," Shaku explored the topic of the first cause, which Western theologians took as proof of the existence of God, since by the logic of regression from effect to cause one had to arrive at a divine point of origin; a physical universe governed by causality had to have a cause outside itself. But Shaku argued otherwise: "The assertion that there is a first cause, is contrary to the fundamental principle of nature, since a certain cause might have an origin in some preceding cause or causes, and there is no cause which is not an effect" (WPR, 2:829–30). Buddhism appears the contrary of deism, with its clockmaker God and clockwork universe; indeed, the universe from the Buddhist perspective has "no beginning, no end. Since, even if we trace back to an eternity, absolute cause cannot be found, so we come to the conclusion that there is no end in the universe." Shaku explained this point with an analogy anyone could understand: "As the waters of rivers evaporate and form clouds, and the latter change [their] form into rain, thus returning once more into the original form of waters, the causal law is in a logical circle changing from cause to effect, effect to cause" (WPR, 2:830). Causality was not a linear chain, but a "logical circle," and the law of karma was comparable to Darwin's theory, since "the moral life of human beings is . . . determined by a logical calculus of evolution driven forth by the actions of particular individuals." Unfortunately, the scientific jargon that Shaku and other Buddhists tried to use did not always come through, partly because of the need for translation, and partly because Blavatsky's and Olcott's theosophy had gotten into American heads well in advance of Buddhism. When the Buddhists used a term like "formless form," for example, they were immediately conflated with the theosophists in the popular press.[50]

This kind of problem did not attach to "The Real Position of Japan toward Christianity," the address given by Hirai Kinzo, a Buddhist layman. Hirai and his fellow layman Noguchi Zenshiro were the only members of the Buddhist delegation whose command of English was sufficient for them to speak on their own before an audience (Barrows had read Shaku's paper "The Law of Cause and Effect"), and Hirai was especially proficient, having lived in California for several years.[51] His talk dealt with the contradictions between Western faith and Western power—which had compelled Japanese compliance with unfair treaties—and with the general hypocrisy of Christian missions in the Far East. He also related the bigoted treatment of Japanese people in San Francisco and Hawaii to the racism he had observed of missionaries in the Orient, adding the biting comment:

"If such be Christian ethics—well, we are perfectly satisfied to be heathen" (*WPR*, 1:449). He shamed his auditors by asking them how they would feel if subjected to the same injustices as those that had been visited upon Japan: "Would not the people of America and Europe think that they were being trampled upon and their rights ignored, if they were denied the application of their judicial power over those cases which occur at home? Would not Western nations be indignant and consider that they were deprived of independence, if they were compelled to renounce their rightful custom duty?" (*WPR*, 1:446). He concluded his talk by quoting from the Declaration of Independence and by insisting that the revolutionary slogan "Give me liberty or give me death" had contemporary relevance in Meiji Japan: "You, who enjoy the fruition of liberty through your struggle for it; you, I say, may understand somewhat our position, and as you asked for justice from your mother country, we, too, ask justice from these foreign powers. . . . We, the forty million souls of Japan, standing firmly and persistently on the basis of international justice, await still further manifestations as to the morality of Christianity" (*WPR*, 1:450).

As the *Chicago Herald* reported, when Hirai concluded, the audience burst into loud applause and cries of "Shame" over "the wrongs which his countrymen had suffered through the practices of false Christianity." The *Chicago Daily Times* said that Hirai's "eloquent utterances" were "like a voice out of darkness, a cry of oppression from a strange land. It came to the thousands of Christians who listened as a thunderblast, and when the priest had finished, the people rose again to their feet and gave him three mighty cheers." The *Chicago Tribune* headline trumpeted the "CRY FROM THE ORIENT: JAPANESE PRIEST STARTLES THE RELIGIOUS CONGRESS." In the article itself the address was called "the sensation of the day and of the whole Parliament so far."[52]

Taken together, Shaku's scientific address and Hirai's political one formed a two-pronged attack against the Anglo-Protestant assumptions of the Parliament's organizers. As a result, Buddhism appeared superior to Christianity from the perspectives of both modernity and morality. Shaku had reconciled Buddhism with science, and Hirai had created the strong sense that the morality of Buddhism was superior to the ethics on display in Christian missions and Christian governments. A third argument strengthened Buddhism and removed it further from the Christian "fulfillment" theory: simply that Buddhism was tolerant of other religions, not exclusionary like Christianity. The Christian minister could not admit a Buddhist to his flock unless the Buddhist converted, but the Buddhist priest welcomed sincere believers of all faiths and saw no contradiction in practicing multiple faiths simultaneously: "Japan has received all teachings with an open mind . . . as is seen by so many temples built in the name of truth with a mixed appellation of Buddhism and Shintoism; as is seen by the affinity among the teachers of Confucianism and Taoism or other isms and the Buddhist and Shinto priests." This was the way the articulate Hirai put it, adding that "though there are many roads at the foot of the mountain, yet, if the top is reached, the same moon is seen" (*WPR*, 1:444).

The idea of Buddhism as a universal faith was the subject of Hirai's second paper at the conference, "Synthetic Religion." He made clear that spiritual truths could be expressed in a variety of ways, but, as one commentator notes, he "left no doubt . . . about where he saw the center of this synthetic religion: 'The one and the same center' of the 'one synthesized religion . . . is called satori or hotoke in Japanese.'"[53] All religions have something in common, said Hirai, but the highest synthesis of all is Japanese Buddhism. He went further than his countryman Shaku, who also made the "synthesis" argument, observing, for example, that Buddha, Jesus, and Confucius all "taught about universal love and fraternity" (*WPR*, 2:1285). Like the Japanese, the Singhalese Buddhist Dharmapala presented his faith as a "synthetic religion" that could easily be aligned with Christianity, as the title of one of his speeches indicated: "Points of Resemblance and Difference between Buddhism and Christianity." But Dharmapala tilted the synthesis in the direction of Buddhism when he quoted passages from the Gospels and termed them "Buddhist teachings as given in the words of Jesus."[54]

Although the Buddhists staked out claims of relevance to the modern world, there was something parochial about those claims, for Buddhism was presented as a religion that was better adapted to modernity than was Christianity. Swami Vivekananda made a different kind of claim, not for the superiority of one religion over another but for the equality of all religions at some deeper level, once the trappings of dogma and ritual had been stripped away: "Every religion is only an evolving [of] a God out of the material man; and the same God is the inspirer of all of them." "Universal Gospel" was the title Vivekananda chose for his theory of spiritual evolution, a title that alludes to the New Testament but ends up suggesting something much more inclusive than the Christian gospel precisely because it *includes* Christianity:

> If there is ever to be a universal religion, it must be one which would hold no location in place and time, which would be infinite like the God it would preach, whose sun shines upon the followers of Krishna or Christ; saints or sinners alike; which would not be Brahman or Buddhist, Christian or Mohammedan, but the sum total of all of these, and still have infinite space for development; which in its catholicity would embrace in its infinite arms

and formulate a place for every human being, from the lowest groveling man who is scarcely removed in intellectuality from the brute, to the highest mind, towering almost above humanity, and who makes society stand in awe and doubt his human nature.[55]

The universality of the message combined with his personal charisma made Vivekananda possibly the most compelling presence at the parliament. Unlike Hirai and Dharmapala (who had scolded his auditors about their ignorance of the Buddha),[56] Vivekananda went out of his way to flatter his audience and to praise America for its tolerance: "It was reserved for America to call, to proclaim to all quarters of the globe that the lord is in every religion" (*WPR*, 2:977). He concluded his lecture on Hinduism with a peroration that brought his audience to its feet: "May he who is the Brahma of the Hindus, the Ahura Mazda of the Zoroastrians, the Buddha of the Buddhists, the Jehovah of the Jews, the Father in Heaven of the Christians, give strength to you to carry out your noble idea. . . . Hail Columbia, mother-land of liberty! It has been given to thee, who never found out that shortest way of becoming rich by robbing one's neighbors, it has been given to thee to march on at the vanguard of civilization with the flag of harmony" (*WPR*, 2:978).

Accounts from every quarter confirm just how compelling a presence Vivekananda was at the parliament. Barrows remarked that when Vivekananda was introduced, audiences gave him the kind of tumultuous applause normally reserved for stage celebrities. The celebrity reception was also reported in the *Daily Inter-Ocean*: "Great crowds of people, the most of whom were women, pressed around the doors leading to the Hall of Columbus . . . for it had been announced that Swami Vivekananda, the popular Hindoo monk who looks so much like McCullough's Othello, was to speak." (The reference is to John Edward McCullough [1832–1885], a popular Irish-born actor who played Othello in blackface.) According to Merwin Marie-Snell, secretary to the liberal American bishop John J. Keane (1834–1921), Vivekananda was "the most popular and influential man in the Parliament."[57] More important, he emerged after the parliament as possibly the most popular and influential participant, for he went on to found the Ramakrishna movement in the United States. The importance of the Ramakrishna centers subsequently established in America is not confined, to be sure, to the realm of popular culture, but Vivekananda has to be regarded as the first in a long succession of swamis and gurus to find a popular following in the United States. Rammohun Roy's fame in the early nineteenth century was confined largely to the Unitarian chapel; besides, he never made a visit to the United States. That distinction belongs to Protap Chandra Majumdar, who went on an American lecture tour for three months in 1874, but he too limited himself to the Unitarian circuit. Majumdar was linked to Roy by Keshub Chandra Sen, who had assumed leadership of the Brahmo Samaj, a humanitarian and religious organization Roy had founded which adapted Hinduism to Western-style church services.[58] But Vivekananda was the first to reach outside the orbit of the church and take a Hindu message directly to the American people. The Ramakrishna movement may have stalled a bit, but its heyday in the 1960s is only one of several testaments to the lasting legacy of the Chicago Parliament of Religions in the United States.

IV

As the example of Vivekananda illustrates, the World's Parliament of Religions is important for a number of historical reasons, among which is the role the parliament played in introducing Asian faiths to an ever expanding American audience. Shaku Soen's post-parliament career is another case in point, mainly because of the influence he exerted on the German immigrant philosopher Paul Carus; Carus, in turn, helped to assure an American audience for D. T. Suzuki, whose long career links the 1893 parliament to the popularization of Zen Buddhism in the 1960s. When Carus heard Shaku's scientifically oriented address at the parliament, he recognized in Buddhism an analogue to the Christian monist philosophy he had been advocating through his two respected journals, *Open Court* and the *Monist*. Monism was mostly the brainchild of the German biologist Ernst Haeckel (1834–1919), who claimed that "the whole universe, including both organic and inorganic matter, and spirit as well as matter, is 'unified' [or 'monistic'] because it is regulated by the same natural laws."[59] Carus also saw himself as the heir of Kant and as a missionary for the religion of science, convictions made evident by "Science a Religious Revelation," the lecture he delivered at the parliament: "It is not true that religion has ceased to be a factor in the evolution of mankind. . . . God is the authority of the moral *ought*. Belief in God must be an unswerving obedience to the moral law" (*WPR*, 2:978). The categorical imperative may be allegorized or personfied in various ways in different religions, but the science of morality underlies them all: hence the rather startling claim that "science is a revelation of God" (*WPR*, 2:980). As Carus explained, given the revelatory status of science, it is inextricably intertwined with religion: "That conception of religion which rejects science is inevitably doomed. It cannot survive and is destined to disappear with the progress of civilization. . . .

Religion is as indestructible as science; for science is the method of searching for truth, and religion is the enthusiasm and good will to live a life of
truth" (*WPR*, 2:981).

After the parliament, Carus began to use Buddhism as a vehicle for
conveying his monist philosophy through a series of scientific and popular
publications, none more important than *The Gospel of Buddha*. The book
was published in 1894 by his Open Court Press and is still in print, with
several million copies sold.[60] The *Gospel* has been called "an archetypal
example of Orientalism, the appropriation of the Orient—in this case Buddhism and the life of the Buddha—to support a decidedly Western and
Christian project."[61] The conscription of Buddhism to the service of Carus's
monistic Christian philosophy becomes clear in the preface to the deluxe
edition of *The Gospel of Buddha,* published in 1915 with illustrations
by the Munich artist Olga Kopetzky. Here Carus explains the distinction
between Hinayana and Mahayana Buddhism in a way that suggests the
prospect of a "Hinayana" version of Christianity. According to Carus, "The
original Buddhism has been called by Buddhists the little vessel of salvation, or Hīnayāna; for it is comparable to a small boat on which a man
may cross the stream of worldliness so as to reach the shore of Nirvāna."
Later Buddhists "popularized the Buddha's doctrines" by constructing "a
large vessel of salvation, the Mahāyāna, in which the multitudes would find
room and could be safely carried over."[62] The principal tenet of Hinayana
Buddhism that Carus is most intent on conveying is monistic: namely, the
understanding that any distinction between temporal self and eternal soul
is mistaken. Buddhism "claims that man's soul does not consist of two
things, of an *ātman* (self) and of a *manas* (mind or thoughts), but that there
is one reality, our thoughts, our mind or *manas,* and this *manas* constitutes
the soul" (Carus, ix). This basic idea, Carus claims, has been obscured by
the religious zeal of Mahayana Buddhism, just as "the dogmatology and
mythological ingredients" of Christianity uphold "the ego-illusion." But
because Christianity is *"the religion of love made easy,"* it is like "a grand
bridge, a Mahāsetu, on which a child who has no comprehension as yet of
self can cross the stream of self-hood and worldly vanity" (xiv). The secondary or functional purpose of Buddhism in *The Gospel of Buddha* becomes
especially clear in the last sentence of the preface: "Above any Hīnayāna,
Mahāyāna, and Mahāsetu is the Religion of Truth" (xv).

In order to convey his Religion of Truth to the Christian reader, Carus
applies the rhetorical devices of the King James version of the Bible to the
story of the Buddha, including chapter-verse format and Elizabethan English. Verse 4 of chapter 1, for instance, sounds like the translated language
of the New Testament: "Ye that suffer from the tribulations of life, ye that

have to struggle and endure, ye that yearn for a life of truth, rejoice at the glad tidings." The "glad tidings" here are the good news that the Buddha "has found the root of all evil; he has shown us the way of salvation" (Carus, 1). That way is given distinctive "biblical" treatment in chapter 2, verse 18: "Yet ye love self and will not abandon self-love. So be it, but then, verily, ye should learn to distinguish between the false self and the true self. The ego with all its egotism is the false self. It is an unreal illusion and a perishable combination. He only who identifies his self with the truth will attain Nirvāna; and he who has entered Nirvāna has attained Buddhahood; he has acquired the highest good; he has become eternal and immortal" (4).

No gospel would be complete without an account of the birth of the savior, which Carus provides in language not so far removed from the sound of the Christian Bible. When Siddhartha was born, "Brahma-angels" took the child and announced to his mother, "Rejoice, O queen, a mighty son has been born unto thee," whereupon "all the worlds were flooded with light. The blind received their sight by longing to see the coming glory of the Lord; the deaf and dumb spoke with one another of the good omens indicating the birth of the Buddha to be. The crooked became straight; the lame walked" (Carus, 8). The impression of the book as a kind of Buddha Bible story is helped along in the deluxe edition by Kopetzky's illustrations. One plate pictures Siddhartha and his mother in the familiar manner of Madonna and child, complete with halos and Caucasian faces. Another shows the Buddha's sermon at Benares that could just as well serve to illustrate Jesus' Sermon on the Mount. Despite the absence of Asian features in her portrayal of the Buddha, Kopetzky claims to have gone to some lengths to ensure "historical fidelity" in her illustrations (Carus, 311), but those efforts are gainsaid by Carus's unmistakable intention to make the life of Buddha the analogue of the life of Christ; the book is a "gospel," after all.

The Gospel of Buddha did not succeed as Carus wished it to. Few American readers made the leap from Buddhism to Christian monism, focusing instead on the story of the Buddha for its own sake. But the book did succeed as a popular introduction to Buddhism, as the ongoing sales figures attest. Strangely, the book also succeeded in Japan when it was published, a few months after the America edition, in a translation by D. T. Suzuki with an introduction by Shaku Soen. As Judith Snodgrass explains, Japanese Buddhists used the book to engage those members of the younger generation who had been educated in the West as part of the Meiji modernization: "Its value was in attracting the attention of the Western-educated elite of the nation[,] introducing them to Buddhist ideas, presented in an accessible form acceptable by Western standards, and reassuring them of Western intellectual interest in and approval of their indigenous religion."

In addition to translating the work as *Buddha no fukuin,* Suzuki provided a biography of Carus in which he explained that the philosopher had turned to Buddhism and rejected Christianity because of his desire to reconcile science and religion.[63] Suzuki did not mention this characterization when he wrote to Carus in March 1895 to introduce himself as the Japanese translator of *The Gospel of Buddha* and a student of the kind of philosophy Carus promoted. Shaku also wrote to Carus and recommended Suzuki to him as a student of philosophy, suggesting that his younger colleague would be invaluable to the spread of monism in Japan. Soon thereafter (March 1897) Suzuki journeyed to LaSalle to work with Carus on a variety of projects, including a translation of the *Tao-te-Ching* (1898), and he remained in America until February 1909.[64]

The Suzuki-Carus translation of the *Tao-te-Ching* is interesting for a number of reasons, not least because it is the first translation of the Chinese classic published in the United States. As such, the book offers additional evidence for the emergence of American curiosity about Taoism during the 1890s, following John La Farge's "artist's letter" titled "Tao: The Way," first published in the July 1891 issue of the *Century Magazine*; an unsigned essay on "Taoism" printed in the second volume of Barrows's history of the Chicago parliament; and a long article by one William Davies in the February 1894 *Atlantic Monthly,* titled simply "Tao."[65] Of these early efforts, La Farge's seems most genuinely appreciative of the fulfilling emptiness of the Tao. The essay from Barrows's collection mainly despairs about the corruption of Taoism into magic and spiritualism, while the *Atlantic* article understands the Tao in the all-too-familiar syncretic terms associated with Emerson's orientalism: "Taoism is a testimony to that transcendent teaching which has been a formative agent in the development of the race from the remotest ages."[66]

The time was ripe for a good American translation of the *Tao-te-Ching,* but Carus's rationalistic philosophy got in the way of the kind of meaningful insights into the ancient text the young Suzuki was prepared to offer. After all, Suzuki could read the Chinese characters; Carus could not. Yet Suzuki is not even named as a collaborator; the title page indicates that "Lao-tze's Tao teh King," renamed *The Canon of Reason and Virtue,* has been "translated from the Chinese by Dr. Paul Carus." While it is true that the word *dào* is not easily rendered into English, "reason" and "virtue" seem to be, at best, several metaphorical removes from the Chinese original, which is usually translated, simply, as "the way." The first line of Carus's version of the *Tao-te-Ching* reads: "The reason that can be reasoned is not the Eternal Reason."[67] By contrast, James Legge's 1891 translation settles on "The Tâo that can be trodden is not the enduring and unchanging Tâo," leaving *dào* untranslated but capturing the concrete sense of "way" or "path" in the original.[68] Carus keeps to his abstract, "monistic" meanings throughout and provides interpretive titles for each of the eighty-one texts that make up the *Tao-te-Ching,* including such gems as "The Virtue of Simplicity," "Trust in Faith," and "Propounding the Essential." If nothing else, Suzuki's long apprenticeship to Carus would have given the young Japanese scholar a thorough familiarity with Western philosophical discourse, knowledge that he certainly put to use in later years when he began to interpret Zen Buddhism for American audiences.

An early opportunity to introduce Americans to Zen came in the summer of 1905 when Suzuki accompanied Shaku on a lecture tour after the abbot returned to the United States at the invitation of Mr. and Mrs. Alexander Russell of San Francisco. Shaku had written a poem on the voyage from Japan which expressed a view of himself oddly consonant with the imperialist sentiments of his official Chicago hosts on his first visit to America in the previous decade, but one that shifted those sentiments from a Christian to a Buddhist context:

> Mountains join into mountains.
> Where is the center of water?
> Where is the destination of clouds?
> I do not know!
> My heart tells me there is a happy field
>   In the American land.
> I presume myself a follower of old Columbus.[69]

The Columbian identification would not have troubled the Russells, who are presumed to have been the first Zen Buddhists in the United States. Shaku stayed with the family at their ocean compound, the House of Silent Light, giving informal lectures there to friends in the Russell circle.[70] He also traveled from San Francisco to speak in several other California cities, including Los Angeles, Sacramento, and San Jose, with Suzuki as translator. In the spring of 1906, with the Russells' backing, Shaku and Suzuki set out for the East Coast, where the Buddhist abbot delivered more formal lectures, often to university audiences, in Washington, Boston, New York, and Philadelphia.[71] Later in 1906 the lectures were collected as *Sermons of a Buddhist Abbot,* published by Carus's Open Court Press. The book went through several editions in the early twentieth century before going out of print, only to reappear in the 1970s with the title *Zen for Americans.* The latter title makes a certain amount of sense, since Shaku seems to have gone out of his way to explain Buddhism in terms that Americans could understand. For example, in reading "What is Buddhism?" before the National

Geographic Society in April 1906, Shaku explained that divinity was not confined to "its highest manifestations" alone (such as the manifestation "Christians call Jesus Christ") "but also in the meanest and most insignificant piece of stone lying in a deserted field"; he added that "the melody of divine reason is heard not only in the singing of a bird or in the composition of an inspired musician, but also in the 'slums of life' as Emerson phrases it" (*Zen*, 83, 84).

In fact, much of the lecture may fairly be called Emersonian, as this passage illustrates: "For the world may pass away, the universe may be shaken out of its foundation, but God will remain and will create a new system out of the former ruins. The ashes of existence will never be scattered to the winds, but they will gather themselves in the ever designing hand of God and build themselves up to a new order of things, in which it [hand of God] is ever shining with its serene radiance" (*Zen*, 84). The continuity of existence and non-existence expressed here is elsewhere explained as the Buddhist recognition of "the coexistence and identity of the two principles, sameness and difference." To support the point, Shaku quoted the opening stanza of Emerson's "Brahma" (*Zen*, 27). Another lecture claimed that "the West is energetic, and the East mystical; for the latter's ideal is to be incomprehensible, immeasurable, and undemonstrative even as an absolute being itself" (*Zen*, 154). The formulation is close to Emerson's in his essay on Plato from *Representative Men,* where East and West are construed in antithetical terms; for example: "If the East loved infinity, the West delighted in boundaries."[72] The language of Shaku's published lectures is, after all, Suzuki's, and Suzuki's English-language education in Japan would have included ample exposure to Emerson, thanks to Ernest Fenollosa.

But the most striking element of the Buddhist abbot's sermons is the consistent case they make for the compatibility of enlightened religion and warfare, both ancient and modern. In "Buddhism and Oriental Culture," another address from April 1906, this one delivered at George Washington University, Shaku reminded his American audience of Nathan Hale's dying regret—that he had "only one life to give for his country"—and claimed that it was a pity that "the officer did not know the truth" of reincarnation, in the Buddhist sense that Shaku then explains: "From his very corpse there have risen so many patriotic spirits breathing the same breath that he breathed. He was not dead, he was never hung, he did not vanish into an unknown region; but he is living a life eternal, he is being born generation after generation, not only in his own country, but also in my country." The persistence of the patriotic spirit embodied by Nathan Hale was enlisted to support Shaku's claim that "Buddhists do not shun struggle and warfare," provided "a cause is worth contending for or defending" (*Zen*, 171, 170).

This remarkable rhetorical maneuver effectively allied the Americans with the Japanese against the Russians, whom Japanese forces had defeated in 1905, ending Tsarist ambitions in Manchuria and Korea.

Besides "Buddhism and Oriental Culture," three additional essays and addresses deal with the Russo-Japanese War, and all of them make the point that the Buddhist belief in reincarnation is not a matter of metempsychosis, or the passing of individual souls from one body to another, whether animal or human. On the contrary, the concept of reincarnation involves the infusion of one consciousness with another:

> Rebirth does not mean the reawakening of the dead. Reincarnation does not mean the resuscitation of a dried-up mummy. The immortality of the soul does not mean the continuation of the individual soul as conceived by most religionists. The spirit is not a thing material and sensual, however ethereally or astrally you may conceive it. It is a transcendental existence, which knows no limiting conditions such as space, time, or causation. Where you feel a noble feeling, where you think a beautiful thought, where you do a self-sacrificing deed, there is the spirit making itself felt in your consciousness. (*Zen*, 210–11)

In addition to articulating the Buddhist basis for Japanese patriotism, such passages also help to explain Buddhist beliefs from the Buddhist perspective. That these sorts of explanations should have been necessary at all is one of the more curious outcomes of the Chicago congress.

The Japanese delegates unsettled the American organizers of the World's Parliament of Religions because they made reasoned arguments—some theological, some political—against Christianity. But they also presented Buddhism in a way that did not harmonize with scholarly opinion, which was based on translation and analysis of the ancient Pali texts. Although he did not attend the Chicago parliament, the esteemed German orientalist Max Müller dismissed Japanese claims to Buddhist authenticity because those claims were not based on "their own canonical books."[73] Likewise, the Pali scholar T. W. Rhys Davids pointed out that Shaku's colleague Ashitsu Jitzusen lacked adequate textual authority for his understanding of nirvana.[74] The scholars put themselves in the position of explaining Buddhism to the Buddhists not only because of their belief in the authority of the text but also because of their insistence on the authenticity of origins: the Eastern or Mahayana development of Southern or Hinayana Buddhism could only be a "corruption" of the original religion. The meaning of nirvana was especially fraught, and Shaku was still taking the fight to Barrows on this front in 1906 by reprinting a letter he had written to the minister ten years before. Shaku's "Reply to a Christian Critic," first published as a letter in *Open Court,* takes Barrows to task for repeating "those errors which are common in the various Western books on Buddhism." He quotes the *Chicago Tribune* of 13 January 1896, where Barrows says that "the goal which made Buddha's teachings a dubious gospel, is Nirvâna, which involves the extinction of love and life, as the going out of a flame which has nothing else to feed upon" (*Zen*, 121–22). Shaku acknowledges that "the word *Nirvâna* means 'extinction,'" but in the sense of "eradication of all evil desires, of all passions, of all egoism, so that the flame of envy, hatred, and lust will have nothing to feed upon" (*Zen*, 122). Shaku makes several other critical corrections to Barrows's skewed view of Buddhism and ends the letter with comparisons of Jesus and Buddha in which Buddha emerges, not surprisingly, as the more enlightened spiritual figure. Strangely, Shaku's reply to Barrows originated with Carus, who drafted the original letter, which Shaku then sent to Barrows (and back to Carus for publication in *Open Court*) after he had Suzuki make a few changes.

Whatever its provenance, the letter fulfilled the purpose, as Shaku wrote to Carus, of correcting "these important misconceptions concerning Buddhism which are cherished by American preachers and scholars."[75] What is important here is the need to correct misapprehensions of Buddhism based on scholarly opinion, and the medium of those corrections: public lectures and magazine articles. In other words, the resistance of the scholarly community to the message of Buddhism carried by living Buddhists left them no choice but to take that message to the public in the form of popular culture. The Japanese Buddhists at the beginning of the twentieth century may have been forced into the arena of popular culture, but later apologists for Asian faiths would look willingly to magazine articles, public lectures, and paperback books as effective media for reaching the American audience. Such media also had the considerable side benefit of being commercially viable, and in the American Orient, at least, profit has proven no impediment to prophecy.

V

American interest in the Orient that followed from the World's Parliament of Religions in 1893 was sustained by popularizers like Paul Carus and by lecturers like Shaku and Vivekananda in the first decade of the twentieth century. That interest received further impetus in the 1910s and '20s from the popular lectures of the Hindu holy man Rabindranath Tagore (1861–1941) and the best-selling books by the syncretic Buddhist Ananda Coomaraswamy (1887–1947). Both these men had one foot in modernism and the other in mass culture, meaning that they were simultaneously appreciated by the modernist authors who promoted them and by a wider American public not necessarily in step with the modernist aesthetic. The phenomenon helps recover an element of that aesthetic which has been largely forgotten: namely, that the iconoclastic culture of modernism nonetheless managed to include a spiritual element of one kind or another. T. S. Eliot simultaneously complicated and validated Christian tradition by means of Hindu religion, but other modernists saw opportunities in the Orient to undercut the traditional authority of Christianity and to represent Asian faiths as somehow more relevant to modern life. Coomaraswamy made that case himself when he managed to find correspondences between the philosophy of Nietzsche and the preachings of Buddha. Tagore did not go that far, but he was, for a time, the next new thing, an avant-garde figure whose spiritual and intellectual musings found their way to both a modernist and a mass audience.

Rabindranath Tagore was awarded the Nobel Prize for literature in 1913, largely on the strengths of *Gitanjali: Song Offerings,* a slim volume of wisdom poetry published in English in 1912 with an introduction by William Butler Yeats. The two poets had been brought together by the portrait painter William Rothenstein, who had met Tagore on a trip to India in the winter of 1910–11.[76] In his introduction to *Gitanjali,* Yeats treats Tagore as a product of the kind of tradition he wished to cultivate in Ireland, "where poetry and religion are the same thing" and where culture "appear[s] as much a growth of the common soil as the grass and the rushes."[77] For this reason, Tagore was an other who was also the same: "A whole people, a whole civilization immeasurably strange to us, seems to have been taken up into this imagination; and yet we are not moved because of its strangeness, but because we have met our own image" (Yeats, 1:40). At first, Yeats's alignment of Indian and Irish imagination might seem an expression of political brotherhood in the face of shared colonial subjugation, but in fact, Yeats's characterization of Tagore and his family as saintly and passive is precisely the view of Indians preferred by the British colonial administration.[78] Tagore is said to "sit immovable in contemplation" for hours at a stretch, while his brother comes across as a Bengali version of St. Francis, with squirrels "climb[ing] on his knees and birds alight[ing] upon his hands" (1:39). Yeats represented Tagore as the voice of "the Indian civilization itself," but that representation was mistaken in several ways: Tagore wrote in Bengali and English, and so could not be understood by millions of speakers of Hindi, Urdu, Tamil, and other Indian languages; also, as a practitioner of the Western-inflected Brahmo Samaj founded by Rammohun Roy, his "philosophy and works were anathema to orthodox

Hindus."[79] Nonetheless, the Irish poet's introduction to *Gitanjali* was highly influential, its sentiments echoed by most of the reviewers of Tagore's book.

The book itself is a curious artifact of the times, especially in the context of literary modernism, whose proponents were the first to advance the Bengali poet's work. Although Yeats made some corrections to Tagore's English as *Gitanjali* was readied for publication, the poetic voice that comes through is thoroughly Victorian in its decorous diction and elevated sentiment. The collection comprises 103 short lyrics gleaned from Tagore's Bengali publications, some of which date back to 1896.[80] Several are directed to "God," most to an unnamed "master" or another paternal spirit best addressed with the biblical "thou," as in the first poem: "Thou hast made me endless, such is thy pleasure. This frail vessel thou emptiest again and again, and fillest it ever with fresh life."[81] The Hindu belief in reincarnation evoked here is complemented by the occasional reference to Indian deities (Vishnu is named in song 53), but more often than not, Tagore eschews allusion to a specific religious system in favor of a more general devotional tone, as in: "Let the cloud of grace bend low from above like the tearful look of the mother on the day of the father's wrath" (Tagore, 18). Both English and American reviewers registered such language as "biblical" and compared the songs in *Gitanjali* to the Psalms of David.[82] The positive reception of Tagore's poetry suggests that the spiritual strain in modern literary and philosophical culture that led such luminaries as William Butler Yeats and William James to involve themselves in theosophy and other cults was very much alive in the years before World War I. The recognition of this spiritual element was probably the key reason Tagore was awarded the Nobel Prize. After all, Alfred Nobel had stipulated in his will that candidates for the annual award should demonstrate an "idealistic tendency."[83] In the deliberations of the Nobel committee, an influential and possibly decisive opinion was offered by the now forgotten Swedish poet Verner von Heidenstam (who won the prize himself in 1917): "The loving and intense religious sense that permeates all [Tagore's] thoughts and feelings, the purity of heart, and the noble and unaffected elevation of the style—all amount to a total impression of deep and rare spiritual beauty."[84]

The religious sentimentality that marked the reception of *Gitanjali* would seem to be well removed from the modernist preference for clarity and precision, yet the modernists as well were taken with Tagore, at least at first. When Tagore visited London in 1912, Yeats introduced him to Ezra Pound, who in his role as literary entrepreneur praised *Gitanjali* in the *Fortnightly Review,* where he treats Tagore as a harbinger of the new poetic renaissance that Pound himself was intent on fashioning. He finds in the poetry a "spirit of curious quiet" which must mean that "we have found our new Greece suddenly. As the sense of balance came back upon Europe in the days before the Renaissance, so it seems to me does all this sense of a saner stillness come now to us in the midst of our clangour of medianisms." While it is hard to say precisely what Pound might have meant by "medianisms," "clangour" at least is clear, for its shows how attentive the American poet was to the sound and rhythm of words. Unlike other reviewers, he took the trouble to ask Tagore to read the poems aloud to him in the original Bengali and reported that he found them "somewhere between the forms of Provencal canzone and the roundels and odes of the Pleiade."[85] When he arranged for the publication of six poems from the book in the third issue of Harriet Monroe's *Poetry*, the avant-garde journal from Chicago, Pound assumed a less elevated tone: "This is *The Scoop*. Reserve space in the next number for Tagore . . . I've known for weeks that he was *the* event of the winter." By the time the poems appeared in the December issue of *Poetry*, Tagore had made his way to Urbana, Illinois, to visit his son, who was a student at the university there. Within ten days of his arrival in Urbana a Unitarian club asked him to speak, prompting Tagore to write to his daughter Bela that "the people of this country are quite crazy about lectures."[86]

Tagore left Urbana for Chicago after his son wrote to Monroe (to request a copy of the December number of *Poetry*) and the editor invited the poet to the city. Thus began the series of contacts with American intellectuals that brought the Indian poet the respect that preceded his celebrity. From Chicago he went to Harvard to lecture on philosophy before returning to England, where *Gitanjali* had gone through ten printings since its March 1913 publication—all before the Nobel Prize was awarded on 13 November. On his first visit to the United States in 1912–13, Tagore had been an Oriental curiosity, known only to a few poets, publishers, and philosophers. On his second, post-Nobel visit in 1916–17, Tagore was a true celebrity, commanding one of the largest lecture fees of the time. The tour had been arranged by the J. P. Pond Lyceum Bureau, whose founder was the only impresario who could really compete with P. T. Barnum. The shift from Pound to Pond was not lost on Pound himself, whose subsequent denunciation of Tagore perhaps gives off the odor of sour grapes: "Tagore got the Nobel Prize because, after the cleverest boom of our day, after the fiat of the omnipotent literati of distinction, he lapsed into religion and optimism and was boomed by the pious non-conformists."[87] This after Pound had compared Tagore's work to "the poetic piety of Dante" in the *Fortnightly Review* (Pound, 114).

Granted, Tagore was popular among the pious, theosophists and Unitarians especially, but in fact he took as his main lecture topic not the pieties of religion but the dangers of nationalism. His lectures set up a contrast between the nation and society, the former mechanistic and dehumanizing, the latter organic and fulfilling: "A nation, in the sense of the political and economic union of a people, is that aspect which a whole population assumes when organized for a mechanical purpose. Society as such has no ulterior purpose. It is an end in itself. It is a spontaneous self-expression of man as a social being. It is a natural regulation of human relationships, so that men can develop ideals of life in cooperation with one another."[88] Tagore's message was anti-imperialist, and he was unstinting in his criticism of the British nation. At the same time he made a distinction between Western nations and Western civilization, and expressed gratitude for certain civilizing institutions adopted in India, such as the rule of law. But as the war in Europe showed, the nation had become ascendant over civilization, which Tagore described as "a moral world." The "cruel war" that "has driven its claws into the vitals of Europe" has come about because "the West has been systematically petrifying her moral nature in order to lay a solid foundation for her gigantic abstractions of efficiency. She has all along been starving the life of the personal man into that of the professional" (RT, 2:430). Tagore ended this lecture with an elevated expression of idealism that makes it easy to see how the man acquired his saintly reputation: "We can still cherish the hope that, when power becomes ashamed to occupy its throne and is ready to make way for love, when the morning comes for cleansing the bloodstained steps of the Nation along the high-road of humanity, we shall be called upon to bring our own vessel of sacred water—the water of worship—to sweeten the history of man into purity, and with its sprinkling make the trampled dust of the centuries blessed with fruitfulness" (RT, 2:435).

The lecture tour began in California, where the *San Francisco Examiner* trumpeted "the cult of Tagore" as something that "has stirred the intellectual world as the thoughts of no other contemporaneous writer have done" and "has taken San Francisco by storm." Among the local Indian population, some revolutionaries in exile construed Tagore's universalist opposition to nationalism as imperialist propaganda against Indian liberation. A plot to assassinate him got as far as the lobby of the San Francisco hotel where Tagore was staying and might have succeeded had not the two would-be assassins disagreed over the murder at the last minute.[89] The *Minneapolis Tribune* picked up the story and ran an account of the event under the headline "Hindu Savant Safe After Wild Flight Under Body Guard."[90] A measure of Tagore's fame on the lecture tour that took him to twenty-five major American towns and cities from September 1916 to January 1917 can be taken by the caption accompanying a photograph of the great man in a Denver newspaper: "Sir Rabindranath Tagore, Hindu Poet, Winner of the 1913 Nobel Prize in Literature, and Apostle of Universal Brotherhood Among Nations, Snapped in Native Garb on His Arrival at the Union Depot in Denver This Morning. Tagore, a Master of Seventeen Languages, and Considered by Many the Most Commanding Personage in Contemporary Literature, Is on a World Tour. 'The Spirit of Peace' Permeates His Writings, While He Would Delete the Word 'Hate' From the Dictionary."[91]

As the blurb "Universal Brotherhood Among Nations" suggests, Tagore's message to American audiences harmonized with the pacifism and internationalism of the incumbent president, Woodrow Wilson, who won reelection in November 1916 by campaigning on the slogan "He kept us out of the war." W. W. Pearson, Tagore's secretary on the lecture tour, opined after the election that the deciding state of California had swung for Wilson because Tagore had spent six weeks there lecturing on the evils of nationalism.[92] Ironically, by the time Macmillan published the lectures as *Nationalism* in 1917, America had entered the war, and political sentiment had shifted in favor of the ideology Tagore had denounced. Moreover, a request from Macmillan to allow Tagore to dedicate the book to President Wilson was refused on the advice of the British ambassador, who suspected Tagore of involvement "in the anti-British plots that were being hatched in America by Indian revolutionaries."[93] In other words, Tagore was accused of collaborating with the very people who had tried to assassinate him.

Tagore's American reputation may have dipped a bit in 1917, but his celebrity helped to establish a permanent place in American culture for Eastern wisdom. Tagore's great fame has to be considered a factor in the American recognition of other Oriental figures of the time, such as Ananda Coomaraswamy. Prior to the second decade of the twentieth century Coomaraswamy was known—outside of India and his native Ceylon—exclusively in England and mainly as a critic of the fine arts, having published numerous articles in the *Burlington Magazine,* published in London. His American career was launched in 1916 with *Buddha and the Gospel of Buddhism,* published simultaneously in London and New York.[94] The bestseller status of the book may have been helped along by the choice of title, which echoes Paul Carus's *Gospel of Buddha,* and by the color plates done by Abanindranath Tagore, Rabindranath's nephew.[95] Coomaraswamy also follows Carus, at least partly: in the preface he promises to present the Buddhist scriptures in relation to "the Brāhmanical systems in which they originate, and, on the other hand, to those systems of Christian mysticism which afford the nearest analogies" (AKC, 1). Further, the syncretic approach that fused Buddhism with esoteric systems of Western mysticism was already familiar to followers of theosophy, even though Coomaraswamy seems not to have had the sort of official relation to theosophy that was enjoyed, if that is the word, by Jiddu Krishnamurti (1895–1986). Nonetheless, through his frequent references to Christian mystics such as Jacob Boehme and William Blake, Coomaraswamy may be the chief exponent of what is usually called the "perennial philosophy," another term for the one-god-fits-all theology first popularized by Vivekananda at the Chicago congress.

But there is also a radical side to Coomaraswamy's Buddhism which attracted a certain species of American middlebrow modernist in the avant-garde culture of the 1910s and '20s. This variant of modernism at issue here is the one whose practitioners interpreted political individualism in terms of the "unique" philosophy propounded by Max Stirner in *Der Einzige und sein Eigentum* (1844). Translated in 1907 as *The Ego and His Own* and published by Benjamin Tucker out of his Unique Book Shop on Fifth Avenue, the book became one of the more important sources for the philosophy of egoism, an antistatist ideology virtually identical with individualist anarchism. Coomaraswamy surely benefited from the prior interest that modernist writers had taken in Tagore's utopian politics, but he went further than Tagore by relating Eastern mysticism to Western radicalism when he likened the Buddha to Nietzsche. However odd the comparison may seem today, it allowed the egoistic modernist to embrace Buddhism as a kind of politico-spiritual avant-gardism. At the time, Stirner was often related to Nietzsche as an anarchist expositor of the value of individual autonomy.[96] Strangely, this ideology seems to have found its way into Coomaraswamy's *Buddha and the Gospel of Buddhism*. An introduction to the book from the late 1960s warns the reader about the author's "frequent comparisons of the Buddha . . . and Nietzsche's Superman."[97] But a certain type of American reader in the second decade of the twentieth century would hardly have regarded Nietzsche as an impediment to the appreciation of Buddhism. Thanks to Emma Goldman and others who appropriated Nietzsche to the anarchist cause by way of Stirner's political egoism, the middlebrow modernist could readily appreciate a Buddha who was also a radical individualist.

Coomaraswamy's Buddha holds in highest regard those who "shall look not for refuge to anyone besides themselves." The sentiment is said to express "the pure individualism of Buddhist thought, here so nearly akin to that of Whitman and Nietzsche" (AKC, 77, 77 n1). Nietzsche is also enlisted to support Buddhist teachings on the nature of pleasure ("in the words of Nietzsche, 'Pleasure is a form of pain'") and on the necessity of avoiding "sentimentality and partiality" ("Gautama had reflected, perhaps, like Nietzsche, 'Ah, where in the world have there been greater follies than with the pitiful?'"). Nietzsche (along with Whitman, again) helps deflect the critique that Buddhism is "a pessimistic faith" (AKC, 92, 144, 176). But the strongest evidence that Coomaraswamy has constructed a Nietzschean Buddha lies in his identification of the Bodhisattva (a term that may refer either to Gautama or to any Buddhist committed to the process of enlightenment) with Nietzsche's *Ubermensch*. The "Bodhisattva ideal" is achieved when "the individual for an end beyond himself takes upon his shoulders the burden of the world's ignorance, and freely spends himself in countless lives of supernatural generosity. The Bodhisattva ideal is practically identical with that of the Nietzschean Superman, with his 'Bestowing Virtue'" (AKC, 179). This last phrase is explained when Coomaraswamy claims that Buddhism has solved the problem that so troubled Emerson, the problem of reconciling self-culture with self-sacrifice: "To achieve this reconciliation, to combine renunciation with growth, knowledge with love, stillness with activity, is the problem of all ethics. Curiously enough, though its solution has often been attempted by oriental religions, it has never been so clearly enunciated in the west as by the 'irreligious' Nietzsche—the latest of the mystics—whose ideal of the Superman combines the Will to Power (*cf. pranidhāna*) with the Bestowing Virtue (*cf. karunā*)" (AKC, 229).[98] The various Nietzschean readings of the Buddha combine with a critique of capitalism that must have been appealing to the radical reader at the time: "At this moment, when the Western world is beginning to realize that it had failed to attain the fruit of life in a society based on competition and self-assertion, there lies a profound significance in the discovery of Asiatic thought, where it is affirmed with no uncertain voice that the fruit of life can be attained in a society based on the conception of moral order and mutual responsibility"; moreover, both Buddhism and Hinduism are said to "stand over against the world of *laissez faire*" (AKC, 2, 3).

Coomaraswamy's official entrance into the cultural field of American modernism is marked by the publication of *The Dance of Siva* in 1918 by the Sunwise Turn Bookshop in New York City. The store was located at East 31st Street and Fifth Avenue, not far from 291, Alfred Stieglitz's avant-garde gallery. Madge Jenison, who founded the business with Mary Mobray Clarke, said she wanted to run "a real bookshop . . . that would pick up all that is related to modern life." During the late teens the Sunrise Turn was a thriving center of avant-garde culture. Peggy Guggenheim worked in the shop for free, and Margaret Anderson was a frequent customer.[99] Anderson is best known as the editor of the *Little Review*, one of the premier organs of the modernist movement in literature. In January 1919 the magazine reviewed *The Dance of Siva* and commended Coomaraswamy for his aesthetic purity. The author of an unsigned review, most likely Anderson herself, observes that "the fashion now to jeer Tagore" is misplaced, that "denial of an art or a civilization proves nothing." The evocation of Tagore is telling, suggesting not only the collapse of his recent American celebrity but also the prospect that his place will be taken by the more "avant-garde" Coomaraswamy. What the reviewer finds most attractive about *The Dance of Siva* is how closely it approximates the editorial opinions of the *Little Review* itself: "Many of our view[s] considered most wildly ex cathedra are calmly endorsed in this history of aesthetics. For instance: beauty is a state, and absolute; a work of art is an outward sign that the artist has discovered the imminence of the Absolute and not that he is trying to regenerate the world or express his opinions, etc."[100] This kind of apolitical, spiritualized aesthetic posture was fully consistent with the Stirnerite anarchism that Anderson, too, promoted. In fact, her interest in Coomaraswamy's book may have been prompted by some of the political ideas in it that approximated her own. In "Cosmopolitan View of Nietzsche," Coomaraswamy attributes "the religion of Idealist Individualism" to the philosopher who is supposed to have cultivated "a selfishness . . . more generous than any altruism."[101]

But the anarchistic sentiments are strongest in the essay that closes the collection, "Individuality, Autonomy, and Function." Here, Coomaraswamy claims that "the repudiation of tyranny must ultimately involve a repudiation of majority rule." He urges "a repudiation of the will to govern" and endorses anarchism outright: "Activity based on anarchic principles may be and often is far more immediately and practically effective than an activity of control" (*Siva*, 137, 138). Oddly enough, the essay makes no reference to Hinduism, Buddhism, or any other Asian faith, with one possible, indirect exception: in considering alternatives to government, Coomaraswamy mentions "a recognition of common interests" and commends "co-operation to achieve them (co-operation is not government)," adding, "This will be an integration founded on the presumed identity of all interests which a monistic philosophy must assert" (*Siva*, 138). We know from Paul Carus that Buddhism was just such a "monistic philosophy."

The Carus connection, however, is insufficient to explain how *The Dance of Siva* managed to cross over from the small-press world of middlebrow American modernism to the wider audience Coomaraswamy enjoyed in the United States. Despite his occasional flirtation with anarchism, he managed to maintain a broad readership because of the universality of his message: his approach is so syncretic that the most esoteric beliefs are made accessible through comparison with more familiar references. He wrote for the general reader, not for the scholar. As Arnold Kunst observes, "Coomaraswamy's treatment of the subject [of Buddhism], unruffled by technical detail and based on the intuitive search for the core of the problems[,] results in the, typical for him, humanistic and broad interpretation offered *sub specie aeternitatis* rather than with a historian's critical outlook."[102]

A less charitable explanation is simply that the American market for Eastern wisdom is not easily exhausted, especially when it is made both mystical and accessible. The merging of the commercial and the mystical is perhaps best illustrated by the long print career of Kahlil Gibran, whose *Prophet* (1923) has sold many millions of copies but was once read, like Coomaraswamy's and Tagore's early works, as a form of modern literature. His books were reviewed in Harriet Monroe's *Poetry*, where critics debated his place in the modern movement. Those critics wound up objecting to Gibran's work, finding its symbolism "too expository" and its "high-sounding easy wisdom" nothing more than a collection of platitudes.[103] Such judgments, however, had no effect on Gibran's popular reputation, probably because the American market for mystical literature had already been tapped by Tagore and Coomaraswamy. Although Gibran's lasting fame among the masses is unthinkable without the prior celebrity of Tagore and Coomaraswamy, he differs from them in at least one important respect: Gibran, a Syrian immigrant, as a child in Boston came under the influence of the pictorialist photographer F. Holland Day, who tutored the youth in symbolist literature, especially Maeterlinck, and introduced him to theosophy and other fin-de-siècle mystical cults. Gibran took this influence to heart and became a mystic himself: a blurb for his first book calls the poet "the William Blake of the Twentieth Century."[104] Hence, Gibran was the source of the wisdom literature he produced, whereas Tagore and Coomaraswamy were largely expositors of long-established traditions. That said, all three had in common the cultivation of a syncretic sensibility that urged mystical alternatives to American materialism.

Such universalism was possibly the only acceptable attitude for an Asian author to take during a period in American history marked by increasing hostility to immigrant groups. Although the Red Scare of 1919 and the Red Raids of January 1920 were driven by paranoia over the anarchist involvement of European immigrants (chiefly Italians), there was an ample supply of hatred and racism to go around among other national groups. The immigrant antagonism peaked in 1924, with the Immigration Act of that year, which included the notorious Asian Exclusion Act, prohibiting people of Asian origin from owning land or becoming naturalized citizens. In this context, the activities of Ananda Coomaraswamy appear either courageous or foolhardy. After all, he had openly advocated anarchism in his 1918 essay at the end of *The Dance of Siva*. And in the same year that the Asian Exclusion bill became law, Coomaraswamy founded the India Culture Center in New York, also serving as its first president. No doubt such activities were made easier by his promotion of a perennial philosophy that could not be tied to a single cultural tradition; at the same time, though, there is no mistaking Coomaraswamy's efforts to overcome American prejudices against the Asian races. He was quite active in the East and West Association, founded in New York by Pearl S. Buck in 1941, which supported the Allied war effort in Asia and called attention to the plight of the peoples of China and India who had suffered the effects of colonialism and racism for so long.[105] In the movement of the American Orient from modernism to mass culture, Coomaraswamy's involvement with Buck in the East and West Association shows that the perennial philosophy is not always limited by eternity or constrained by transcendence.

VI

Pearl S. Buck's *The Good Earth* is perhaps the premier example of the American Orient in the form of popular culture. The book was the best-selling novel in the United States in both 1931, the year of its publication, and the following year. Buck was awarded the Pulitzer Prize when the book came out, and she received the Nobel Prize for Literature in 1938, largely on the merits of *The Good Earth*. The reasons for the book's success have long been linked to the Great Depression of the 1930s, since Buck's narrative of the northern Chinese farmer Wang Lung and his hard-working wife O-Lan gained topical relevance during the Dust Bowl years. The Chinese landscape recalls the Great Plains, and some of the crops that Wang Lung plants, notably wheat and corn, were likewise staples of farms in Kansas and Nebraska. The Chinese farmers in Buck's fictional world also struggle to overcome floods, drought, and locusts, just as their real-life American counterparts did as the Dust Bowl decade wore on. The Dust Bowl began the year of the book's publication, so the ultimate triumph of Wang Lung and his family over difficulties similar to those American farmers faced had understandable appeal. But the book is far more interesting and complex than this simple explanation of its popularity, or its simple style, suggests.

The comparison of Buck's China to Dust Bowl America is complicated by the novelist's firsthand experience of agricultural methods. The daughter of Presbyterian missionaries, Buck had grown up in China and spoke fluent Chinese. She met her first husband, John Lossing Buck (called "Lossing"), in Nansuzhou, in the northern province of Anhui (spelled "Anhwei" in the novel), where he had gone to study Chinese farming after his graduation in 1914 from Cornell University, originally a land-grant college devoted to the study of agriculture. After their marriage in 1917, he got a job at the University of Nanjing, eventually becoming a professor in its Department of Agriculture. Although he was an expert in modern agricultural methods and taught courses in farm engineering, farm management, and the like, he developed the view that the Chinese farmer could not fully benefit from modernization. In 1930, after studying close to 3,000 farms, he published his findings in book form as *Chinese Farm Economy,* which recognized that the kinds of modern agricultural methods practiced in the United States might not serve the Chinese farmer well at all: "Progress in Chinese agriculture does not depend solely, as so many think, upon the introduction of expensive farm machinery of the West."[106] Because Chinese peasants were "too poor to purchase—and their farms too small to accommodate—US reapers, mowers, steam plows, seed drills, and harrows," Lossing Buck recommended that they continue to use "the preindustrial methods that had traditionally enabled [them] to farm so efficiently."[107] His wife, Pearl, was very familiar with this book because she had helped to type the reports on which it was based, and may even have helped to write some parts of it.[108]

Buck appears to incorporate in her novel a number of the observations about farm life made in her husband's scholarly study, but she departs from some of those observations in significant ways. The fictional farm in *The Good Earth* follows the basic facts outlined in *Chinese Farm Economy*: Wang Lung acquires his land through inheritance, uses an ox to pull the plough, and requires two people to work the farm (*CFE,* 37, 219, 231). Early on, O-Lan is the second hand, which would have been unusual, because most women would not have been expected to work, having undergone the ordeal of foot binding, which, Lossing tells us, "is much more prevalent in Northern China" (*CFE,* 235) where the novel is set. But because O-Lan had been raised as a slave she was not required to have the dainty feet expected of women from wealthy families.

Although Pearl would hardly have required *Chinese Farm Economy* for information about climate, Lossing's description of the weather in the plains area of northern China verifies its fictional representation: "Irregularity of rainfall is typical of both North and East Central China but more so in Northern China, and this accounts for either floods or droughts. Such conditions may affect large areas in North China during the same season and thus cause famine" (*CFE,* 11–12). When such conditions strike the Wang Lung farm, the family has inadequate food reserves to survive the famine and so is forced to abandon the property. Lossing's book mentions the problem of insufficient reserves a number of times, a situation "aggravated by the absence of . . . credit" (*CFE,* 425). Access to capital is certainly a problem for Wang Lung, a problem that is rectified only by the accidental acquisition of wealth when the revolution breaks out in Nanjing. Later in the novel, and mainly through the savvy machinations of his second son,

Wang Lung is sufficiently wealthy to make loans to other farmers, and at a high rate of interest. The son's business acumen is attributable to his education, and the fact that he and his older brother are both literate is quite unusual in the farming communities that Lossing describes. According to *Chinese Farm Economy,* most farmers in the north of China "object to sending their children to school . . . because of the need for them on the farm" (*CFE,* 236).

Buck seems to have recognized the problems faced by the farmers identified in her husband's study, but she does not necessarily advocate all the solutions he recommends. Her fictional representation agrees with his factual analysis insofar as Wang Lung's primitive agricultural methods are perfectly adequate for success, mainly because of the enormous labor he expends in working the farm. But Buck raises doubts about her husband's recommendation that what the Chinese farmer needs is greater access to credit and capital. There is no mistaking the moral position she takes toward Wang Lung's over-enterprising sons at the end of the novel, and in this context it is perhaps telling that Buck referred to the common people in her book as "the proletariat."[109] In general, however, the representation of farming in *The Good Earth* could never be mistaken for the kind of farming that exhausted the soils of the plains states and led to the Dust Bowl. Possibly, the appeal of Buck's novel was not simply that its readers could recognize an analogue of America in China; they could also see how they might recover from the problems of modern life by rejecting them and returning to a simpler age. Once again, the Orient offered something America lacked, only here the offer was rather paradoxical, since what America lacked was lack itself: that is, the problem involved too much modernity, and the remedy was all in the relinquishing.

The nostalgic appeal of an earlier agrarian age might very well have been an element of the book's initial popularity, but Buck makes clear that such preindustrial dreams are doomed, even in China. Throughout the novel, Wang Lung's single-minded insistence on the value of the land and on the importance of forming a deep connection to the good earth pays dividends over and over again. The house in which the farmer lives with his aged father is fashioned out of the land itself, "great squares of earth dug from their own fields, and thatched with straw from their own wheat."[110] When Wang Lung gives his wife O-Lan money to buy cloth, he thinks about how "it had come out of the earth, this silver, out of his earth that he ploughed and turned and spent himself upon" (*Earth,* 35). The sexual connotations of this last phrase are played out in Wang Lung's marriage, for both O-Lan and her first child seem to have emerged from the land itself: they are "brown as the soil" and look like "figures made of the earth" (41).

Despite drought, flood, and locusts, the land remains the only reliable basis for family life and human society. Two contrasting episodes make this point: the family's exile to a city to the south, where they beg to avoid starvation caused by a terrible drought; and Wang Lung's dalliance with a young woman whom he takes for his second wife once he becomes somewhat wealthy. In both cases, the land offers cure and comfort: "As he had been healed of his sickness of heart when he came from the southern city and comforted by the bitterness he had endured there, so now again Wang Lung was healed of his sickness of love by the good dark earth of his fields and he felt the moist soil on his feet and he smelled the earthy fragrance rising up out of the furrows he turned for the wheat" (*Earth*, 212).

But as the family acquires greater wealth and the children mature, social pressures cause Wang Lung to remove himself ever further from the land. The pressures are nourished by his eldest son's insistence that it is not appropriate for the family to continue to live like peasants. At the end of the novel, this son and his younger brother contemplate selling parts of the land to exploit the financial opportunities opened up by the modern world, as one tells the other, "This field we will sell and this one, and we will divide the money between us evenly. Your share I will borrow at good interest, for now with the railroad straight through I can ship rice to the sea and I . . ." At this point Wang Lung protests, "We will never sell the land. . . . Out of the land we came and into it we must go." The sons then assure their father that "the land is not to be sold," but the assurance is false: "Over the old man's head they looked at each other and smiled" (*Earth*, 357). American readers in the 1930s would have been in a position to experience this ending as more complex than we do now, since they had experienced how modernity had all but destroyed both farming and finance. The Dust Bowl and the Wall Street crash could both be seen as the products of the kinds of initiatives that Wang Lung's sons contemplate at the end of *The Good Earth*.

Even the simple style of the novel is not so simple as it seems. Buck's language is partly a mirror of her principal characters, illiterate peasants who could not be expected to communicate complex ideas in complex language. The simplicity of the style has made the book a fixture of American high school and junior high school curricula, but Buck clearly did not set out to write a book for juveniles. Nor can the style be explained solely as a reflection of the characters' psychology and social status. Rather, the style seems calculated to represent the feel of the Chinese language for readers of English, and so functions in the service of verisimilitude. Buck had experimented with the technique in her first novel, *East Wind, West Wind* (1930), and had defended certain phrases that seemed odd to English ears but, she believed, accurately captured the flavor of Chinese idioms.

Buck often claimed "that she first composed her novels mentally in Chinese, and then translated them into English" in order "to reproduce in English the altogether different cadences of Chinese speech."[111] More often than not in *The Good Earth*, Buck's language suggests the subject-verb-object (SVO) syntax of Chinese. Of course, SVO is also the basic syntax of English, but Chinese employs subordination to a lesser degree than English does, a syntactical feature that Buck conveys by limiting or simplifying subordination in the novel. She avoids subordinating adverbs like "therefore" and "however" in favor of "when" and "if," but mostly she employs the coordinating conjunctions "and" and "but," especially to represent speech. A good example of the "Chinese" style occurs when Lotus, Wang Lung's second wife, expresses dissatisfaction with her situation: "Now and I have no one except you and I have no friends and I am used to a merry house and in yours there is no one except the first wife who hates me and these children of yours who are a plague to me, and I have no one" (*Earth*, 206). The sentence also captures the morphology of Chinese, which tends to be monosyllabic. Even the bi-syllabic words in the sentence—"except," "merry," and "children"—are each a single morpheme (with the partial exception of "children," which employs the rare pluralizing morpheme -*en*).

In addition to imitating the syntax and morphology of Chinese, Buck also occasionally imitates semantic features unique to the language. For example, instead of the English word "train," she uses the term "fire-wagon" (93), an exact translation of the Chinese compound *huǒchē* (lit., "fire-carriage"). Instead of "rifle" she writes "firestick" (*Earth*, 297), a coinage which suggests either *huǒqì* "firearm" (lit., "fire-tool") or *qiāng*, which means both "rifle" and "spear."

The Chinese feel of the text is further conveyed by the use of proper names and place names in their Chinese forms. In addition to the principals Wang Lung and O-Lan, the elder and younger sons are given the names Nung En and Nung Wen, whose meaning is explained: "The first word of each name signified one whose wealth is from the earth" (*Earth*, 164). One passage is remarkable not only for the use of place names in their Chinese forms but also for Buck's comparison of country language with city language:

> But Anhwei is not Kiangsu. In Anhwei, where Wang Lung was born, the language is slow and deep and it wells from the throat. But in the Kiangsu city where they now lived the people spoke in syllables which splintered from their lips and from the ends of their tongues. And where Wang Lung's fields spread out in slow and leisurely harvests twice a year of wheat and rice and a bit of corn and beans and garlic, here in the farms about the city men urged their

land with perpetual stinking fertilizing of human wastes to force the land to a hurried bearing of this vegetable and that besides their rice. (*Earth*, 106)

The extension of the language comparison into an analogy of one type of agriculture to another adds meaning to the "simple" style that Buck has created: it is the very language of the earth.

The verisimilar style, then, also has a metaphorical purpose that is of a piece with the idealization of preindustrial farming as preferable, in many ways, to modern agriculture. And if modern agricultural methods, like the farms surrounding Kiangsu city, "force the land to a hurried bearing" and exhaust the soil, as happened in the years leading up to the Dust Bowl, then both the style and the subject of *The Good Earth* could be read as a remedy for the ills of Depression-era America. In some ways the film version, released in 1937 as the Dust Bowl period was nearing its end, exploits the comparison of premodern China and modern America that is implicit in Buck's novel. But it largely oversimplifies the complexities of Buck's "simple" novel, not only by subjecting her story to the studio formulae required to ensure box-office success but also by offering modern solutions to the problems of peasant farming, solutions which neither Buck nor her husband sanctioned.

MGM purchased the rights to *The Good Earth* at the end of May 1932 and, after more than a year of initial planning, sent a production crew to China in December 1933. The slow pace of the production schedule was to mark the project throughout; it was beset by any number of delays and difficulties, including the suicide of George Hill, the first of three directors assigned to the film. Hill had overseen the production in China and had met with Buck in Shanghai. Although she had no official role in the making of the film once she signed away the rights to her book, she must have made a number of suggestions to Hill about locations and casting. In August 1932, long before he arrived, Buck had written to an MGM studio executive in New York offering detailed recommendations, advising, for instance, that the southern city of Suzhou be used as the site of the 1911 revolution depicted in the novel, even though she had imagined the action in Nanjing (her reasons for the shift were convenience of access and the cityscape of Suzhou, relatively unchanged between 1911 and 1932). She also advised using an all-Chinese cast.

As things developed, both ideas—location shooting and Chinese casting—became problematic as the production team, supervised by Irving Thalberg, struggled to reconcile the demands of authenticity and accessibility. Using a Chinese cast presented language problems because most Chinese actors were not fluent English speakers (the studio flirted with the idea of an all-Chinese version with subtitles); further, the Chinese Exclusion Laws would have led to problems with any post-location shooting back in Hollywood. Location shooting was also complicated by the political treatment of some scenes, which were more overtly handled in the film than in the book. In the novel, Wang Lung has little or no understanding of the nationalist uprising in the southern city, and the reader, likewise, cannot grasp the full significance of the events because they are presented from the character's limited perspective. In the film, the republican politics of the soldiers is quite explicit; moreover, they repress the looting in the southern city by sending peasants to the wall to die by firing squad. The Chinese government would never have permitted such a scene to be shot in China; in fact, the government later insisted that the scene be cut from the completed film when it was shown in China. In the end, then, the studio decided against location shooting: "It is not exactly practical to make the whole picture in China," Hill reported to Thalberg, "as our facilities will be limited by distance." So the crew packed up and returned to Hollywood.[112]

The return to Hollywood did not mean that the studio had sacrificed its original goal of authenticity. On the contrary, Hill had overseen a massive effort to acquire a stock of properties from Chinese farms and towns to make the film a realistic depiction of Chinese life. Sidney Franklin, the film's third director (who received screen credit), recalled that "the cargoes of properties" included everything "from costumes covering every period in a quarter of a century, with idols and farm implements, carts and rickshaws, the principal parts of the Chinese sampans, waterwheels, utensils, dishes—in fact everything possibly used in daily life in China, both in big cities and on the farms."[113]

The use of these properties in the final film assured authenticity in the mise en scène, while audience accessibility was assured by the decision to use English-speaking actors. Although Chinese Americans were cast as extras and in some secondary parts, such as the roles of Wang Lung's sons and the backward daughter, all the principal roles went to Anglo-European actors of some renown. The Austrian-born Paul Muni played Wang; the Viennese actress Luise Rainer played O-Lan; the American comic actor Walter Connoly played Wang's uncle; the ballet dancer Tilly Losch, also from Vienna, played the temptress Lotus; another American, Charley Grapewin, played Wang's father. With the exception of Losch, whose Hollywood career was rather limited, the cast by any measure was made up of extremely well known actors, which all but guaranteed the success of the film. Muni had won the Academy Award in 1935 for the title role in *The Story of Louis Pasteur*; he had also received three previous nominations, including the best-actor nomination for his work in *I Am a Fugitive from a Chain Gang* (1932). Rainer had won the best-actress Oscar in 1936 for her second American film, *The Great Ziegfeld,* in which she played the great showman's common-law wife, who, like O-Lan, has to make way for another woman. Connoly had been a fixture in a number of 1930s screwball comedies, including *It Happened One Night* (1934); Grapewin was a veteran of numerous westerns and detective films.

Grapewin's greatest success came after *The Good Earth,* when he played Dorothy's Uncle Henry in *The Wizard of Oz* (1939), which was directed by Victor Fleming, who succeeded George Hill as director of *The Good Earth.* Peter Conn observes that Wang's "entrance into the magnificent House of Hwang anticipates Dorothy's entry into Oz in the classic scene that Fleming would direct just two years later. (Even the musical background is similar.)."[114] Once inside the palace, Wang's bride is given away by the ancient mistress of the house, who speaks in a wheedling voice quite similar to the one used by Margaret Hamilton as the Wicked Witch of the West in the later film. Fleming may have had a hand in planning some of the scenes in *The Good Earth,* but he fell ill and was replaced by Franklin before actual shooting began.[115] But regardless of whether the scenes are attributed to Fleming or to Franklin, certain elements of *The Wizard of Oz* were evidently inspired by *The Good Earth.* The connections might be used to argue that *The Good Earth,* despite the attempts at realism and authenticity, remains as much a fantasy as *The Wizard of Oz,* albeit a fantasy of a different sort.

Another conflict between authenticity and accessibility arose when the screenwriters tried to turn Buck's plot into a workable scenario. In the novel, Wang Lung is at times rather craven in his drive to acquire more land, and his relationship with O-Lan can hardly be described as romantic. Neither character, then, is wholly sympathetic, and neither fit the standard studio profile that required all male leads to be heroic and all female leads to be glamorous. Likewise, the conclusion of the novel, in which the sons secretly conspire against their father's wishes, is hardly the uplifting ending that audiences of Hollywood films had been trained to expect. Clearly, something had to be done if the film version of *The Good Earth* were to become the kind of Hollywood product that would succeed at the box office. James L. Hoban has examined the script files in the MGM archives and detailed the process that led to two key changes in the plot of the novel which mark the finished film: greater attention to O-Lan, and the expansion of the locust plague into the climactic scene of the film. Hoban also notes that the scenario of the film follows the basic four-act structure of the stage adaptation of 1932 written by Owen Davis and his son Donald: "The first act focuses on the marriage of Wang and O-Lan and the birth of their first son; the second act shows the consequences of the drought and the removal to the southern city; the third presents a wealthy Wang, returned to his land, but growing restive and seeking the diversions of Lotus; and the fourth act shifts attention to the ailing O-Lan, the coming of the locusts (off-stage, of course), the marriage of the Eldest Son, and the renewed commitment of Wang to the land."[116] The film is not an adaptation of the play, but the theatrical version does receive screen credit and may have influenced the movie scenario in other ways besides plot structure.

The play opened the fifteenth season of the Theater Guild on 17 October 1932 with a strong cast led by Claude Raines as Wang, Alla Nazimova as O-Lan, and Sydney Greenstreet as Wang's uncle.[117] Whereas Raines and Greenstreet are still known to audiences today for their roles in *Casablanca* and other films, Nasimova has slipped into obscurity, yet she was probably better known at the time because of her long career on the silent screen, including the lead role in *Salome* (1923), which she also produced. The Theatre Guild staging of *The Good Earth* was a major production, with thirty-six named characters, plus another forty-seven parts made up of "Slaves and Servants in the Great House of Hwang, Villagers, Soldiers and Citizens in the city, Mourners, etc." Buck was deeply involved and had final say over "all points of racial and national accuracy" to ensure that the production conformed to the facts of Chinese peasant life as she knew them from her many years in China.[118] It is not clear whether she advised the playwrights on the script, but certainly the play adheres much more closely to the language of the novel than does the film. In a program note titled "Mrs. Buck and the Play," the producers said that "in co-operating with Owen and Donald Davis, the playwrights, Philip Moeller, the director, and Lee Simonson, who designed the sets and the costumes, Mrs. Buck demonstrated not only the keen comprehension of the Oriental psychology, shown with amazing skill in her book, but a knowledge of the Chinese scene, down to the most minute detail, which has been invaluable in bringing her story to life upon the stage." The note includes a rather telling quotation from Buck herself: "During these days while I have been watching the rehearsals of 'The Good Earth,' I have come to realize that the book I wrote has grown and taken on a new life of its own in a new country, a life beyond my conception and almost apart from me. . . . So I see this creation, at once mine and not mine, take on life in an art foreign to me, but which I appreciate."[119]

These rather tepid public comments belied stronger private reservations about the capacities of European and American actors "to impersonate her Chinese characters credibly." Sure enough, when the notices came in, the critics voiced Buck's concerns precisely. The *New York Evening Post* review was typical: "Dragged indoors; played by white actors with English accents and Occidental hearts, who wear pigtails and Chinese costumes; set before a wrinkled cyclorama that is supposed to represent the sky . . . 'The Good Earth' does little more than demonstrate the limitations of the theater as a medium."[120] Obviously, the film would not be constrained by such limitations, but the film would also perpetuate most of the non-Chinese elements of the play, including a makeover in the character of O-Lan.

Certainly the version of O-Lan that appears in the play is closer to the character in the film than to the one in the novel. For example, in the novel Wang Lung is resolute when, during the famine, he refuses the offer to sell the land after his uncle has made the arrangements to do so, shrieking at the would-be buyers, "We will die on the land that has given us birth!" O-Lan simply agrees with her husband and quietly reinforces his resolve (87). In the play, Wang's lines are effectively given to O-Lan when her husband hesitates: "Though we die. . . we will never sell our land!"[121] In the film, Wang decides to sell, but O-Lan, haggard and exhausted from childbirth, emerges from the bedroom to insist that they will never sell the land. In Act I of the play, she shows the sort of savvy business sense that belongs to Wang's second son in the novel: she tells Wang not to sell his wheat immediately after harvest "but save until the snow comes when the people of the town will pay well for it" (1–26). On more than one occasion in the play certain male characters—such as the surly gatekeeper at the House of Hwang—are struck by O-Lan's confident behavior and look at her with awe, "amazed by [her] authoritative tone" (1–21). As Conn says, such respect is "almost completely at odds with the traditional patriarchal assumptions that guided Pearl in writing her novel."[122] Possibly, the character of O-Lan was affected by the casting: Nazimova was a strong-willed, independent woman and something of a nonconformist, to say the least (her production of *Salome* featured a mostly homosexual cast in tribute to Oscar Wilde).[123] In any case, O-Lan is certainly a more knowing, assertive figure in the film than in the novel, but that modification in the character was first made by the playwrights, not the screenwriters.

The second major modification of the novel as adapted for the screen has partial precedent in the play. In the theatrical version, just before she dies, O-Lan says to Ching: "Promise to lead my husband's men against this plague—against the Locusts, I could not rest easily in our good earth knowing it had been given over to them" (3–25). Given the limitations of the stage, the battle against the plague of locusts is not dramatized, but the victory of the farmers is implied in the next and final scene when O-Lan is put to rest in the earth, and shortly thereafter, Wang takes up a hoe and delivers the curtain lines: "Now where is the plough? And where is the seed for the rice planting? Come, Ching, my brother . . . come . . . call the

men . . . I go out to the land" (3–29). The play asks the audience to understand the plague of locusts in metaphorical terms as some combination of
forces that has distracted Wang from the land and has alienated him from
O-Lan. The locust plague functions in a similar metaphorical way in the
novel to reconnect Wang to the land, only there the distraction comes from
his uncle's involvement with the group of bandits known as Redbeards.
After Wang fights the locusts with fire and water, the narrator comments:
"The locusts did this for him. For seven days he thought of nothing but
his land, and he was healed of his troubles and his fears" (*Earth*, 233). The
locust episode takes up a scant two pages in the novel and informs only a
few lines of the play, but it occupies some fifteen minutes of screen time in
the film. It also performs the same metaphorical function of reestablish-
ing Wang's dedication to the good earth by helping him overcome both
his decadent attachment to Lotus and his estrangement from his second
son, who has also come under Lotus's spell. Indeed, right before the locust
plague, Wang catches his son with Lotus, beats him, and orders him out of
his house. But the son helps his father in the struggle against the locusts,
and they are reconciled when the pests are defeated.

As this summary shows, Wang remains a strong paternal figure at the
end of the film, and his sons wholly support him. This ending is completely
contrary to the one orchestrated by Buck at the end of the novel, which
presents Wang as a doddering, old-fashioned figure who is merely patron-
ized by his sons as they scheme to modernize the farm and even sell parts
of it. The film version of the first son, like the one in the novel, receives
a formal education. But unlike the son in the novel, he uses his modern
knowhow to defeat the swarm of locusts and save the traditional farm. In
the novel, Wang takes charge, and, with the help of Ching, fights the locusts
and finds that "the best of his fields were spared" when the cloud of locusts
moves on (233). In the film, when Wang learns that locusts are on the way,
he is resigned to the loss of his fields as the will of heaven. His elder son
rejects such superstition, saying, "It's a thing of nature. We can fight it!"
When an older man recounts the terrible effects of an earlier plague that
he had the misfortune to experience, Wang asks his son, "And can you fight
that with your books?" But the son is undaunted: "I speak of what I heard
at school. And I heard this: that a man is slave to the earth, or its master."
Wang is finally convinced: "If this thing can be done," he says, "show us
how to do it." The son then tells his father and the other farmers exactly
what will happen when the locusts arrive: they will be driven by the wind
to a specific spot, where they can be held off with a firebreak until the wind
changes. His solution is technological: "We'll get kerosene—the fire stuff."
Given the stilted dialogue and the wooden acting, the first-time modern

viewer might reasonably expect more Hollywood bathos to follow; but the locust sequence turns out to be truly spectacular, a masterful piece of filmmaking.

The sequence was shot on the 500-acre working farm that MGM specially created for the film in the Santa Clara hills near Chatsworth, California, complete with wheat crops, pigs, chickens, and water buffalo descended from animals brought from China. The locust plague was cinematically manifested in three ways: through documentary footage of locust swarms, through special effects (bits of burned cork blown by a wind machine), and, most remarkable, through shots of an actual outbreak of locusts filmed in Utah as the movie was being made. The documentary and special effects footage was double-exposed against the farmers frantically fighting the plague in the fields, while the shots of the Utah locusts were intercut with the California footage.[124] As Franklin tells it, his second unit director "took close-ups of Chinese men lying on the ground, with thousands of grasshoppers crawling all over them. A hand would come in and pull the man out of the picture—in Utah. A cut, and the man would rise to his feet in Chatsworth. Combining these scenes with the special effects work created an exceptionally realistic sequence."[125]

The realism was heightened and dramatized by the camerawork of Karl Freund, a veteran of Weimar filmmaking (he was the cinematographer for F. W. Murnau's *Der Letzte Mann* [1924] and for Fritz Lang's *Metropolis* [1927]) and the montage work of Slavko Vorkapich (celebrated for experimental montage sequences in *Manhattan Cocktail* [1928] and *Sins of the Fathers* [1928]). The power of the sequence, which is, again, set up by some truly awful acting and writing, reveals once more the curious combination of authenticity and accessibility in *The Good Earth*. No viewer can fail to appreciate that there is something profoundly true in the struggle of the Chinese peasants against the forces of nature which the sequence captures; at the same time, many viewers are bound to sense something profoundly false in the relationship of father to sons as conveyed by the dialogue. Buck's story is made to fit a formula that has nothing to do with the novel. As one critic put it, "The film edits out and replaces Buck's message, substituting the notion that progress improves on tradition."[126]

The revisions in Buck's story are partly due to the fortuitous resemblance of the trials her Chinese peasants endure to those the American farmer encountered during the Dust Bowl. Clearly, the studio worked this resemblance for all it was worth. The famine sequence begins with shots of dry, cracked earth, and a starving water buffalo nuzzling the mud of a depleted watering hole. Later, shots of dust blowing in the wind appear through the wooden grid of a farmhouse window, suggesting a view from within a prison cell. These details support a reading of the film as the Chinese cognate of the Dust Bowl years, especially when Wang says, "The earth has forgotten us." And when Wang and his family journey south to escape the famine, they hop aboard a train very like a gang of Depression-era hobos, whereas in the novel Wang pays for their transport with his last pieces of silver. The locust plague, another real-life reference to the Dust Bowl (as the Utah outbreak during filming proves), therefore gains in metaphorical force, functioning as a symbol not only within the film but outside of it as well. A filmgoer in the 1930s would have had no difficulty understanding the Chinese triumph over the locusts in allegorical terms, as a hopeful sign that Americans too might overcome the challenges of the Depression and the Dust Bowl. Paradoxically, by being true to the times, the film wound up misrepresenting and oversimplifying the story of *The Good Earth* as Buck had written it.

A further contradiction emerges in the publicity campaign built around the film, which claimed absolute fidelity to the novel. By the late 1930s, Buck was recognized as an authority on China, so any claim of faithfulness to her vision was bound to create a sense in the mind of the public that the film was of historical importance. This much is implied by a title card at the beginning which announces that "the soul of a great nation is expressed in the life of its humblest people. In this simple story of a Chinese farmer may be found something of the soul of China—its humility, its courage, its deep heritage from the past and its vast promise for the future." The trailer for the film is the strongest evidence of a publicity strategy built on the borrowed prestige and presumed authority of Buck's novel: it promises "the glorious screen reproduction of the most vital novel of our time"—the use of the word *reproduction* rather than *adaptation* is telling, as is the montage that superimposes a title and images over the turning pages of the book itself—and continues: "Line by line, page by page, chapter by chapter, the screen unfolds this magnificent drama." The "proof" of this assertion comes with a close-up of the first page of *The Good Earth*—"It was Wang Lung's marriage day"—and a dissolve to the early scene showing Wang making his nuptial preparations and saying, "This is the day!" Next, the cover of the "Pulitzer Prize Novel" appears over a shot of Chinese farmworkers with the superimposed title: "Just as you read it . . . so will you see it. . . ."

Curiously, the preview does provide a fairly faithful synopsis of the novel, up to a point: "Wang and O-Lan are married"; "O-Lan presents Wang with his first-born son"; "Grim famine ravages the north of China"; "Revolution flames in the south"; "Terrifying legions of locusts hide the sun," and so on. The Hollywood formula emerges, however, when the trailer foretells the story of a conventional love triangle: "But the love of

Wang and O-Lan endures until hunger for the lips of Lotus makes Wang forget the heart of O-Lan!" The trailer draws to a close by returning to the revolution sequence—"Frenzied mobs loot the great house"—and the promise that "These . . . and other memorable events from the great book will strike your very soul." The concluding claim is quite remarkable: "This picture *is* the book! The drama that Pearl S. Buck tore from the heart of a man . . . his women . . . and a people!" The end of the four-minute trailer calls *The Good Earth* "a Metro-Goldwyn-Mayer triumph."[127]

As it turned out, the film was a triumph, and the critics did think that it was true to the book. Frank Nugent in the *New York Times* declared it "one of the finest things Hollywood has done this season or any other," adding that it "does full justice to the novel." He did comment that "some liberties" had been taken "with the novel's text," but "none with its quality or spirit," and he had no problem with the "new climax" the studio had invented: "a terrifying locust plague which threatens to destroy his crops and makes Wang realize that the land and O-Lan meant more to him than being the lord of the Great House."[128] Buck made the same kind of public comments about the film that she had earlier made about the play; in fact, she repeated them almost verbatim, telling a reporter for the *New York Evening Post*: "The book I wrote has taken on a new life of its own . . . a life beyond my conception . . . in an art foreign to me but which I appreciate."[129] In private, she expressed doubts about the film that exceeded those she had earlier expressed about the play: "As to the film . . . it's too long . . . and it is so intense with noise and drama . . . that one is exhausted after it. . . . It's too *much*—too much storm, too much locusts, too much looting . . . everything is overdone. . . . The end is changed from the book. O-Lan gets the pearls, the second wife is dismissed, Wang returns to the land—the American romance in other words." Even so, "it's so carefully worked out as to details that it is really authentic in setting in spite of some Hollywood garishness."[130] In short, Buck was pleased about the authenticity of the mise en scène, but she was not happy that the studio had made her story more accessible by turning it into "the American romance."

Buck was right: Hollywood had Americanized her novel. This may seem a strange assertion, given that it was in fact written by an American, but *The Good Earth* did capture a culture utterly foreign to most of Buck's fellow citizens. Moreover, Buck provided little explanation of Chinese customs and traditions, maintaining a voice within the culture, as her English mimicry of Chinese diction and syntax shows. The foreignness of this hybrid world led the producers of the theatrical adaptation to provide program notes "From Various Sources" to help the audience understand the Chinese way of life: the deep connection to the land ("A peasant, thigh-deep in water, plough[s] his field with a plough as primitive as those his fathers have used for forty mortal centuries"); the threat of famine ("Even when there is no famine in China fully 2,000,000 Chinese die annually from starvation"); and the role of women ("Women in China have accepted the position of having husbands chosen for them because they have believed that matches are made in Heaven").[131] The film version got around the problem of unfamiliarity by showing traditional agricultural methods on screen, by illustrating the effects of famine in vivid detail, and by reworking the scenario and the principal characters to conform to audience expectations.

The Americanization of the Chinese in the film version of *The Good Earth*, not to mention the enormous popularity of both the book and the movie, is evidence of changing attitudes toward China in the late 1930s and early 1940s. How much the MGM film actually contributed to this change is hard to say, but there is no denying the growing sympathy of Americans for the Chinese people during that period. The Japanese attacked China in July 1937; the film opened in August; and the hostilities continued to grow through the late summer and fall, so *The Good Earth* was playing in theaters as the second Sino-Japanese War escalated. One critic commented that "*The Good Earth* humanized the Chinese people for the American public; when Japan bombed and invaded China, the public was outraged as if their own neighbors had been invaded."[132] The critic referred to the humanizing effect of the novel, not the film, but surely the film gave added impetus to American sympathies at a critical time. Meanwhile, Pearl S. Buck was tireless in her advocacy of Chinese and Chinese American causes through the several institutions she had created for that purpose. She and her second husband, Richard Walsh, urged repeal of the Chinese exclusion laws through articles in their magazine *Asia,* through their foundation, the East and West Association, and, most important, through the Citizens Committee to Repeal Chinese Exclusion, with Richard as chairman and Pearl as public spokesperson. In this capacity she testified before the House Committee on Immigration and Naturalization in May 1943. Her testimony helped gain the support of Eleanor Roosevelt (with whom she had earlier worked to advance the NAACP) and eventually the president. Thanks in large part to Buck's efforts, the exclusion laws were repealed on 22 October 1943.[133]

If the MGM film did have a role in the momentous repeal of Chinese exclusion, that fact is beset with any number of paradoxes. Chinese actors had after all, been excluded from the main roles in favor of American actors of European extraction. Mainly for that reason, the film has not aged well at all (cinematography excepted), and certainly Chinese Americans today would have a hard time watching it, except as a case study in

Hollywood orientalism. In *Donald Duk* (1991), a novel by the Chinese American author Frank Chin, a character holds Buck accountable for Chinese stereotypes when he says, "I wish Pearl Buck was alive and walk into my restaurant so I can cut out her heart and liver. That's how much I hate that movie."[134] In the late 1930s, however, a number of Chinese Americans, including some prominent figures, were eager to appear in the film. Moy Ming, known as the "patriarch of Chinatown," made his services available, as did Chester Gan, leader of the Young China Movement in Southern California, and Ching Wah Lee, editor of the *Chinese Digest* (he took the role of Ching). Sidney Franklin says in his memoirs that "many of the Chinese regarded it as a patriotic duty to aid in the production."[135] He does not say whether they felt a sense of patriotic duty to China or to the United States, but at the time the film was made, the distinction may not have been that important. What is important is that the film spoke to all Americans, including those of Chinese descent, appearing as it did at a pivotal moment in American history. In one way or another, MGM's *The Good Earth* touched on recent American experiences through its evocation of the Dust Bowl and the Great Depression, even as contemporary events introduced new meanings into the film by way of the Sino-Japanese conflict and the growing threat of an expanding war in Asia. If those meanings have been largely lost today (as the quotation from Chin's novel shows), they are nonetheless worth recalling, because they helped to usher in a new phase in the history of the American Orient, which, thanks to Pearl S. Buck, Irving Thalberg, and other practitioners of the popular, has taken a permanent and prominent place in American culture.

Afterword

AFTER MORE THAN two centuries, the American Orient remains a steady presence in the social and cultural life of the nation. From the earliest conflation of Confucianism with absolutist politics and rationalist morality to the nineteenth-century incorporation of Hinduism into Unitarian theology and transcendentalist philosophy; from the scholarly investigations of ancient Sanskrit and Pali texts to the fin de siècle explorations of Japanese aesthetics; from the modernist revision of almost all the prior treatments of Far Eastern traditions to the exploitation of those traditions by means of mass culture: the American Orient has undergone myriad transformations but continues to attract adherents of various stripes, from sincere believers to bogus promoters. The greatest transformation occurred in the 1940s, with the end of Chinese exclusion and Japanese internment. The period since that time has seen an extraordinary saturation of Asian culture into American experience. Given these changed historical circumstances, the problem of describing the American Orient in a meaningful way has become more difficult. After all, the "Oriental" is a fantasy figure, an ideological delusion derived from books and bias, whereas there is nothing fantastical about the millions of Chinese, Japanese, Korean, and other Asian American citizens who have immigrated to the United States in the wake of the liberal legislation of the 1960s and 1970s.

That said, earlier forms of orientalism continued to circulate in American culture well after their initial appearance, and in some instances it is possible to trace the genealogy of certain ideas and attitudes that persist into the present. That genealogy runs mainly in the realm of popular culture, with early postwar developments like the Beat Generation producing a second Buddhist boom with clear links to the first, mainly by way of the 1893 Parliament of Religions. The Chicago parliament also allows us to observe an unmistakable family resemblance between the New Age gurus who began to appear in the late 1960s and Swami Vivekananda, founder of the Ramakrishna Mission. Similarly, Rabindranath Tagore acted well in advance of the Beatles and the Maharishi Mahesh Yogi when he told Americans in the run-up to World War I to give peace a chance, since all they needed was love. Even the current yoga vogue has precedent in the late nineteenth century through the recently discovered activities of Pierre Bernard (1876–1955), aka "The Great Oom," a combination showman and guru who ran an ashram with a celebrity clientele in Nyack, New York.

Although the imaginary territory of the American Orient has indeed expanded since the end of World War II, the need to imagine the Far East as the counter to or the cure for American ills has by now been far outstripped by hard social realities. Principal among these are the Korean and the Vietnam Wars, Cold War conflicts that made American citizens strategic allies with major segments of two Asian populations against a common ideological enemy. The second of these conflicts had significant social impact, not only because of the antiwar protests against it but also because of the policy of resettling Vietnamese refugees in the United States after the fall of Saigon at the end of April 1975. Special legislation by the Ford administration, known as the Indochina Migration and Refugee Act, assured that increasing numbers of Vietnamese people would be able join other Asian immigrants (Chinese, Filipino, Indian, and Korean, mainly) who had been free to enter the United States after the Immigration Act of 1965. According to government sources, in 1964 the immigration quota from all Asian countries was only 3,690 persons (compared with 149,597 from all European countries). In 1965, Asian immigrants (including Filipinos) totaled almost 20,000, a number that has escalated year after year so that as of the 2000 census, more than 2 million residents of American communities speak Chinese at home; 1.5 million speak Hindi, Gujarati, or some other Indic language; another 1.5 million speak Vietnamese; a million speak Korean; and a half-million, Japanese.[1] The aggregate impact of all these Asian groups on American culture is incalculable, and the kind of categorical analysis used in the earlier chapters of this book (based on politics, theology, scholarship, aesthetics, and so on) can no longer be brought to bear in any meaningful way. The lone category that retains some special relevance is mass culture, but it is strange how many of the Asian elements in the commercial mainstream today owe their origins to an earlier counterculture. That counterculture, in turn, has roots in the fin de siècle infusion of Eastern faith and philosophy into the intellectual and religious life of the United States.

American openness to Oriental culture is something that the fin de siècle has in common with the post–World War II period. The distinction between "American" and "Oriental," however, has become fairly meaningless today, not only because of the outmoded ideological meanings that cling to the word *Oriental* but also because of the ongoing process of Asian assimilation to American ways. But there is another reason to be skeptical of the dichotomy that goes back to the earlier period: much of the culture that passed for Asian from the Chicago congress onward was not itself "authentically" Asian but a kind of hybrid culture that deployed Western contexts to convey Eastern ideas. Vivekananda, Dharmapala, and Shaku Soen were all, to some degree, Oriental orientalists: that is, they presented "native" Asian cultures from Western ideological perspectives.

To be sure, in most cases the choice to frame Hinduism or Buddhism within a familiar Western context such as "progress" or "science" was a conscious, strategic measure designed to reach the American audience. But it is also true that the most popular speakers at the Chicago conference, especially the Buddhists, had experienced considerable exposure to Western ideas before they came to the United States. As a result, they presented versions of their Eastern faiths not fully consonant with traditional practices in their home countries. Anagarika Dharmapala, for example, had met Henry Steel Olcott in Ceylon and accompanied the celebrated Theosophist-cum-Buddhist on his tour of Japan. Olcott had been invited to Japan in 1889 by Hirai Kinzo, the layman who gave the stirring nationalist speech in Chicago criticizing Western imperialism and evangelicalism. No doubt he was attracted to Olcott's criticism of Christianity, but he would also have been interested in Olcott's standing as a man of science whose imprimatur could help promote Buddhism as a modern-day religion.[2] Shaku Soen, whose lecture in Chicago emphasized the compatibility of Buddhism with modern science, had attended Keio Gijuku University after his monastic training—an extremely unusual thing for a Buddhist monk to do, especially since the university experience would have involved no small measure of Westernization.[3] Shaku's student D. T. Suzuki, who had translated the paper his master presented in Chicago, also translated Paul Carus's *The Gospel of Buddha* into Japanese before moving to La Salle and working with Carus on other translation projects over a ten-year period (1897–1908). All these activities give credence to Martin J. Verhoven's claim that "the immense popularity that Oriental religions and philosophy enjoyed in the West can be attributed somewhat to the strange fact that the hybrid forms of Asian thought exported to the Occident were already customized for Western consumption."[4]

The lone figure who spans both the fin de siècle and the post–World War II period is D. T. Suzuki. And although the movement of Eastern thought into the American counterculture is a complex phenomenon involving many players, possibly no single figure is more important to the early phases of that movement than Suzuki. After serving as Shaku's interpreter on the 1905 lecture tour and translating the lectures for Open Court Press as *Sermons of a Buddhist Abbot* (1906), Suzuki himself gave at least one lecture on Buddhism, in Maine, before publishing his first book in English, *Outlines of Mahayana Buddhism* (1907). In 1908 he left La Salle for a year in Europe, and, after working on ancient Buddhist manuscripts at the Bibliothèque Nationale in Paris, he did a Japanese translation of Swedenborg's *Heaven and Hell* at the request of the London Swedenborg Society. The translation appeared in 1910, the year after he returned to Japan at age thirty-nine. In 1913 Suzuki published a book about Swedenborg and, in the years following, did three more translations of the Swedish mystic's work: *The New Jerusalem* (1914), *The Divine Love and the Divine Wisdom* (1914), and *The Divine Providence* (1915). To be sure, during this period the prolific Suzuki was also doing Japanese translations of Chinese classics and writing original works in both Japanese (*Zengaku Taiyo,* an outline of Zen [1913]) and English (*A Brief History of Early Chinese Philosophy* [1914]).[5] But the early work with Swedenborg, the translation of Carus's *Gospel of Buddha,* and Suzuki's first original publication, an "Essay on Emerson" from 1896, merit emphasis here because all these projects show the depth of Suzuki's involvement with esoteric Western traditions. The connection with Emerson seems particularly strong: Suzuki's *Essays in Zen Buddhism (First Series)* (1927) and *Essays in Zen Buddhism (Second Series)* (1933) are evidently so titled as an homage to Emerson's two essay collections, likewise subtitled *First Series* and *Second Series.*[6] Although Suzuki published a number of works in English, intended for the Western reader, over the first half of the twentieth century, he did not return to the United

States until 1950, when he moved to New York City and began lecturing at Columbia University at the age of eighty. He remained at Columbia until 1957, moved to Cambridge to lecture at Harvard, M.I.T., and other universities, then returned to Japan in 1958. In 1959 he published *Zen and Japanese Culture,* a substantially revised version of his 1938 book, *Zen Buddhism and Its Influence on Japanese Culture.* The 1959 edition may serve as a rough guide to Suzuki's thinking on Zen Buddhism during the 1950s, the critical decade of his influence on the emerging American counterculture.

Suzuki is so mindful of Western contexts in *Zen and Japanese Culture* that the book could almost be retitled *Zen and American Culture.* The point can be partly illustrated by his bibliography, divided into "Ancient Chinese Sources" and "Books in English." Ezra Pound's *The Great Digest and the Unwobbling Pivot* appears on both lists; the second list features such American classics as T. S. Eliot's *Complete Poems and Plays,* Emerson's *Complete Writings,* Thoreau's *Walden,* and Whitman's *Leaves of Grass.* Pound excepted, all these writers are enlisted to support Suzuki's comments about Zen in the text itself. After recounting an anecdote from Baso Doichi (d. 788) in which the master chides a student for failing to recognize that reality is "not outside but within his person," Suzuki comments that "this person is Rinzai's 'true man in all nakedness going in and out through your senses.'" He then wonders if this "true man" is analogous to "the third who always walks beside you" in Eliot's evocation of the apostles' anguished perception of the risen Christ in *The Waste Land.*[7]

In the chapter "Zen and Swordsmanship," Suzuki quotes Emerson's "Brahma" in full because the poem "fittingly illustrates the perfect swordsman's psychology" (*Z & J,* 207). Verses from the same poem are quoted again later in connection with a passage from the *Bhagavad-Gita.* But the most remarkable reference to Emerson comes near the end of the book, when Suzuki indulges in an autobiographical reflection, something he rarely does: "I am now beginning to understand the deep impressions made upon me while reading Emerson in my college days. I was not then studying the American philosopher but digging down into the recesses of my own thought, which had been there ever since the awakening of Oriental consciousness. That was the reason why I had felt so familiar with him—I was, indeed, making acquaintance with myself then. The same can be said of Thoreau" (*Z & J,* 343–44). Thoreau is earlier used to explain the Japanese concept of *wabi,* abstractly defined as "transcendental aloofness in the midst of multiplicities" but illustrated practically as the capacity to be "satisfied with a little hut, a room of two or three *tatami* (mats), like the log cabin [*sic*] of Thoreau" (*Z & J,* 23). The East-West comparison is made more explicit when Suzuki quotes a poem by Dogen (1200–1253), founder of one branch of Zen Buddhism, and a passage from the "Solitude" chapter of *Walden*, both involving the sound of rainfall and both illustrative of "what is sometimes designated as cosmic consciousness" (*Z & J*, 342).

The lone reference to Whitman, though brief, is in some ways the most significant of all the references to American writers whom Suzuki cites to clarify the meaning of Zen. In "Love of Nature," the final chapter of *Zen and Japanese Culture,* Suzuki recounts several anecdotes about the Zen Lunatic Ryokwan, described as a "lover of trees," children, and the vermin on his own body, all to make the point that "independence and spontaneity" are to be valued above all else. Whitman joins Ryokwan as an exemplar of the kinds of values Suzuki believes are needed to counter the deadening conformism of the 1950s:

> These days we live under such varied rules of convention. We are really slaves to ideas and notions, fashions and traditions, which constitute the psychological background or what is now popularly called the ideology of modern people in the organization. We can never act as Whitman advises. We are in a state of complete slavery, although we may not realize it or, rather, are not willing to admit it. When we see Ryōkwan giving himself up to the free movement of his feelings, which are thoroughly purged, to follow the conventional parlance of all egotistically oriented defilements, we feel as refreshed as if we were transported into another world. (*Z & J*, 373–74)

The language that Suzuki uses here, notably the phrase "modern people in the organization," strongly suggests that he is setting up the Zen experience as a counter to the sensibility famously described by William H. Whyte in his best-selling study of 1956, *The Organization Man.*

The basic thesis of Whyte's book is that conformism and collectivity stifle creativity and individuality, a claim few would dispute today but one that had to be argued then. In his introduction Whyte pointed out that the problem he had identified was not limited to the corporation but influenced other institutions as well: "The corporation man is the most conspicuous example, but he is only one, for the collectivization so visible in the corporation has affected almost every field of work. Blood brother to the business trainee off to join Du Pont is the seminary student who will end up in the church hierarchy, the doctor headed for the corporate clinic, the physics Ph.D. in a government laboratory, the intellectual on the foundation-sponsored team project, the engineering graduate in the huge drafting room at Lockheed, the young apprentice in a Wall Street law factory."[8]

Shortly after the book was published, the Du Pont Corporation took out a magazine advertisement showing a group of well-groomed, purposeful-

looking junior executives in suits and ties juxtaposed to an image of a
solitary, disheveled figure in worn-out jeans, wearing sandals and holding a guitar. The solitary figure was captioned "Bernie the Beatnik," an
obvious failure compared with the corporate types, who had not given up
their freedom when they went to work for Du Pont, as Bernie the Beatnik
thought, but, rather, had taken action to ensure it: the organization men
were "pursuing a freedom that can be enjoyed only so long as [we] have a
strong, creative and productive nation."[9] The Cold War anxieties expressed
here are also implied by the term *beatnik* itself, one of many late 1950s
coinages inspired by the satellite Sputnik, which the Soviet Union launched
on 4 October 1957. The pejorative, Russianizing suffix attached to *beat*
meant that the beatnik, like Sputnik, was a sign of something ominously
threatening to American values. Even though the lines between the organization man and the beatnik, between corporate conformism and rebellion
against it, were already being drawn when Suzuki published his influential
book on Zen, he nonetheless helped to identify the counterculture of the
Beat Generation with Far Eastern thought.

Suzuki was not, of course, the only writer of the 1950s advocating Far
Eastern means of overturning Western materialism and conformism. The
year after Whyte published *Organization Man,* Alan Watts (1915–1973)
published *The Way of Zen.* Born in Great Britain, Watts came to the United
States in 1938, after publishing *The Spirit of Zen* in 1936, a book that
Watts himself described as "a popularization of Suzuki's earlier works."[10]
The twenty-one-year-old Watts had been inspired to write his first book on
Zen after meeting Suzuki at the World Congress of Faiths at the University of London. Watts's long and varied American career included service
in the Episcopal Church early on, but he is best known as having been a
popularizer of Asian thought. Millions of Americans were introduced to
Taoism, Mahayana Buddhism, and Zen Buddhism through his numerous
books, his six-part series *Eastern Wisdom and Modern Life* (which aired
on National Education Television in the early 1960s), and a long-running
weekly radio broadcast for KPFA in Berkeley, California, which he kept up
from 1953 until his death in 1973.[11] His 1957 *Way of Zen* made an effort
to break free of the influence of Suzuki, citing the need for a book on Zen
that would supply more background and history than Suzuki had provided.
Suzuki's *Zen and Japanese Culture,* published two years after *The Way of
Zen,* may have been a partial response to this criticism. In any event, what
is important is that two substantial books on Zen Buddhism appeared
within two years, both published at a time when the postwar paradigm of
institutional life was being questioned. Indeed, part of the appeal of Zen,
Watts says in his 1957 book, lies in its refusal "to be organized, or to be

made the exclusive possession of any institution"; moreover, its exponents "never sought the acknowledgment of any formal authority" (xiv). No sooner had Whyte diagnosed the illness of the 1950s than Suzuki and Watts suggested a possible cure in Zen Buddhism.

Watts, however, went further than Suzuki by cautioning against the conformism and authoritarianism that he saw evident in some forms of Zen Buddhism itself. His "Beat Zen, Square Zen, and Zen" warns that the organization man might even turn up in the Buddhist temple as the practitioner of "square Zen": that is, "the Zen of established tradition in Japan with its clearly defined hierarchy, its rigid discipline, and its specific tests of *satori*." Watts finds "beat Zen" also lacking, since all too often it is used "to justify a very self-defensive Bohemianism." He insists instead on a type of Zen that is neither beat nor square: "For Zen is above all the liberation of the mind from conventional thought, and this is something utterly different from rebellion against convention, on the one hand, or adapting foreign conventions, on the other."[12]

This important essay first appeared in the summer 1958 issue of the *Chicago Review,* prior to the publication of Jack Kerouac's *The Dharma Bums* in the fall. When Watts expanded the essay for publication as a City Lights pamphlet in 1959, he added several pages on the relationship of Zen to different art forms, including the music of John Cage, the painting of Mark Tobey, and, of course, the fiction of Kerouac. (He is especially hard on Cage, calling his experiments with blank scores and random noises "therapy" but not art [95]). Watts updated the essay again for book publication in 1960, adding a long introductory note correcting the impression that his criticism of the beat variety of Zen meant that he was a spokesman for the square version. He makes clear that he is no advocate for anything "that can be organized, taught, transmitted, certified or wrapped up in any kind of system" (80). Quite the contrary: "Let Zen soak into the West informally, like the drinking of tea" (81). Where the earlier *Way of Zen* had criticized Suzuki for his "unsystematic" presentation, that defect now appears as a virtue, given the way Zen Buddhism resists being organized by any kind of system. The book version of "Beat Zen, Square Zen, and Zen" includes a footnote characterizing Suzuki as "a very rare bird among contemporary Asians—an original thinker." As such, "people in square Zen and academic sinology have their qualms about accepting him" (105 n5). Suzuki's status as a layman in the Zen hierarchy of Japan was certainly no impediment to his being accepted in the United States. Together with Watts, Suzuki has to be regarded as a significant impetus to America's second Buddhist boom.

The second boom differs from the first one, inspired by Sir Edwin Arnold's *The Light of Asia,* in two important respects. First, the historical circumstances that marked the entrance of Buddhism into American culture in the late nineteenth century could not have been more unlike those of the late 1950s. Arnold's poem appeared at a time when Americans had grown weary of strenuous achievement and were cultivating a more spiritual, aesthetic, and "feminine" ethos. Suzuki's and Watts's books came to national attention at a deeply anxious period of the Cold War, a period that made the pacifist appeal of Buddhism especially attractive. And for the fatalistic, the prospect of nuclear annihilation may have been easier to reconcile with Buddhist nirvana than with the promises of conventional Christianity. Second, the social resonance of the second Buddhist boom was notably different from that of the first. Aside from a few fundamentalist ministers, most of the Victorian-era Americans who read *The Light of Asia* found the poem only mildly controversial, and its great popularity suggests that Arnold succeeded in his goal of melding morality and exoticism; in fact, the morality was sufficiently familiar to make the exotic both socially acceptable and intellectually interesting. The mid-twentieth-century Americans who were attracted by the second Buddhist boom differed from their nineteenth-century ancestors in that they had no real interest in the alleged similitude of Buddhism and Christianity (Jack Kerouac excepted). Rather, they used Buddhism as a vehicle to reject not just Christianity and other forms of middle-class morality but the very idea of the middle class itself, which validated the corporate, conformist, and consumerist values Whyte had so eloquently described.

Unease over the corporate lifestyle, the attraction of Zen Buddhism as an alternative to that lifestyle, and the emergence of the Beat Generation were closely interrelated developments in postwar America. One of the simplest ways of characterizing the members of the Beat Generation is to say that they were all alienated from their middle-class origins and chose to live their lives apart from the social structures readily available to them—or, at least, that was the way their alter egos behaved in their fiction and poetry. Jack Kerouac may have ended up living with his mother in the depths of alcoholism and Catholicism, but his persona was always on the road as a mostly Mahayana Buddhist. Of Kerouac's several road novels, *The Dharma Bums* (1958) is probably the most representative of the counterculture lifestyle guided by an Eastern sensibility. The Kerouac character in this novel is named Ray Smith, a kind of hobo Bodhisattva who gravitates to the Bay Area during the San Francisco Poetry Renaissance. In fact, the book itself is a document of that important cultural moment, a roman à clef that features fictional versions of now canonized poets such as Kenneth Rexroth, Gary Snyder, and Allen Ginsberg.[13] The novel contains an account of Ginsberg's reading of "Howl" at Gallery Six on the evening of 13 October 1955, "the night of the birth of the San Francisco Poetry Renaissance."[14] Ginsberg is called "Alvah Goldbrook," and his poem is called "Wail," but Kerouac works in a knowing allusion to the actual title when he refers to all the participants at the legendary reading as "the whole gang of howling poets" (*Bums*, 288, 289). The principal poet in *The Dharma Bums*, however, is not Ginsberg but Snyder, who goes by the fictional name "Japhy Ryder." An avid proponent of Zen Buddhism, Ryder lives near the Berkeley campus in a twelve-by-twelve shack fitted out in Asian style, with straw mats instead of chairs and a collection of books, "some of them in Oriental languages," such as "all the great sutras [Buddhist scriptures], comments on sutras, the complete works of D. T. Suzuki and a fine quadruple volume edition of Japanese haikus" (292). Smith is never without a copy of the *Diamond Sutra* himself, for the book contains invaluable counsel for someone whose life is lived on the road. For example, a shared meal with a fellow freight-hopper prompts this reflection: "I reminded myself of the line in the Diamond Sutra that says, 'Practice charity without holding in mind any conceptions about charity, for charity after all is just a word'" (*Bums*, 282).

Kerouac singles out the Christian virtue of charity in the sutra, and in the novel, numerous times, suggesting a measure of acceptance of Christianity in the narrator which is generally absent from the character Japhy Ryder. In fact, the contrasting spiritual attitudes of these two characters is sounded many times. For example, they sit in a park in Chinatown listening to a black female preacher (a dramatic situation already suggestive of several layers of cultural and religious synthesis) and have an argument about "all that Jesus stuff she's talking about." Smith asks, "What's wrong with Jesus? Didn't Jesus speak of Heaven? Isn't Heaven Buddha's Nirvana?" and confesses to Ryder that he is troubled by "this schism we have about separating Buddhism from Christianity, East from West" (363). Shortly thereafter, Smith hops another freight train, this time to begin a cross-country journey to visit his mother in North Carolina for Christmas, and invokes both religious traditions as he rides: "O Buddha thy moonlight O Christ thy starling on the sea" (*Bums*, 365).

Kerouac thus emerges as a major exception to the midcentury impulse to use Buddhism as a counter to Christianity, possibly because his variety of Buddhism is far less inflected with the Zen perspective represented by Snyder, Watts, and other Bay Area residents who are more closely identified with the San Francisco Renaissance than is Kerouac. *The Dharma Bums* itself offers ample evidence of this claim. The distinction between two types of Buddhism is drawn early in the novel when Smith calls Zen Buddhism "silly," and, seeing that the comment "took Japhy back a bit," goes on to explain:

"I'm not a Zen Buddhist, I'm a serious Buddhist, I'm an oldfashioned dreamy Hinayana coward of later Mahayanism," and so forth into the night, my contention being that Zen Buddhism didn't concentrate on kindness so much as on confusing the intellect to make it perceive the illusion of all sources of things. "It's *mean*," I complained. "All those Zen Masters throwing young kids in the mud because they can't answer their silly word questions." (*Bums*, 288)

However much the two characters may differ over the precise form that Buddhism should assume in the United States, they agree that it must be part of a countercultural revolution, the purpose of which is not to destroy American values but to revive them.

This theme, which is also the theme of this book, is so pronounced as to beggar commentary. One passage in particular sets up Buddhism as the vehicle of both spiritual and political renewal, when Ryder describes the meaning that Eastern belief has for him:

You know, when I was a little kid in Oregon I didn't feel that I was American at all, with all that suburban ideal and sex repression and dreary newspaper gray censorship of all our real human values but and when I discovered Buddhism and all I suddenly felt I had lived in a previous lifetime innumerable ages ago and now because of faults and sins in that lifetime I was being degraded to a more grievous domain of existence and my karma was to be born in America where nobody has any fun or believes in anything, especially freedom. That's why I was always sympathetic to freedom movements, too, like anarchism in the Northwest. (*Bums*, 301–2)

The speech prompts one character to declare that "Japhy Ryder is a great new hero of American culture" (302). What is heroic here is the capacity for enlightenment, construed as acute awareness of the here and now. The meaning becomes clear when Ryder announces that "frontiersmen are always heroes and were always my real heroes and will always be. They're constantly on the alert in the realness which might as well be real as unreal, what difference does it make, Diamond Sutra says 'Make no formed conceptions about the realness of existence nor about the unrealness of existence'" (*Bums*, 350).

One obvious American hero, a frontiersman of the spirit, is Walt Whitman, and in the novel Kerouac follows Suzuki when he describes the poet as "the Zen Lunacy bard of old desert paths." Whitman is enlisted to support the Beat rebellion against consumer culture, a "rucksack revolution" of "Dharma Bums refusing to subscribe to the general demand that they consume production and therefore have to work for the privilege of consuming, all that crap they didn't really want anyway such as refrigerators, TV sets, cars, at least new fancy cars, certain hair oils and deodorants and general junk you finally always see in the garbage anyway" (*Bums*, 351). The characters even imagine communities "of pure holy men" living in "small huts with religious families, like the old days of the Puritans" (*Bums*, 352). The evocation of America's founding by the Puritans and of the country's expansion by the frontiersmen places a burden on Buddhism that is almost comic, but there is no mistaking the notion that Eastern beliefs hold the key to the nation's renewal: "'Just think how truly great and wise America will be, with all this energy and exuberance and space focused into the Dharma.'" Ironically, Ryder's claim here is immediately undercut: "'Oh'—Alvah—'Balls on that old tired Dharma'" (*Bums*, 351). The irony is retrospective because spoken by the Ginsberg character, for it was Ginsberg, more than any other member of the Beat Generation, who became known for his close ties to Buddhism.

Around the time he wrote "Howl," Ginsberg had only a passing interest in Buddhism, seeing it as merely derivative of Taoism, which he professed to practice. In September 1954 he wrote to Kerouac, "Yes of course I am a *Taoist*," adding that "Zen Buddhism is also a very *late* sharp humorous version" of the Tao. He also commented on the problems of Beat fellow-traveler Neal Cassady's long-suffering wife Carolyn by saying that she could use "some real force of compassion or insight or love or Tao, or whatever." But in the same letter Ginsberg asks Kerouac, "When you send me essay on Buddha?" And in November he wrote to Kerouac again asking for "the Buddha book to read" and mentioned that he was reading a book on Zen by the Anglo-German translator Edward Conze (1904–1979).[15] Ginsberg went to New York the next month for his brother's wedding and met up with Kerouac there, whereupon Kerouac assumed the role of Buddhist teacher in earnest. A measure of this earnestness can be taken by the letter Kerouac had written to Ginsberg earlier: "For your beginning studies of Buddhism you must listen to me carefully and implicitly as tho I was Einstein teaching you relativity or Eliot teaching the Formulas of Objective Correlation on a blackboard in Princeton."[16]

Ginsberg always thought of Kerouac as his first Buddhist teacher, but such instruction can hardly be regarded as formal. The poet did not undergo formal study until 1972, when he took his Bodhisattva vows and became a follower of Chogyam Trungpa Rinpoche, a practitioner of the "Crazy Wisdom" school of Tibetan Buddhism.[17] He wrote his French translator that his "lovely guru . . . reminds me of Kerouac," not only because of Chogyam Trungpa's alcoholism but also because "he's turned me on to . . . improvisation." The letter goes on to describe Ginsberg's meditation practice and Buddhist beliefs in some detail. Meditation is a matter of "just sitting at the moment following breath out nostril dissolving into space thus mixing breath with space, mind with breath, thus mixing mind with space in front of face thus short-circuiting discursive thought daydream & sleepiness with each attentive breath thus opening up awakened space, more precisely, wakening awareness of space around the room, the planet, etc." Ginsberg also mentions having received a mantra from the guru for use at "Miami antiwar conventions . . . for mass protection against police," and, finally, he updates the terminology of "classic Buddhist" ideas for his French correspondent when he describes the proper Bodhisattva attitude regarding politics: "Any action taken in hostile emotion or with aggression as motive leads to more hostility & aggression, & aggression in form of capital monopoly or psychic monopoly is root of personal & social woe—aggression to maintain & reinforce illusion of separate egohood & its powers."[18] By planning to incorporate Buddhism into political protest, Ginsberg is entirely typical of the general tendency in American cultural life to deploy Eastern thought as a means to the betterment of that life.

While the role of Buddhism in Ginsberg's life was complex but clear, the place of Buddhism in his poetry is problematic, in at least two ways. First, Western influences on his art are understandably pervasive, so much so that Eastern sources and meanings appear far less important than, say, the mystical humanism of William Blake, the Americanism of Walt Whitman, or the prophetic voice of the Old Testament. Even in his *Indian Journals*, a record of travels and impressions in India and Southeast Asia from March 1962 to May 1963, the poet refers to "Blake my Guru," and in a poem from 1965 he describes himself as a "Buddhist Jew."[19] Such phrases might suggest the kind of East-West synthesis favored by Kerouac, but they also point to a second problem: a sometimes cavalier tendency to ignore the cultural specificity of Eastern traditions in favor of what one critic calls an "almost breezy interchangeability" of, say, Hinduism and Buddhism, a tendency that recalls Emerson's nineteenth-century indifference to the distinctiveness of such traditions. An example of the latter issue is Ginsberg's conflation of the Buddhist refuge prayer and the Hindu Hare Krishna in the long poem "Angkor Wat" (1963).[20] Although that poem and "The Change" (also 1963) are cited as evidence of a greater sensitivity to Buddhism in Ginsberg's evolving aesthetic, the aesthetic itself still seems firmly grounded in the vatic voice of that incantatory Hebraic tradition which also includes Blake and Whitman. Although there is no denying that a fuller understanding of Ginsberg's art can be gained by detailing the ways in which the poet incorporated elements of Buddhism into the bardic tradition—as Tony Triglio has done in the only book-length study of the subject—it is also true that Ginsberg's Buddhism is not solely or simply limited to his poetics. Buddhism, and Eastern traditions generally, were also critical to the public image he maintained from the early 1960s onward.

The public and performative nature of his Eastern enthusiasms, more so than his poetry per se, is what makes Ginsberg a pivotal figure in the history of the American Orient. As "the PR genius of the Beat Generation,"[21] he was a much more substantial figure in the development of the postwar counterculture than either Kerouac or Snyder, but he also had a role in the transformation of that counterculture into consumer culture on the strength of his public persona alone. The claim strains credulity at first, because Ginsberg himself was a relentless critic of the consumerism and conformism of the 1950s, a hero of the antiwar hippies of the 1960s, and an inspiration to the gay liberation movement of the 1970s. But where Kerouac's and Snyder's roles in the counterculture were mostly personal and local, Ginsberg's was political and national: he became a major public figure and a far-left celebrity during one of the most intensely radical periods in American political life. Besides, given Ginsberg's own media-savvy attention to his iconic image as a self-described "folk hero," the commercial manipulation of that image was inevitable.[22] A widely circulated photograph of the poet dancing ecstatically at the 1967 Human Be-In at Golden Gate Park in San Francisco captured his iconic standing in the counterculture as only a photograph can. The following year saw Ginsberg adding to his mythic status as a counterculture celebrity when he appeared on *Firing Line*, the television interview program hosted by William F. Buckley, founding editor of the *National Review*. Ginsberg's spirited debate with the lion of the modern conservative movement on such issues as censorship, drug use, and the Vietnam War has become legendary, but what stands out most in the memories of those who saw the program is the moment when Ginsberg sang the "Hare Krishna" while accompanying himself on a harmonium. He prefaced his performance with these words: "For the preservation of the universe instead of its destruction, Krishna returns, in the *Bhagavad Gita*, every time there's fire, original sin leading to atom bombs."[23]

The fusion of Far Eastern thought, counterculture protest, and celebrity status in the person of Allen Ginsberg at a watershed moment in American life has some far reaching implications. While it may seem rather quaint to refer to Ginsberg as "bohemian," there is no question that sometime in the 1960s his counterculture persona took on the mythic quality associated with Baudelaire, Artaud, and other bohemian heroes. Ginsberg at the San Francisco Be-In, Ginsberg on *Firing Line*, and Ginsberg at the 1968 Democratic National Convention in Chicago all contributed to the growing myth. The relation of Ginsberg's bohemian status to the consumer culture which conferred that status on him can be understood as an individual instance of a more general cultural dynamic. As Elizabeth Wilson has observed, "The figure of the bohemian personifies the ambivalent role of art in industrial society; and Bohemia is a cultural *Myth* about art in modernity, a myth that seeks to reconcile Art to industrial capitalism, to create for it a role in consumer society. The bohemian is above all an idea, the personification of a myth."[24] Critics such as Triglio are quick to point out that the public, mythic version of Ginsberg's bohemian Buddhism is far from the whole story. Besides performance, there was also practice: Ginsberg may have chanted mantras and played the harmonium on television programs, but he also meditated in private for hours at a time on a regular basis. That said, the key point remains valid: the public, performative Ginsberg was part of the change in American culture whereby Buddhism and other Eastern religions become subject to commercial exploitation. This is so mainly because Ginsberg acquired celebrity status around the same time that Hinduism, Buddhism, and less respected variants of "Eastern Wisdom" were gaining followers among members of the music and entertainment industries.

The most celebrated example of this trend is without doubt the Beatles, who began studying with the Maharishi Mahesh Yogi at his ashram in the Himalayas in early 1968. Other celebrities who accompanied the Beatles on this now notorious retreat included the singer-songwriter Donovan, the singer Mike Love of the Beach Boys, and the actress Mia Farrow. Although the retreat was cut short amid reports that the Maharishi, sworn to celibacy, had behaved in sexually inappropriate ways, the great publicity generated by the episode secured the success of the yogi's patented brand of meditation for years to come. Ten years before the Beatles and other celebrities made the Maharishi a household name, he had come to the United States and tried, without notable success, to introduce Americans to his transcendental meditation movement. That movement took off, commercially and culturally, only after the Maharishi's highly visible association with the Beatles and other pop-culture celebrities. Around the same time, the American "channeler" David Spangler began working "clairvoyantly with a group of non-physical beings from the inner worlds of spirit," as he put it, a practice subsequently described in his book *Revelation: The Birth of a New Age* (1976).[25] Spangler's term "New Age" gained currency in the 1970s as a descriptive epithet for all kinds of counterculture activities, from the neo-theosophical mysticism that Spangler himself advocated to ancient Eastern practices like yoga or more recent ones like transcendental meditation.

Indeed, transcendental meditation is one of the more enduring examples of New Age spirituality, its countercultural panache having been successfully reified by the forces of the market. Trademarked as TM, the transcendental meditation technique involves the silent chanting of a mantra twice a day for twenty minutes, "while sitting comfortably with eyes closed," as the TM website puts it, for the purpose of allowing "the mind to settle inward, beyond thought, to experience the silent reservoir of energy, creativity, and intelligence." A seven-step course of instruction in TM over four days costs $2,000, including follow-up sessions.[26] The TM technique is licensed by the Maharishi Vedic Education Development Corporation, a nonprofit educational organization whose assets were valued at $300 million in early 2008, when the Maharishi died.[27]

The death of the founder, however, has caused no abatement in the corporation's enterprises. From its headquarters in Fairfield, Iowa, the organization runs a college, the Maharishi University of Management, and oversees a branch in lower Manhattan, Global Financial Capital of New York. In October 2008, John Hagelin, the executive director of Global Financial Capital and heir-apparent to the Maharishi, responded to the worldwide financial crisis by sending out a press release that offered a "bailout" to Wall Street consisting of "Vedic technologies of consciousness," which, he claimed, "can bring calm and stability to the markets, stimulate the economy, and promote good fortune for the country."[28] Like that of most corporations in the early twenty-first century, the TM business model also includes a "green" component, but one based on Vedic beliefs. One of the Maharishi's last public initiatives was a call to demolish or relocate all toxic structures, including historic landmarks, not built along the lines of "Vedic architecture in harmony with Natural Law." He insisted that the White House was one of these toxic structures and recommended relocating the nation's capital to the town of Smith Center, Kansas (population 1,931, according to the 2000 census). Possibly, one of the things Smith Center has to recommend it is its relative proximity (a day's drive) to Maharishi Vedic City, Iowa, which TM followers incorporated in July 2001. A New Age community planned according to Vedic principles, every building in the town faces east, and each one "has a central silent space called a *Brahmastan* and a golden roof ornament called a kalash."[29]

The TM movement continues to attract celebrity followers, among them the filmmaker David Lynch, who has established his own foundation (with John Hegelin as president) to promote transcendental meditation "for consciousness-based education and world peace." Former Beatles Paul McCartney and Ringo Starr, as well as hip-hop mogul Russell Simmons, have lent their celebrity to support Lynch's foundation.[30] Although critics have called the Maharishi Vedic Education Development Corporation "a cult business enterprise," the ongoing appeal of TM to Americans in search of more satisfying lives is undeniable. And the fact that many are willing to pay substantially for such satisfaction shows that Asian religion can be as easily adapted to commercial culture as can the big-box Christianity of American megachurches.

The TM phenomenon, however, is obviously not the same as the commercialization of Christianity. For one thing, Vedic tradition involves nothing like the Calvinist doctrine of election, which political economists understand as one of the wellsprings of capitalism. If material success is understood as validation of spiritual election, then there is really no conflict between commercial ambition and Christian faith. Besides, one of the things missing from commercial versions of Christianity but so important to TM and other brandings of Indian religion is some prior connection to the counterculture. That is the critical question here: why did Asian religious traditions migrate in America from counterculture to consumer culture? Two closely related sociological explanations, neither fully satisfactory, might be advanced on the basis of either generational development or generational competition. The first theory is simpler: members of the counterculture generation grew up, got jobs, and spent money, but rationalized their relationship to the establishment they had once opposed by continuing to cultivate their countercultural tastes. The second theory is similar but more complicated: the conflict of the hippie generation of the 1960s and the yuppie generation of the 1980s has led to a combination or synthesis of interests, a blending of countercultural tastes and professional attitudes.

Neither of these two theories is limited to the transformation of the American Orient—especially the second one, which was spelled out by David Brooks in his best-selling study of 2000, *Bobos in Paradise* ("bobo" is short for "bourgeois bohemian"). Brooks saw "a new and amorphous establishment" emerging, one whose members had "learned from both 'the sixties' and 'the eighties'" and had managed to create "a new balance of bourgeois and bohemian values." He begins his book with an anecdote about returning to the United States after a four-year absence and being "confronted by a series of peculiar juxtapositions," including this one: "Suddenly massive corporations like Microsoft and the Gap were on the scene, citing Gandhi and Jack Kerouac in their advertisements."[31] This reference, which construes the counterculture in Oriental terms (directly, though Gandhi, and indirectly, through Kerouac), is one of only a handful by which Brooks advances his thesis, evoking establishment exploitation of Far Eastern thought. Had he written the book only a year or two later, there would have been many more opportunities to draw on the American Orient to argue for counterculture consumerism, because that is when the yoga vogue really gained momentum in the United States.

In April 2001 the journalist Richard Corliss published a long article in *Time* magazine profiling the yoga industry. At that time, some 15 million Americans were said to "include some form of yoga in their fitness regimen," double the number of only five years previously, with 75 percent of all health clubs in the United States offering yoga classes. The emphasis on health and fitness is telling, because yoga was not always understood in those terms. Corliss makes the perceptive comment that back in the days of the Beat Generation, yoga "signaled spiritual cleansing and rebirth, a nontoxic way to get high. Then it was seen as a kind of preventive medicine that helped manage and reduce stress." The "third wave" was the incorporation of yoga into fitness regimes. Corliss also notes that the yoga industry has received a great deal of free publicity from "movie idols and rock stars" whose patronage of this or that form of yoga makes them effective "salesmen" for the practice, and he names the 1968 Beatles retreat with the Maharishi Mahesh Yogi as a seminal event. He also names a truly staggering number of celebrities who have made a point of incorporating yoga into their professional lives and their public images: "Today yoga is practiced by so many stars with whom audiences are on a first name basis—Madonna, Julia, Meg, Ricky, Michelle, Gwyneth, Sting—that it would be shorter work to list the actors who don't assume the asana [pose]." To be sure, Corliss does not dwell exclusively on the celebrity element of the yoga vogue; his article contains much evidence for the long-term health benefits of regular yoga exercise. Actually, that aspect of yoga is consistent with its original place in the American counterculture, whose suspicion of Western medicine led to the cultivation of Far Eastern alternatives. Indeed, the yoga industry makes up part of the $27 billion that Americans spend annually on alternative or supplementary medical treatment. This form of consumption is supplemented by two others for which hard numbers are not readily available from the trade associations devoted to the yoga industry: instructional books and videos, and yoga apparel and paraphernalia. The latter are available from Nike, J. Crew, and many other upmarket vendors, or from any one of the several celebrity gurus who have capitalized on the yoga vogue in recent years.[32]

Since the 2001 article in *Time*, the guru who has attracted the most attention in the United States has been Rodney Yee. Even at the time of the article, Yee was not just a yogi who ministered to the stars; he was a celebrity himself, that honor having been conferred on him by no less a starmaker than Oprah Winfrey. After Yee appeared on *Oprah* in early 2001, his *AM/PM Yoga for Beginners* became the second-best-selling video for the year in all categories from Amazon.com. The son of a U.S. Air Force colonel, Yee dropped out of Berkeley to study ballet, then yoga, so he is

not some Far Eastern exotic but an all-American success story.³³ And like
many successful men of the professional class, his career has been dotted
with scandal, mainly in the form of several high-profile affairs with students. The most recent of these involved leaving his wife of twenty-four
years, the woman with whom he established a yoga empire headquartered
in Oakland, California, to begin a new venture in Sag Harbor, New York,
with Colleen Saidman, a yoga instructor herself who had also been married
to her spouse for a quarter-century.³⁴ The affair generated a certain amount
of moral opprobrium in the press, like any other celebrity scandal, but the
new couple soon settled into their new life, with Ms. Saidman becoming
Mr. Yee's business partner in the lucrative yoga retreat industry. A domestic
weekend retreat costs around $500 per participant, while international
retreats run from $1,000 to $6,000 or more (not counting airfare), depending on location. The Saidman-Yee "experience" in Bali, for instance, comes
with a pricetag of $3,650 single occupancy, $5,640 double.³⁵ A recent
advertisement for one of these retreats, if I read it correctly, promises a
selfless sense of self that is both amorphous and androgynous:

> Masculine energy is typified as being more gross, while feminine energy is typi-
> fied as more subtle. In this workshop, we move from vinyasa (linking move-
> ment with breath) to integrated alignment; from chanting to silence; from
> pranayama (breath exercises) to pratyahara (withdrawal of the senses toward
> the self); and from philosophy to meditation, creating a profound experience
> of movement from the gross to the subtle.
>
> This expertly-guided practice enables us to refine our attention and begin
> to dissolve the illusion of the boundary between male and female and between
> us and the world. As a result, we move in the direction of joyful, selfless service
> in all of our relationships, beginning with our relationship to self.³⁶

While there can be no question about Mr. Yee's and Ms. Saidman's special expertise on the subject of dissolving boundaries, their joint enterprise
is only one of many such concerns offering spiritual and physical well-
being to the well-heeled. Surf Goddess Retreats, for example, provides a
"unique style of yoga which is designed to enhance your surfing and facili-
tate mind, body and spirit connection." Instruction adheres to "the classic
yogic traditions of Hatha, Iyengar, Kundalini and Tantra to weave a flowing
and relaxing experience designed especially to stretch and rejuvenate the
muscles used for surfing."³⁷ This retreat too is on the Indonesian island of
Bali, which seems to be particularly amenable to the high-end yoga and
eco-tourist trade. To be fair, Surf Goddess Retreats appears to be a grossly
commercial operation, unlike many of the institutes and organizations with
which modern American yoga gurus are affiliated. Many of Rodney Yee
and Colleen Saidman's retreats, for example, are run through nonprofit

outfits like the Omega Institute for Holistic Studies, Inc., a tax-exempt organization under Section 501(c)(3) of the Internal Revenue Code. But regardless of whether yoga vendors provide their products and services through nonprofits or private corporations, yoga consumers pay hard cash, and pay handsomely. What they get for their money varies with the amount. The yoga classes that come with membership in a gym or the local Y may involve nothing more than the basic asanas or poses, but the yoga weekend in the Catskills or the yoga retreat in the tropics offers much more: tantric awareness, full-body massage, gourmet meals, wine tasting. The ad copy for these sorts of high-end retreats does not always make clear the distinction, if any, between yogic and hedonistic experiences, since the call to "pamper yourself" (a common admonition in the ads) appears to involve both.

This latest understanding of the meaning of yoga in the United States could not contrast more strongly with the earliest: recall that Hannah Adams and her contemporaries thought that yoga was a form of self-torture, and it is hard to imagine "torture yourself" as much of an entice-ment to a modern yoga retreat. But it was precisely the capacity for self-torture that brought the first American yoga guru to national prominence. His name was Pierre Bernard, who had the good fortune in 1889 to meet an Indian man by the name of Sylvais Hamati, in Lincoln, Nebraska, of all places. Originally from Calcutta, Hamati became Bernard's guru and began to teach the young American the ancient body-control techniques of hatha yoga.[38] After studying with Hamati for several years, Bernard became so proficient in these techniques that he was able to put himself into a coma-like trance so deep that he was insensitive to the pain of having his body pierced with foot-long surgical needles. He gave a demonstration of what he called his "Kali Mudra" death trance in San Francisco on 26 January 1898 before an audience of medical doctors and other distinguished guests. As Robert Love tells it, once Bernard had disappeared into the Kali Mudra, a Dr. D. McMillan pushed a surgical needle "slowly through one of Ber-nard's earlobes. The doctors watched as he pushed another needle through the young man's cheek. He inserted a third through Bernard's upper lip and then ran a fourth through his nostril, sewing the ends of the metal together with thread." Local newspapers ran headlines like "Sewed His Lip to His Nose" and "Tortured While Asleep."[39]

Over the first third of the twentieth century, Bernard parlayed his remark-able abilities into a yoga empire with great celebrity appeal, despite numer-ous run-ins with the law and with the purity leagues (men and women exercising together in scanty outfits caused suspicion enough, not to men-tion rumors of secret tantric sex cults). He began calling himself "the great Om," which the press initially mangled into "the Great Oom" and later enhanced to "the Omnipotent Oom." After relocating to the East Coast, Bernard first started a successful yoga studio amid the row of millionaires' houses on Fifth Avenue in New York City, then established a yoga retreat in the Hudson Valley hamlet of Nyack, New York. The retreat attracted such luminaries as the conductor Leopold Stokowski, the actress Helen Hayes, the playwright Maxwell Anderson, and more than one Vanderbilt heiress.[40] In addition to yoga, Bernard had a passion for sports, especially baseball and boxing. The Hollywood screenwriter Ben Hecht describes a 1935 celebrity baseball game on a diamond owned by "Oom, the Omnipotent." The game's opening festivities featured a parade of performing elephants that "were also part of Oom's yoga enterprise," a touch of showmanship that reveals Bernard's cultural kinship with America's first master of Oriental spectacle, P. T. Barnum. Among the stars on Hecht's side were the future TV impresario Ed Sullivan, Harpo Marx, and Jack Dempsey, the heavyweight boxer.[41] In 1939, *Life* magazine ran a photo feature showing heavyweight hopeful Lou Nova training at Bernard's Nyack retreat. The portly, middle-aged yogi is shown in the lotus position instructing the boxer "to get in touch with reality," as the caption has it, by "learning to control his stomach muscles."[42] Nova used a "yoga stance" in the ring to deliver what he called his "Cosmic Punch." It worked against Max Baer but not against Joe Louis, who knocked out Nova to retain his championship. "I got an 'Earth Punch,'" he said.[43]

The biography of Pierre Bernard may be a bit bizarre, but the man's unusual career offers further evidence for the claim that postwar American interest in Far Eastern thought has its roots in the fin de siècle. After all, Bernard studied with his master Hamati during the 1890s and came to national attention just as the century turned. Unlike Suzuki, whose roots in the American Orient are also traceable to the fin de siècle, Bernard was not a cultural presence in the 1950s, but his many students and disciples most assuredly were. Principal among those who followed the Omnipotent Oom to become yoga teachers themselves was his wife, Blanch DeVries (1891–1984), sometimes called "the mother of yoga in America." DeVries kept up yoga studios in Nyack and New York City until 1982 and, like her husband, attracted a celebrity following, including the actors Frederic March, Anthony Quinn, Henry Fonda, and Claire Bloom. Also like her husband, she numbered wealthy and powerful members of the social aristocracy among her clients, and it was through their agency that the now celebrated yogi B. K. S. Iyengar first came to the United States from India in 1956, the year after Bernard's death (*Oom*, 339).

Bernard also had a roundabout relationship to the second Buddhist boom of the 1950s by way of Ruth Fuller Sasaki (1892–1967), who, as

Ruth Everett, had studied with Bernard in the 1920s. Her son-in-law Alan Watts says in his autobiography that the "phenomenal rascal-master" Bernard first acquainted Everett with Zen Buddhism at his retreat in Nyack; she was so inspired that she "decided then and there to take off for Japan and study it first hand." In the 1930s she made several trips to Japan and met with D. T. Suzuki, who arranged for her to study Zen with a master in Kyoto.[44] She eventually became "the only westerner, and the only woman, ever to be made a priest of a Daitoku-ji Temple in its many centuries." Through her work at the First Zen Institute in New York City (founded by her second husband, Sasaki Sokei-an) and her many translations and original books about Zen Buddhism, notably *Zen Dust* (1967), Ruth Fuller Sasaki joins Suzuki and Watts as an influential popularizer and expositor of Zen for Americans. But she would never have traveled the route she did without Pierre Bernard's unorthodox encouragement.[45]

As the fascinating story of the Great Oom shows, the contemporary mixture of yoga practice and celebrity culture is nothing new. What is new or, at least, recent is the extraordinary degree to which Far Eastern faiths characterized by selfless asceticism have entered the mainstream of American consumerism. In his 2000 preface to his 1992 book *The American Encounter with Buddhism*, Thomas Tweed expresses astonishment over the remarkable emergence of Buddhist influence during the last decade of the twentieth century: "Buddhism's cultural impact now is everywhere—in medicine, painting, music, poetry, publishing, psychotherapy, film, fashion, advertising, and television." He lists numerous examples of the ways in which American entrepreneurs have been able to profit from what appears to be yet another Buddhist boom in the United States. Among many examples, he names the fashion designer Vivienne Tam, whose spring 1997 collection sought to promote the kind of "spiritually balanced life . . . the Buddhas represent." The image of the Buddha soon wound up on children's T-shirts when her designs were copied and sold as ready-to-wear apparel by Sears and other department stores. Heather Aponick, a New York designer known as "Zoe Metro," took note of the Buddhist prayer-bead bracelet traditionally worn by the Dalai Lama and began selling copies in Chinese takeout containers for $25 to $30 apiece. Tweed says she "grossed $1 million by the end of 1999" before switching "from wooden beads to semiprecious stones, each with its own spiritual significance" (e.g., purple stones for truth, pink for love, black for courage). Color-coded spirituality, of course, has nothing to do with the traditional function of the plain wooden beads, or *juzu*, that Buddhist monks and lay persons use as Catholics use the rosary, to count off prayers or mantras.[46]

Buddhism, it seems, is good business, and one can only wonder what D. T. Suzuki would make of this development in the Eastern tradition he helped to introduce to the United States. One of the oddest examples of the adaptation of Buddhism to business is *Presentation Zen: Simple Ideas on Presentation Design and Delivery* (2008), a book by Garr Reynolds, an associate professor of management at Kansai Gaidai University in Japan. The purpose of Reynolds's book is to enliven and simplify corporate slide presentations by employing "the same ethos as Zen." He explains that "the essence or the spirit of many of the principles found in Zen concerning aesthetics, mindfulness, connectedness, and so on can be applied to our daily lives, including presentations."[47] In other words, the corporate conformism that W. H. Whyte cautioned against in *The Organization Man* and the alternative to such conformism that D. T. Suzuki counseled Americans about in *Zen and Japanese Culture* in the late 1950s are now seen as complementary: no contradiction obtains between the corporate clone and the Zen Koan.

This latest turn in American culture linking conformism and consumerism to yoga practice and Buddhist religion seems especially disorienting, not least because yoga and Buddhism were first seen, however indistinctly, as a means of *countering* materialist ambitions in the United States. Most of what Henry David Thoreau knew about Buddhism he got from the fragments of the *Lotus Sutra* that Elizabeth Peabody translated for *The Dial*, but that was enough for him to set the Buddha up as a defense against "sharpers in trade and in society," as one of his Harvard classmates put it.[48] And Thoreau may not have had a clear sense of what yoga was, but he knew it was something simple, something well removed from the modern industrial economy that threatened the natural life. Possibly, even without knowing much about it, Thoreau got something right, for the practice does seem more compatible with a simple cabin than with a million-dollar resort. That said, the pencilmaker from Concord does have something in common with his consumerist cousins of the twenty-first century, for they, too, have responded to the stresses of American life by looking Eastward for relief. The difference lies not in the impulse but in the context. In Thoreau's day it really was possible (more nearly possible, anyway) to find a place apart from the capitalist, commercial world and the artificial desires that form the false self necessary to sustain that world. If there is a wheel of *samsara* in American life, that would be it: the circular thinking which assumes that artificial desires can be satisfied by the same emptiness that generates them. And if there is a veil of *maya* in America life, that would be it as well: the illusion that satisfaction of that sort is somehow real.

The meaning of the American Orient for Thoreau (and Emerson, and Fenollosa, and Pound, and others) inhered in the separation of Western and Eastern values, combined with the belief that the latter could be used to improve the former. But when the former suffuses the latter—that is, when Western consumerism contaminates Eastern spiritualism to the degree that it has done in contemporary culture—there is no hope of improvement, no help for the self. And there is no stronger proof of this claim than the fact that transcendental meditation, yoga, and the rest are securely branded now as sectors of the self-help industry.

Thoreau, of course, saw it all coming a century and a half ago, when the capitalist retreat of choice was not Bali or the Caribbean but Newport, where, he suspected, wealthy Americans of the time thought "more of the wine than the brine." The observation is made in the concluding paragraph of Thoreau's *Cape Cod*, the last line of which has the author looking eastward once again, but for different reasons than he did in the 1840s. Imagining the view from Cape Cod over the dark Atlantic, Thoreau turns his back on the West and announces that "a man may stand there and put all America behind him." Thoreau had Darwin to thank for this final prospect, which makes the east just that—a direction, not a destination.

And so it is today: not much is left of the American Orient as a political, moral, or aesthetic alternative to the mantra of the market.

 NOTES

Introduction

1. Edward Said, *Orientalism* (New York: Vintage, 1978), 1–2. Further references are cited parenthetically in the text.

2. "Orientalism," *Knickerbocker Magazine* 41.6 (July 1853): 478–79. Further references are cited parenthetically in the text.

3. Robert McClellan, *The Heathen Chinee: A Study of American Attitudes toward China, 1890–1905* (Columbus: Ohio State University Press, 1971), 8.

4. The preceding information about the immigration legislation of 1882, 1888, 1892, 1902, 1917, and 1924 is taken from the *Congressional Record,* as follows: 47th Congress, 1st Sess. (6 May 1882): chap. 126; 50th Congress, 1st Sess. (1 October 1888): chap. 1064; 57th Congress, 1st Sess. (5 May 1892): chap. 60; 57th Congress, 1st Sess. (29 April 1902): chap. 641; 64th Congress, 2nd Sess. (5 February 1917): chap. 29; 68th Congress, 1st Sess. (26 May 1924): chap. 190.

5. "Coolidge Proclaims Immigrant Quotas," *New York Times,* 1 July 1924.

6. See McClellan, *The Heathen Chinee,* 47–52.

7. For an account of the Japanese American internment experience from the perspective of someone who was a child at the time, see Mary Matsuda Gruenewald, *Looking like the Enemy: My Story of Imprisonment in Japanese-American Internment Camps* (Troutdale, Ore.: NewSage Press, 2005).

8. Paul R. Spickard, *Japanese Americans: The Formation and Transformations of an Ethnic Group,* rev. ed. (New Brunswick, N.J.: Rutgers University Press, 2009), 105–6.

9. For an excellent treatment of this little-discussed aspect of Japanese internment, see "A New Deal for Asians," chapter 4 of Colleen Lye, *America's Asia: Racial Form and American Literature* (Princeton, N.J.: Princeton University Press, 2005), 141–203.

10. See Holly Edwards, ed., *Noble Dreams, Wicked Pleasures: Orientalism in America, 1870–1930* (Princeton, N.J., and Williamstown, Mass.: Princeton University Press and Sterling and Francine Clark Art Institute, 2000); and Alexandra Munroe, ed., *The Third Mind: American Artists Contemplate Asia, 1860–1989* (New York: Solomon R. Guggenheim Foundation, 2009).

11. See Carl T. Jackson, *Oriental Religions and American Thought: Nineteenth-Century Explorations* (Westport, Conn.: Greenwood Press, 1981); and Beongcheon Yu, *The Great Circle: American Writers and the Orient* (Detroit: Wayne State University Press, 1983).

12. Jackson's book does include an excellent chapter on scholarship, though that is obviously not his main concern. See Jackson, "The Emergence of the Oriental Scholar," in *Oriental Religions and American Thought,* 179–99.

13. See Alfred Owen Aldridge, *The Dragon and the Eagle: The Presence of China in the American Enlightenment* (Detroit: Wayne State University Press, 1993); Thomas A. Tweed, *The American Encounter with Buddhism, 1844–1912: Victorian Culture and the Limits of Dissent* (1992; Chapel Hill: University of North Carolina Press, 2000); Lawrence W. Chisolm, *Fenollosa: The Far East and American Culture* (New Haven: Yale University Press, 1963); Judith Snodgrass, *Presenting Japanese Buddhism to the West: Orientalism, Occidentalism, and the Columbia Exposition* (Chapel Hill: University of North Carolina Press, 2003); Christopher Benfey, *The Great Wave: Gilded Age Misfits, Japanese Eccentrics, and the Opening of Old Japan* (New York: Random House, 2003); and Lye, *America's Asia.*

1. The Eighteenth Century

1. J. P. Rao Rayapati, *Early American Interest in Vedanta: Pre-Emersonian Interest in Vedic Literature and Vedantic Philosophy* (New York: Asia Publishing House, 1973), 40.

2. L. J. Gallagher, S.J., trans., *China in the Sixteenth Century: The Journals of Matthew Ricci, 1583–1610* (New York: Random House, 1953), xix, quoted in Raymond Dawson, "Western Conceptions of Chinese Civilization," in *The Legacy of China* (Oxford: Oxford University Press, 1964), 9.

3. Voltaire, *Philosophical Dictionary,* 2 vols., trans. Peter Gay (New York: Basic Books, 1962), 1:145, 169.

4. Herrlee Glessner Creel, *Confucius: The Man and the Myth* (New York: John Day, 1949), 259.

5. Dawson, "Western Conceptions of Chinese Civilization," 13, 14.

6. Quoted in G. F. Hudson, "China and the World," in *The Legacy of China* (Oxford: Oxford University Press, 1964), 358. Leibniz is quoted also in Adolf Reichwein, *China and Europe: Intellectual and Artistic Contacts in the Eighteenth Century,* trans. J. C. Powell (New York: Knopf, 1925), 47–48.

7. Hudson, "China and the World," 350.

8. Edmund S. Morgan, *Benjamin Franklin* (New Haven: Yale University Press, 2002), 211.

9. Benjamin Franklin, "From the Morals of Confucius," *Pennsylvania Gazette,* 28 February–7 May 1738, 2.

10. Benjamin Franklin to George Whitefield, 6 July 1749, in *Benjamin Franklin: Representative Selections,* ed. Frank Luther Mott and Chester E. Jorgenson (New York: American Book Company, 1936), 198.

11. Carl T. Jackson, *The Oriental Religions and American Thought: Nineteenth-Century Explorations* (Westport, Conn.: Greenwood Press, 1981), 14.

12. Franklin to Sarah Bache, 26 January 1784, in *Benjamin Franklin: Representative Selections,* 461.

13. Although the preface is unsigned, Franklin is widely believed to have had a hand in its authorship. See Jackson, *The Oriental Religions and American Thought,* 14; and Robert S. Ellwood, introduction to *Eastern Spirituality in America: Selected Writings* (New York: Paulist Press, 1987), 7.

14. Preface to *Transactions of the American Philosophical Society* 1 (1 January 1769–1 January 1771): iv. Further references are cited parenthetically in the text as Pref.

15. Alfred Owen Aldridge, *The Dragon and the Eagle: The Presence of China in the American Enlightenment* (Detroit: Wayne State University Press, 1993), 32. Aldridge, 32–33, summarizes Bartram's "Life and Character of the Chinese Philosopher Confucius," unpublished manuscript at the Morgan Library in New York City.

16. Creel, *Confucius,* 267.

17. Ian McMorran, "Chinese: Literary Translation into English," in *Encyclopedia of Literary Translation into English,* ed. Oliver Classe (London: Fitzroy Dearborn, 2000), 279.

18. Aldridge, *The Dragon and the Eagle,* 23.

19. Ibid., 25.

20. *A Catalogue of the Books Belonging to the Library Company of Philadelphia* (Philadelphia: Bartram and Reynolds, 1807), 64.

21. "Discourse the Eleventh on the Philosophy of the Asiaticks," in *Sir William Jones: A Reader,* ed. Satya S. Pachori (Delhi: Oxford University Press, 1993), 195.

22. Jonathan Gross, ed., *Thomas Jefferson's Scrapbooks: Poems of Nation, Family, and Romantic Love* (Hanover, N.H.: Steerforth Press, 2006), 163.

23. See *Poeseos Asiaticae Commentariorum, The Works of Sir William Jones* (London: Walker, 1807), 6:6–7.

24. "On the Second Classical Book of the Chinese," in *The Works of Sir William Jones,* 4:119–20.

25. Jefferson to Adams, 28 October 1813, in *The Adams-Jefferson Letters,* ed. Lester J. Capon (1959; Chapel Hill: University of North Carolina Press, 1987), 388. Further references are cited parenthetically in the text as A-J.

26. Creel, *Confucius,* 276. For a discussion of the Confucian and Jeffersonian systems, see Hisaotung Niu, *Comparison of Educational Thoughts: Confucius and*

Thomas Jefferson (Meerut, India: Anu Books, 1990). Niu's pamphlet explores only analogues, not influences.

27. Thomas Jefferson, "A Bill for the More General Diffusion of Knowledge," in *Political Writings,* ed. Joyce Appleby and Terence Ball (Cambridge: Cambridge University Press, 1999), 236.

28. Reichwein, *China and Europe,* 107–8; François Quesnay, *Physiocratie: Droit naturel, Tableau économique et autres textes,* ed. Jean Cartelier (1765; Paris: Flammarion, 1991), 84.

29. François Quesnay, *Œuvres économiques et philosophiques,* ed. A. Oncken (Frankfurt-Paris, 1888), 636.

30. Creel, *Confucius,* 326 n16.

31. Robert D. Richardson, introduction to *A New Translation of Volney's Ruins,* 2 vols. (1802; New York: Garland, 1979), 1:v; Jackson, *The Oriental Religions and American Thought,* 13–14.

32. *The Papers of Thomas Jefferson,* ed. John Cantanzariti (Princeton, N.J.: Princeton University Press, 1997), 27:390n.

33. *A New Translation of Volney's Ruins,* 1:56. Further references are cited parenthetically in the text as Volney.

34. *The Papers of Thomas Jefferson,* ed. Barbara B. Oberg (Princeton, N.J.: Princeton University Press, 2005), 32:441–42n.

35. Richardson, introduction to *A New Translation of Volney's Ruins,* 1:vi.

36. Volney complied with the burning instructions. Oberg, *The Papers of Thomas Jefferson,* 32:442n.

37. *The Selected Writings of John and John Quincy Adams,* ed. Adrienne Koch and William Peden (New York: Knopf, 1946), 51.

38. Ibid., 87.

39. See "John Adams and the Gods," in Frank E. Manuel, *The Eighteenth Century Confronts the Gods* (Cambridge, Mass.: Harvard University Press, 1959), 271–80.

40. Burton Feldman, introduction to Paul Henri Mallet, *Northern Antiquities,* 2 vols. (1770; New York: Garland, 1979), v, vi.

41. Mallet, *Northern Antiquities,* 1:58.

42. "Discourse the Eleventh on the Philosophy of the Asiaticks," in *Sir William Jones: A Reader,* ed. Satya S. Pachori (Delhi: Oxford, 1993), 193. Further references are cited parenthetically in the text as Pachori.

43. Manuel, *The Eighteenth Century Confronts the Gods,* 264, 266, 267.

44. Charles Dupuis, *Origine de tout les cultes; ou, Religion universelle* (Paris, An III [1795]), 1:416. Quoted in Manuel, *The Eighteenth Century Confronts the Gods,* 269.

45. Adams was convinced, for example, that Pythagoras had journeyed to India and that it was through Pythagoras that "modifications and disguises of the Metampsichosis had crept into Egypt and Greece and Rome and other Countries. Have you read Farmer on the Dæmons and Possessions of the New Testament?" Adams to Jefferson, 25 December 1813, in A-J, 413.

46. Joseph Priestley, *A Comparison of the Institutions of Moses with Those of the Hindoos and Other Ancient Nations* (Northumberland, Pa.: A. Kennedy, 1799), 407. Further references to this edition are cited parenthetically in the text as *Comparison*.

47. Robert E. Schofield, *The Enlightenment of Joseph Priestley: A Study of His Life and Work from 1733 to 1773* (University Park: University of Pennsylvania Press, 1997), 274. Schofield takes up the latter part of Priestley's life in an epilogue.

48. See Raymond Schwab, *The Oriental Renaissance:Europe's Rediscovery of India and the East, 1680–1880,* trans. Gene Patterson-Black and Victor Reinking (New York: Columbia University Press, 1984). Schwab singles out Wilkins's 1784 translation of the *Bhagavad-Gita* as the first of several "authentic texts" and "major breakthroughs" in the understanding of Sanskrit (51), and he singles out Schlegel as "literally the inventor of the Oriental Renaissance" because of his 1808 essay, *Uber die Sprach und Weisheit der Indier* (72).

49. Quoted in Garland Cannon, *The Life and Mind of Oriental Jones: Sir William Jones, the Father of Modern Linguistics* (Cambridge: Cambridge University Press, 1990), 100–101.

50. Quoted in Cannon, *Oriental Jones,* 135.

51. Pachori , *Sir William Jones: A Reader,* 30–31.

52. Rayapati, *Early American Interest in Vedanta,* 43.

53. Cannon, *Oriental Jones,* 147. Pachori, *Sir William Jones: A Reader,* 31 n1.

54. Cannon, *Oriental Jones,* 176, 183.

55. Gay Wilson Allen, *Walt Whitman Handbook* (New York: Hendricks House, 1957), 458.

56. Schwab, *Oriental Renaissance,* 55.

57. Rayapati, *Early American Interest in Vedanda,* 49.

58. Jones, "A Hymn to Narayena," in Pachori, *Sir William Jones: A Reader,* 53.

59. Ralph Waldo Emerson, *Collected Poems and Translations* (New York: Library of America, 1994), 159.

60. Quoted in Cannon, *Oriental Jones,* 16–17.

61. Nancy F. Cott, *The Bonds of Womanhood: "Women's Sphere" in New England, 1780–1835* (New Haven, Conn.: Yale University Press, 1977), 7.

62. For an account of this first edition of Adam's dictionary, see Gary D. Schmidt, *A Passionate Usefulness: The Life and Literary Labors of Hannah Adams* (Charlottesville: University Press of Virginia, 2004).

63. Hannah Adams, *A Dictionary of All Religions and Religious Denominations: Jewish, Heathen, Mahometan, Christian, Ancient and Modern,* 4th ed. (1817; Atlanta: Scholars Press, 1992), n.p. Further references are cited parenthetically in the text as 4th ed.

64. Hannah Adams, *A Memoir of Miss Hannah Adams, Written by Herself with Additional Notices by a Friend* (Boston: Gray and Bowden, 1832), 11, quoted in Thomas A. Tweed, introduction to Adams, *Dictionary,* xiii.

65. Thomas A. Tweed, "An American Pioneer in the Study of Religion: Hannah

Adams (1933–1831) and Her Dictionary of All Religions," *Journal of the American Academy of Religion* 60.3 (Autumn 1992): 454.

66. Jackson, *The Oriental Religions and American Thought*, 18.

67. Thomas Maurice, *The History of Hindostan*, 3 vols. (1795–1798; rpt. New York: Garland, 1984), 2:vi.

68. Jackson, *The Oriental Religions and American Thought*, 17–18.

69. Hannah Adams, *A View of Religions*, 3rd. ed. (Boston: Manning and Loring, 1801), 275. Further references are cited parenthetically in the text as 3rd ed.

70. Jackson, *The Oriental Religions and American Thought*, 142.

71. Washington Irving,, *A History of New York*, ed. Michael L. Black and Nancy B. Black (1809; Boston: Twayne, 1984), 22. Further references are cited parenthetically in the text as Irving.

72. Jacob Bryant, *A New System; or, An Analysis of Ancient Mythology*, 2nd. ed., 3 vols. (1775–1776; rpt. New York: Garland, 1979), 2:251.

2. The Nineteenth Century

1. Charles Wilkins, trans., *The Bhagvat-Geeta* (1785; Delmar, N.Y.: Scholars' Facsimiles and Reprints, 1959), 52. Further references to this edition are cited parenthetically in the text as B-G.

2. Charles Wilkins, "Observations on the Seeks and their College," in *Asiatic Researches* (1788; London: Vernor and Hood, 1798), 1:290.

3. "Important Documents Relating to the Seeks in India," *Christian Disciple* 2.9 (September 1814): 269. Further references are cited parenthetically in the text as "Important Documents."

4. "Unitarianism and Universalism," *Encyclopaedia Britannica*, 2009, Encyclopaedia Britannica Online, http://search.eb.com/eb/article-9109455 (accessed 25 June 2008).

5. "On the Gods of Greece, Italy, and India," in *Sir William Jones: A Reader*, ed. Satya S. Pachori (Delhi: Oxford University Press, 1993), 179–80.

6. "Remarkable Extracts," *Christian Disciple* 2.11 (November 1814): 343–44. Further references are cited parenthetically in the text as "Remarkable Extracts."

7. "A Shocking Procession" and "The Views of Dr. Doddridge in Relation to Heresy," *Christian Disciple* 2.11 (November 1814): 342–43, 345–46.

8. Anna Letitia LeBreton, ed., *Correspondence of William Ellery Channing, D.D., and Lucy Aiken from 1826 to 1842* (Boston, 1874), 19, quoted in Bruce Carlisle Robertson, *Raja Rammohan Ray: The Father of Modern India* (Delhi: Oxford University Press, 1995), 50. The biographical sketch of Roy (or Ray) is also taken from Robertson, 11, 13, 18–19, 22–23.

9. "Theology of the Hindoos, as taught by Ram Mohun Roy," *North American Review and Miscellaneous Journal* 6.3 (March 1818): 386. Further references are cited parenthetically in the text as Roy.

10. The official website of the American Unitarian Conference gives the dates of the *Christian Register* as 1821–1957 but also notes that publication continued, with

a change of title to the *Unitarian Register*, from 1957 until 1961, when the journal merged with the *Universalist Leader* and became known as *UU World*. "Unitarian Christian Journals," http://www.americanunitarian.org/journals.htm (accessed 14 May 2009).

11. J. P. Rao Rayapati, *Early American Interest in Vedanta* (New York: Asia Publishing House, 1973), 77–78. Further references are cited parenthetically in the text as Rayapati.

12. Quoted in Igbal Singh, *Rammohun Roy: A Biographical Inquiry into the Making of Modern India*, 2nd ed. (Bombay: Asia Publishing House, 1983), 1:217–18. Further references are cited parenthetically in the text as Singh.

13. Adrienne Moore, *Rammohun Roy and America* (Calcutta: Brahmo Mission Press, 1943), 41.

14. Thomas Jefferson, ed., *The Life and Morals of Jesus of Nazareth* (1803; St. Louis, Mo.: Thompson, 1902), 168.

15. Rammohun Roy, *The Precepts of Jesus: The Guide to Peace and Happiness* (1820; London: Unitarian Society, 1824), 98.

16. "Unitarian Christians in India," *Christian Register* 1 (20 April 1821): 2.

17. "Religious Intelligence: Rammohun Roy," *Christian Register* 1.17 (7 December 1821): 65, 66.

18. Editorial, *Christian Register* 1 (17 May 1822): 158.

19. Ralph Waldo Emerson to Mary Moody Emerson, 10 June 1822, quoted in James Elliot Cabot, *A Memoir of Emerson* (Boston: Houghton, Mifflin, 1887), 1:80–81.

20. Kenneth Walter Cameron, *Emerson's "Indian Superstition"* (Hartford, Conn.: Transcendental Books, 1977), 18.

21. Russell B. Goodman, "East-West Philosophy in Nineteenth-Century America: Emerson and Hinduism," *Journal of the History of Ideas* 51.4 (October-December 1990): 625, 641. Further references are cited parenthetically in the text as Goodman.

22. Ralph Waldo Emerson, *Essays and Lectures* (New York: Library of America, 1983), 57, 59.

23. *The Letters of Ralph Waldo Emerson*, ed. Ralph L. Rusk (New York, 1939), 3:290.

24. Arthur Christy, *The Orient in American Transcendentalism: A Study of Emerson, Thoreau, and Alcott* (New York: Octagon Books, 1969), 285. Further references are cited parenthetically in the text as Christy. Information about Emerson's reading of orientalist texts is taken from Christy's appendix, "Books and Marginalia," 275–323.

25. Carl T. Jackson, *The Oriental Religions and American Thought: Nineteenth-Century Explorations* (Westport, Conn.: Greenwood Press, 1981), 183.

26. "The Divinity School Address," in *Emerson: Essays and Lectures*, 88, 78, 89. Further references are cited parenthetically in the text.

27. Quoted in "Chronology," in *Emerson: Essays and Lectures*, 1129.

28. "Veeshnoo Sarma," *The Dial* 3.1 (July 1842): 82, 85 Further references are cited parenthetically in the text as VS.

29. Charles Wilkins quotes from Jones on this point in his "Translator's Preface" to *Fables and Proverbs from the Sanskrit, being the "Hitopadesa"* (1787; London: Routledge, 1885), 10.

30. William Bysshe Stein, introduction to *Hitopadesa: Fables and Proverbs from the Sanskrit* (1787; Gainesville, Fla.: Scholars' Facsimiles and Reprints, 1968), v–vi.

31. "Lectures on the Times," in *Emerson: Essays and Lectures*, 164. Further references are cited parenthetically in the text.

32. W[illiam] T. Harris, "Emerson's Orientalism ," in *The Genius and Character of Emerson: Lectures at the Concord School of Philosophy*, ed. F. B. Sanborn (Boston: Osgood, 1885), 372.

33. "Plato; or, The Philosopher," in *Representative Men, Emerson: Essays and Lectures* 634–35. Further references are cited parenthetically in the text as Plato.

34. Goodman, "East-West Philosophy," 641.

35. Frederic Ives Carpenter, *Emerson and Asia* (1930; New York: Haskell House, 1968), ix. Further references are cited parenthetically in the text as Carpenter.

36. Quoted in Frederick Augustus Braun, *Margaret Fuller and Goethe* (New York: Henry Holt, 1910), 73, 37, 68–69.

37. "Goethe; or, The Writer," in *Representative Men, Emerson: Essays and Lectures*, 758. Further references are cited parenthetically in the text.

38. Information about who selected what for the "Ethical Scriptures" series in *The Dial* is taken from Christy, *The Orient in American Transcendentalism*, 11–13.

39. Alan D. Hodder, *Thoreau's Ecstatic Witness* (New Haven, Conn.: Yale University Press, 2001), 211. Further references are cited parenthetically in the text as Hodder.

40. Henry David Thoreau, *A Week on the Concord and Merrimack Rivers* (1849), ed. Carl F. Hovde et al. (Princeton, N.J.: Princeton University Press, 1980), 67. Further references to this edition are cited parenthetically in the text as *Week*.

41. James Russell Lowell, review of *A Week on the Concord and Merrimack Rivers, Massachusetts Quarterly Review* 9 (December 1849): 47.

42. *The Journal of Henry David Thoreau*, 2 vols., ed. Bradford Torrey (1906; New York: Dover, 1962), 1:279.

43. Thoreau to Harrison Blake, 20 November 1849, in *The Writings of Henry David Thoreau: Familiar Letters*, ed. F. B. Sanborn (Boston: Houghton Mifflin, 1906), 6:175.

44. Hodder, *Thoreau's Ecstatic Witness*, 203, notes that the Asian "texts to which [Thoreau] had access do not explain the detail of such practices."

45. Henry David Thoreau, *A Week on the Concord and Merrimack Rivers; Walden; The Maine Woods; Cape Cod* (New York: Library of America, 1985), 411.

46. Christy, *The Orient in American Transcendentalism*, 195.

47. "Sayings of Confucius," *The Dial* 3.4 (April 1843): 493, 494. Thoreau's source was Joshua Marshman, *The Works of Confucius, containing the original text, with a translation* (Serampore, India: Mission Press, 1809).

48. For a discussion of the importance of silence in Thoreau, see Hodder (231): "Asian conceptions of language—the eloquent silence of Confucius or the trans-

cendental hymns of the Vedas—proved instructive. Silence for Thoreau was the source of speech, of thought, of time, of creation, in much the same way as it was depicted in these traditions."

49. "Chinese Four Books," *The Dial* 4.2 (October 1843): 205, 207, from David Collie, *The Chinese Classical Work Commonly Called the Four Books* ([Malacca, Malaysia]: Mission Press, 1828).

50. Thoreau is here (137) quoting from Warren Hastings's preface to Wilkins's translation of the *Bhagavad-Gita.*

51. Robert D. Richardson Jr., "Thoreau and Concord," in *The Cambridge Companion to Henry David Thoreau* (Cambridge: Cambridge University Press, 1995), 19.

52. Walter Harding, *The Days of Henry Thoreau: A Biography* (Princeton, N.J.: Princeton University Press, 1982), 429.

53. Although Arnold's poem was written in the early 1850s, prior to the 1859 publication of the *Origin of Species,* it was not published until 1867 and therefore begs for interpretation in the light of Darwin's theory. But Arnold certainly did not need to wait for the full controversy about Darwin to emerge to feel anxiety about the relation of religion and science, which was a lifelong concern, as it was for many Victorians. See Laurence W. Mazzeno, *Matthew Arnold: The Critical Legacy* (Rochester, N.Y.: Camden House, 1999), especially chapter 8, "The Critical Reception of Arnold's Religious Writings" (125–35).

54. Mathew Arnold, *The Poems of Matthew Arnold* (London: Oxford University Press, 1909), 402.

55. Klaus K. Klostermaier, *A Survey of Hinduism,* 3rd ed. (Albany: State University of New York Press, 2007), 498.

56. Megan Marshall, *The Peabody Sisters: Three Women Who Ignited American Romanticism* (Boston: Houghton Mifflin, 2005), 425, 436. The attribution of the Burnouf translations to Thoreau originates with George Willis Cooke, "*The Dial:* An Historical and Biographical Introduction, with a List of the Contributors," *Journal of Speculative Philosophy* 19 (July 1885): 265. Cooke concludes his article with a note asking that readers send corrections to any errors they happen to notice. On page 322 of the same volume of the journal he prints this correction: "The extracts made from 'The White Lotus of the Good Law' were by Miss E. P. Peabody, and translated from Burnouf." The correction went unremarked until Elizabeth Witherell of the Textual Center for the Writings of Henry David Thoreau noticed it and communicated the discovery to Wendell Piez, who published an article about the misattribution, "Anonymous Was a Woman—Again," in *Tricycle: The Buddhist Review* 3 (Fall 1993): 10–11. The correction is also discussed in Thomas A. Tweed's preface to the paperback edition of *The American Encounter with Buddhism, 1844–1912* (Chapel Hill: University of North Carolina Press, 2000), xvi–xvii, xxi n12.

57. Quoted in Christy, *The Orient in American Transcendentalism,* 321.

58. Hongbo Tan, "Confucius at Walden Pond: Thoreau's Unpublished Confucian Translations," *Studies in the American Renaissance* 17 (1993): 282–83.

59. Quoted in Robert Sattlemeyer, *Thoreau's Reading: A Study in Intellectual History* (Princeton, N.J.: Princeton University Press, 1988), 68.

60. Dale Riepe, *The Philosophy of India and Its Impact on American Thought* (Springfield, Ill.: Thomas, 1970), 22; Shalom Goldman, *God's Sacred Tongue: Hebrew and the American Imagination* (Chapel Hill: University of North Carolina Press, 2004), 164–65.

61. Riepe, *The Philosophy of India and Its Impact on American Thought*, 12; *Dictionary of American Biography*, ed. Dumas Malone (1934; New York: Scribner, 1962), 9:308. Further references are cited parenthetically throughout the book as *DAB*.

62. Quoted in R. K. Gupta, *The Great Encounter: A Study of Indo-American Literary and Cultural Relations* (Riverdale, Md.: Riverdale, 1987), 96, 97.

63. Jackson, *The Oriental Religions and American Thought*, 180–81.

64. *Journal of the American Oriental Society* 1 (1849): iii, v. Further references to this journal (*JAOS*) are cited parenthetically in the text by volume and page number (e.g., 1:iii, v).

3. The Fin de Siècle

1. Earl Miner, *The Japanese Tradition in British and American Literature* (Princeton, N.J.: Princeton University Press, 1958), 5–6.

2. Hermann Melville, *Moby Dick* (1851; New York: Random House, 1981), 498.

3. Quoted in Miner, *The Japanese Tradition*, 20.

4. J. M. Roberts, *The New History of the World* (Oxford: Oxford University Press, 2003), 843. Further references are cited parenthetically in the text as Roberts.

5. Raphael Pumpelly, *Across America and Asia* (New York: Leypoldt and Holt, 1870), 67, 68, 76, 143. Further references are cited parenthetically in the text as *AA&A*.

6. Raphael Pumpelly, *My Reminiscences*, 2 vols. (New York: Henry Holt, 1918), 1:281. Further references are cited parenthetically in the text as *R*.

7. Carl T. Jackson, *The Oriental Religions and American Thought* (Westport, Conn.: Greenwood Press, 1981), 206. Further refernces are cited parenthetically in the text as Jackson.

8. For the other biographical details in this paragraph, see the Morse and Bigelow entries in *DAB*.

9. Edward S. Morse, *Japan Day by Day: 1877, 1878–79, 1882–83*, 2 vols. (1917; Atlanta: Cherokee, 1990), 1:339–40. Further references are cited parenthetically in the text as *JDD*. The dates in Morse's title should be noted, since some critics seem confused about the periods of his Japanese residence. He arrived in 1877 and was contracted to teach zoology at the University of Tokyo shortly thereafter, in July 1877. But he had to request a five-month leave of absence from his two-year appointment because he had already committed to a series of public lectures "at home for the coming winter" (*JDD*, 1:139). He gave his first lecture at the university on 12 September 1877; returned to the United States at the end of the fall term, lectured there over the winter months, and came back to Japan in the spring, probably sometime in April (the first date recorded in *JDD* upon his return is 1 May 1878 [1:371]). So he

evidently taught in the fall of 1878 and the winter of 1879, which, together with fall 1877 and the leave of absence in winter 1878, rounds out the two-year appointment. He arrived for his third period of residency on 5 June 1882 and left sometime in 1883 (the exact date is not indicated).

10. Dorothy G. Wayman, *Edward Sylvester Morse: A Biography* (Cambridge, Mass.: Harvard University Press, 1942), 248.

11. Quoted in ibid., 251.

12. The alternate Sunday schedule was not without exception. Morse's four lectures on Darwinism were given on 27, 28, 31 October and 2 November.

13. Wayman, *Edward Sylvester Morse*, 248–49.

14. Morse adds that the Burke volume has sold "over ten thousand copies" (*JDD*, 2:318).

15. Wayman, *Edward Sylvester Morse*, 234.

16. Ibid., 259.

17. Ibid.

18. T. J. Jackson Lears, *No Place of Grace: Antimodernism and the Transformation of American Culture* (Chicago: University of Chicago Press, 1994), 232.

19. William Sturgis Bigelow, *Buddhism and Immortality* (Boston: Houghton Mifflin, 1908), 44. Further references are cited parenthetically in the text as Bigelow.

20. Beongcheon Yu, *The Great Circle: American Writers and the Orient* (Detroit: Wayne State University Press, 1983), 80.

21. Henry Adams, "John La Farge's Discovery of Japanese Art: A New Perspective of the Origins of *Japonisme*," *Art Bulletin* 67.3 (September 1985): 453–54, 450. The 1878 letter that Adams quotes was written to Richard Watson Gilder, editor at Scribner.

22. Quoted in Royal Cortissoz, *John La Farge: A Memoir and a Study* (Boston: Houghton Mifflin, 1911), 112–13. Details of La Farge's biography are taken from the entry in *DAB*, 5:530–35.

23. Christopher Benfey, *The Great Wave: Gilded Age Misfits, Japanese Eccentrics, and the Opening of Old Japan* (New York: Random House, 2003), 132–33.

24. John La Farge, "An Essay on Japanese Art," in Raphael Pumpelly, *Across America and Asia* (New York: Leypoldt and Holt, 1870), 195. Further references are cited parenthetically in the text.

25. Kathleen Pyne and D. Scott Atkinson, "Landscapes of the Mind: New Conceptions of Nature," in *The Third Mind: American Artists Contemplate Asia, 1860–1989* (New York: Solomon R. Guggenheim Foundation, 2009), 89–93.

26. One watercolor is in the San Francisco Museum of Art, and the other in the Metropolitan Museum in New York City.

27. James L. Yarnell, "John La Farge and Henry Adams in Japan," *American Art Journal* 21.1 (1989): 67–69.

28. Edward Chalfant, *Better in Darkness: A Biography of Henry Adams: His Second Life, 1862–1891* (Hamden, Conn.: Archon Books, 1994), 511.

29. Adams to Gaskell, 25 April 1886, quoted in Chalfant, *Better in Darkness*, 511.

30. Adams to Theodore Frelinghuysen Dwight, 28 June 1886, in *Henry Adams and His Friends: A Collection of His Unpublished Letters,* ed. Harold Dean Cater (1947; New York: Octagon, 1970), 163.

31. Adams to Dwight, 17 July 1886, in ibid., 165.

32. Adams to Dwight, 10 August 1886, in ibid., 168.

33. John La Farge, *An Artist's Letters from Japan* (New York: Century, 1897), ix. Further references to this edition are cited parenthetically in the text as *ALJ*.

34. Okakura Kakuzo, *The Book of Tea* (New York: Fox Duffield, 1906), [v].

35. Victoria Weston, *Japanese Painting and National Identity: Okakura Tenshin and His Circle* (Ann Arbor: Center for Japanese Studies, University of Michigan, 2004), 5-6, 7.

36. Ezra Pound, *ABC of Reading* (1934; New York: New Directions, 1960), 81.

37. Hannah Adams, *A View of Religions, in Three Parts,* 3rd ed. (1801; London: Button and Son, 1805), 416.

38. Odell Shepard, ed., *The Journals of Bronson Alcott,* 2 vols. (1938; Port Washington, N.Y.: Kennicat Press, 1966), 1:xxiii, 2:388, 1:180.

39. La Farge concludes the chapter "Tao: The Way" with a translation of "Tchouang-tsee" from the Latin of Joseph Henri Prémare's *Notitia Linguae Sinicæ, ALJ,* 117 n1. Prémare (1666–1736) was a Jesuit missionary to China; his *Notitia Linguae Sinicæ* was a Chinese grammar that included examples from classic Chinese texts. The book circulated in manuscript for a century or so before being published in 1839 (see Christoph Harbsmeier, *Science and Civilization in China,* ed. Joseph Needham, vol. 7, pt. 1 [Cambridge: Cambridge University Press, 1998], 16). Giles's translation of several passages from Chuang Tse was published by Quarich in 1889; Legge's translation of the *Tao-te-Ching* appeared in volume 39 of *The Sacred Books of the East,* ed. F. Max Müller (Oxford: Oxford University Press, 1891). La Farge's chapter on the Tao was first published in *Century Magazine* 42.3 (July 1891): 442–48, but most of it was written in Nikko in 1886. La Farge's essay therefore appeared around the same time as the Giles and Legge translations, but there is no evidence that he was aware of these scholarly efforts. Also, La Farge's *Century* essay appeared in advance of "Tao," an article in *Atlantic Monthly* 73.436 (February 1894): 182–98, by William Davies, who does not mention La Farge.

40. James Legge, trans., *Tao te Ching,* in Müller, *Sacred Books of the East,* 39:49.

41. Okakura Kakuzo, *The Awakening of Japan* (1904; New York: Japan Society, 1921), 65.

42. Henry Adams, *The Education of Henry Adams* (1906; Mineola, N.Y.: Dover, 2002), 272, 239.

43. Adams to John Hay, 21 October 1886, in *Henry Adams and His Friends,* 174.

44. Lawrence W. Chisolm, *Fenollosa: The Far East and American Culture* (New Haven: Yale University Press, 1963), 30–31, 25, 40.

45. Quoted in G[eorge] B[ailey] Sansom, *The Western World and Japan: A Study in the Interaction of European and Asiatic Cultures* (New York: Knopf, 1962), 396–97, 398.

46. Chisolm, *Fenollosa,* 41.

47. G. W. F. Hegel, *Lectures on the Philosophy of History*, trans. J. Sibrew (London: Bohn, 1861), 90. Further references are cited parenthetically in the text as *Lectures*.

48. If Fenollosa interpreted Hegel's vision of future history to mean that it would involve a synthesis of East and West, as he clearly did, then he went against the suppositions of Hegel himself, who said that "the burden of the World's history" might reveal itself "in a contest between North and South America" (*Lectures*, 90).

49. Chisolm, *Fenollosa*, 26.

50. William H. Goetzmann, with Dickson Pratt, *The American Hegelians: An Intellectual Episode in the History of Western America* (New York: Knopf, 1973), 3, 354. Further references cited parenthetically in the text as Goetzmann.

51. Chisolm, *Fenollosa*, 42.

52. Ibid., 47, 28, 50, 51.

53. Weston, *Japanese Painting and National Identity*, 6–7.

54. Quoted in Benfey, *The Great Wave*, 145.

55. Percival Lowell, *The Soul of the Far East* (Boston: Houghton, Mifflin, 1888), 2, 3. Further references are cited parenthetically in the text as *Soul*.

56. Calling Hearn peripatetic is a bit of an understatement. He was born on the British-controlled Greek island of Leukas in 1850 to an Anglo-Irish father in the English navy and a mother of Greek, or possibly Maltese, lineage. When the father was ordered to the West Indies, he sent his wife and son to Dublin. The marriage foundered over the father's infidelity, whereupon Hearn's parents separated, with Major Hearn assigned to India and Mrs. Hearn returning to Greece. The boy, aged seven, was left in Dublin to be raised by relatives. They sent him to boarding school, first in England, where he lost an eye in a schoolyard altercation (almost all the photographs of the adult Hearn are in profile to hide the missing eye), and then in France. At age nineteen he was sent to Cincinnati to live with a distant relative but wound up living on his own when the distant relative kept his distance. He was taken in by a printer named Henry Watkin, who nicknamed Hearn "The Raven" because of the young man's fascination with Edgar Allan Poe, whose style he imitated in some early stories. With Watkin's help, the young Hearn landed a job as a night reporter for the *Cincinnati Enquirer*. He worked for the *Enquirer* and other Cincinnati papers until 1877, when he departed for Memphis on his way to New Orleans. By 1881 he was on the staff of one of the most important newspapers in the South, the *New Orleans Times Democrat*. Hearn wrote stories mainly about the Creole community of the city while also becoming fascinated with the Orient, reading parts of Max Müller's series, *Sacred Books of the East* (1879–1894), and, of course, Percival Lowell's *Soul of the Far East*. In 1887 he published an orientalist volume of his own, *Some Chinese Ghosts*, a book that combined his old interest in the supernaturalism of Poe with his new interest in the Far East. Also in 1887 he left New Orleans for New York to make arrangements for a sojourn in the West Indies; there he stayed, off and on, for two years, starting out in Trinidad and ending in Martinique. Finally, in 1890, he left the United States for good, arriving in Yokohama on 4 April. He lived in Japan for the rest of his life, married a Japanese woman named Setsu Koizumi, and became a Japanese citizen after their son was born in 1893. This sketch of Hearn's life is

taken mostly from *Lafcadio Hearn,* Nina H. Kennard's old-fashioned but thorough biography (New York: Appleton, 1912), and also from Benfey, *The Great Wave,* esp. 221, 214–15.

57. Lafcadio Hearn, *Glimpses of Unfamiliar Japan,* 2 vols. (London: Osgood, McIlvane, 1894), 1:vi–vii.

58. Lafcadio Hearn, *Kokoro: Hints and Echoes of Japanese Inner Life* (Boston: Houghton Mifflin, 1896), n.p. The full explanation of *kokoro* is that the "word signifies also mind, in the emotional sense; spirit; courage; resolve; sentiment; affection; and inner meaning,—just as we say in English, 'the heart of things.'" Further references to this edition of *Kokoro* are cited parenthetically in the text as *K.*

59. The intellectual contrast between Hearn and Fenollosa was matched by personal antipathy, at least on the part of Hearn. As Benfey explains, Hearn met Fenollosa in April 1898 but, quickly tiring of the man's "pomposity and dogmatism," sent him a letter that put an end to the friendship: "My dear Professor—I have been meditating, and after the meditation I came to the conclusion not to visit your charming new home again—not at least before 1900. I suppose that I am a beast and an ape; but nevertheless I hope to make you understand." Quoted in Benfey, *The Great Wave,* 233.

60. Ernest Fenollosa, "Chinese and Japanese Traits," *Atlantic Monthly* 69 (1892): 774. Further references are cited parenthetically in the text as "Traits."

61. For a discussion of *The Knight Errant* and the Boston decadents, see chapter 3 of David Weir, *Decadent Culture in the United States* (Albany: State University of New York Press, 2008). Fenollosa published "The Significance of Oriental Art" in *The Knight Errant* 1 (1892): 65–70.

62. Ernest Fenollosa, preface to *East and West, the Discovery of America, and Other Poems* (Boston: Crowell, 1893), vi. Further references are cited parenthetically in the text as *EW.*

63. The poem, by Charles G. D. Roberts, is titled "A Ballad of Manila Bay"; "The Rescue of the 'Winslow'" is by Lt. Ernest E. Mead, identified as "navigating officer of the 'Hudson.'" *Harper's New Monthly Magazine* 98 (December 1898): 114–15, 123–29.

64. Ernest Fenollosa, "The Coming Fusion of East and West," *Harper's New Monthly Magazine* 98 (December 1898): 116. Further references are cited parenthetically in the text as "Fusion."

65. Ibid., 120: "Today China is buying up large numbers of Japanese textbooks and translations of European literature, employing Japanese in many of her offices, and sending one hundred and fifty selected students not to Europe but to the care of the Tokio government for education in Japanese universities."

4. The Twentieth Century I

1. Noel Stock, *The Life of Ezra Pound* (New York: Avon, 1970), 201–2. Further references are cited parenthetically in the text as Stock.

2. The information in this paragraph concerning "Philadelphia Orientalism" is

taken from Ira B. Nadel, "Constructing the Orient: Pound's American Vision," in *Ezra Pound and China,* ed. Zhaoming Qian (Ann Arbor: University of Michigan Press, 2003), 13–14.

3. Ibid., 23.

4. Erza Pound, *Selected Prose, 1909–1965,* ed. William Cookson (New York: New Directions, 1973), 145. Further references are cited parenthetically in the text as *SP.*

5. Ralph Waldo Emerson, *Emerson: Essays and Lectures* (New York: Library of America, 1983), 20. Further references to *Nature* are cited in the text with the abbreviation *N.*

6. Lawrence W. Chisolm, *Fenollosa: The Far East and American Culture* (New Haven, Conn.: Yale University Press, 1963), 218.

7. Erza Pound, *The Selected Letters of Ezra Pound, 1907–1941,* ed. D. D. Paige (New York: New Directions, 1971), 49.

8. Nadal, "Constructing the Orient," 17. Nadal quotes Murray Cohen, *Sensible Words: Linguistic Practice in England, 1640–1785* (Baltimore: Johns Hopkins University Press, 1977), 143.

9. Ernest Fenollosa, *The Chinese Written Character as a Medium for Poetry,* ed. Erza Pound (1936; San Francisco: City Lights Books, n.d.), 22. Further references are cited parenthetically in the text as *CWC.*

10. Ernest Fenollosa, "The Nature of Fine Art," *The Lotus* 9 (April 1896): 756, quoted in Chisolm, *Fenellosa,* 216–17.

11. Ezra Pound, *Gaudia Breska* (London: Lane, 1916), 106.

12. Ernest Fenollosa, "Chinese and Japanese Traits," *Atlantic Monthly* 69 (1892): 771.

13. Ezra Pound, *Jefferson and/or Mussolini: L'Idea Statale: Fascism as I Have Seen It* (New York: Liveright, 1935), 45, 63. Further references cited as *JM.*

14. Feng Lan, *Ezra Pound and Confucianism: Remaking Humanism in the Face of Modernity* (Toronto: University of Toronto Press, 2005), 4–5. Pound's expression of belief in the *Ta Hio* is taken from *Literary Essays of Ezra Pound,* ed. T. S. Eliot (New York: New Directions, 1968), 86. Further references are cited parenthetically in the text as *LE.*

15. "Bomanji Pestonji Wadia (1881–1958)," Stiftelsen Teosofiska Kompaniet Malmö, 27 January 2009, http://www.teosofiskakompaniet.net/BPWadiaBiografi.htm.

16. Ezra Pound, trans., *Confucius* (New York: New Directions, 1951), 29. Further references are cited parenthetically in the text as *C.* The translation here is Pound's revision of his 1928 translation of Pauthier's *Ta Hsio,* done in 1947 and based on Legge's Chinese edition.

17. Ezra Pound, *ABC of Reading* (New York: New Directions, 1960), 29.

18. See David Weir, *Anarchy and Culture: The Aesthetic Politics of Modernism* (Amherst: University of Massachusetts Press, 1997), 154–55, 178–79.

19. Feng Lan, *Ezra Pound and Confucianism,* 88. Further references are cited parenthetically in the text as Lan.

20. Quoted in Lan, 86.

21. Ezra Pound, "The Words of Ming Mao 'Least among the Disciples of Kung-Fu-Tse,'" in *Ezra Pound's Poetry and Prose: Contributions to Periodicals* (New York: Garland, 1991), 1:320.

22. Cleo McNelly Kearns, *T. S. Eliot and Indic Traditions: A Study in Poetry and Belief* (Cambridge: Cambridge University Press, 1987), 21. Further references are cited parenthetically in the text as Kearns.

23. T. S. Eliot, "What Is Minor Poetry," in *On Poetry and Poets* (New York: Farrar, Straus and Giroux, 1957), 38. Further references are cited parenthetically in the text as *OPP*.

24. Lyndall Gordon, *Eliot's Early Years* (New York: Noonday, 1977), 11–13.

25. Robert E. Spiller, "The Battle of the Books," in *Literary History of the United States,* 3rd ed., ed. Robert E. Spiller et al. (New York: Macmillan, 1963), 1149.

26. Irving Babbitt, "Democracy and Standards," final chapter of *Democracy and Leadership* (1924), rpt. in *Irving Babbit: Representative Writings,* ed. George A. Panichas (Lincoln: University of Nebraska Press, 1981), 158.

27. Quoted in Beongcheon Yu, *The Great Circle: American Writers and the Orient* (Detroit: Wayne State University Press 1983), 128.

28. Quoted in Kearns, *T. S. Eliot and Indic Traditions,* 23.

29. Jeffrey M. Perl and Andrew P. Tuck, "The Hidden Advantage of Tradition: On the Significance of T. S. Eliot's Indic Studies," *Philosophy East and West* 35.2 (April 1985): 116.

30. Quoted in ibid., 117. (The notebook cited is in the Houghton Library, Harvard University.)

31. Ibid.

32. T. S. Eliot, *Knowledge and Experience in the Philosophy of F. H. Bradley* (New York: Columbia University Press, 1989), 142. Further references are cited parenthetically in the text as *KE*.

33. Piers Gray, *T. S. Eliot's Intellectual and Poetic Development, 1909–1922* (Sussex, U.K.: Harvester Press, 1982), 156.

34. Jeffrey M. Perl, *Skepticism and Modern Enmity: Before and after Eliot* (Baltimore: Johns Hopkins University Press, 1989), 49.

35. Ibid., 52–53. The description of Nagarjuna's philosophy is taken from P. T. Raju, *The Philosophical Traditions of India* (London: Allen and Unwin, 1971), 128–29. Perl (183 n44) says that Raju's book "is a conventional university text, and may represent the kind of reading of Mādhyamika that Harvard offered Eliot."

36. T. S. Eliot, *Selected Essays* (New York: Harcourt, Brace and World, 1964), 201. Further references are cited parenthetically in the text as *SE*.

37. Harish Trivedi, *Colonial Transactions: English Literature and India* (Manchester, U.K.: Manchester University Press, 1995), 68, 123. Further references are cited parenthetically in the text as Trivedi.

38. Gordon, *Eliot's Early Years,* 115.

39. T. S. Eliot, *Collected Poems: 1909–1962* (New York; Harcourt, Brace and World, 1963), 76. Further references are cited parenthetically in the text as *CP*.

40. Trivedi is here citing Edmund Wilson, "The Poetry of Drought," *The Dial* 73 (December 1922): 611–16; rpt. in *T. S. Eliot: The Critical Heritage*, ed. Michael Grant (London: Routledge, 1982), 1:140.

41. This information comes from Trivedi, *Colonial Transactions*, which cites *The Principal Upanishads*, ed. and trans. S. Rhadhakrishnan (London: Allen and Unwin, 1953), 289–90.

42. Trivedi's source is the entry for "S[h]anti" in Sir Monier Monier-Williams, *A Sanskrit-English Dictionary*, new ed. (Oxford: Clarendon Press, 1951), 1064.

43. T. S. Eliot, *The Idea of a Christian Society* (1939); rpt. in T. S. Eliot, *Christianity and Culture* (New York: Harcourt, Brace, 1949), 50–51.

44. Peter Ackroyd, *T. S. Eliot: A Life* (New York: Simon and Schuster, 1984), 229. Further references are cited parenthetically in the text as Ackroyd.

45. Narsingh Srivastava, "The Ideas of the *Bhagavad Gita* in *Four Quartets*," *Comparative Literature* 29.2 (Spring 1977): 99.

46. Kristian Smidt, *Poetry and Belief in the Work of T. S. Eliot* (New York: Humanities Press, 1961), 213.

47. T. S. Eliot, introduction to Nagendranath Gangulee, ed., *Thoughts for Meditation: A Way to Recovery from Within* (Boston: Beacon Press, 1952), 13–14.

48. T. S. Eliot, "A Brief Introduction to the Method of Paul Valéry," in *Le Serpent*, trans. Mark Wardle (London: Cobden-Sanderson, 1924), 14.

49. Ibid., 13–14.

50. Marianne Moore, *Complete Poems* (New York: Macmillan, 1967), 29. For a discussion of the early influence of Chinese art on Stevens and Moore, see Zhaoming Qian, *The Modernist Response to Chinese Art: Pound, Moore, Stevens* (Charlottesville: University Press of Virginia, 2003), especially chapter 2, "Chinese Art Arrives in America: Stevens and Moore," 22–46.

51. Sara Teasdale, *Sonnets to Duse and Other Poems* (Boston: Poet Lore, 1907), 22.

52. C. David Heymann, *American Aristocracy: The Lives and Times of James Russell, Amy, and Robert Lowell* (New York: Dodd, Mead, 1980), 164; Sanehide Kodama, *American Poetry and Japanese Culture* (Hamden, Conn.: Archon, 1984), 38–39.

53. Amy Lowell to Tsunejiro Miyaoka, 13 January 1921; quoted in Kodama, *American Poetry and Japanese Culture*, 40.

54. John Gould Fletcher, *Selected Essays*, ed. Lucas Carpenter (Fayetteville: University of Arkansas Press, 1989), 57.

55. See Stephen Maxfield Parrish, *Currents of the Nineties in Boston and London: Fred Holland Day, Louise Imogen Guiney, and Their Circle* (New York: Garland, 1987), especially chapter 2, "The American Memorial to Keats," 96–209.

56. Amy Lowell, *A Dome of Many-Coloured Glass* (1912; New York: Macmillan, 1915), 111.

57. Heymann, *American Aristocracy*, 188.

58. Ibid., 192.

59. Amy Lowell, *Sword Blades and Poppy Seeds* (1914; Boston: Houghton Mifflin, 1921), 244, 245.

60. Quoted in Charles Norman, *Ezra Pound* (New York: Macmillan, 1969), 106.

61. Mari Yoshihara, *Embracing the East: White Women and American Orientalism* (New York: Oxford University Press, 2003), 104.

62. Adrienne Munich and Melissa Bradshaw, *Amy Lowell, American Modern* (New Brunswick, N.J.: Rutgers University Press, 2004), xxii.

63. Review of *Des Imagistes: An Anthology,* in *Poetry: A Magazine of Verse* 5.1 (October 1914): 38.

64. Preface to *Some Imagist Poets* (Boston: Houghton Mifflin, 1916), viii.

65. Mari Yoshihara, *Embracing the East,* 50–51.

66. Percival Lowell, *The Soul of the Far East* (Boston: Houghton, Mifflin, 1888), 148–49.

67. Amy Lowell, *Pictures of the Floating World* (New York: Macmillan, 1919), 11, 12, 11. Further references are cited parenthetically in the text as *Pictures.* I have drawn on Sanhide Kodama, *American Poetry and Japanese Culture,* 45–49, for the discussion of Lowell's Japanese sources for "Lacquer Prints."

68. William N. Porter, *A Hundred Verses from Old Japan* (Oxford: Clarendon Press, 1909), n.p.

69. Ibid.

70. A notice in *Poetry* 9.6 (March 1917): 331, announcing the forthcoming publication of "Lacquer Prints" in *Some Imagist Poets 1917,* says that "Miss Lowell wishes to express her indebtedness to Mr. Arthur Davidson Ficke, for his prose translation of *Streets,* by Yakura Sanjin, which appeared in his *Chats on Japanese Prints*"; 18 poems from the "Lacquer Prints" series were first published in this issue of *Poetry.*

71. Arthur Davidson Ficke, *Chats on Japanese Prints* (1915; New York: Stokes, 1917), 129. Further references are cited parenthetically in the text as Ficke.

72. Julius Kurth, *Suzuki Harunobu* (Munich: Piper, 1910).

73. For an account of the spectrist hoax, see Louis Untermeyer, *The New Era in American Poetry* (New York: Henry Holt, 1919), 320–23; also see John Hall Wheelock, *The Last Romantic: A Poet among Publishers: The Oral Autobiography of John Hall Wheelock* (Columbia: University of South Carolina Press, 2002), 99.

74. Amy Lowell to Walter Bynner, 5 June 1918; quoted in S. Foster Damon, *Amy Lowell: A Chronicle* (Boston: Houghton Mifflin, 1935), 457.

75. Amy Lowell to Arthur Davidson Ficke, 20 April 1916; quoted in Damon, *Amy Lowell,* 354.

76. Kodama, *American Poetry and Japanese Culture,* 46.

77. See Hokusai Katsushika, *Fugaku Hiyaku-kei; or, A Hundred Views of Fuji (Fusiyama),* trans. Frederic Victor Dickins (London: Batsford, 1880), 37: "A hunter or wayfarer . . . is resting under a pine tree, and with exaggerated gesture shows his delight at the image of the Mountain, of which he has caught an unexpected glimpse, reflected on the surface of the water with which he has just filled the saucer." According to Kodama, *American Poetry and Japanese Culture* (46), Lowell bequeathed her copy of this book to Harvard University in 1926.

78. Damon, *Amy Lowell,* 505.

79. Amy Lowell, preface to *Can Grande's Castle* (1918; New York: Macmillan, 1919), xii–xiii. Further references to this edition are cited parenthetically in the text as *Castle*.

80. For a discussion of the short-lived *Seven Arts* (1916–1917), see Paul R. Gorman, *Left Intellectuals and Popular Culture in Twentieth-Century America* (Chapel Hill: University of North Carolina Press, 1996), 55–65.

81. Editors' note to Seichi Naruse, "Young Japan," *Seven Arts* 1 (April 1917): 616. Further references are cited parenthetically in the text as Naruse.

82. Quoted in Damon, *Amy Lowell*, 420.

83. Amy Lowell to Linda Hawley Brigham, 4 November 1919, quoted in Damon, *Amy Lowell*, 475.

84. Marleigh Grayer Ryan, "Guns as Keys: James McNeill Whistler as a Metaphor for Japan in a Poem by Amy Lowell," *Currents in Japanese Culture: Translations and Transformations*, ed. Amy Vladeck Heinrich (New York: Columbia University Press, 1997), 375.

85. Ibid., 376. Ryan points out that Lowell gets the title of the first painting wrong; it is *Nocturne: Blue and Silver—Battersea Reach*, not "Battersea Bridge" (377).

86. Ernest Fenollosa, "The Place in History of Mr. Whistler's Art," *The Lotus* 1.1 (December 1903): 16.

87. Amy Lowell, foreword to *Pictures of the Floating World*, vii. For the claim that Lowell focused on Whistler's *Variations on Green and Violet* because of Fenollosa's essay in *The Lotus*, see Ryan, "Guns as Keys," 382–85.

88. Damon, *Amy Lowell*, 434, 586.

89. Amy Lowell, preface to *Fir-Flower Tablets* (Boston: Houghton Mifflin, 1921), vi–vii. Further references to this edition are cited parenthetically in the text as *Tablets*.

90. Quoted in Heymann, *American Aristocracy*, 255.

91. For a sketch of Giles's career, see Robert Kern, *Orientalism, Modernism, and the American Poem* (Cambridge: Cambridge University Press, 1996), 172–73; for the influence of Giles on modernist poets, see Zhaoming Qian, *Orientalism and Modernism: The Legacy of China in Pound and Williams* (Durham, N.C.: Duke University Press, 1995), 26–34, 120–24.

92. Herbert Allen Giles, *Chinese Poetry in English Verse* (London: Quarich, 1898), 200 n6. Further references are cited parenthetically in the text as Giles.

93. Erza Pound, *Personæ: Collected Shorter Poems* (New York: New Directions, 1971), 108. Further references are cited parenthetically in the text as *Personæ*.

94. Qian, *Orientalism and Modernism*, 41.

95. Quoted in Kern, *Orientalism, Modernism, and the American Poem*, 197.

96. Arthur Waley, trans., *A Hundred and Seventy Chinese Poems* (1919; New York: Knopf, 1922), 70.

97. Qian, *Orientalism and Modernism*, 42.

98. Ibid., 41.

99. Mari Yoshihara, *Embracing the East*, 106.

100. Quoted in Harley Farnsworth MacNair, ed., *Florence Ayscough and Amy Lowell: Correspondence of a Friendship* (Chicago: University of Chicago Press, 1945), 104.

101. Biographers are divided on the question of Lowell's sexuality; see Heymann, *American Aristocracy,* 209–11.

102. Amy Lowell to the Boston Equal Suffrage Association for Good Government, 7 October 1918, quoted in Heymann, *American Aristocracy,* 247.

103. Amy Lowell to Louis Untermeyer, 11 August 1916; quoted in S. Foster Damon, *Amy Lowell,* 365–66.

104. Ezra Pound, introduction to *"Noh," or Accomplishment: A Study of the Classical Stage of Japan* (1917; New York: Knopf, 1927), 5.

105. Pound's admiration for Mussolini has been analyzed at length by many critics, but see especially Tim Redman, *Ezra Pound and Italian Fascism* (Cambridge: Cambridge University Press, 1991). Heymann, *American Aristocracy,* calls Lowell a "silent but ardent supporter of Mussolini" who "feared for the future of her clan" (279).

5. The Twentieth Century II

1. Phineas Taylor Barnum, *Life of P. T. Barnum, Written by Himself, including His Golden Rules of Money Making* (Buffalo, N.Y.: Courier, 1888), 134.

2. A. H. Saxon, *P. T. Barnum: The Legend and the Man* (New York: Columbia University Press, 1989), 99. For an account of the Fejee Mermaid—a monkey and a fish sewn together—see Saxon, 119–23.

3. Bluford Adams, *E. Pluribus Barnum: The Great Showman and the Making of U.S. Popular Culture* (Minneapolis: University of Minnesota Press, 1997), 165–66.

4. P. T. Barnum, *Struggles and Triumphs; or, Fifty Years of Recollections of P. T. Barnum, Including His Golden Rules for Money-Making, Illustrated and Brought up to 1889, Written by Himself* (Buffalo, N.Y.: Courier, 1889), 271.

5. Adams, *E. Pluribus Barnum,* 167, 175.

6. Barnum, *Struggles and Triumphs,* 349. The first *Oxford English Dictionary* (*OED*) entry for *ethnological* is dated 1849, but a cite from the *Daily News* of 19 September 1873 captures the sense of the term as Barnum used it: "A collection of ethnological curiosities from New Guinea."

7. Barnum had been alert to this necessity at least from the 1850s; see Adams, *E. Pluribus Barnum,* 21.

8. Philip B. Kunhardt Jr. et al., *P. T. Barnum: America's Greatest Showman* (New York: Knopf, 1995), 274.

9. Quoted in Adams, *E. Pluribus Barnum,* 178.

10. Kunhardt et al., *P. T. Barnum,* 274.

11. Adams, *E. Pluribus Barnum,* 178–79; Kunhardt et al., *P. T. Barnum,* 289.

12. Brijraj Singh, "Henry Willard French and India," *New England Quarterly* 64.4 (December 1991): 579; Judith Snodgrass, *Presenting Japanese Buddhism to*

the West (Chapel Hill: University of North Carolina Press, 2003), 101–2; Thomas A. Tweed, *The American Encounter with Buddhism, 1844–1912: Victorian Culture and the Limits of Dissent* (1992; Chapel Hill: University of North Carolina Press, 2000), 29.

13. Russell Roberts and Rich Youmans, *Down the Jersey Shore* (New Brunswick, N.J.: Rutgers University Press,1993), 154; Emil R. Salvini, *Boardwalk Memories: Tales of the Jersey Shore* (Guildford, Conn.: Globe Pequot Press, 2006), 174.

14. Oliver Wendell Holmes, "The Light of Asia," *International Review* 7 (October 1879): 345–46, 347.

15. W. C. Brownell, "Recent Poetry," *The Nation* 29 (1879): 314.

16. The quotations from the *Boston Evening Transcript* and the *New York Evening Post* are excerpted in the back matter of the twenty-eighth edition of *The Light of Asia* (London: Trübner, 1885).

17. Edwin Arnold, preface to *The Light of Asia: The Life and Teaching of Gautama, Prince of India and Founder of Buddhism* (Twickenham, U.K.: Senate, 1998), viii. Further references to this edition, first published in 1908, are cited parenthetically in the text as Arnold.

18. Tweed, *The American Encounter with Buddhism,* 29.

19. Samuel Henry Kellogg, introductory notes to *The Light of Asia and the Light of the World* (London: Macmillan, 1885), xv–xviii. Further references are cited parenthetically in the text.

20. William Cleaver Wilkinson, *Edwin Arnold as Poetizer and as Paganizer* (New York: Funk and Wagnall's, 1884), 11. Further references are cited parenthetically in the text.

21. Holmes, "The Light of Asia," 346, 347.

22. Elizabeth Cady Stanton, obituary notice for Charles de Berard Mills, *Free Thought Magazine* 18 (January-December 1900): 413.

23. Charles D. B. Mills, *The Indian Saint; or, Buddha and Buddhism* (Northampton, Mass.: Journal and Free Press, 1876), v. Further references are cited parenthetically in the text.

24. Mary Warner Blanchard, *Oscar Wilde's America: Counterculture in the Gilded Age* (New Haven: Yale University Press, 1998), 4.

25. For a discussion of the American reaction to the "achievement ethos" in the late nineteenth century, see T. J. Jackson Lears, *No Place of Grace: Antimodernism and the Transformation of American Culture, 1880–1920* (Chicago: University of Chicago Press, 1983), especially chapter 6, "From Patriarchy to Nirvana: Patterns of Ambivalence."

26. The comment is from the *Edinburgh Courant* and is printed in the back matter of the 1880 edition of *The Light of Asia.*

27. J. A. Smith, "Sacred Books of the East," *Old Testament Student* 4.3 (November 1884): 140.

28. Quoted in Tweed, *The American Encounter with Buddhism,* 104.

29. Ibid., 46.

30. Peter Washington, *Madame Blavatsky's Baboon: A History of the Mystics, Mediums, and Misfits Who Brought Spiritualism to America* (New York: Schocken, 1995), 83. The sketch of theosophy in this paragraph is based on Washington, *Madame Blavatsky's Baboon*, 10, 82; Robert S. Ellwood, *Eastern Spirituality in America* (Mahwah, N.J.: Paulist Press, 1987), 17; Carl T. Jackson, *The Oriental Religions and American Thought* (Westport, Conn.: Greenwood Press, 1981), 157–77.

31. Washington, *Madame Blavatsky's Baboon*, 85.

32. W. Michael Ashcraft, *The Dawn of a New Cycle: Point Loma Theosophists and American Culture* (Knoxville: University of Tennessee Press, 2002), 17–18.

33. H. P. Blavatsky, *An Abridgment of the Secret Doctrine*, ed. Elizabeth Preston and Christmas Humpreys (Wheaton, Ill.: Theosophical Publishing, 1967), xxix–xxx, xxx n7. Further references are cited parenthetically in text as *SD.*

34. "The Nature and Office of the Buddha's Religion," *The Path* 1.1 (April 1886): 24.

35. Blavatsky, *Abridgment of the Secret Doctrine*, xv.

36. Washington, *Madame Blavatsky's Baboon*, 53.

37. Jackson, *The Oriental Religions and American Thought*, 169.

38. See David M. Earle, *Re-covering Modernism: Pulp, Paperbacks, and the Prejudices of Form* (Farnham, Surrey, U.K.: Ashgate, 2009).

39. *New York Times*, 19 June 1893, 9, quoted in Adams, *E. Pluribus Barnum*, 194.

40. Snodgrass, *Presenting Japanese Buddhism*, 157.

41. "Theosophy at the World's Fair," *The Path* 8.6 (September 1893): 191.

42. Quoted in Richard Hughes Seager, *The World's Parliament of Religions: The East/West Encounter, Chicago, 1893* (Bloomington: Indiana University Press, 1995), 13.

43. Ibid., xvii.

44. John Henry Barrows, "Results of the Parliament of Religions," in *A Museum of Faiths: Histories and Legacies of the 1893 World's Parliament of Religions*, ed. Eric Z. Ziolkowski (Atlanta: Scholars Press, 1993), 133. Barrows is probably quoting from newspaper reports, though he gives no indication of his source. Further references to Barrows's report are cited as "Results."

45. Seager, *World's Parliament*, 22–23.

46. Vivekananda, "Hinduism," in *The World's Parliament of Religions*, ed. John Henry Barrows (Chicago: Parliament Publishing, 1893), 2:969. Further references are cited as *WPR.*

47. Barrows, "Review and Summary," *WPR* 2:1572.

48. Quoted in Snodgrass, *Presenting Japanese Buddhism to the West*, 211.

49. Barrows, "Results," 139 n23.

50. James Edward Ketelaar, "The Reconvening of Babel: Eastern Buddhism and the 1893 World's Parliament of Religions," in Ziolkowski, *Museum of Faiths*, 293, 294–95.

51. Snodgrass, *Presenting Japanese Buddhism*, 76; Ketelaar, "The Reconvening of Babel," 280.

52. The newspaper accounts are taken from Snodgrass, *Presenting Japanese Buddhism,* 183; Ketelaar, "The Reconvening of Babel," 299; and Seager, *World's Parliament,* 75.

53. Snodgrass, *Presenting Japanese Buddhism,* 185–86.

54. Anagarika Dharmapala, "Points of Resemblance and Difference between Buddhism and Christianity," *WPR* 2:1289. quoted in Ziolkowski, *Museum of Faiths,* 320–21.

55. Vivekananda, "Hinduism," *WPR* 2:977.

56. According to Barrows, Dharmapala asked how many in his audience had read the life of Buddha, and only five raised their hands, whereupon he said, "Five only! Four hundred and seventy-five millions of people accept our religion of love and hope. You call yourselves a nation—a great nation—and yet you do not know the history of this great teacher. How dare you judge us!" Barrows adds: "If Mr. Dharmapala had inquired of the three thousand people at the Parliament, 'How many of you have read, in whole or in part, Arnold's Light of Asia, with its account of Buddha?' many hundreds of hands would have been held up. The ignorance is not as dense and wide as imagined" (*WPR,* 2:1571).

57. The comments on Vivekananda's popularity from Barrows, the *Daily Inter-Ocean,* and Marie-Snell come from Marie Louise Burke, *Swami Vivekananda in America: New Discoveries* (Calcutta: Advaita Ashrama, 1958), 85, quoted in Seager, *World's Parliament,* 111.

58. Carl T. Jackson, *Vedanta for the West: The Ramakrishna Movement in the United States* (Bloomington: Indiana University Press, 1994), 8, 4.

59. Tweed, *The American Encounter with Buddhism,* 66.

60. Snodgrass, *Presenting Japanese Buddhism,* 227, 224.

61. Ibid., 222.

62. Paul Carus, *The Gospel of Buddha: Compiled from Ancient Records* (Chicago: Open Court, 1915), xiii. Further references are cited parenthetically in the text as Carus.

63. Snodgrass, *Presenting Japanese Buddhism,* 245–46.

64. For an account of Suzuki's work with Carus, see ibid., 262–67.

65. John La Farge, "Tao: The Way," *Century Magazine* 42.3 (July 1891): 442–48; "Taoism," in *WPR,* 2:1355–58; William Davies, "Tao," *Atlantic Monthly* 73.436 (February 1894): 181–98.

66. Davies, "Tao," 183.

67. Paul Carus [and D. T. Suzuki], trans., *The Canon of Reason and Virtue (Lao-tze's Tao teh King)* (Chicago: Open Court, 1903), 97.

68. James Legge, trans., *The Texts of Taoism: The Tao te Ching, The Writings of Chuang-tzu; The Thai-Shang* (New York: Julian Press, 1959), 95.

69. Quoted in Nyogen Senzaki, *Like a Dream like a Fantasy: The Writings and Translations of Nyogen Senzaki,* ed. Eido Shimano (Tokyo: Japan Publications, 1978), 109, quoted in Seager, *The World's Parliament,* 158.

70. Ibid.

71. Daisetz Teitaro Suzuki, preface to *Zen for Americans* (New York: Metrobooks, 2002), iii–iv. Further references are given parenthetically in the text as *Zen.*

72. Ralph Waldo Emerson, "Plato; or, the Philosopher," *Representative Men,* in *Emerson: Essays and Lectures* (New York: Library of America, 1983), 640.

73. Max Müller, "The Real Significance of the Parliament of Religions," *Arena* 11 (1894): 10, quoted by Snodgrass, *Presenting Japanese Buddhism,* 226.

74. T. W. Rhys Davids, *Buddhism: Its History and Literature: American Lectures on the History of Religions 1894–95,* (London: Putnam, 1904), 208, quoted in Snodgrass, *Presenting Japanese Buddhism to the West,* 225.

75. Quoted in Snodgrass, *Presenting Japanese Buddhism,* 318 n8.

76. Krishna Dutta and Andrew Robinson, *Rabindranath Tagore: The Myriad-Minded Man* (London: Bloomsbury, 1995), 160.

77. William Butler Yeats, introduction to *Gitanjali* (1912; New Delhi: Sahitya Akademi, 1994), 1:39. Further references to Yeats's introduction are cited parenthetically in the text as Yeats.

78. On this topic, see Mary M. Lago, *Rabindranath Tagore* (Boston: Twayne, 1976), 67.

79. Ibid., 67–68.

80. Ibid., 58.

81. Rabindranath Tagore, *Collected Poems and Plays* (New York: Macmillan, 1945), 3. Further references are cited parenthetically in the text as Tagore.

82. See May Sinclair, "The Gitanjali; or, Song Offerings of Rabindra Nath Tagore," *North American Review* 197 (1913): 659–76; and *Times Literary Supplement,* 7 November 1912, 492.

83. Quoted in Dutta and Robinson, *Rabindranath Tagore,* 185, 186.

84. Quoted ibid., 186.

85. Ezra Pound, "A Review of Gītanjalī," in *Tagore Centenary Volume,* ed. Mahendra Kulasrestha (Hoshiarpur, India: Vishveshvaranand V.R. Institute, 1961), 111–12. Further references are cited parenthetically in the text as Pound.

86. Dutta and Robinson, *Rabindranath Tagore,* 166, 171.

87. Ezra Pound to Iris Barry, 25 January 1917, in *Selected Letters of Ezra Pound* (New York: New Directions, 1971),106.

88. Rabindranath Tagore, "Nationalism in the West," in *The English Writings of Rabindranath Tagore,* ed. Sisir Kumar Das (New Delhi: Sahitya Akademi, 1996), 2:421 (cited parenthetically in the text as RT).

89. Dutta and Robinson, *Rabindranath Tagore,* 204.

90. Sujit Mukherjee, *Passage to America: The Reception of Rabindranath Tagore in the United States, 1912–1941* (Calcutta: Book Land, 1964), 77.

91. Cited in Dutta and Robinson, *Rabindranath Tagore,* 205.

92. Ibid., 208.

93. Mukherjee, *Passage to America,* 80, cited in Das, *The English Writings of Rabindranath Tagore,* 2:770 n20.

94. Ananda K. Coomaraswamy, *Buddha and the Gospel of Buddhism* (1969; Secaucus, N.J.: Citadel Press, 1988). Hereafter cited as AKC.

95. See the Coomaraswamy chronology and bibliography in Vishwanath S. Naravane, *Ananda K. Coomaraswamy* (Boston: Twayne, 1978), 11, 169–81.

96. David Weir, *Anarchy and Culture: The Aesthetic Politics of Modernism* (Amherst: University of Massachusetts Press, 1997), 146, 154–55.

97. Arnold Kunst, introduction to AKC, viii.

98. In his glossary in AKC, 355, 353, Coomaraswamy defines *pranidhana* as a Sanskrit noun meaning "vow, self-dedication, firm persuasion, of a Bodhisattva"; *karuna* is the Pali term for the Sanskrit cognate *karma,* defined as "compassion, the bestowing virtue—the leading passion in a Bodhisattva."

99. Mary V. Dearborn, *Mistress of Modernism: The Life of Peggy Guggenheim* (New York: Houghton Mifflin Harcourt, 2004), 34.

100. "The Dance of Siva," *Little Review* 5.9 (January 1919): 65.

101. Ananda K. Coomaraswamy, *The Dance of Siva: Essays on Indian Art and Culture* (New York: Dover, 1985), 115, 120. Further references are cited parenthetically in the text as *Siva.*

102. Kunst, introduction to AKC, iv.

103. Harriet Monroe, "Journeyman Poets," *Poetry: A Magazine of Verse* 14 (August 1919): 278.

104. David Weir, *Decadent Culture in the United States: Art and Literature against the American Grain, 1890–1926* (Albany: State University of New York Press, 2008), 82–84, 178–79.

105. See Robert Shaffer, "Pearl S. Buck and the East and West Association: The Trajectory and Fate of 'Critical Internationalism,' 1940–1950," *Peace & Change* 28.1 (January 2003): 1–36.

106. John Lossing Buck, *Chinese Farm Economy* (Chicago: Chicago University Press, 1930), 314. Further references are cited parenthetically in the text as *CFE.*

107. Blake Allmendinger, "Little House on the Rice Paddy," *American Literary History* 10.2 (Summer 1998): 365.

108. Ibid.

109. Peter Conn, *Pearl S. Buck: A Cultural Biography* (Cambridge: Cambridge University Press, 1996), 127.

110. Pearl S. Buck, *The Good Earth* (1931; New York: Washington Square Press, 1958), 2. Further references are cited parenthetically in the text as *Earth.*

111. Conn, *Pearl S. Buck,* 113.

112. Kevin Brownlow, "Sidney Franklin and *The Good Earth,*" *Historical Journal of Film, Radio and Television* 9.1 (1989): 80, 81; James L. Hoban Jr., "Scripting *The Good Earth*: Versions of the Novel for the Screen," in *The Several Worlds of Pearl S. Buck,* ed. Elizabeth J. Lipscomb et al. (Westport, Conn.: Greenwood Press, 1994), 130, 136.

113. Brownlow, "Sidney Franklin and *The Good Earth,*" 81–82.

114. Conn, *Pearl S. Buck,* 194.

115. Brownlow, "Sidney Franklin and *The Good Earth,*" 83. Franklin said Fleming "had handled the location details and done most of the preparation for filming the story" before becoming "seriously ill."

116. Hoban, "Scripting *The Good Earth,*" 129.

117. The program is bound with the typescript of the play in the archives of the Theatre Division of the New York Public Library at Lincoln Center.

118. Conn, *Pearl S. Buck,* 146.

119. *The Good Earth* program, 8.

120. Quoted in Conn, *Pearl S. Buck,* 146–47.

121. Owen Davis and Donald Davis, "The Good Earth," New York Public Library Theatre Division, typescript, 2–17. Further references are cited parenthetically; since the typescript is paginated by act, 2–17, for example, refers to page 17 of the second act.

122. Conn, *Pearl S. Buck,* 192.

123. Elaine Showalter, *Sexual Anarchy: Gender and Culture at the Fin de Siècle* (New York: Penguin, 1991), 163.

124. Allmendinger, "Little House on the Rice Paddy," 373.

125. Quoted in Brownlow, "Sidney Franklin and *The Good Earth,*" 84.

126. Allmendinger, "Little House on the Rice Paddy," 373.

127. Trailer for *The Good Earth,* special feature, *The Good Earth,* dir. Sidney Franklin, 1937, DVD, Warner Brothers.

128. Frank S. Nugent, "The Good Earth," *New York Times,* 3 February 1937, accessed online at http://movies.nytimes.com/.

129. Quoted in Conn, *Pearl S. Buck,* 196.

130. Pearl S. Buck to Emma Edmunds White, 5 February 1937, Nora Stirling papers, Randolph College archives, quoted in Hoban, "Scripting *The Good Earth,*" 141.

131. *The Good Earth* program, 22.

132. Charles W. Hayford, "*The Good Earth,* Revolution, and the American Raj in China," in Lipscomb et al., *The Several Worlds of Pearl S. Buck,* 22.

133. Conn, *Pearl S. Buck,* 273–74.

134. Frank Chin, *Donald Duk* (Minneapolis: Coffee House Press, 1991), 136.

135. Brownlow, "Sidney Franklin and *The Good Earth,*" 84.

Afterword

1. See U.S. Bureau of the Census, "Immigration and Naturalization," *Statistical Abstract of the United States: 1965,* 86th ed. (Washington, D.C.: U.S. Government Printing Office, 1965), 91; U.S. Bureau of the Census, "Immigration and Naturalization," *Statistical Abstract of the United States: 1970,* 91st ed. (Washington, D.C.: U.S. Government Printing Office, 1970), 92; and U.S. Bureau of the Census, "Section 1: Population," *The 2008 Statistical Abstract,* 19 December 2008, http://www.census.gov/compendia/statab/2008/2008edition.html (accessed 4 July 2010).

2. Judith Snodgrass, *Presenting Japanese Buddhism to the West* (Chapel Hill: University of North Carolina Press, 2003), 155–56.

3. D. T. Suzuki, "An Autobiographical Account," in *A Zen Life: D. T. Suzuki Remembered,* ed. Masao Abe (New York: Weatherhill, 1986), 19.

4. Martin J. Verhoven, "Americanizing the Buddha: Paul Carus and the Transformation of Asian Thought," in *Faces of Buddhism in America,* ed. Charles S. Prebish and Kenneth K. Tanaka (Berkeley: University of California Press, 1998), 220.

5. Information about Suzuki's career and bibliography is taken from Abe, *A Zen Life*, 219–24 and 235–46.

6. For a fuller discussion of this point and Suzuki's relation to Emerson generally, see Lawrence Buell, *Emerson* (Cambridge, Mass.: Harvard University Press, 2003), 196–97.

7. D. T. Suzuki, *Zen and Japanese Culture* (Princeton, N.J.: Princeton University Press, 1959), 8–9, 9 n4. Further references are cited parenthetically in the text as *Z & J*.

8. William H. Whyte, *The Organization Man* (1956; Philadelphia: University of Pennsylvania Press, 2002), 3.

9. Quoted in Joseph Nocera, foreword to Whyte, *The Organization Man*, viii.

10. Alan Watts, preface to *The Way of Zen* (New York: Vintage, 1957), xi.

11. Robert S. Ellwood, s.v. "Watts, Alan Wilson," *American National Biography Online* http://www.anb.org/articles/08/08-01880.html February 2000 (accessed 4 July 2010).

12. Alan Watts, "Beat Zen, Square Zen, and Zen," in *This Is It* (Toronto: Collier, 1967), 103–4, 85, 91. Further references are to this edition cited parenthetically in the text by page number.

13. For a list identifying characters with their real-life counterparts, see Douglas Brinkley, ed., *Jack Kerouac: Road Novels 1957–1960* (New York: Library of America, 2007), 854 n279.1.

14. Jack Kerouac, *The Dharma Bums*, in Brinkley, *Road Novels 1957–1960*, 292. Further references to this edition are cited parenthetically in the text as *Bums*.

15. Allen Ginsberg to Jack Kerouac, 5 September and 9 November 1954, *The Letters of Allen Ginsberg*, ed. Bill Morgan ([Cambridge, Mass.]: Da Capo, 2008), 102–8, 110–13.

16. Quoted in Tony Triglio, *Allen Ginsberg's Buddhist Poetics* (Carbondale: Southern Illinois University Press, 2007), 34.

17. Ibid., x, xii. Of the Bodhisattva vow, Triglio says it "is one of the most serious commitments to Buddhism a lay practitioner can make. The practitioner vows to continue taking rebirth as a bodhisattva, a saint-like being with a devotion to continued altruistic rebirths until all sentient beings attain enlightenment" (199 n2). Of the "Crazy Wisdom" school, Triglio says that it simultaneously "claim[s] the authority of a lineage (so crucial as a form of currency in Tibetan Buddhism) and . . . work[s] actively to undermine the authority of lineage making" (xi).

18. Allen Ginsberg to Jean Jacques Lebel, 6 January 1974, in Morgan, *The Letters of Allen Ginsberg*, 375–76.

19. Allen Ginsberg, *Indian Journals* (New York: Grove Press, 1970), 153; *Selected Poems: 1947–1995* (New York: HarperCollins, 1996), 148.

20. Triglio, *Allen Ginsberg's Buddhist Poetics*, 31.

21. Ann Douglas, introduction to *The Dharma Bums* (New York: Penguin, 2006), xvi.

22. Allen Ginsberg to Charles Rothschild, in Morgan, *The Letters of Allen Ginsberg*, 406.

23. Allen Ginsberg, *Spontaneous Mind: Selected Interviews,* ed. David Carter (New York: HarperCollins, 2001), 98.

24. Elizabeth Wilson, *Bohemians: The Glamorous Outcasts* (New Brunswick, N.J.: Rutgers University Press, 2000), 3.

25. See David Spangler, *David Spangler,* http://www.davidspangler.com/. For a scholarly estimate of the New Age, see Wouter J. Hanegraaff, *New Age Religion and Western Culture: Esotericism in the Mirror of Secular Thought* (New York: Brill, 1996).

26. "The Transcendental Meditation Program," *Maharishi Vedic Education Development Corporation,* 2009, http://www.tm.org/.

27. Lily Koppel, "Maharishi Mahesh Yogi, Spiritual Leader, Dies," *New York Times,* 6 February 2008. Unless otherwise noted, all the information about the Maharishi Mahesh Yogi and TM in this paragraph is taken from the *Times* obituary.

28. "New Billion Dollar Bailout," *Global Financial Capital,* 28 October 2009, http://www.gfcny.net/press_release/2008_10_26.html.

29. See *Maharishi Vedic Center, Iowa,* 2008, http://www.maharishivediccity.com/.

30. *David Lynch Foundation,* 2009, http://www.davidlynchfoundation.org/.

31. David Brooks, *Bobos in Paradise: The New Upper Class and How They Got There* (New York: Simon and Shuster, 2000), 256, 9.

32. Richard Corliss, "The Power of Yoga," *Time,* 15 April 2001.

33. Deirdre Donahue, "Look at This Man's Body: This Is What Yoga Can Do for You," *USA Today,* 24 April 2002.

34. Abigail Pogrebin, "An Illicit Yoga Love Story," *New York Magazine,* 21 May 2005.

35. "Rodney Yee and Colleen Saidman to Host Yoga Retreat in Bali," *ASIATravelTips.com,* 3 June 2008, http://www.asiatraveltips.com/news08/36-YogaRetreat.shtml.

36. "A Weekend of Yoga with Colleen and Rodney," *Omega Institute for Holistic Studies,* 16–18 October 2009, http://eomega.org/omega/.

37. "Surf Goddess Yoga," *Surf Goddess Retreats,* http://www.surfgoddessretreats.com/yoga.html.

38. Robert Love, *The Great Oom: The Improbable Birth of Yoga in America* (New York: Viking, 2010), 12–13.

39. Ibid., 20, 21.

40. Ibid., 54, 141, 257, 101–2, 111–15.

41. Ben Hecht, *A Child of the Century* (New York: Simon and Schuster, 1954), 509; Love, *The Great Oom,* 269.

42. "Prizefighter Trains by Yoga Methods," *Life,* 15 May 1939, 69.

43. Ferdie Pacheco, *Blood in My Coffee: The Life of the Fight Doctor* (Champaign, Ill.: Sports Publishing, 2005), 116.

44. Alan Watts, *In My Own Way: An Autobiography* (1972; Novato, Calif.: New World Library, 2007), 119–20.

45. Isabel Stirling, *Zen Pioneer: The Life and Works of Ruth Fuller Sasaki* (Emeryville, Calif.: Shoemaker and Hoard, 2006), xxii, xvii, 6.

46. Thomas Tweed, preface to *The American Encounter with Buddhism, 1844–1912: Victorian Culture and the Limits of Dissent* (1994; Chapel Hill: University of North Carolina Press, 2000), xiii–xiv.

47. Garr Reynolds, *Presentation Zen: Simple Ideas on Presentation Design and Delivery* (Berkeley, Calif.: New Riders, 2008), 8.

48. John Weiss, "Thoreau," in *Pertaining to Thoreau* (Detroit: Hill, 1901), 147. This appreciation of Thoreau by one of his Harvard classmates was originally published in the *Christian Examiner* of July 1865.

INDEX

wisdom literature, 34, 37, 38, 215
wisdom poetry, 145, 150–51, 207
Witherell, Elizabeth, 265n56
Wizard of Oz, The, 223
Wordsworth, William, 35
World's Parliament of Religions, 8, 191, 192–
    99; Buddhism at, 193, 194–97, 205, 234;
    Hinduism at, 193, 194, 197–99; influence
    on mass culture of, 176, 191, 199
World War I, 8, 210
World War II, 145, 230; Japanese American
    internment during, 9–10, 119, 233

Yates, William, 54–55
Yeats, William Butler, 191, 207–8
Yee, Rodney, 250–52
yoga: and Buddhism, 255; and Hinduism,
    41; modern-day commercialism around, 8,

234, 250–52; as self-punishment, 41, 252;
    Thoreau on, 65
Yoshihara Mari, 156, 170
Yoshimitsu Ashikaga, 157
"Young Japan" (Naruse), 162, 166
Yu, Beongcheon, 12, 94–95

Zen and Japanese Culture (Suzuki), 237,
    239, 255
Zen Buddhism, 199, 254, 255; and Beat
    Generation, 240, 241, 244; Ginsberg and,
    244–47; Kerouac on, 242–43; Shaku on,
    8, 203–4; Suzuki on, 237–38; Watts on,
    239–40. *See also* Buddhism
Zen Dust, 254
Zen for Americans (Shaku and Suzuki),
    203–4
Zhong yong (Mencius), 68